BLOOD
AND
IRONY

Blood & Irony

Southern
White
Women's
Narratives
of the
Civil War,
1861–1937

The University
of North
Carolina
Press

CHAPEL

HILL &

SARAH E. GARDNER   LONDON

© 2004 The University of North Carolina Press
All rights reserved

Designed by Kristina Kachele
Set in Minion by Tseng Information Systems, Inc.

Manufactured in the United States of America

The paper in this book meets the guidelines for
permanence and durability of the Committee on
Production Guidelines for Book Longevity of the
Council on Library Resources.

Library of Congress Cataloging-in-Publication Data
Gardner, Sarah E.
Blood and irony: Southern white women's narratives
of the Civil War, 1861–1937 / Sarah E. Gardner.
p. cm.
Based on the author's doctoral thesis, Emory
University.
Includes bibliographical references and index.
ISBN 0-8078-2818-1 (cloth: alk. paper)
1. Confederate States of America — Historiography.
2. United States — History — Civil War, 1861–1865 —
Historiography. 3. Southern States — Intellectual
life — 1865- 4. Group identity — Southern States —
History. 5. United States — History — Civil War,
1861–1865 — Personal narratives, Confederate.
6. United States — History — Civil War, 1861–1865 —
Literature and the war. 7. American literature —
Women authors — History and criticism. 8. Women
and literature — Southern States — History.
9. Southern States — In literature. 10. Group identity
in literature. I. Title.
E487 .G27 2003
973.7'13'072 — dc21   2003012777

08 07 06 05 04   5 4 3 2 1

Contents

Illustrations

Acknowledgments

This project began as a doctoral dissertation at Emory University under the direction of Elizabeth Fox-Genovese. It benefited immeasurably from her attentive reading, keen historical sense, and many helpful suggestions. Betsey continues to be an important mentor and friend; I cannot possibly thank her enough for all that she has done for me over the years. I also thank Patrick Allitt, Dan Carter, Eugene D. Genovese, Jack Kirby, Michael O'Brien, and James Roark, all of whom read all or portions of this work and offered insightful criticism.

Many archivists and librarians have provided me with much-needed assistance. I would like to single out the staffs at the Atlanta History Center, Duke University, Emory University, the Southern Historical Collection, and the University of Virginia for their help along the way. I am particularly indebted to David Moltke-Hansen, who listened to me drone on about his project during my stays in Chapel Hill. Ginger Cain, Barbara Mann, Linda Matthews, Naomi Nelson, and Kathy Shoemaker proved important allies while I worked in Emory University's Special Collections and offered me steady employment during those lean graduate school years.

I am grateful to the American Historical Association, the Manuscript Society, and Duke University for partially funding my research.

Many friends and family members offered me invaluable moral support. Susan Anderson and Mark Ledden were always ready to suggest diversionary tactics to draw me out of the library. Jeff Young made sure that I returned to my work. Vate Powell provided places for me to stay during my research trips to Boston, Charlottesville, and New York. More important, he has seen me through rough times, and for that I am forever grateful. Margaret Storey and Jonathan Heller both gracefully withstood my slovenly tendencies and my long-suffering devotion to the Cleveland Indians. Their culinary skills, witty breakfast table banter, and continued friendship have served me well. Houston Roberson has proven a great friend and the best road-trip companion a scholar could want. Mary Ann Drake provided me with sage advice on making the transition from graduate student to faculty member and colleague. I thank her for her constant support over the years. I thank my friends at Manuel's Tavern for always leaving a space for me at the table on Sunday nights. I especially thank Anastasia Christman and her parents, Michael and Joann Jackson, for always being there for me and guiding my way. Finally, I thank my parents, Ann L. Gardner and the late Donald C. Gardner, who have placed a great deal of faith in my abilities to do good work.

My colleagues in the history department at Mercer University surely deserve some kind of award for refraining from pestering me about the inordinately long time it has taken me to finish this project. Many of my former students failed to show similar restraint and shamelessly questioned whether I would finish this book in their lifetimes. To them all I am grateful — for obviously different reasons.

I have received a great deal of assistance from the staff at the University of North Carolina Press. Ellen D. Goldlust-Gingrich copyedited my manuscript with great care. I would especially like to thank Pam Upton, who helped me finalize my manuscript, and David Perry, who stuck with this project.

My greatest debt surely belongs to Todd Leopold, who has lived with this project almost as long as I have. Although I have not always followed his suggestions for "improving" my manuscript, I have benefited from his counsel and his companionship more than he realizes.

Everywoman
Her Own
Historian

*"He was the cavalry general Jeb Stuart.... I danced
a valse with him in Baltimore in '58," and her voice
was proud and still as banners in the dust.*
—WILLIAM FAULKNER, Flags in the Dust

The speaker was Virginia Du Pre, the eighty-year-old woman who fondly re-
members General Jeb Stuart in William Faulkner's 1927 novel, *Flags in the Dust*.
Her interest in the story of the dashing Confederate officer is deeply personal,
for it tells not only of Stuart's bravery in the face of fifteen thousand Yankees but
also of her brother Bayard Sartoris's "brief career" as a cavalryman in the Confederate Army. Aunt Jenny had first told her story in 1869, and she had subsequently told it many more times—"on occasions usually inopportune." Indeed,
as Aunt Jenny grew older, "the tale itself grew richer and richer, taking on a mel-
low splendor like wine; until what had been a hair-brained prank of two heedless
and reckless boys wild with their open youth, was become a gallant and finely
tragical focal point to which the history of the race had been raised from out the
old miasmic swamps of spiritual sloth by two angels valiantly and glamorously
fallen and strayed, altering the course of human events and purging the souls
of men." Faulkner correctly understood the importance of stories to southern

1

culture. More important, he understood the crucial role women played as disseminators of southern stories of the Civil War. "Years ago we in the South made our women into ladies," he explained elsewhere. "Then the War came and made the ladies into ghosts. So what else can we do, being gentlemen, but listen to them being ghosts."[1] Indeed, Faulkner knew that Aunt Jenny's version of the story of Jeb Stuart, Bayard Sartoris, and the "anchovies" remained uniquely her own.

Although evocative, Aunt Jenny's tale remains eclipsed by a more familiar tale of the Civil War. Nine years after Aunt Jenny told her story in *Flags in the Dust*, Margaret Mitchell, following in the long line of southern white women who penned narratives of the Civil War, introduced Scarlett O'Hara to American audiences in her 1936 Pulitzer Prize–winning novel, *Gone with the Wind*. That Scarlett so ably and so fully captured the imagination of the national reading public was no minor literary coup for the numerous southern white women who had been telling their tales of the war as early as the Federal reinforcement of Fort Sumter in 1861. What had started out as an attempt to tell a distinctly southern story of the war had evolved, by Scarlett's incarnation, into a remarkably successful effort to tell the national story of the war. Indeed, the southern story had become the national story, with Scarlett O'Hara displacing Henry Fleming, John Carrington, Basil Ransom, and even Aunt Jenny as the character whose stories the nation was reading.[2] This book explores the emergence of a discourse that permitted Mitchell's story to attain cultural hegemony by chronicling the efforts of countless southern white women who actively competed for the historical memory of the Civil War during the first seven decades following Appomattox. The narratives of these diarists, novelists, historians, and clubwomen built the stage on which Scarlett would be the star.

Midway through the Civil War, a Virginia woman nervously awaited news about the besieged city of Vicksburg, Mississippi. Knowing that other women throughout the South shared her anxiety, Judith McGuire readily assumed that they, like she, sought comfort from wartime tensions by recording their experiences. More to the point, she predicted that "almost every woman of the South . . . will have her tale to tell when this 'cruel war is over.'" Knowing also that the tide had begun to turn against the South, she bemoaned that these war narratives would stand as the sole remnant of the Confederate civilization that surrounded her. McGuire did not doubt southern women's ability or authority to chronicle the Civil War, but she regretted the reduction of vibrant experiences to mere narrative: "The life of too many will be, alas! as a 'tale that is told'; its interest, its charm, even its hope, as far as this world is concerned, having passed away." Virginia's Cornelia Peake McDonald echoed McGuire's concern. Writing after the war, McDonald noted, "I had seen so much of real suffering, of conflict, danger and death, that for years I could read neither romance or history, for nothing equaled what I had seen and known. All tales of war and carnage, every story of sorrow and suffering paled before the sad scenes of misery I knew."[3] Decades before Faulkner wrote, McGuire, McDonald, and many others feared that although the story of the South would be full of sound and fury, it would ultimately signify nothing. Their fears proved groundless.

Events amply confirmed McGuire's prediction that white southern women would tell their stories of the war. Even the most cursory glance at finding aids and collection descriptions from archives throughout the South betrays the abundance of unpublished manuscripts penned by southern white women between 1865 and 1936. Family papers swell with titles such as "My Recollections of the War" and "A Confederate Girlhood." Numerous southern white women, however, refused to settle for this circumscribed, private reading audience. With firm conviction in the accuracy and marketability of their accounts, these women sent unsolicited manuscripts to regional and national magazines, hoping to see the stories in print. Some such writers even founded journals in order to ensure publication of these wartime narratives. Widows of Confederate leaders and statesmen published biographies of their husbands, taking the opportunity to advance personal interpretations of the war. These narratives, including their distinct interpretive contributions, easily wove themselves into the fabric of the white South's attempt to come to terms with the meaning of defeat. Women born in the decades following the war could take this emerging account of the southern experience for granted as an integral collective memory. They, in turn, could contribute to its development through imaginative stories. By the 1930s, readers curious about the Civil War faced a mountain of literature written by southern white women.

Scholars have examined men's war narratives but have yet to explore systematically the mass of writings by southern women. To be sure, writers have prodded a bit, poking around in isolated areas. Historians and literary critics alike have mined Mary Boykin Miller Chesnut's *Diary from Dixie*, extracting a wealth of information about one woman's life in South Carolina society. Margaret Mitchell's novel, *Gone with the Wind*, has enjoyed even more attention from scholars and the general public.[4] The position of Chesnut's diary or

Scarlett O'Hara's story relative to the body of war literature by other southern women, however, remains unclear. Here, through an examination of southern white women's published and unpublished narratives of the Civil War from 1861 to 1936, I hope to redress this oversight. Novels, diaries, biographies, histories, and reminiscences all reveal the ways in which southern women conceptualized the war. Moreover, these narratives demonstrate the manner in which southern women, in carving out new public roles for themselves, fashioned a new cultural identity for the postbellum South.

My first task is deceptively simple: to illustrate the transformative impact of the Civil War on southern women's historical imaginations. From the outset of my research, I was struck with the prodigious body of war literature written by southern white women. A mere survey of these titles, however, would not begin to capture the authors' achievements. The ways in which these writers understood the origins, meanings, and implications of war and defeat for themselves and southern society traced a view of the tragedy that directly contested northern historians' dominant interpretations. Indeed, southern white women did not entrust even their own menfolk with the telling of war. Katherine Anne Porter insisted, for example, that Stark Young took stories from her family's history "and then got them all wrong or used them badly" in his 1934 Civil War novel, *So Red the Rose*. Porter noted that her cousin, Gertrude Beitel, whose "brains" Young had "picked" for his novel, "detests the book, said she never knew a Southerner could so miss the point of what the old Southerners really were."[5] From the start, southern white women demonstrated a firm grasp of the war's decisive importance to American and southern history. In addition, these women's particular interpretations of the war colored their attempt to comprehend postbellum realities.

Second, I wish to demonstrate the continuing dialogue between interpreters and interpretations of the Civil War. In some cases, the narrators maintained direct and personal communication with each other. Virginia novelists Ellen Glasgow and Mary Johnston, for example, frequently read each other's drafts and finished novels and commented on them in personal correspondence. The voluminous correspondence among members of the United Daughters of the Confederacy (UDC) suggests that they read each other's pamphlets and listened to each other's addresses with great interest and acumen. In other cases, the dialogue was less direct. Some women would comment on other authors' works when writing in diaries or to editors. Other authors would borrow or parody plotlines and scenes from previously published works. In all cases, however, it is evident that these women writers constantly referred to other works, built on accounts that were already a part of the public discourse, and thereby continually altered the narratives of war and defeat.

Third, I hope to elucidate the ways in which these women contributed to the creation of the southern myth of the Lost Cause. This myth has generated a voluminous historiography, beginning with journalist Edward J. Pollard's often rambling and always turgid and polemical 1867 history of Confederate defeat, *The Lost Cause*.[6] Since Pollard's publication, scholars have argued over the specific functions of the myth. Whether addressing its political, religious, psychocultural, or literary manifestations, however, all these discussions center on the question of southern identity.[7] This relentless pursuit of the meaning of Confederate defeat, both by scholars and by proponents of the myth, has had more to do with white southerners' need to create a viable history than with pure intellectual curiosity. Indeed, this creation lay at the heart of postbellum southern culture and political consciousness. Historians, it seems, have been no more immune to the need to reconcile the past with the postwar American culture than have the southerners being studied.[8]

Southern women participated directly and influentially in this conscious effort to fashion a distinctly southern story of the war. They, along with the more familiar heroes of the Confederacy and men of the New South, actively combated northern accounts of the war.[9] For the participants in this paper battle over the authoritative version of the war, the spoils of victory were nothing less than the ultimate triumph in the war itself. To the winners went the assurance of popular acceptance and influence of a culturally sanctioned representation of the past. For many Americans, the Civil War has been the crucible of U.S. history, challenging each new generation to come to terms with its meaning. As Gary Gallagher notes, "few episodes in American history match the Civil War in its power to make the people who lived through it think seriously about a suitable public memory."[10] Southern white women were as susceptible as their men to the grandeur, pathos, sentiment, emotion, curiosity, tragedy, and romance of the war. Beginning with the years of Reconstruction, these women produced a steady flow of celebratory accounts, in both fiction and prose, to consecrate a "proper" southern understanding of antebellum society and the tragedy that had felled it. And each succeeding generation of southern white women vigorously entered the war of words.

Southern white women did not question the standard southern interpretation of the war's causes. Most of these authors did not consider their narratives to be the proper venue to express distaste for the war, if they harbored such sentiments at all. Nor did these women consider their writings the place to explore cowardice or treachery. They did not cast themselves or their heroines as Cassandras whose foreknowledge of the fate of the Confederacy went unheeded by the recalcitrant leaders of the southern cause.[11] Nevertheless, the myth of the Lost Cause did not persist in its original rendition but emerged from, flowed into, and continually revised this emerging collective memory of the war as southerners rebuilt and reassured their position in the world. That memory, as it took shape, never offered a single static representation of the war but rather included multiple and constantly shifting versions.[12] Central to the understanding of the historical narration of that collective memory is an appreciation of what elements changed and what remained constant. At the turn of the twentieth century, for example, Helen Dortch Longstreet, the widow of General James Longstreet, of Gettysburg fame, staged a valiant effort to resuscitate the reputation of her husband, who had been vilified immediately following the war. Southerners had so altered the boundaries of the Lost Cause myth that Helen Longstreet could, with her fellow southerners' approval, attempt to include her formally reviled husband in the pantheon of Lost Cause heroes. Perhaps even more telling, author Caroline Gordon, following the canons of the epic, suggested in her 1937 novel *None Shall Look Back* that the Confederacy fell because of the tragic flaws of individuals—of men such as General Nathan Bedford Forrest—who manipulated the fates of those around them. Gordon's vision allowed for the possibility that the fall of the Confederacy had been predetermined, but assuredly not because of some nostalgic myth of moonlight and magnolias. Rather, she seems to have believed that war might uniquely test a man's mettle and character and thus reveal something important not about a specific historical event but about human nature.[13]

The relationship between a "documented" past and a "created" past can illuminate the motives, intent, audience, and context that shaped discourses about the Civil War and the ways in which those discourses were read. Judith McGuire's concern that accounts of the war would serve as the only remnant of the Confederacy suggests the dangers of reducing a tragic event to mere narrative. The Civil War cannot be reduced to consciousness. Real battles were fought, and lives were lost. These battles and losses inspired southern white women to explain the meaning of these events, but I do not seek to judge accuracy by comparing these accounts with "actual" or "real" events. Nor do I intend to expose these writers' constructions of the past as romantic, escapist, or delusional. I do, however, assert that the reality of the postwar South informed narratives of the past.

I have arranged the following chapters chronologically. While I do not argue for a teleological, or natural, progression from the earlier works to the later ones, I do maintain that postbellum politics and culture shaped narratives of the war as much as did the events of the conflict itself. The first chapter, "Pen and Ink Warriors, 1861–1865," considers southern women's writing during the war, taking as emblematic Augusta Jane Evans's *Macaria; or, Altars of Sacrifice* (1864). These wartime writers exposed many of the themes, such as the causes and inevitability of the war, that other novelists and historians explored in later works. Since many later writers accepted Confederate defeat as a foregone conclusion, they infused their stories and histories with a sense of loss. To contemporary writers, however, the fate of the Confederacy had yet to be determined, and their narratives exude a sense of optimism, excitement, and uncertainly, thereby conveying an existential reality that is unequaled in postbellum works. At the same time, these wartime narratives identified the issues to be explored in postwar works and underscored the highly malleable nature of the postwar discourse.

In the second chapter, "Countrywomen in Captivity, 1865–1877," I turn to works published during Reconstruction, as exemplified by Alabama novelist Mary Ann Cruse's 1867 novel, *Cameron Hall*. Cruse's characters face the immediacy and the reality of Confederate defeat and must come to grips with the ensuing torpor. Their seeming paralysis captures the psychic shock experienced by southern white women. For example, Evans, who had so enthusiastically supported the Confederacy's efforts with her writings, now felt unable to lift her pen on the subject of the South. She abandoned a planned history of the Confederacy, and decades passed before her novels again even broached the subject of the war or the Confederacy.[14] The narratives published during Reconstruction have a distinct tone: if they lack the anxiety about the war's outcome that pervaded the wartime writings, they also lack the familiarity with the notion of defeat that characterizes subsequent chronicles. For while the outcome of the war was as obvious to these writers as it was to their readers, the future of the South was not. Forced to abandon their roles as mere supporters of the Confederacy, southern white women shouldered the responsibility of creating the region's postwar consciousness. They began that work in the narratives they published during Reconstruction.

The third chapter, "A View from the Mountain, 1877–1895," examines works published between the "southern redemption" and the founding of the UDC. In many respects, works from this period underscore a tension between the literature of Reconstruction and that of the turn of the twentieth century. With the chaos of the immediate postwar era settled and the white South "redeemed," New South boosterism flourished, and publications began to appear from a second generation of women who had been young children or had not yet been born at the outbreak of the Civil War. This generation's writings reflect the possibilities for the future they saw in the newly industrializing South. While these authors could not alter the outcome of the war, they could dispel the sense of gloom and despondency that permeates the narratives written during Reconstruction and could hint at the promise of a resurgent white South.

But for many southern white women, all was not well with the New South. For some, like Mary Anna Jackson and Varina Davis, the glory of the South still rested with the Confederacy, not with some elusive dream of a New South. For others, like Mary Noailles Murfree, promises of industrialization had an ugly underside. Murfree's 1884 novel, *Where the Battle Was Fought*, suggests that while the Confederacy was not the embodiment of southern grandeur, neither was the New South. The land "where the battle was fought" was barren, no longer able to sustain the family that had once lived on it. In Murfree's mind—and indeed, in the minds of many others of this period—the war neither symbolized a glorious cause nor paved the way for the South's salvation.

The fourth chapter, "The Imperative of Historical Inquiry, 1895–1905," surveys the literature published at the turn of the twentieth century. With the founding of the UDC came one of the largest official organizations for the mobilization of memories of the Civil War. The Daughters understood their mission in human affairs to be divinely inspired: "For do not fail to realize," admonished UDC President-General Cornelia Branch Stone to a large audience of Daughters, "that we are no accidental thing. God has brought us into existence for specific purposes. Purposes which no other people on the face of the earth can or will do. So that if we fail in them, they will go undone. God will hold us accountable," she warned, "for this work which he means for us to do."[15] The formation of the UDC decisively influenced southern women's narratives of the Civil War, giving southern white women the strength of a major organization to support and direct their efforts. The UDC's sense of a divine imperative to write the true history of the war compelled its members to pen personal accounts, while its conviction of a providential history provided the tone of a larger, collective narrative. Writing the antitheses to northern Whiggish interpretations of the war, and at odds with the historicists who explained away all events as mere points on a timeline, the UDC and its supporters ensured that the reading public had access to alternative visions of history. The guidelines issued by the UDC's Historical Committee organized the members' papers into uniform, familiar accounts. The Textbook Committee compiled reading lists, offering examples for the Daughters to follow. And although the UDC never dictated specific content to be included in members' accounts, the organization did present firm structural rules, thereby guaranteeing that the women wrote in similar ways and told similar stories.

The literature of Ellen Glasgow, who published her "social histories" of Virginia during this period, seems to contrast with UDC's rhetoric. While the UDC and like-minded women writers such as Constance Cary Harrison, Mary Seibert, and Louisa Whitney waxed rhapsodic on the virtues of the Old South and the Confederacy, Glasgow presented a grimmer view. Her novels — *Voice of the People* (1900), *The Battle-Ground* (1902), and *Deliverance* (1904) — as well as her private writings suggest that she believed that the South's future rested neither with the old wartime generation nor with the leaders of the New South. Instead, the future depended on the common people. Her character Pinetop, a nonslaveholding farmer from Tennessee, sacrifices his life for a cause in which he ostensibly has nothing invested. The Blakes, the formerly aristocratic, slaveholding family in *Deliverance*, would have died out had it not been for the infusion of new, common blood, symbolized by the marriage of the planter's son to the overseer's daughter. And in *Voice of the People*, Glasgow asserted that the Populist movement, the final hope for the South, was the last stage of the Civil War. As an angry mob guns down Virginia's Populist governor, the one man who stands between the crowd and the object of its terror, the rioters symbolically obliterate the palliative to all of the South's ills. The death of Populism, according to Glasgow, delivered a severe blow to the South's attempts to extract itself from the morass of its postbellum malaise. Yet even Glasgow could never escape the dominant southern narrative of defeat and vindication. Despite her intentions, she could not write against the grain and frequently fell back on stock characters and plotlines. This tension between Glasgow's intent, her finished works, and the UDC vision of the Confederacy and its history ran through turn-of-the-century Civil War literature.

The fifth chapter, "Righting the Wrongs of History, 1905–1915," assesses the war narratives of the early twentieth century. While the UDC continued to praise the glory brought to the Southland by the Confederacy's noble martial spirit, others, most notably Mary Johnston, held different opinions. To be sure, Johnston celebrated the South's role in the formation of American civilization, championed the South's distinct culture, and professed its right to secede. In this respect, she did not break completely with the past. But she did not glorify the war itself. In her view, the war brought only destruction, and a Confederate triumph would in no way have mitigated the devastation to the southern landscape. No matter how compelling postwar white southerners found the Confederacy's claim to independence, no matter how seductive the idea of secession, according to Johnston, the war qua war had been a disaster for the South. Where some saw the Civil War as the ultimate expression of the Confederacy, Johnston saw only death.

The sixth chapter, "Moderns Confront the Civil War, 1916–1936," examines the immediate cultural and literary backdrop for Margaret Mitchell's phenomenally successful novel, *Gone with the Wind*. The narratives of this period suggest that southern authors offered a new perspective on the Civil War to their fellow southerners as well as to the nation as a whole. The recent experience with World War I gave a new impetus to southerners' preoccupation with reconstructing the memory of the Civil War. Members of the UDC, generations removed from the Civil War, found compelling connections between their wartime work and that of Confederate women. Douglas Southall Freeman cautioned his readers that his disgust with modern warfare, engendered by his participation in World War I, might creep into his 1934 Pulitzer Prize–winning biography of Robert E. Lee. Indeed, the pressing need to relive, in both positive and negative ways, the Civil War led William Faulkner, one of the South's greatest tellers of tales, to fashion himself a hero of the Great War. The number of works published on the Civil War eclipsed the previous mark set in the post-Reconstruction years, aided by the release of novels by Faulkner, Stark Young, and Evelyn Scott. Mitchell capitalized on America's renewed interest in Civil War literature; in so doing, she nationalized the southern story of the war.

The epilogue, "Everything That Rises Must Converge," examines Caroline Gordon's 1937 novel, *None Shall Look Back*, published less than a year after the release of *Gone with the Wind*. Gordon realized her misfortune, commenting frequently on the poor timing of her novel's appearance and complaining of Mitchell's success in cornering the literary market. Gordon also recognized the profound differences between the two novels. Gordon and others of her cohort, notably Scott, laid claim to a new literary style that became increasingly compelling as southern authors moved away from the didactic mode and toward the symbolic. The previous generation of southern women novelists had begun to experiment with technical and stylistic innovation, but not even Johnston, perhaps the most successful of the group, had fully transformed the sentimentalized, romanticized, and idealized artifact that the Civil War novel had become. To be sure, a more skeptical, jaundiced view of war had emerged with Stephen Crane's *Red Badge of Courage*, but even it was unable to counter the romantic account of war that remained popular at the turn of the twentieth century. Johnston's great contribution lay in her depiction of the repetitive and destructive futility of all war, even when it was fought for the noblest of causes. Gordon, in contrast, self-consciously pursued the formal and stylistic innovations of modernism and in so doing not merely succeeded where others had failed but provided a model for later southern writers.

With rare exceptions, modern readers will find that most of these war narratives seem like second-rate romances.[16] We are, after all, familiar with Margaret Mitchell's account of Sherman's March to the Sea and descriptions of Scarlett O'Hara's pluckiness in the face of adversity. Yet what strikes us as derivative, sentimental, or simply false affected late-nineteenth- and early-twentieth-century readers differently. They were reading something new. For even when relying on previously told narratives that had already become part of the common stock of war stories, southern white women writers were fashioning new tales in an effort to explain and vindicate southern defeat. In doing so, they created a new cultural identity for the postbellum South. For these women and their readers, history and its telling mattered.

1

Pen and Ink Warriors, 1861–1865

In February 1861, Emma E. Holmes of Charleston, South Carolina, contemplated the future of her country and became incensed. The "Black Republicans," through their "malignity and fanaticism," had fragmented the United States. To Holmes, Abraham Lincoln's 1860 election to the presidency had signaled a sea change in American politics, and she remarked on the mounting tensions between the North and the South since that fateful November day. Although Holmes wished mightily that a civil war might be averted, she feared that bloody battle was inevitable. "A revolution, wonderful in the rapidity with which it has swept across the country," had captured her imagination and fired her spirit. "Doubly proud am I of my native State," she boasted, "that she should be the first to arise and shake off the hated chain which linked us with 'Black Republicans and Abolitionists.'" Holmes admitted only one regret as the country inched toward war: "How I wish I had kept a journal during the last three months of great political change." To compensate for her previous laxity, she would in future chronicle in her diary what she deemed to be "the most important events" in national affairs since the election of Lincoln, a time that had been "fraught with the happiness, the prosperity, nay, the very existence of our future." She recognized at once the importance of her work. She soon boasted of her journal's value "as a record of events which mark the formation and growth of our glorious Southern Confederacy."[1]

Hundreds of white women throughout the South followed suit. The art of diary keeping certainly was not new to white southern women. As Elizabeth Fox-Genovese notes, journaling allowed women to reflect on their lives and to ponder their place in antebellum southern society. Most journals, she remarked, functioned "as chronicles of personal, intellectual, or spiritual progress." The Civil War engendered a transition in journal keeping, as southern white women increasingly turned to their journals to comment on the surrounding world. Significantly, as Steven Stowe suggests, the diary form allows the diarist to interpret events. "A diary by its nature," Stowe explains, "encourages an intellectually active, organizing voice, putting the diarist legitimately at the center of determining the meaning of things."[2] The war, then, provided Confederate women the opportunity to analyze political events to a heretofore unprecedented degree.

Louisiana Burge, a young student at Wesleyan Female College in Macon, Georgia, pithily captured this transition in diary keeping. Burge began her journal in 1860, pledging "to keep a 'journal'—not so much as a record of my own thoughts, feelings, and acts solely—but mostly as they occur in connection with the events of the time." Rocked by the tumultuous affairs that threatened daily existence, southern white women like Burge shifted the focus of their journals from themselves to national politics and local battles. Journal keeping had never been entirely a private affair, and women expected that at the very least, their families would read their journals.[3] Knowing that their journals would be read, Confederate women, like Holmes, capitalized on the opportunity to preserve for future generations an "accurate" record of this "revolution."

Southern white women who wished a wider reading audience than their immediate families turned their talents to fiction, using the Civil War as the catalyst for their novels. Like journal keeping, novel writing was familiar ground for at least a small group of southern women. Introduced as a literary form in New England in the 1820s, domestic fiction became immensely popular with American women in the ensuing decades. According to historian Elizabeth Moss, "Typically chronicling the trials and tribulations of an intelligent, emotional, and exceedingly virtuous female temporarily forced to make her way alone, the domestic novel as formulated in the American North explored the problems and possibilities of domesticity, using stilted language and convoluted plots to emphasize the importance of home and community." Such antebellum southern authors as Caroline Gilman, Caroline Hentz, and Augusta Jane Evans, among others, put their own spin on this standardized, sentimental literary genre, using the plantation as the center of their fiction; portraying the Old South as a well-ordered, harmonious society; and creating a particular brand of southern literature.[4]

The outbreak of the Civil War forced many of these authors, and others who entered the literary market for the first time, to abandon such overtly domestic plots in favor of a more explicitly political fiction. Evans, an exceedingly popular antebellum domestic novelist from Alabama, began her 1864 war novel *Macaria; or, Altars of Sacrifice* with a standard domesticity plot but ended it in a most unconventional way. Evans, and her contemporaries, including Sallie Rochester Ford and Maria McIntosh, were no longer writing solely for the moral uplift of southern women. These writers had become propagandists, fighting for their civilization. Like the contents of their novels, the authors' motives had shifted from the domestic to the political.

Although southern white women could neither throw themselves on the fiery altar to save their society, as the heroine of *Macaria* lamented, nor become men and enter into the fray, as Wadley noted, they could write — and that is precisely what they did. Diaries, correspondence, and fiction suggest that southern white women wrote for myriad reasons. Some women immediately sensed the need to tell a distinctly southern story of the war and began by maintaining a eyewitness record. Others sought release from wartime tensions by noting impressions and opinions in journals or in correspondence to loved ones. Still others wrote, perhaps for the first time, for explicitly political reasons. Some wrote war novels and poetry to bolster Confederate soldiers' spirits and to remind those on the home front of the sacred cause for which their menfolk were fighting and dying. Whatever the motivations, southern white women recorded their responses to key battles, voiced opinions on statesmen and generals, and offered informed discussions about the war's causes and implications for the future of the South. "It is not my privilege to enter the ranks," explained a somewhat disingenuous Evans to General Pierre Gustave Toutant Beauregard, "wielding a sword, in my country's cause, but all that my feeble, womanly pen could contribute to the consummation of our freedom, I have humbly, but at least, faithfully and untiringly *endeavored* to achieve." Evans and other southern women had become pen and ink warriors.[5]

This Book Will Always Be of Peculiar Interest to Me

Southern white women clearly recognized the transformative importance of the Civil War and wished from the start to preserve its record. Cornelia Peake McDonald of Winchester, Virginia, faithfully maintained a diary for her husband, who was away fighting for the Confederacy, and for her children, who were too young at the war's start to appreciate fully the magnitude of events. McDonald's husband encouraged her to keep a diary, and according to an 1875 preface to her diary, she believed "that my children will take interest in the record of that time" and wished "them to remember the trials and struggles we endured and made and the cause in which we suffered." Consequently, she took pen to paper and recorded the events of the war, later reconstructing those pages that were destroyed in the fray.[6]

The departure of Kate Rowland's husband, Charles, a wealthy planter from Augusta, Georgia, prompted his wife to begin her journal. In late October 1863, Kate admitted that she had often thought of writing but had put it off until her husband left to serve under General Joseph E. Johnston: "It has been a long desire of mine to keep a journal . . . only I have never done so." She regretted "not having commenced at the beginning of this war, as so many stirring events have been transforming around us, I should like to have noted them down." Margaret Junkin Preston, Stonewall Jackson's sister-in-law by his first marriage, offered a similar lament: "I regret now that I did not, a year ago, make brief notes of what was passing under my eye," she confessed. "Not write a journal,—I have no time nor inclination for that—but just slight jottings as might serve to recall the incidents of this most eventful year in our country's history. It is too late now to attempt the review." Unlike Rowland and Preston, however, many southern white women began their wartime journals in late 1860, with Lincoln's election as president, or with the 1861 secession crisis.[7]

Loula Kendall Rogers, a young woman from Barnesville, Georgia, who began her journal in 1861, believed that the first year of the war would "long, long be remembered as the commencement of our great struggle for Freedom, the formation of a new Republic, and the 'night that brings the stars.'" Rogers continued to chronicle the events of the war because she believed that her account would provide a storehouse of tales for future generations: "I am proud to be living in such an era in Southern history," she proclaimed on the last day of 1861, "for it will be something worth telling to our *grand children* who will listen with more interest than we do to those good old tales of the Revolution."[8] Rogers, who later became an active member of the United Daughters of the Confederacy and poet laureate for the state of Georgia, undoubtedly referred to her wartime journal for inspiration for the hundreds of essays and poems she wrote about the South and the Confederacy.

Rumors, inaccuracies, and false reports constantly befuddled Rogers, and indeed most diarists who wished to maintain a "true" account of the war. George C. Rable notes that Confederate women's isolation from public life fostered a high degree of susceptibility to conflicting reports of "great victories and crushing defeats." Writing from a refugee home in Wilcox County, Georgia, in late 1864, Rogers lamented the latest rumors that "general Hood was killed, and President Davis is dead! If it is true," she noted, "I shall feel as if we *are* really *forsaken* by Heaven and given up to be lost." Mary Loughborough, who sought refuge in a cave near Vicksburg during the city's siege, commented on the particular difficulty of obtaining accurate information while in hiding: "Rumors come to us of the advance of the Federal troops on the Black River; yet so uncertain were the tidings, and so slow was the advantage gained, we began to doubt almost everything." An exuberant Wadley recorded the resignation of General Winfield Scott as commander of the U.S. Army so that he might aid his native Virginia, only to note five days later that Scott had neither resigned nor intended to defect to the Confederacy. Scott's refusal to join the Confederacy needled Wadley, and she reserved special vituperation for him, recording in her diary his real and fictional exploits in all manner of battles. On 10 May 1864, Tennessee's Belle Edmondson sadly noted that General James Longstreet had suffered a mortal wound at the Battle of the Wilderness: "Heaven forbid the correctness of the report," she added, recognizing its possible inaccuracy. Indeed, Edmondson later refused to record the latest news from the front, doubting its veracity yet fearing the worst: "No late news except Yankee lies," she wrote on 16 May 1864, "which say that we are beaten in Va, and I do not believe one word of it—never will hear the truth until we get the Southern account." Grace Elmore, a prominent young woman from Columbia, South Carolina, summarized the crippling effects of rumors on the psyche of women left on the home front: "All day we [women] are anxious and gloomy from the rumors and facts, and then when our men come they laugh at our fears and reassure us even against our judgments."[9]

Loula Kendall Rogers, 1865. (Courtesy Special Collections Department, Robert W. Woodruff Library, Emory University)

More frustrating than the myriad of rumors, however, was the absence of reports. "There is a lull now," Rogers recorded in the summer of 1862, anxious to hear from her brothers and her fiancé on the front line. "No telegrams are allowed to be sent from the west, so we can hear nothing either by mail or by telegraph. It is dreadful, this harrowing suspense, how long must I bear it?" Similarly, Rowland, fearing General William T. Sherman's imminent passage through Georgia, admitted, "I feel particularly anxious to-day, not having had any news since Sunday when it was thought the great fight in Georgia would come off yesterday." Despondent over the fate of the Confederacy during the last year of the war, disgusted at reports of lawlessness and desertion among southern soldiers fighting in the western theater, and filled with contempt for the Confederate leadership, Wadley believed that the armies in the east were her country's only possible salvation: "I hope all from there, but we hear nothing."[10] The news blackouts continually stymied women's efforts to record the latest information. Faced with maddening silences from the front, diarists anxiously filled many a page with supposition, innuendo, and sheer fantasy.

In addition to providing southern white women with a way to record the events of the war, diary keeping afforded a means for personal reflection and for questioning the providential hand that was believed to guide the South's war efforts. Rogers titled her 21 February 1862 entry "Darkness." Noting the Confederacy's reversal at Fort Donelson, Tennessee, Rogers begged, "has our nation which at first seemed under the watchful care of a kind Providence been guilty of some great sin?" "Have we erred," she continued, "have we forgotten the God who made us and has that God forsaken us? Is the enemy to be permitted to take all our Forts and Cities to sprinkle our lands with our own blood, and make themselves masters of all we have?" She finally asked despondently, "Is that to be the end of this war?" Equally confused, Elmore queried, "What is life without a country and what is our country without freedom to enjoy all its beauties and blessings with which God has surrounded us the land of our birth?" Indeed, Elmore was so distraught at the reversals of the Confederacy that she confessed in her diary that she would consider suicide preferable to life under Yankee rule.[11] Diary keeping provided Elmore and many other southern women with a means for coming to terms with their crises of faith, their dark nights of the soul.

Southern white women also questioned forces much more earthly than Providence. Never one to censure her criticisms of the "evil" spirit that infected the Confederacy, Wadley assessed the state of the Confederacy at the end of 1863. "Our sky looks so dark, our foes within, our inefficient and false officers and the luke warmness of the people are what we have to contend with," she bleakly noted. "These are foes far more powerful than the Yankees," she continued, "and when I think of the corruption in our midst and see no genius powerful enough to crush it, I fear that we shall gain our liberty only after years of war and perhaps anarchy." More directly, Wadley unhesitatingly levied blame on Confederate soldiers, whom she believed had earned her scornful pen. Although piqued at a recent rampage of Union forces in Delhi, Louisiana, her anger at the Yankees did not match the ire she reserved for the Confederate general who was unable to stave off the attack. "All this damage done by a few contemptible Yankees, while our own contemptible Gen'l Blanchard was shivering with fright in Monroe, *and* there was a company of our soldiers in the [area] but they happened to be *watching* the wrong place, if we only had a *man* here for a Gen'l instead of the effeminate creature we have, these raids might be prevented and this important railroad left open for the benefit of the whole country." Her evaluation of John C. Pemberton's defense of Vicksburg was equally damning, as she placed the blame for the city's fall squarely on the general's shoulders: "May every true patriot execrate the name of Pemberton," she pleaded. Wadley hoped, however, that Pemberton's actions would not sully the "glorious" southern cause.[12]

Not surprisingly, southern white women frequently turned to their diaries to record their ill will toward the Yankees. As Rable argues, "condemning the Yankees as the most hateful of God's creatures masked [southerners'] hatred" and allowed them to "rationalize, modify, or abandon long-held ideas about Christian charity." Wadley proclaimed in her diary, "rather will every man, woman, and child perish upon the soil that gave them birth, than call down the curses of our Free Forefathers upon the degenerate race" that attempted to force the South into the Union. Northern soldiers were called "perfidious," "treacherous," "murderous," "vile," "contemptible," and "traitorous." In a particularly strong passage, Rogers spat out her absolute hatred for the Union Army. Anticipating a Union raid, Rogers considered the likelihood of her diary falling into enemy hands: "I want them to know that *I hate, loathe, and abhor the very scent, sight, and name of a Yankee* with all my *heart, soul, mind, and body* and this assertion I would stick to if they were to point a thousand bayonets at me at once."[13]

While Rogers slung epithets at the entire "Yankee race," most southern women reserved the harshest words for those Federal soldiers who raided southern civilians' homes. Those raids quite literally brought the front line to the home front. This intrusion into southern women's personal space shattered any notions they might have harbored about a separate domestic sphere or about Confederate men's ability to protect their women. Confederate women believed that Union soldiers deemed nothing sacred, noting that they destroyed livestock, larders, and personal possessions while marching across the South. McDonald, who lived with her nine children during the war, contemptuously recalled the Federal occupation of her town. McDonald's anger flared when she found a soldier rifling through her desk. "He . . . turned out the contents of my writing desk," she wrote, "read some notes aloud in a mocking tone (for which I could have shot him.)" Similarly, Rowland listed the livestock and provisions burned by Yankee raiders but found their wanton destruction of women's personal possessions most egregious: "They burnt all gin houses and cotton and in many instances dwellings, destroyed all horses, cows and stock of every kind and worst [sic] than all destroying ladies wardrobes and tearing their clothes to pieces." Learning that the Union raiders planned to "starve out the women and children," Elmore questioned the tactic of bringing the war to noncombatants: "God in Heaven! Even Satan in his war with the hosts of heaven was nearer to God than these; he bravely met his equals in strength, but these creatures slay the poor, dumb, helpless beasts and insult the women and children and say in this way they will conquer our men."[14] The intrusion of war into the home shocked, frightened, and frustrated women, who turned to their diaries to record these emotions.

Diary keeping provided southern white women with a sense of calm during troubling times. Wadley noted the tremendous comfort she received from recording events in her journal. On the last page of the third volume of her Civil War journal, she wistfully recalled that her diary "has been with me, and been my faithful confident [sic] in so many scenes and in so many different moods, I don't know what I should do without my journal, it is such a relief to me to write here." Because the volume contained Wadley's documentation of her family's exodus across the war-ravaged South in search of a safe haven, it was especially dear to her: "This book will always be of peculiar interest to me as the one which holds the record of our eventful, of our important journey, I shall always like to be able to recall it in all the particularities which I have written down here, and which I might gradually forget without this record." Elmore echoed Wadley's sentiments. "There is a great pleasure in writing the thoughts and actions of yourself and those around you," she acknowledged, "a pleasure that is often purely selfish, for much that is written gratifies only the feeling of the moment, and whether the feeling be good or bad it is naught to you since you have the pleasure of expressing it." Whatever other purposes diary keeping may have served, at the very least it provided southern women an enjoyable leisurely activity.[15]

Under These Circumstances, Writing Is Like
Taking My Brains Out with Pinchers

Private correspondence offered southern women another avenue for expressing their doubts, concerns, hopes, and criticisms of the Confederacy to trusted recipients. Assuming that only the intended reader would be privy to the letter's contents, corresponding proved especially cathartic for socially prominent women, who might have felt that their position in Confederate society constrained them from speaking publicly. Although many of these women vigorously championed the Confederacy until the bitter end, their correspondence evidences fluctuations in support and confidence. Writing from her home, Bivouac, in Louisiana, Elsie Bragg confided to her husband, General Braxton Bragg, that even the "most sanguine" women were beginning to lose faith in the Confederacy. Especially concerned with the Confederacy's 1862 reversals in her home state, Elsie Bragg noted that she and her compatriots felt despondent not because their homes were "in the hands of the invaders" but because the Confederacy has "*never regained a foot of ground lost*. Slowly and surely," she continued, "states and cities are taken but never *retaken*."[16] Like diary writing, corresponding was a cultivated art form in the nineteenth-century South, yet the prose is often less stilted and conventional than in diaries. Women could dash off their most immediate and pressing concerns in letters more facilely than in diaries because the writers were unconcerned with fashioning a coherent document that would chronicle their spiritual and personal growth. In this particular letter, Elsie Bragg entrusted her frustrations to her husband, believing that only he would read her letter and therefore remaining unconcerned that her words would later come back to haunt her.

Just as distressing as Elsie Bragg's crisis of faith was her disillusionment with the behavior of southern soldiers, and again, she confided in her husband. Angered at reports that Confederate soldiers had abandoned their posts at Fort Pillow, Tennessee, Elsie spilled out, "I thought southern men were at least *brave*." As an afterthought, she added, "I believe we [women] bear up better than our men," and perhaps only half jokingly suggested going to Fort Pillow herself, shaming "soldiers to stand their posts by showing what women could brave and endure." Similarly, in July 1862, a thoroughly disgusted Mary Ann Cobb wrote to her husband, Howell, about the rumors rocking Athens, Georgia, that Generals John B. Magruder and Robert Toombs were drunk on the battlefield during the Seven Days' Battles in Virginia.[17] Such behavior hardly matched the public image of the virtuous Confederate soldier nobly fighting for the honor of his country. Although Bragg and Cobb might not have wished to tarnish the reputation of the southern soldiers, they could well express their anger in private correspondence.

Even Evans, a celebrated propagandist for the Confederacy who would later glorify the pure and noble southern soldier in her 1864 novel, *Macaria*, used an 1862 letter to vent her disgust at the attitude of Confederate soldiers. "You have doubtless become to some extent acquainted," she seethed, "with the spirit of subordination and disaffection which is rife in our armies and which has attained in this section of the Confederacy melancholy and alarming proportions." For this "spreading spirit of defection," Evans blamed the Exemption Bill, which allowed wealthy southerners to pay substitutes to fight. "Moreover," she continued, "one unfortunate clause (though designed I know to guard against servile insurrection) has resulted most unhappily in the creation of an anti-slavery element among our soldiers who openly complain that they are torn from their homes and families consigned to starvation, solely in order that they may protect the property of slaveholders, who are allowed by the 'bill' to remain in quiet 'enjoyment of luxurious ease.'" Two years later, when Evans drafted *Macaria*, she wrote of a wealthy planter, Mr. Huntingdon, who at the news of Fort Sumter unhesitatingly joined the Confederate Army. Although Evans conceded that "a stern sense of duty does not prevent people from suffering at separation and thought of danger," she nonetheless made no reference to the Exemption Bill in her novel, preferring instead to memorialize the soldiers who rushed to defend their country.[18]

Varina Davis, the wife of Confederate President Jefferson Davis, expressed her frustration not at the fate of the Confederacy but at the trials of being married to a leader of a country at war: "How do you spend your time?" she asked Mary Boykin Chesnut, the wife of James Chesnut, a South Carolina politician and aide to Jefferson Davis. "I live in a kind of maze. How I wish my husband were a dry-goods clerk," she confessed. "Then we could dine in peace on a mutton scrap at three and take an airing on Sunday in a little buggy with no back." Davis seemingly felt secure in sharing her frustrations with a confidant, trusting that such sentiments would not be made public. "This dreadful way of living from hour to hour depresses me more than I can say," Davis later admitted.[19] She undoubtedly recognized her precarious position as wife of the president of the Confederacy: publicly expressing her fears and frustrations would be tantamount to treason. Corresponding with Chesnut allowed Davis privately to unburden her heart, without fear of repercussions.

Of course, southern white women did not write letters only to vent frustrations. Like diary keeping, corresponding allowed southern women to express their hopes for the new nation, their assessments of battles, their policy recommendations, their hatred of Union soldiers, and their evaluations of Confederate leaders. Writing letters also fostered "unprecedented intimacy, new frankness, heightened self-awareness, and self-revelation," as Drew Gilpin Faust argues. And as with diaries, the exigencies of warfare often interfered with the writing of letters. As Cobb noted early in the war, "under these circumstances, writing is like taking my brains out with pinchers."[20] Cobb and her compatriots continued to write, however, sharing their thoughts with trusted friends and family, drawing solace and comfort from the effort.

A Dangerous Experiment

Some women who wrote during wartime sought a reading audience beyond their immediate families. A friend "urged" Loughborough, who spent the early months of 1863 hiding in a cave near Vicksburg, Mississippi, "to dispatch the papers as speedily as possible while public interest in the siege was still vivid" and published her account in 1864. The preface to the second edition of Loughborough's work, published in 1881, noted that "words cannot express the wonder and admiration excited in [Loughborough's] mind by the conduct of those brave [Confederate] men at Vicksburg; how they endured with unflinching courage the shower of ball and shell, how they confronted the foe with undaunted resolution . . . how they endured with steadfast perseverance, the hunger, the wet, the privation." But words of admiration apparently did, in fact, fail Loughborough, for the original account contains scenes of angry and frightened women accusing their Confederate "protectors" of desertion. As the men of the town fled a Union attack on 17 May 1863, the women scornfully yelled after them, "we are disappointed in you. . . . who shall we look to now for protection?" As if to mock the fleeing men, Loughborough recorded her escape through enemy fire from her cave to the house where her husband was stationed. The Confederate soldiers camped nearby "stood curiously watching the effect of the sudden fall of metal around me. I would not for the world have shown fear; so braced by my pride,

I walked with a firm and steady pace, notwithstanding the treacherous suggestions of my heart that beat a loud 'Run, Run.'" Indeed, Loughborough seemed more concerned with detailing the hardships and privations of noncombatants in a town under siege than with glorifying southern soldiers.[21]

In 1863, Confederate spy Rose O'Neal Greenhow published an account of her exploits and eventual arrest. Initially skeptical of her story's appeal, a reluctant Greenhow was persuaded by friends to make her story known. Unlike Loughborough, however, Greenhow reserved her most scathing comments for Union soldiers and "black Abolitionists." She intended her narrative "to excite more than a simple feeling of indignation or commiseration," she noted, "by exhibiting somewhat of the intolerant spirit in which the present crusade against the liberties of sovereign states was undertaken, and somewhat of the true character of that race of people who insist on compelling us by force to live with them in bonds of fellowship and union." Greenhow's work was unabashedly political. A passage describing her equanimity during a search of her private correspondence could very well summarize her confidence in entering the public realm of political debate. "I had a right to my own political opinions," she offered, "and to discuss the questions at issue, and never shrank from the avowal of my sentiments." She later credited John C. Calhoun for helping her formulate her first, rudimentary "ideas on State and Federal matters" but noted that "these ideas have been strengthened and matured by reading and observation. Freedom of speech and thought," she declared, belonged to her by birthright and by the Constitution, "signed and sealed by the blood" of the South's fathers. Although Greenhow yielded slightly in her final chapter, noting that she was not a "philosophical historian," she nonetheless entered into a discussion of the war's causes, "a subject which does not properly come within my text."[22] According to Greenhow, the North's usurpation of power, not the extension of slavery into the territories, provoked disunion. Greenhow's account suggests the facility with which southern women bandied about familiar, contemporary political rhetoric and the degree to which they were willing to enter public discourse.

Other southern white women who published their stories of the war during the early 1860s, however, shied away from eyewitness accounts and published fictional versions, thereby transforming the genre of the antebellum domestic novel into an overtly political form. Critics were quick to pick up on the transformation. Reviewing Evans's *Macaria*, poet J. R. Randall commented that the author had "ventured on a dangerous experiment." Rather than writing the story of one woman's life, Evans had "endeavored to write a story of American life — our hard, bare, prosaic, unnovelistic American life—in an ultra classic and super-erudite style." As propagandists for the southern cause, Evans and her contemporaries not only reached large reading audiences but also carried moral authority with their readers, thereby shoring up their position. Along with Evans, Kentucky's Sallie Rochester Ford, author of the 1864 novel *Raids and Romance of Morgan and His Men*, reached the greatest popular and critical success of this new breed of women writers. In addition to the expected female readership for women's novels, Evans and Ford garnered a captive male reading audience, as Confederate camps across the South devoured Evans's and Ford's works.[23] Breaking with the traditional form of domestic fiction, both Evans and Ford broadened the scope of the novels, not merely examining the heroines' inner lives but also addressing larger sociopolitical issues.

Both Evans and Ford discussed the antebellum American political climate, cataloging northern abuses perpetrated against the South and outlining the irreconcilable philosophical and cultural differences between the two sections. Foreshadowing secession, Russell Aubrey, lawyer, politician, and Confederate hero of Evans's *Macaria*, proclaimed that northern demagoguery, or "the hydra-headed foe of democracy," threatened the existence of the United States. In a later scene, Irene Huntingdon, the novel's heroine, echoed Russell's sentiments, warning southerners to be ever vigilant in the newly founded Confederacy lest demagoguery creep "along its customary sinuous path, with serpent eyes fastened on self-aggrandizement." Similarly, Ford wrote of the "dark injustice and lawless tyranny" that presided over the antebellum United States. "The heel of the despot crushes her sons to the earth," she explained, "his cruel hand has torn from them their liberties, and dyed itself in their blood."[24] Simply put, the North had trod on the South's constitutionally guaranteed liberties, thereby ensuring a bloody war.

Faced with such abuses from an outrageous foe, asserted Ford, southerners naturally clung to a theory of states' rights, believing that southerners "*were right*; *their cause just*, and . . . they could do and dare, suffer and die, rather than be crushed beneath the fragments of a broken Constitution, rent by the hand of a vulgar despot." Evans, too, asserted that the North had abrogated the Constitution, forcing the South to strike out on its own. Although the South had formerly revered the federal government and cherished the region's position in the United States, "'Union' became everywhere the synonyme of political duplicity," forever severing its link with the South. "The Confederacy realized that the hour had arrived when the historic sphinx must find an Oedipus," Evans explained, "or Democratic Republican Liberty would be devoured, swept away with the *debris* of other dead systems."[25] For both women—and, indeed, for future southern writers—the Civil War had been engineered by the North's annulment of constitutionally guaranteed liberties, not, as northerners argued, by the South's adherence to the institution of slavery.

Although southerners believed that they had been compelled to break away from the Union, they did not feel unequal to the task of participating in an organized government. Indeed, they thought themselves better prepared for the challenge after having separated from the North. Free from the conflicting cultures and antagonistic labor systems that had ripped apart the Union, these southern women authors believed the Confederacy to have a viable, independent government. "We are now . . . a thoroughly homogeneous people," explains Irene in *Macaria*. Because the South completely identified itself with "commerce and agriculture," it need not feel threatened by outside interests. In a final burst of patriotic enthusiasm, Irene proclaims, "purified from all connection with the North and with no vestige of the mischievous element of New England Puritanism, which, like other poisonous Mycelium, springs up perniciously where even a shred is permitted, we can be a prosperous and noble people."[26]

In addition to including protracted discussions on political theory, Evans and Ford and their lesser-known contemporaries transformed the antebellum domestic novel by describing battles, a realm traditionally reserved for male writers. Evans particularly concerned herself with the July 1861 Battle of Manassas, the first great Confederate victory. She exhibited the same apprehension as did the diarists about falsely reporting the events of the war. Determined to offer her readers an accurate account of the battle, Evans consulted General Beauregard, a hero in what proved to be one of the South's most important psychological victories. "The chapter to which I allude is the *XXXth*," she informed the general, "and before I *copy it*, I am extremely desirous to know that I am *entirely accurate* in all my statements relative to the Battle." To avoid factual errors and misrepresentations, Evans posed a number of questions to Beauregard:

1. That you and General Johnston were not acquainted with the fact that [General Irwin] McDowell had left Washington with the main Federal army to attack you at Manassa's Junction *until* a young Lady of Washington (I give no name), disguised as a market women, and engaged in

selling milk to the Federal soldiers succeeded in making her way through their lines to *Fairfax Courthouse* and telegraphed you of the contemplated attack.

2. That you immediately telegraphed to General Johnston, then at Winchester, and in consequence of this information he hastened to Manassa?

3. At what hour did you learn that your Order for an advance on Centreville by your right wing had failed to reach its destination?

4. Did *you* not *lead* in *person* the second great charge which recovered the plateau and took the Batteries that crowned it?

"Fearful" as Evans may have been at "intruding" on the general in the middle of the war, she nevertheless thought her chapter on Manassas sufficiently important to solicit Beauregard's aid with her manuscript.[27]

Evans infused detailed accounts of troop movements with her own anti-Union rhetoric and painted a vivid portrait of the Battle of Manassas. "In July, 1861, when the North, blinded by avarice and hate, rang with the cry 'On to Richmond,' our Confederate Army of the Potomac was divided between Manassa and Winchester, watching at both points the glittering coils of the union boa-constrictor, which writhed in its efforts to crush the last sanctuary of freedom." While Union General Robert Patterson threatened to attack General Johnston's Confederate troops in the Shenandoah Valley, McDowell expected to overwhelm Beauregard at Manassas. "But the Promethean spark of patriotic devotion burned in the hearts of Secession women," Evans boasted, "and resolved to dare all things in a cause so holy, a young lady of Washington, strong in heroic faith, offered to encounter any perils, and pledged her life to give General Beauregard the necessary information." According to Evans, Beauregard telegraphed Johnston at Richmond, "and thus, through womanly devotion, a timely junction of the two armies was affected, ere McDowell's banners flouted the skies of Bull Run."[28] Evans apparently overcame her concerns about the accuracy of her depiction of the battle.

For Evans, writing in 1863, Manassas set the tone for what she hoped would be the eventual triumph of the Confederacy. Nevertheless, Evans astutely recognized the debasing and dehumanizing qualities of warfare. "At half past two o'clock the awful contest was at its height," Evans began, "the rattle of musketry, the ceaseless whistle, the hurtling hail of shot, and explosion of shell, dense volumes of smoke shrouding the combatants, and clouds of dust boiling up on all sides, lent unutterable horror to a scene which, to cold, dispassionate observers, might have seemed sublime." Evans might have reveled in the outcome of the battle, but she saw nothing glorious or romantic on the battlefield. "Hideous was the spectacle presented — dead and dying, friend and foe, huddled in indiscriminate ruin, walking in blood, and shivering in the agonies of dissolution; blackened headless trunks and fragments of limbs, ghastly sights and sounds of woe, filling the scene of combat." Evans believed that the price of warfare would be justified, however, by the South's overthrow of "puritanical hypocrisy."[29]

Ford chose not to memorialize the celebrated Battle of Manassas in her novel but wrote instead of the border skirmishes in Kentucky and Tennessee and General John Morgan's attempts to win the state for the Confederacy. "Poor degraded, subjugated Kentucky," Ford lamented, "thine is a sad story of vacillation and fear; of wrong and oppression." Early in *Raids and Romance*, Ford wrote of a February 1862 battle at Fort Donelson, located on the Cumberland River, in which Federal troops prevailed. Ironically, Ford writes first of the pomp and grandeur of the battle: "With banners proudly waving, and officers splendidly uniformed cheering their men to victory, they dash on-on-on!" Just as the Confederacy found its position impossible to sustain at the Battle of Fort Donelson, however, so too did Ford find it difficult to maintain her romantic image of warfare. "All through that long, dread day," she continued, describing the fighting before the tide turned against the Confederates, "the battle raged most fearfully and as night closed in upon sickening carnage, the enemy, repulsed, cut to pieces, slain in hundreds, was driven to seek his position of the morning, leaving the field covered with dead and dying."[30] Although both authors offered readers literary, stylized depictions of battle, Ford and Evans nonetheless eschewed glorifying warfare, preferring instead a more brutal portrayal of the war that was rending the United States.

Ford not only described battles but evaluated the effectiveness of Confederate officers in particular missions. Since *Raids and Romance of Morgan and His Men* was a work of Confederate propaganda, it is not surprising that Ford almost always praised the work of the Confederacy's leaders. And, given the title of the novel, readers could correctly expect Ford to crown Morgan with the laurels she believed he so richly deserved. To deflect any criticism leveled against Morgan for failing to secure Kentucky for the Confederacy, Ford admitted that "the campaign has been pronounced a failure, a sad, sad *faux pas* and the commanding general has been solely censured for want of ability and oversight of points which would have insured to the Confederate arms a glorious victory." Because General Morgan's invasion of the state failed, General Bragg's army was unable to occupy Kentucky, and the Confederacy failed to gain any territory in the West. Ford asked her readers to consider Morgan's ill-fated invasion from a different perspective, however. "If the object was to withdraw the Federal forces from their threatening position to North Alabama, relieve East Tennessee, obtain a supply of provisions and clothing for the men, and give the Southern sentiment of the state an opportunity to enlist under the Southern flag," she suggested, Morgan's invasion had not failed, "even though the expectations of the friends of the South might not have been fully realized in any of these particulars."[31] Confident of her ability to assess the progress of the Confederacy and eager to rally support for the southern cause, Ford offered her readers alternative readings of the South's setbacks, unable to face the possibility of defeat.

Although both Evans and Ford strayed far from the conventions of the antebellum domestic novel, their wartime novels provided a degree of comfortable familiarity for the works' primarily female reading audience. Both authors developed love interests for their Confederate heroes. Both celebrated the virtues of traditional southern womanhood. Both waxed rhapsodic about southern women's potential contributions to the Confederacy, and this point might have been their works' prime attraction for female readers. In one of the final scenes of *Macaria*, Irene, the novel's heroine, explains to her friend Electra, "You and I have much to do, during these days of gloom and national trial—for upon the purity, the devotion, and the patriotism of the women of our land, not less than upon the heroism of our armies, depends our national salvation." Irene then chronicles the duties of southern women: "to jealously guard our homes and social circles from the inroads of corruption, to keep the fires of patriotism burning upon the altars of the South, to sustain and encourage those who are wrestling the border for our birthright of freedom." Once the Confederacy had secured the South's independence, women would be guaranteed "long-life usefulness" to the new republic. This passage must have been particularly inspiring to those women who fretted over their inability to participate directly in the Confederate cause. After reading the novel, Ellen Gertrude Clanton Thomas of Augusta, Georgia, recorded in her diary that she felt ashamed of her own complacency and resolved to do her part for the war. "*The next evening I visited the hospital!*" she boasted. "The best commentary upon the good Miss Evans' book effected," Thomas added. Evans and Ford stretched the boundaries of the domestic novel but were unwilling to abandon their tested base of support and included scenes that were guaranteed to please female readers.[32]

Of course, all southern white women writers did not capture the same wide critical and popular response as did Evans and Ford. Military service removed many men from their customary roles as heads of families, forcing women to run their households and thus severely limiting the time available for writing. Furthermore, the exigencies of the war taxed most publishers' everyday operations, sharply curtailing the quantity and quality of works in print. Northern publishers, which before the war had been at best reluctant to print works penned by southern women writers, were now completely cut off, forcing southern authors to turn to smaller southern firms. Even the major southern literary houses, such as West and Johnston of Richmond, Virginia, and S. H. Goetzel of Mobile, Alabama, faced supply shortages, runaway inflation, and disrupted shipments of their finished products.[33] Even when minor southern women's novels were published—for example, Florence J. O'Connor's *Heroine of the Confederacy* and Maria McIntosh's *Two Pictures*—it remains unclear whether Confederate soldiers read these works with the same voracity with which they read *Macaria* and *Raids and Romance*. Like Evans and Ford, these lesser-known authors broadened the definitions of traditional domestic fiction and developed a new genre of women's war narratives, offering discussions of politics and battles.

McIntosh and O'Connor garnered only small reading audiences, but their messages were powerful. Ford and Evans did not corner the market on women's wartime propaganda. O'Connor, for example, recognized the importance of foreign support for the Confederate cause. In a direct plea to Europeans who backed the North, O'Connor begged near the end of her 1864 novel, *The Heroine of the Confederacy; or, Truth and Justice*, "will you not learn wisdom from the past? Will you still madly rush on death and suffering, when you know the award which awaits your generous conduct? Have you not heard already of Knownothingism—of the many isms which ere the war sprung up in the North, had for their aim the depriving of foreigners of any of the rights of citizenship? Are you blind to the treachery of former conduct?" O'Connor had chronicled the North's abuses, established the necessity of southern secession, and described the ugliness of battle before appealing to Europeans for aid. She had intended her novel to convince Europeans that their support for that North was tantamount to genocide, adding a bit of authorial prodding toward the end to ensure that her message would be understood. Interestingly, O'Connor had demurely approached her readers early in her novel, assuring them that she had not metamorphized into "the female politician, the literary lady who affects the Madame de Stael." Instead, O'Connor claimed, she had intended her work "to portray a few (to some perhaps interesting) events that will probably be lost sight of by more worthy 'gray goose quills' than mine, but which are not the less *true or valuable*."[34] O'Connor well understood the precarious position of polemical women writers in nineteenth-century society and wished to ease her readers' minds while convincing them of the righteousness of the Confederacy.

McIntosh, who had achieved a measure of critical and popular success in the 1840s and 1850s with her novels *Charms and Counter-Charms* (1848) and *The Lofty and the Lowly* (1851), wished to counter the prevailing opinion of the South, which had been heavily influenced by Harriet Beecher Stowe's *Uncle Tom's Cabin*. Although born in Georgia, McIntosh was a frequent traveler north of the Mason-Dixon line and harbored warm sentiments toward the North. Indeed, she had championed sectional harmony in her previous novels, especially *The Lofty and the Lowly*, in which sets of southern and northern heroes and heroines wed and pledge to promote peaceful coexistence. By the mid-1860s, however, McIntosh had abandoned her position as sectional healer and set out to explain the failings of her previous literary efforts to meld the North with the South as well as to challenge Stowe's depiction of southern culture and the institution of slavery. McIntosh's ninth and final novel, *Two Pictures; or, What We Think of Ourselves, and What the World Thinks of Us*, published in 1863, offered a pointed look at the near incompatibility of northern and southern cultures. McIntosh relied once again on a favorite literary strategy, the marriage between a southern belle and a Yankee, but here the marriage does not symbolize the union of the two cultures but instead represents the triumph of the southern position. Despite Hugh Moray's initial reluctance to take over the family plantation of his bride, Augusta, he soon settles into his role as planter and master. Speaking to his northern law partner, Hugh justifies the institution of slavery and explains his plans for the improvement of his slaves. Despite some abuses in the system, "in the essential features, the dependence of the slave, the rule and authority of the master, I believe it to be divinely appointed for the noblest ends. . . . I shall be a king on my own land," Hugh continues, "but, with my views, I must be a priest as well as a king. Instead of these people living for me, I must live for them." Hugh's neighbors soon begin to emulate his style of slave management, much to the satisfaction of the new master. Along with Hugh, southern planters begin to realize that "not England, not their northern neighbors, but God, who rules on earth as in heaven, according to the counsel of His own righteous will, had brought to their doors these beings, so ignorant and degraded, yet none the less His children and their brethren, that they might lead them to that truth which should form them anew in the image of God." Slaveholders begin to repent not their positions as masters, for that was not a sin, but their failure to live up to the responsibilities entrusted in them as masters.[35] To atone for their failings, according to McIntosh, southern slave owners began to minister to the slaves' souls as well as their bodies, providing spiritual guidance as well as comfortable living quarters.

In McIntosh's view, despite these improvements in slave management, Stowe slandered the South with the publication of *Uncle Tom's Cabin*. In the final scene of *Two Pictures*, Augusta expresses her horror at a favorable northern newspaper review of Stowe's novel. *Uncle Tom's Cabin* can only further divide the country, surmises Augusta, suggesting that all of McIntosh's earlier literary efforts were in vain. Although Augusta hopefully notes that southerners will discount Stowe's portrayal of them, McIntosh's character nonetheless concedes that the novel will strengthen antislavery sentiment both in the North and abroad. Hugh agrees, adding, "the world's picture of us is seldom just, to look at it would either inflate us with vanity, or irritate us by a sense of wrong, we will turn from it, and try to see ourselves as God sees us, this will make us at once humble and hopeful."[36] In the end, McIntosh's novel warned southerners against being seduced into self-doubt and self-loathing by outside accounts of their culture. Remain constant, she counseled, and trust that the southern position is divinely sanctioned.

More important than these authors' efforts to sway outside opinion about the South and the Confederacy, however, were their attempts to bolster southerners' faith in their sacred cause. O'Connor carefully explained that the North was wholly responsible for the bloody conflict, inciting the peace-loving South into war. The "Black Republicans," she informed her readers, "broke in upon the peace of our country and killed it with bayonets, angry blood, desperate boils, confusion and wrong." She reserved special vituperation for the Beechers and other northern preachers who used their pulpits to slander the South and agitate the North into a frenzy of war fury. Though northerners feigned "despair and grief" over the destruction of the Union, she claimed, they had sought to rip the country apart. "Nero-like, they now sit upon their tower, fiddling over the conflagration of their country, and singing paeans of triumph over the success of their vile project."[37] Here and throughout the novel, O'Connor assured her readers of the North's position as transgressor, championing one of the Confederacy's chief rallying cries.

In addition to designing her novel as a piece of Confederate propaganda, O'Connor had further transgressed the boundaries of domestic fiction by including camp and battle scenes in her novel. Like Evans, O'Connor wrote of the Battle of Manassas, using the Confederate victory as a rallying point for her readers. Claiming knowledge of both the history of warfare and the merits of Confederate leaders, O'Connor exclaimed, "Victory is ours! Let us proclaim it far and wide, until hills and dales re-echo the sound, and all honor, fame, and praise to the great general whose wonderful Napoleonic genius has this, with desperate, overwhelming odds against him, achieved so glorious and brilliant a victory — a victory unrivaled in the annals of America, North or South, not only for its magnitude, but its effulgence." Lapsing into the conventions of the epistolary novel, O'Connor conveyed the horrors of war by including an imaginary letter from a soldier at Manassas to his sister. In melodramatic terms, O'Connor depicted the brutal conduct of northern soldiers: "The ravages and devastation's of Atilla [sic] the Hun, the fanatical rage of Omar, the Turks oppression, the Sepoy's revenge, have been humane and charitable compared with the conduct of these hyenas."[38] O'Connor did not restrict herself to the Battle of Manassas but also gave accounts of Bethel, Rich Mountain, Belmont, and Shiloh, always glorifying the southern soldier and proclaiming the righteousness of the southern cause. Although O'Connor's overly emotive conceptualization of war did not match Evans's in popularity, O'Connor nevertheless entered into a discourse that many had thought unseemly — or at least uninteresting — for women.

Accounts of camp life and battles allowed McIntosh and O'Connor to break free from the boundaries of domestic fiction, making their novels more accessible to men. Like Evans and Ford, however, these women understood that southern women would largely constitute the reading audience and targeted the novels accordingly. Both McIntosh and O'Connor effusively praised the virtues of southern women, extolling their beauty, charm, and devotion: "Let others talk of woman's rights as they will," a train conductor tells Augusta, "you know that you are enjoying woman's highest privilege, and exercising her noblest duty, while you are thus keeping human soul true to the best instincts which God has implanted within it." Rather than allow other characters to comment on the myriad of southern women's virtues, O'Connor let her heroine boast of her and her compatriots' worthiness and usefulness to the Confederacy. In a letter to a soldier at the front, Natalie, the title character in *The Heroine of the Confederacy*, assures him of the constancy of the women at home: "We are prepared for all emergencies, and even our women, in devotion to their country's cause, will stand unparalleled in history," she comforts. "Each and every southern woman's cry is 'give us but a crust of bread and a cup of water from the running brook, but, oh, give us liberty. . . . Yes, like the Spartan Mothers of old." Natalie concludes, "Our women say to their husbands, sons, fathers, and lovers, 'Come with your shield, or on it.'"[39]

Natalie sings the praises of southern women not only to Confederate soldiers but also to her female companions. Like Evans, O'Connor imagined women occupying a position of importance within the Confederacy. Shortly after re-assuring the soldier at the front, Natalie addresses a group of women, detailing their specific tasks for the good of the southern cause. "Now is the time to judge friend from foe," she counsels. "Now is the time the pruning knife should be placed at the root, to eradicate the budding imperfections of the glorious Con-federate tree, whose branches shall o'ershadow the earth, and whose blossoms shall be 'defiance,'—whose fruit 'victory.'"[40] By positioning women as the Con-federacy's moral arbiters, the judges of worthiness and devotion, O'Connor af-forded women a great deal of cultural weight, a tactic that undoubtedly appealed to her female readers.

In addition to speechifying on behalf of southern women, Natalie appears as the true heroine of the Confederacy. During the course of the novel, Natalie as-sumes the identity of three other characters, with her role as Confederate nurse and spy not revealed until the tale's end. As "Miss Clayton," Natalie aids her country by carrying dispatches from deep within the Confederacy across enemy lines. Inviting female readers to place themselves in Miss Clayton's position, the author titillates and shocks her readers, offering them some of the excitement of combat. Describing Miss Clayton's daring escape, O'Connor wrote, "imagine . . . gentle ladies . . . yourselves thus, and seated back in the corner of a dilapidated vehicle, with your hand grasping a revolver, and your thumb upon the trigger, not daring to close your eyes[, and] you can form some idea of what one of your own sex suffered in her character of Confederate emissary." O'Connor asserted that not even the renowned exploits of Belle Boyd, the real-life spy who kept Stonewall Jackson informed while he was positioned in the Shenandoah Valley of Virginia, could surpass the deeds of Miss Clayton.[41]

Without any sort of transition, readers leave the woman spy in the Shenan-doah Valley and encounter a nurse, "Sister Secessia," at a Richmond hospital. "Like a new star, she beamed in the clouded firmament of the sick and suffering, she was welcome everywhere," O'Connor wrote of this briefly seen character. Finally, near the end of the novel, Natalie disguises herself as "Miss Laval," an-other spy who risks her life to aid her country.[42] Through these three heroic char-acters, O'Connor offers her women readers the opportunity to identify them-selves with the heroine, setting out to save the Confederacy. Although women's roles on the home front were circumscribed by convention, through the fantasy of fiction, O'Connor's readers found themselves on the battlefield.

There Is No Longer a "Luxury of Woe"

Although later writers would explore many of the themes developed by the war-time diarists, correspondents, and authors, these early narratives differ because the ending had yet to be written: the outcome of the war remained unknown. "The future of the Southern country is as glorious as ever were those of Italy or Greece," wrote O'Connor early in *Heroine of the Confederacy*, "and her brightness and best days are but dawning. Her sun is but beginning to cast its early beams around, her noon will awaken the world."[43] Unburdened by defeat, war-time writers could imagine a future for the independent southern nation. Although these narratives form the foundation for the dominant trope in postwar southern writing, the myth of the Lost Cause, they remain free from the myth they created. Because postwar authors knew the ending, they could infuse their narratives with a pervasive sense of defeat. In contrast, wartime diarists could delight in news from the front, confident that every Confederate victory ensured eventual triumph and equally confident that every Confederate setback would be rectified by the hand of Providence.

Novelists were even more unfettered by the story's ending. Writing to bolster the spirits of both fighting men and noncombatants, southern women novelists reveled in the possibility of a triumphant Confederate nation, encouraging their readers to do likewise. "That day approaches," announced Ford near the end of *Raids and Romances*, when the South will be free from the North's tyrannical grip. "Let us hope for this glorious realization of our desires," she encouraged her readers, "pray for it, and above all, let us put forth every energy, strain every nerve, avail ourselves of every resource, endure every hardship, surmount every obstacle, vanquish every difficulty, until this blessed era shall burst upon us, and we, a free and independent people[,] shall unite as with one voice in paean and of triumph and thanksgiving."[44] The outlook seemed bleak for the novel's characters: Charley and Henry, the two heroes, have been recaptured by the Union troops and sent back to a foul prison camp, and General Morgan's fate remains even more endangered. But because the soldiers and politicians had yet to provide Ford with the true ending for her novel, she could still write of a victorious Confederate nation.

The events at Appomattox Courthouse stripped these women of the luxury of writing their own endings to the war. For some, news of the Union victory provided the ending not only to their stories but also to their desire to write new stories. "I used to live to write sometimes, and put in words either the thoughts of my mind or in the heart in that way of superfluous emotion," Elmore sadly confessed. "Now everything seems so worthless, even the events and pains of my life seem unworthy of *being felt*." The Confederacy had ceased to unite southerners, she remarked, and had been replaced by pain and suffering. "Grief has in these present days lost all individuality, it is the common property of my countrymen;—so surrounded are we by it, so universally is its language spoken, so darkly does its shadow rush upon us all, so constant and real is its presence, that there is no longer a 'luxury of woe.'" And Elmore's sense of despair was now shared by the South as a whole. "What is the use of words," she asked, "when I've but to look in the face of my neighbors and see there the shadow that rests upon mine?"[45]

In fact, the end of the war did not signal the end of Elmore's activities as a writer. Nor did it prevent other women from writing. It did, however, so capture the imagination of southern white women writers that no story of the war could be told without the pervading sense of Confederate defeat. From 1865 on, the end of the story loomed large from the opening paragraphs.

2

Country-women in Captivity, 1865–1877

Here indeed . . . ruin reigned supreme.
—MARY ANN CRUSE, Cameron Hall

Sarah L. Wadley had just heard of the South's defeat in the Civil War when she opened her diary on 20 April 1865. An ardent supporter of the Confederacy, Wadley now experienced a profound sense of remorse that seemed almost debilitating. "I am depressed almost to despair," she confessed. "Life seems to have lost its interest, earth its beauty." Although Wadley assiduously followed the events of the war, chronicling in her diary the Confederacy's victories and setbacks, she professed genuine surprise at the surrenders of Generals Robert E. Lee and Joseph E. Johnston. Confused about and frightened by the South's uncertain future, Wadley experienced a shock that might have stemmed more from a sense of displacement than from actual disbelief over the war's outcome, which had seemed apparent for months. Wadley's stamina had waned. "What use is courage under difficulties, hope in misfortune," she asked, "when courage can no longer avail, hope can no longer cheer?" She ended her Civil War diary with the simple plea, "Oh God, help me."[1]

Like other southerners, Wadley had heard rumors and stories about north-ern plans for reunification, yet she could not envision a future for herself or her country under northern rule. The North's failure to hammer out a single, co-herent plan complicated Wadley's and other white southerners' conceptions of life after the war. Indeed, northern politicians had bandied about proposals as early as 1863 without reaching a compromise.[2] These profound disagreements stemmed from contradictory constitutional and legal interpretations of seces-sion. Terms of surrender, reunification, and the authority for jurisdiction and administration of these terms all hinged on the successful resolution of these complicated questions. The first to articulate a formal plan for reunification, President Abraham Lincoln argued that the South had not in fact seceded and, therefore, its constitutional status had never been compromised. More impor-tant, according to this position, terms of surrender fell to the office of the presi-dency. Lincoln's 1863 Proclamation of Amnesty and Reconstruction offered full pardons to any southerner, except high-ranking civil and military Confederates, who had pledged future loyalty to the Union and agreed to accept the aboli-tion of slavery. Any state could establish a new state government, provided its constitution explicitly abolished slavery, once 10 percent of its 1860 voters ac-cepted these terms of loyalty. Lincoln's plan then entitled the state government to representation in the national government.

Although never ratified, Lincoln's "10 percent plan" generated a great deal of discussion, most of it unfavorable. Some abolitionists expressed dissatisfaction over the plan's silence on the subjects of black equality, suffrage, and participa-tion in the process of Reconstruction. Lincoln designed his proposal to shorten the war and marshal white support for emancipation, not as a blueprint for re-unification, however. Radical Republicans who challenged Lincoln's interpreta-tion of secession expressed far more fundamental concerns about the 10 per-cent plan. Massachusetts Senator Charles Sumner, Pennsylvania Representative Thaddeus Stevens, and other Radicals maintained that the southern states had seceded, thereby abrogating their constitutional status. Under this interpreta-tion, because the states had been conquered by the North, they had been reduced to provinces with territorial status. Since territories fall under the jurisdiction of Congress rather than the president, the legislative branch commanded the power to devise a plan for Reconstruction.

Radical Republicans shared a reading of the Constitution but did not share a vision for the postwar South. Sumner, Stevens, and Indiana Representative George W. Julian pushed for a hard peace. Their plan demanded the confiscation of southern plantations and the redistribution of the land to the freed slaves and white southerners who had remained loyal to the Union. Most members of Congress, however, feared that this plan violated constitutional protections of property rights and refused to support the bill. The debates generated by the Sumner, Stevens, and Julian plan, however, did lead to a consensus among Republicans on certain elements that they believed any reunification plan should incorporate. First, the Republicans agreed that high-ranking civil and military Confederates should be barred from returning to power. Second, the Republican Party should be established as the dominant party in southern political life. Finally, freed slaves should receive full civil equality, and the federal government should guarantee this full equality.

In 1864 moderate and radical Republicans hammered out a compromise between Lincoln's plan and Sumner, Stevens, and Julian's plan. By midsummer, Congress had passed the Wade-Davis Bill, which stated that a majority (not 10 percent, as Lincoln had proposed) of a state's white male adult population would have to swear an "ironclad" oath of allegiance to the Union. The state could then hold a constitutional convention, but those who fought for or aided the Confederacy were prohibited from voting in the Convention, thereby reserving the state's future for those explicitly opposed to the Confederacy. Although the Wade-Davis Bill was far more radical than Lincoln's proposal, the president did not oppose the measure. The president then engaged selected members of Congress in informal talks, but the two camps had not reached an agreement when the president was assassinated on 14 April 1865.

It is no wonder, then, that white southerners such as Sarah Wadley felt a deep sense of confusion about the South's future. In less than one week in April 1865, the Confederacy had been defeated, the president of the United States had been assassinated, and Vice President Andrew Johnson had suddenly assumed the office of the chief executive. Meanwhile, northern politicians continued to haggle over vastly different plans for the South. Although Wadley believed that a divine justice was exacting its vengeance when Lincoln was assassinated, her anxiety regarding the South's future was not alleviated. Indeed, Wadley grew more concerned. Others shared her befuddlement. Ella Gertrude Clanton Thomas of Augusta, Georgia, remarked in a particularly vindictive diary entry that her hatred of the North had only increased since the end of the war. The seemingly endless debates in the North over the terms of peace fostered Thomas's renewed sense of frustration. "We have been imposed upon," she recorded, "led to believe that terms of treaty had been agreed upon which would secure to us a lasting and honorable peace. The treaty entered into between Sherman and Johnston, the Northern president refuses to ratify—Now that we have surrendered—are in a great degree powerless we can count with certainty upon nothing. Our lands will be confiscated and imagination cannot tell what is in store for us."[3] Clarification did not appear to be forthcoming.

Like Lincoln, the new president maintained that the South had never seceded and therefore retained its constitutional rights. According to Johnson, Reconstruction fell completely under the purview of the office of the president. When Congress adjourned for its summer recess in 1865, Johnson acted unilaterally and implemented his own plan for Reconstruction, demanding only that southern states revoke their ordinances of secession, nullify war debts, and ratify the Thirteenth Amendment. In return, Johnson offered complete amnesty and a return of all property except slaves to most white southerners in exchange for an oath of allegiance. Like most other plans, Johnson's excluded high-ranking Confederates and southerners who owned taxable property amounting to more than twenty thousand dollars, although those exempted could directly petition Johnson, which they hastily did. By December 1865 all former Confederate states had met Johnson's requirements to rejoin the Union and had functioning governments.

While southern white men went about the business of securing their property by swearing their allegiance to the Union, southern white women reviled the entire process. "It makes my whole being fierce," seethed Wadley, "to think that we now stand in the condition of criminals waiting for pardon, of erring brothers to be forgiven and received." Loula Kendall Rogers, of Barnesville, Georgia, was even more contemptuous: "I sincerely trust Southern women may not be so double faced," she confessed, "but remain true to their first principles and unshaken in their steadfast desire to be *distinct* and *separate* people from the North."[4] Southern white women soon realized that the end of the war had not signaled an end to their suffering, a release of hatred, an acceptance of the terms of surrender, or a willingness to reintegrate into the Union.

An Ambitious Venture for a Woman

For some women, the news of Confederate defeat and rumors about Reconstruction paralyzed writing efforts, at least temporarily. Emma Holmes of South Carolina remarked in a brief journal entry dated 17 April 1865 that the "rush of events" and the "whirl of excitement" had so bewildered her that she could scarcely write. "It is almost absurd to pretend to write up a journal in times as these," she apologized. Five days later, Holmes bemoaned language's inadequacy to convey southerners' emotional pain. "To go back to the Union!!!" she screamed. "No words can describe all the horrors contained in those few words." Rogers also faced this paralysis, confessing on 11 May 1865, "I have no heart to write in my journal now—we are a broken spirited people almost."[5]

Both women soon overcame their initial inability to write about southern defeat, filling their once-neglected journals with invectives against the North and praise for the Confederacy, just as in wartime writings. Rogers also transferred her need to write about the war to other genres, eventually becoming the poet laureate for the state of Georgia, largely because of her poetry about the Confederacy. She also helped organize the Barnesville Chapter of the United Daughters of the Confederacy, became an officer in the Georgia Division of the United Daughters of the Confederacy, and penned many essays on the southern cause.

Professional writers shared in this initial crisis of ability. Augusta Jane Evans, one of the Confederacy's most effective propagandists, ceased to write publicly about the war for almost forty years. For Evans, more was at stake in the Civil War than merely the political and cultural identity of the southern nation. She had perceived her personal identity as inextricably linked with that of the Confederacy. With the South's loss came a near deathblow to her psyche. "All my hopes, aims, aspirations were bound up in the success of that holy precious cause," lamented Evans. "Its failure has bowed down and crushed my heart as I thought nothing earthly could do."[6] The future offered nothing to Evans, and she was despondent.

Evans had initially thought of writing a history of the Confederacy. Despite her reservations about a woman's ability to write critically on "military matters," she explained to former Confederate Vice President Alexander H. Stephens shortly after the war that "my heart vetoes the verdict of my judgment, and prompts me to offer some grateful testimonial, some tribute, however inadequate, to the manes of our heroes." Three months later, however, she declared that "the past — our hallowed past is too unalterably mournful to be dwelt upon." By the following year she had abandoned altogether her projected history, deferring to Stephens, who planned his own study of the war. Her decision might have stemmed in part from her capitulation to her "better judgment" on women's inability to write about war. This choice might also have stemmed from her desire

Loula Kendall Rogers. (Courtesy Special Collections Department, Robert W. Woodruff Library, Emory University)

to shore up a wounded patriarchal gender order that demanded that women re-affirm traditional antebellum gender roles in the wake of defeat.[7] More likely, her decision resulted from her intense feelings about the death of the Confederacy.

Evans's reluctance to publish her views on the Civil War, Confederate defeat, and Reconstruction by no means signaled her disengagement from the subject matter. To Pierre Gustave Toutant Beauregard, with whom she had corresponded for her novel *Macaria*, Evans expressed her indignation at Republican rule. In an 1867 letter, she compared the South with other conquered lands, claiming that the South had suffered the greatest abuses: "More pitiable than Poland or Hungary," she wrote, "quite as helpless as were the Asia Minor provinces when governed by Persian Satraps, *we* of the pseudo '*territories*' sit like Israel in the captivity; biding the day of retribution,—the *Dies Irae* that must surely dawn in blood upon the nation that oppresses us." The South's conquerors had so incensed Evans that she applauded what appeared to be their "demoralization" and decay. Although Evans counted General Beauregard among her friends, she worried about his reaction to her sentiments. "What will you think of me,—if I tell you candidly" of the North's impending demise, she asked. Beauregard was privy to opinions that Evans cautiously censored from her reading public. After all, "in these *uncertain times* it is perhaps best to be reticent."[8]

Time did not quell Evans's hatred for the North or the Republican Party or ease her soul regarding Confederate defeat. Outraged by the obvious Republican bent of *Harper's* magazine during the 1860s and 1870s, Evans voiced her anger most explicitly in an eight-page 1876 letter to Colonel W. A. Seaver. A recent spate of articles designed to bolster the African-American vote for the Republican ticket in the upcoming national election piqued Evans's ire. "While the mere business aspect of the matter may be quite unimportant," she snidely commented, "as the Mess'rs Harper can doubtless smile and afford to incur the loss of Southern patronage for their periodicals,—there are principles involved, for which dollars and cents furnish no standard." She later questioned what she perceived to be the insidious motives behind the magazine's editorial policy: "Have ten years of serfdom to Radical rule and proscription entitled the Southern States no sympathy," she queried, "or do the Mess'rs Harper hate us so intensely, so unrelentingly, so everlastingly—that they merge all other aims in that of maligning,—caricaturing and persecuting their white countrymen."[9]

Evans, a noted and respected author, no doubt could have chosen a more public forum to express her disgust at the "Mess'rs Harper." She had certainly demonstrated her willingness to enter national political discussions during the war. Yet Evans largely shielded her views during Reconstruction. Although she never explicitly commented on her withdrawal from public political debate, she did suggest that her emotions were too raw, her feelings too intense, to divulge them to an anonymous reading public. In her letters to Beauregard, Seaver, and others, she first reminded her correspondents of their long-standing personal relationships. Perhaps only then could Evans reveal these deep, ugly, unreconstructed thoughts. Perhaps she deemed it unsavory for a southern lady, even one with a national reputation such as hers, to be on record as inviting a plague on the North.[10] For whatever reason, this previously vocal supporter of Confederate nationalism decided to refrain from public discussion of the Civil War and its results for the next forty years.

The postwar malaise and torpor that descended on Evans, however, did not prohibit all southern white women from publicly commenting on the war. Although better remembered for her novels, Sarah A. Dorsey, a member of the "literary Percy" clan, penned a biography of former Louisiana governor and Confederate General Henry Watkins Allen. Dorsey shared Evans's contention that the South should record its version of the Civil War. "It is very essential," Dorsey wrote in 1866, "for the sake of southern honor, and the position which may be accorded us in the future pages of impartial history, that we, Southern people, should also put on record on the files of Time, so far as we can, our version of the terrific struggle in which we have so recently engaged, and from which we have emerged, — after four years of unparalleled suffering, gallant resistance, and stern endurance of all the fiercest vicissitudes of any war ever waged by any peoples, broken in fortunes, defeated in battle, crushed, bleeding, and subjugated!"[11]

Dorsey had ample reason to be anxious about the South' position in the nascent Civil War historiography. A number of northern accounts of the war appeared during the early years of Reconstruction, offering interpretations of the "great rebellion" that southerners found unpalatable. Southern writers, who had spilled a great deal of ink claiming that a desire to perpetuate and extend the institution of slavery had not impelled them into war, agreed with little in these early northern accounts, despite the northerners' reluctance to single out slavery as the sole cause of the war. J. T. Headley, writing in 1865, argued that slavery was not the root cause of the war but was merely a "means to an end — a bug bear to frighten the timid into obedience, a rallying cry for the ignorant, deluded masses." Rather, southerners' "accursed lust for power" caused the war. Famed New York journalist Horace Greeley concurred. A southern oligarchy, according to Greeley, "resolved to rend the Republic into fragments." George Lunt similarly wrote that "self-seeking and ambitions demagogues, the pest of republics, disturbed the equilibrium, and were able, at length, to plunge the country into that worst of all public calamities, civil war." Early northern chroniclers of the war may have belonged to the "bungling generation" school of Civil War historiography, but they placed the blame squarely on the shoulders of southern politicians and fire-eaters.[12] Dorsey and countless other southern white women felt compelled to counter this argument.

But Dorsey also shared Evans's reservations about women's ability to write such a history. A mere four pages after calling for a southern account of the war, Dorsey excluded women from the enterprise: "It is an ambitious venture for a woman with her feminine mind, which, though often acute, subtle, penetrating, and analytic, is too entirely *subjective* to attempt in any way the writing of history." Dorsey distinguished biography from history, however, thereby justifying her current project. Just as women "paint best" still lifes, women might write biographies because they "require close, refined, loving scrutiny, in which affection and patience may be useful in giving accuracy and penetration to the eye and which require fine, dainty touches of the pencil, and minute, careful elaboration." In contrast, Dorsey believed that general history was far too panoramic for women to grasp, requiring "the broad, objective grasps of the masculine soul."[13]

Despite Dorsey's protestations about women's inability to write "history," however, she resisted her self-imposed restrictions and used her biography of Allen to comment on the war in general. Indeed, Dorsey fully intended to transgress her own rules, for she informed readers in the preface that she had relied heavily on "official documents and contemporary journals" for sections in which she touched "upon the story of the War." In no way did Dorsey intend to restrict her discussion to Allen's involvement in the fighting. She thus commented extensively, for example, on the devastating importance of the fall of Vicksburg. Moreover, she attempted to clear General John C. Pemberton of any fault for the South's loss. Contemporary wisdom had held that Pemberton, urged by General Joseph Johnston to attempt either a breakout attack from the besieged city or to escape across the river, surrendered solely because of cravenness. "I believe myself," wrote Dorsey, "after careful examination and impartial observation, that General Pemberton has been greatly wronged by us all." To vindicate Pemberton, she included portions of his correspondence and reports: "I use them without asking permission," she explained, "but knowing how pure and disinterested is my own search after the truth of history, I have ventured to trespass so far on the indulgences of my friends, and have made such use . . . as I thought discreet and valuable to history, holding myself responsible for all I say in these pages."[14] Dorsey not only broke free from the boundaries of strict biography but also offered informed opinions about the course of the war, claiming responsibility for her own formulations. Under the guise of biography, then, Dorsey employed her "feminine mind" to write history.

Not all agreed with Dorsey's gendered conceptions of genre. Southern men who wrote biographies of Confederate soldiers and statesmen apparently did not find the task emasculating. For example, during the war and the Reconstruction era, John Esten Cooke published biographies of Generals Stonewall Jackson and Robert E. Lee. Not surprisingly, Cooke, a former Confederate officer, found no compelling need to justify his project, as Dorsey had. He did extol the benefits of his craft, concluding the biography of Jackson by stating that the work represented a "truthful" record of Jackson's career. "It is impossible," Cooke therefore noted, "that the main occurrences have not been understood, or that the reader has not formed a tolerably clear idea of the military and personal traits of the individual. From the narrative, better than from any comment, those characteristics will be deduced." Cooke also wrote that his biography of Lee "will necessarily be 'popular' rather than full and elaborate." Cooke intended his biography to give "out full justice to all — not to arouse old enmities, which should be allowed to slumber, but to treat [the] subject with the judicial moderation of the student of history." Cooke did not distinguish between biography and history or find the task of writing biography particularly suited to women. Moreover, Cooke seemed much more willing to play down sectional hatreds than did the white southern women who penned their narratives of the Civil War during Reconstruction. Cooke appealed to his readers, whom he presumed to be largely, if not exclusively, male, to form their opinions of Jackson and Lee based on the generals' consummate military ability and personal integrity rather than on their sectional affiliation. Cooke wrote as a military man for other men who "unite[d]" in their appreciation of military genius. Southern white women could not — and did not — make such appeals.[15]

Other women entered the literary scene following the war not by publishing biographies but by making public their memoirs of the war. Confederate spy Belle Boyd wrote her account as a exile living in England and published it in 1865, after the war ended. Boyd's active participation in the war — dressed as a man, no less — liberated her, allowing her, she believed, to enter the male realm of political discourse. Recognizing that she treaded on dangerous territory, a familiar position for her, Boyd tried to tailor her narrative to her immediate reading audience, hoping to offend as few readers as possible. "I will not attempt to defend the institution of slavery, the very name of which is abhorred in England," Boyd conceded early in her narrative, "but it will be admitted that the emancipation of the negro was not the object of Northern ambition." Boyd ended her account by noting that although many people had urged her to suppress her volume, she had refused to do so, believing "that in this fiery ordeal, in this suffering, misery, and woe, the South is but undergoing a purification by fire and steel that will, in good time, and by His decree, work out its own aim." As Sharon Nolle-Kennedy noted in the introduction to her edition of Boyd's memoirs, however, the British press attacked the former Confederate spy for inappropriately entering political discourse.[16] In this respect, Boyd's strategy failed, at least in part.

Writing as "A Lady from Virginia," Judith B. McGuire published her *Diary of a Southern Refugee during the War* in 1868. Like Dorsey and Boyd, McGuire chose a circumscribed subject, in this case her personal wartime experience, rather than the broad canvas of "history" as a vehicle for interpreting the war. McGuire hoped that her record would resonate with her readers. "They will hear much of the War of Secession," she professed, "and will take special interest in the thoughts and records of one of their own family who had passed through the wonderful scenes of this great revolution." Like many of her compatriots, McGuire had believed that divine providence guided the South, blessing her homeland "with the fairest land, the purest social circle, the noblest race of men, and the happiest people on earth." The war, however, engendered a crisis of faith for McGuire: "Is it God's purpose to break up this system?" she asked in the preface to her volume. "Who can believe that it was His will to do it by war and bloodshed? Or that turning this people loose without preparation, a rapid demoralization, idleness, poverty, and vice should doom so many of them to misery, or send them so rapidly to the grave?" McGuire offered her book as a sort of poultice for those who suffered the same crisis. Through her account, readers could examine and reexamine the course of the war and evaluate the South's position "in the sight of God." McGuire fervently hoped that her work would "be agreeable and useful to her readers."[17]

Cornelia Phillips Spencer of Chapel Hill, North Carolina, certainly did not share others' apprehension about women's ability to write history. Immediately following the war, Spencer contributed a series of articles to the religious newspaper *The Watchman*, expanding and publishing these writings in 1866 as *The*

Last Ninety Days of the War in North Carolina. Spencer acknowledged the difficulties she faced in writing her book, although she felt herself stymied not because of her gender but because of her temporal proximity to the war. Spencer assured North Carolina Governor John W. Graham that she was fit for the task of writing their state's history in the war: "I am particularly obliged by such a mark of confidence," she proclaimed, "and whatever ability I possess shall be exerted to show that I am neither insensible nor unworthy." She later boasted that Graham would be hard-pressed to find a "more zealous" annalist than she. Of the war, however, Spencer wrote elsewhere, "The passions that have been evoked by it will not soon slumber, and it is perhaps expecting too much of human nature, to believe that a fair and candid statement of facts on either side will soon be made." Spencer nevertheless wrote a passionate account of the war, believing that her greatest achievement rested with the collection of source material. Later historians, she contended, could consult these documents and produce a "fair . . . representation . . . of the conflicts of opinion" and "motives of action." Such a treatment, according to Spencer, would ensure justice not only to history but also to the South.[18]

Spencer's fellow North Carolinians supported her endeavor with singular vigor, sending her their manuscripts regarding Sherman's March and Federal raids for inclusion in her book. "It gives me great pleasure," publisher E. J. Hale prefaced his account of Sherman's March, "to assist you in the patriotic work which you have undertaken and which I know you will perform admirably well." Thomas Atkinson, worried that he might be criticized for his role in the war, confessed his reluctance to put himself on public display. "But it seemed to me," he continued, "important not only for the interests of Justice, but of Humanity, that the Truth should be declared concerning the mode in which the late Civil War was carried on, and I did not see that I was exempted from this duty rather than anyone else who had personal knowledge of facts bearing on that subject." Atkinson thus felt "bound" to send Spencer his version of the war. Verina M. Chapman forwarded to Spencer an account of Stoneman's raid, paying special attention to the Union army's treatment of women, despite Chapman's fears that gross inaccuracies regarding specific events marred her narrative. "The terms 'rambling' and 'desultory' are descriptive of all my rehearsals of events," Chapman warned. She later acknowledged that her passions had been so riled by the Federal raids that she believed herself "utterly unable to give anything like a circumstantial or business like account of anything."[19] Chapman nonetheless marshaled her evidence, penning an emotional account. Others followed suit, as Spencer received scores of replies to her initial inquiries.

Contributors willingly aided Spencer because they desired that a "true" history of the war be written. "Withhold nothing," Zebulon B. Vance, former governor of North Carolina, counseled Spencer, "of the outrages of Sherman's army," for to do so would be criminal. "History," he added, "personating the righteous anger of the Gods, is to avenge us with the scorn of posterity upon our despoiless memories; and I pray that no Southern pen may help to turn its consuming fierceness from its legitimate prey." Spencer apparently heeded Vance's advice, for *The Last Ninety Days* contains vivid descriptions of the North's "outrageous" conduct during the war. Following a particularly gruesome account of Sherman's atrocities, Spencer argued that the way in which the North waged war roused the South's bitter contempt for its enemy and not merely for the Union victory. "Hard blows do not necessarily make bad blood between generous foes," she explained. "It is the ungenerous policy of the exulting conqueror that adds poison to the bleeding wounds." Lest her readers object to the inclusion of such painful details, Spencer provided a palliative: because the South had fallen victim to a peculiarly brutal oppressor, heretofore unmatched in the annals of warfare, southerners themselves had to "tell the mournful story" lest the North remain unaccountable for its egregious sins.[20]

Distasteful as it might have been, then, Spencer filled her pages with "crimes" committed against the South during the war. She appears to have had more difficulty confronting the abuses of Reconstruction, however. Although only in the first year of what would be a twelve-year occupation of the South, Spencer found much to offend her, in particular the Howard Amendment, which effectively banned antebellum officeholders from returning to their posts, and presidential pardons. Although in her book she expressed concern about the effects of Reconstruction on southern women, especially widows, her private correspondence suggested a more fundamental concern with southern manhood. "The whole system of bringing gentlemen of the South to their knees," she confessed to Vance, "as petitioners at the bar of Federal Government is to me, the expressed essence of meanness—which only the Universal Yankee nation would have been guilty of." Unlike in the *Last Ninety Days*, however, Spencer was unwilling entirely to blame the North for the present state of affairs. "I am not in spirits to say what I think of the North," she continued in her letter to Vance, "for there is among our own people such an amount of servility—such a want of manliness and decent self-assertion." Southern cowardice, then, was the true cause of alarm. "The men are so thoroughly cowed and prostrated that it won't do to throw stones northwards."[21] In both private and printed forms, then, Spencer professed her belief that the South indeed faced dire straits.

Despite the gloomy portrait drawn by Spencer, readers and critics enthusiastically received *The Last Ninety Days*. Unlike Boyd, who at times fictionalized her encounters with Stonewall Jackson to suggest the general's support of her "masculine" endeavors as a Confederate spy, Spencer had documented support from those who championed her entry into the "masculine" realm of political discourse. Vance praised Spencer's efforts, claiming that "the real value of your sketches does not consist so much in stringing together the prominent events of the war in chronological order, but in the graphic setting forth of the feelings and sufferings of our people." Further validating her project, he added, "the truth is it is a woman's task, & I know but one woman who could do it!!" "It is unnecessary for me to add anything to the deservedly high encomiums of the press on your work," wrote R. L. Beall of Lenoir, North Carolina. He finished his letter wishing Spencer a "rich . . . harvest of pecuniary profit" to match her fame. Local newspapers echoed these readers' responses, praising Spencer for her truthfulness and candor.[22]

A year after the publication of Spencer's history of North Carolina, Sallie Brock Putnam published a similar account of Richmond, Virginia. A native of the city, Putnam had witnessed the continuing struggle for control of the Confederate capital. Although she published *Richmond during the War* in 1867, only two years after the cessation of hostilities, she likened the history of the war to a carefully guarded secret that begged disclosure. Assuming that she spoke for all white southerners, Putnam claimed, "there is something in the locked chamber that will interest us — something that the world will be wiser and better for knowing — and hesitatingly we turn the key, to reveal the secrets held by the Confederate Capital during the four years of the terrible Civil War."[23] Even though most southerners undoubtedly remembered the events of the war, the history of the war still held a degree of mystery, at least to Putnam, and the South, she believed, needed to be included in the secret.

Putnam's unabashed enthusiasm for the Confederacy and her hopes for its success permeate the early chapters of her book. Indeed, her admission that she and her fellow southerners believed in the viability of the Confederacy, and not just in its righteousness, distinguishes *Richmond during the War* from later histories. To be sure, Putnam cited familiar reasons for the South's defeat: "When we reflect upon the weakness of the South, her utter insufficiency, compared with the numbers and resources with which she presumed to contest," she confessed, "we are lost in amazement at the very inception, to say nothing of the continuation of the struggle through four long years of difficulties, that grew and thickened at every step—of impediments which arose, unlooked for, and everywhere."[24] Yet this wisdom came only after the war. Unlike later writers who grafted onto pre-Appomattox southerners a sense of doom from the very beginning, Putnam did not ascribe to Richmond's inhabitants the ability to predict history. Although Putnam subscribed, at least in part, to the increasingly resonant Lost Cause readings of southern history, she did not infuse her work with it.

The events of the war soon shocked white southerners out of their ignorance, according to Putnam, leaving them "to muse on the mutability of human events." Putnam credited a divine power with the ultimate outcome: "We were driven to reflect on the strange and mysterious dealings of the wonder-working hand of God, and wiping the film from our eyes of faith, to steer clear of the wrecking reefs of infidelity."[25] Yet she did not deny human agency. Unlike many of her contemporaries, who blamed Confederate defeat on divine retribution against real or imagined sins, and later writers, who seemed more willing to ascribe events to a preordained script, Putnam maintained a remarkable sense of historicism. The South lost but did so because of its own weakness, not because of a vengeful God.

Moreover, Putnam exhibited a hopefulness for the future that stemmed not from a longing for divine intervention but from a faith in her fellow Virginians. While her contemporaries moaned about federal occupation of their land, Putnam optimistically imagined the possibilities for a restored Richmond. "The energy, the enterprise, the almost universal self-abnegation, and complete devotion, with which the people of the South entered into and sustained the cause of the war, to all but a successful termination, prove that they are capable of still grander, and higher, and nobler enterprises."[26] Putnam exhibited none of the war weariness that her contemporaries so keenly felt and apparently remained unaware of the malaise that inflicted many white southerners after the war: while she eagerly anticipated the rebuilding of her homeland, others looked more resignedly on their fate.

Despite only modest sales, *Richmond during the War* was "admirably received by the Press and [was] very much quote[d] from." More important for Putnam, however, the foray into the literary world kindled a burning interest in her newfound career. Confiding in Rogers, a friend, Putnam confessed, "I am beginning to feel the restless stirring of Ambition and have had a slight taste from her dissatisfying cup." Although Putnam felt both inclined and eminently qualified to write history, the unrewarding sales of *Richmond during the War* persuaded her to attempt another genre for the "undigested mass" that tormented her imagination. "I must adopt a 'Specialty,'" she realized, "and I am inclined to think that 'Specialty' will sooner or later be 'fiction.'" Putnam calculated her move carefully: "My taste runs upon History, but fiction is more expedient," she continued, "and more profitable and therefore I shall cultivate a taste for it." Putnam never returned to the Civil War as the catalyst for her writing. She did, however, successfully make the transition to fiction.[27]

Dorsey, McGuire, Spencer, and Putnam pioneered the enterprise of southern white women writing histories of the Civil War. Although other Reconstruction-era women shared these authors' desire to tell a "true" representation of the war, most chose to do so through fiction or poetry. Perhaps most women considered history outside the realm of women's expertise, as Evans and Dorsey not too convincingly claimed. Perhaps other women felt too burdened by the historical record and wanted to re-create the freedom of uncertainty that had existed before the war's outcome was known. Or perhaps eulogies, in the form of poetry, offered the only solace. By the end of the nineteenth century, southern women would increasingly turn to history as a medium for telling their Civil War stories. During Reconstruction, however, southern women almost completely neglected the genre.

The Romance of Sectionalism

Some woman, distraught over the South's loss, imagined divine retribution against the North for its crimes against the Confederacy. Four years after the war ended, Cora Ives published a book marketed to the South's white youth, *The Princess of the Moon: A Confederate Fairy Story*, in which Randolph, a disheartened Confederate soldier, entreats the goddess of the moon to relieve his sorrow. She grants his request by giving him a flying horse named Hope. Randolph flies over the United States during his first two voyages, witnessing first "his own desolate land" and then "the homes of the conquerors abounding in plenty and decked in the spoils they had so cruelly acquired." He finally flies to a far-off fairyland, where he marries the goddess of the moon. As the couple stands in the receiving line, "several most singular looking objects" descend to the ground, issuing forth men with "carpet-bags" and "traps of all descriptions." Once Randolph's faithful old servant exposes the treachery of these "demons of cruelty," the goddess grants Randolph the power to torture them at will. He declines her offer.[28]

With this magnanimous gesture, the Confederate soldier becomes the salvation for the fallen South. "Had you taken advantage of my offer to wreak vengeance upon your enemies," the goddess informs Randolph, "you would have again been stained with sin." Although the South had suffered, the goddess continues, Randolph's merciful action has purified his homeland, ensuring it "greater blessings than before." The goddess then turns to the carpetbaggers, admonishing them, "Repent your ways while you have time." Randolph has granted them a stay of execution, she counsels, allowing the carpetbaggers the chance to return home and warn the Radical Republicans that Nemesis's hand is poised above, "ready to strike the blow that will carry destruction in its wake." The goddess urges the carpetbaggers to "unshackle the race of heroes they have enslaved . . . before it is too late."[29]

Ives's tale of the Lost Cause fit perfectly with journalist Edward Pollard's contemporary explication of southern defeat, and her readers would have recognized the familiar elements. According to both Ives and Pollard, the Confederates had been the virtuous soldiers, conquered only by the Union's superior resources. If the South had sinned, then Randolph's gesture of charity toward the carpetbaggers has redeemed the nation. Furthermore, Randolph's action proves that southerners are the "noble race." Because he was a Confederate soldier, he "spurn[ed] to trample on fallen foes." Having suitably atoned for its sins, the South can now rightfully expect divine retribution against the North. "Live hereafter in peace and happiness," the goddess proclaims, "and know that your fallen country will yet arise from her ashes in greater glory than ever."[30]

Significantly, Ives began her story not with the action of the war but with Confederate defeat. As she pointed out in her introduction, southerners were painfully aware of the events of the war and the "crimes" of Reconstruction. Instead, hers was a story of redemption. South Carolina writer Sallie F. Chapin, who published her novel *Fitz-Hugh St. Clair* in 1872, three years after Ives wrote her fairy tale, scoffed at Ives's conviction that southerners were well versed in the history of the war. Indeed, Chapin believed it her duty systematically, if a bit unevenly, to redress the sin of ignorance. Unlike Ives, then, Chapin set out to explain the virtues of slavery, the evils of abolitionism, the grandeur of southern plantations, the heroism of southern leaders, the wickedness of the northern army, and the pain of defeat. Of northerners who instructed southerners to resign themselves to defeat, Chapin asked, "Have we not accepted it, with its disgrace, degradation, and torture?" To critics who believed that she should accept her situation with quiet equanimity, Chapin stormed, "Why, if we should keep silence, while our children were being taught that their hero-fathers were 'fiends, brutes, thieves, and murderers,' the very stones would cry out against us." Lest Chapin's readers remain unclear about her intent, she declared that "every line written in this book" demonstrated the righteousness of the southern cause and the valor of the Confederate soldier. "One day the world will acknowledge," she asserted confidently, that the Confederacy had crumbled "because We were Outnumbered! Not Outbraved!" The editors of the *Southern Historical Society Papers* publicly thanked Chapin for her work, noting that the novel "holds up a model for the young men of the South which we could wish them all to read and imitate."[31]

Like Ives, Chapin embraced Pollard's reading of southern defeat. Indeed, Chapin's novel includes from the beginning her understanding of the Lost Cause myth, a tactic that would become more common with later writers. Before the events at Fort Sumter trigger the main action of the novel, General St. Clair "predicts" the Confederacy's loss, detailing to his young son, Fitz-Hugh, the dire repercussions promised for the South: "Negroes will occupy our high places and ignorance and vice will hold a violent sway." "In less than four years after we are subjugated," the elder St. Clair continues with remarkable accuracy, "South Carolina will have negro legislators and senators and plantation darkies will be sent to Congress and sit where Calhoun, McDuffie, Hugh S. Legare, and Hayne sat." Radical Republicans would reap what they had sown, however, "for when it is too late" they would understand "that in trying to ruin the South they have brought about destruction upon the entire country."[32]

The novel races along, highlighting the major events and battles of the war, bitterly describing the results of southern losses. But like *The Goddess of the Moon, Fitz-Hugh St. Clair* is a novel of vengeance. Immediately following the war, the hero, Fitz-Hugh, travels to New York to raise capital to save his once-considerable South Carolina estate, Glendaire. Besieged on all sides by "Yankee" temptations—gambling, women, alcohol—the sturdy Fitz-Hugh remains pure, works diligently, and sends his four-dollar paycheck home to his family, now living in a Confederate widow's home. He soon encounters Mr. Winthrop, an old friend of his father's from before the war. Launching into a discussion on postwar politics, Winthrop admits to Fitz-Hugh, "I was a Union man . . . but, God

"A Fifteenth Amendment Taking His Crops to Market." Illustration from Sallie F. Chapin's 1872 novel, *Fitz-Hugh St. Clair: The South Carolina Rebel Boy; or, It's No Crime to Be Born a Gentleman.*

knows, every sentiment of my nature revolts at the enslavement of my own race and their subjugation to ignorant negroes and irresponsible and unscrupulous riff-raff from every quarter of the globe."[33] General St. Clair's early prediction has been fully realized. Winthrop, the stand-in for the North, understands at last the national implications of Confederate defeat, but his awareness comes too late. The "noble" white race has been enslaved by "reprobates." Faced with the monumental task of regaining their land and government, Chapin suggested, southerners might nevertheless take small comfort in forcing the North to confront its wickedness and atone for its sins.

The novel ends with Fitz-Hugh St. Clair married to Winthrop's daughter, Lucie, and the couple returning to the restored St. Clair estate. Chapin, however, by no means participated in the reconciliation romance culture epitomized by such northern authors as John De Forest and M. A. Avery and described in various contexts by historians Paul Buck, Joyce Appleby, and Nina Silber. De Forest's 1867 novel, *Miss Ravenel's Conversion from Secession to Loyalty*, perhaps best represents these reconciliation romance novels. Here, De Forest equated loyalty to the Confederacy with feminine insensibility. Lillie Ravenel is the South's

"Glendaire." Illustration from Sallie F. Chapin's 1872 novel, *Fitz-Hugh St. Clair: The South Carolina Rebel Boy; or, It's No Crime to Be Born a Gentleman.*

staunchest supporter despite the opinions of the men who surround her, especially her father. Only the constant didactic lectures of a northern gentleman and wooer, Edward Colburne, coupled with the events of the war, persuade Lillie to abandon her Confederate convictions, an action symbolized by her romantic union with Colburne. In *The Rebel General's Loyal Bride: A True Picture of Scenes in the Late Civil War*, Avery reversed the conventional plot of the reconciliation romance — the northern soldier wooing the southern belle. Hotheaded, lustful Confederate General Atherton forces Catherine Hale, a sweet northern governess who supports abolition, to marry him in exchange for rescuing her

"The Negro Quarters at Glendaire." Illustration from Sallie F. Chapin's 1872 novel, *Fitz-Hugh St. Clair: The South Carolina Rebel Boy; or, It's No Crime to Be Born a Gentleman.*

brother, a captured northern soldier, from the Confederate gallows. Although Catherine considers the arrangement a "price beyond all computation," she consents. Catherine fails to persuade the general to abandon his pernicious convictions until he is on his deathbed, when he realizes his "folly and madness" and Catherine acknowledges her love for him. At the war's end, Atherton is dead, the South lies in ruins, and Catherine marries Lloyd Hunter, a southerner who had defected from the Confederate camp long before Atherton did. The newlyweds remain on Atherton's plantation, where they teach the former slaves to be good, independent Christians. Unlike the northern novelists, who symbolized the South's reintegration into the Union with marriages between penitent southerners and righteous northerners, Chapin depicted a repentant northerner seeking forgiveness and guidance from the South. Fitz-Hugh and Lucie return to South Carolina, ready to tackle the Radical Republicans, rebuild the family estate, and reclaim southern politics. Rather than participate in the culture of reconciliation, Chapin and scores of women like her celebrated the politics of "redemption."[34] White southern women had yet to form a regional organization to mount a defense against the culture of reconciliation, but they nonetheless rejected the northern trend.

Some southern white men supported their women's refusal to participate in the reconciliatory mood. Indeed, during 1876, the year of the U.S. centennial celebration, the Southern Historical Society (SHS), founded in 1869 by former Confederate officers, began publishing its papers. The organization sought to collect, classify, preserve, and publish "all the documents and facts bearing upon the eventful history of the past few years illustrating the nature of the struggle from which the country has just emerged, defining and vindicating the principles which lay beneath it, and marking the stages through which it was conducted to its issue." SHS officers solicited material to support the organization's collection in a number of divisions, including:

- The histories and historical collections of the individual States from the earliest periods to the present time, including travel, journals, and maps.
- Complete files of the newspapers, periodicals, literary, scientific and medical journals of the Southern States, from the earliest times to the present day, including especially the period of the recent American civil war.
- Works, speeches, sermons and discourses relating to the recent conflict and political changes. Congressional and State reports during the recent war.
- Official reports and descriptions, by officers and privates and newspaper correspondents and eye-witnesses of campaigns, military operations, battles and sieges.
- Names of all wounded officers, soldiers, and sailors. The nature of the wounds should be attached to each name, also the loss of one or more limbs should be carefully noted.
- The conduct of the hostile armies in the Southern States. Private and public losses during the war. Treatment of citizens by hostile forces.
- Southern poetry, ballads, songs, etc.

Despite the SHS's claim that its goals were not sectional and its labors were not partisan, its published papers suggested otherwise. The SHS recognized that "the generations of the disinterested must succeed the generations of the prejudiced before history, properly termed such, can be written." Its archives, filled with impassioned, sectional accounts of the war, were to serve future "objective" historians.[35]

During the first two years of the papers' run, the SHS published articles such as "A Vindication of Virginia and the South," by Commodore M. F. Maury; "Reminiscences of the Confederate States Navy," by Captain C. W. Read; and "General J. E. B. Stuart's Report of Operations after Gettysburg," as well as a series on "Causes of the Defeat of General Lee's Army at the Battle of Gettysburg—Opinions of Leading Confederate Soldiers." The society also published short reviews of leading popular accounts of the Civil War. Of General H. V. Boynton's *Sherman's Historical Raid*, a refutation of Sherman's memoirs, the editorial staff of the SHS explained, "We cannot . . . accept all that General Boynton has written; but we rejoice to see this well merited rebuke to the 'General of the Army,' who not only makes himself 'the hero of his own story,' but oversteps all bounds of delicacy and propriety (not to say common decency), and well illustrates in his Memoirs the proverb 'Oh, that mine enemy would write a book!'"[36] Something other than national reconciliation clearly motivated the SHS, and its decision to begin publishing its papers during the nation's centennial anniversary was significant.

Like Chapin, most southern white women authors during this period eschewed the reconciliation romance plot and offered instead stern prohibitions against intersectional marriages. Helena J. Harris penned her morality tale, "Cecil Gray; or, the Soldier's Revenge" shortly after the war. The short story opens with the antiheroine, Cecil Gray, marrying Walter Earnest, even though she loves another man, Elbert Grant. The respectable Walter had enlisted with the Army of Virginia at the outset of the war. Cecil informs Elbert, a Union man, that her husband died at Manassas, implying that she is now free to marry Elbert. Walter discovers his wife's machinations and rushes home, arriving as the wedding ceremony is about to begin. He hides and uses his well-honed sharpshooting skills to pick off Elbert before the ceremony is completed. Walter then rescues his children from their unfaithful mother, and Cecil dies, a suitable punishment for her disloyalty to her husband and the Confederate cause. Not given to the fine art of subtlety, Harris handed her readers an unmistakably clear message: betrayal of the southern cause, in any form, would meet with swift and appropriate justice.[37]

Sarah J. C. Whittlesey, author of the 1872 novel *Bertha the Beauty: A Story of the Southern Revolution*, was no less severe in her condemnation of intersectional marriages. Whittlesey's novel of the war includes conventional romantic plots. Bertha, the pretty yet tragically poor and unfortunate daughter of a transplanted Connecticut Yankee, unflaggingly supports the southern cause. Her unenlightened father refuses to abandon his support for the Federal government's design to squelch the liberties of the southern states and, worse, forces Bertha to marry Horace Stanhope, a scurrilous Yankee who deserted his wife after their first year of marriage. As further proof of Stanhope's depravity, he joins the Union army, not out of any loyalty to the Federal cause but because it takes him away from Bertha. "Day after day, his atheistic and tyrannical Soul had crept from the deceptive covering that concealed it until it stood forth in all its deformity and hideousness," Whittlesey contemptuously wrote of her villain.[38]

Fortunately for Bertha, Horace dies in battle at the hand of the brave Confederate Colonel Percy Ormund, leaving Bertha free to marry her true soul mate, Percy. Safely in his arms, Bertha explains to her family, "I don't think it advisable for the two sections to intermarry. They are too unlike in every respect, and never can coalesce—always a house divided against itself, I don't care where you find them; like ours, two against two." To further demonstrate the irreconcilable nature of the North and the South, Whittlesey described Bertha and Percy's trip north immediately following the war. The journey fills the couple with "regret, as it furnished them with proofs of Yankee bitterness and yearning for Southern blood that was highly displeasing to Christian minds." The hostility of northern noncombatants particularly shocks the southern couple: "Men who had not shouldered a gun in defense of the Union, and did all their fighting with their tongues, were not satisfied that the war should end until the South was utterly crushed by confiscation and Northern emigration, and every Rebel of rank had dangled at the end of a rope!"[39] National reconciliation was impossible both symbolically, through intersectional marriage, and in reality, through culture or politics.

Although other novelists were not as explicit in their proscriptions against intersectional marriages, their messages resounded clearly. Sarah Dorsey turned her pen to fiction after she finished her biography of Allen and in 1867 published *Lucia Dare*, a novel that painstakingly delineates the differences between the North and the South. Although British by birth, the heroine, Lucia Dare, has a sympathetic nature that will prove crucial later in the novel. In an early scene, Dorsey approvingly described Lucia's character, suggesting that Lucia would be favorably inclined toward the South and its most cherished institutions: "In spite of Plato, John Stuart Mill, and Miss Anna Dickenson [sic], mankind generally prefer[s] the strong-hearted women to their abler, iron-nerved, powerful muscled sisters, who never do go into hysterics, have contempt for nerves, weakness, and softness of all kinds, especially for fragile, delicate, daintily, dimpled . . . women like Lucia Dare." At boarding school in Paris, Lucia meets Louise Peyrault, a southerner who so eloquently defends slavery that Lucia soon begins to examine her own views on the subject. Louise also rails against northerners and their poor manners. Speaking of another student, Grace, who hails from the North, Louise virtually hisses, "I dislike her with an A; because she is artful, ambitious, and an abolitionist. . . . She is cool, cultivated, smart, acute, intelligent, ill-tempered, malicious Yankee. She is maneuvering, bites her fingernails. . . . I don't like her morals, her taste, her birth, nor her dress." In short, states Louise, Grace "does not suit me." To punch up her argument further, Louise later decries the entire abolitionist movement, even casting aspersions on the English, who first brought slaves to the colonies and then castigated the system, a point that Lucia takes to heart.[40]

By the time Lucia arrives in Louisiana in 1861 to look for her brother, from whom she had been separated as a young child, she is favorably disposed toward the South. Moreover, Lucia sympathizes with the South's attempt at independence, understanding that the South had opposed war, "and it was not until she had been goaded to frenzy like Io with the perpetual gad-fly of radicalism, that, in utter desperation, in the extremity of hopelessness of any better things or of being able to retain her personal and domestic rights, her *republican* government, she seized her arms and stood upon the defensive, not willing to resign all that she believed made her prosperity and her vitality without striking one blow for it." With her newly cemented political views, Lucia renews her friendship with Louise, who had returned to the South and married a Confederate soldier. Distraught that she cannot fight for her country, bereaved over the death of her husband, and determined not to submit to "that detested race" of northerners, Louise disguises herself as a man, enters the fray, and dies in battle.[41] Lucia, who had also married a southerner, returns to England after the war, unable to live in a conquered land.

Dorsey never overtly denounced intersectional marriages in her novel but nevertheless made it clear that the North and South were incompatible. Louise sacrifices her life rather than live under northern rule. Less dramatically, Lucia and her family return to England to avoid Federal occupation of the South. National reconciliation did not interest Dorsey. Indeed, reintegration was impossible both symbolically and politically. For Dorsey, the end of the war brought neither romance nor reunion.

Virginia's Mary Tucker Magill shared her countrywomen's contempt for intersectional marriages. For Mary Holcombe, the heroine of Magill's 1871 novel, *Women; or, Chronicles of the Late War*, marriage to a northerner is so completely incomprehensible that she remains virtually silent on the issue. Equally abhorrent, but at least worthy of some discussion and explication, is the possibility of a marriage between a southern belle and a southern man who fled the Confederacy. Mr. Dallam, Mary's fiancé, agrees to go north at his father's behest to be with his ailing mother, who had left the South before the war, although Dallam promises Mary that he will not take up arms against his former homeland. Mary grapples with the implications of Dallam's move. "I have studied the matter out myself, turning it backward and forward to find some favorable light for you," she tells him. "But the end of the whole was this: You have sold your birthright for a mess of pottage."[42] Furious, Mary severs her engagement to Dallam, and she remains single at the end of the novel.

The Holcombe women were not immune to spurious Yankee advances, however. While Mary questions Mr. Dallam's intentions, her sister, Margaret, spurns the affections of Captain Brown of the U.S. Army and instead gives her love to a dashing Confederate, Captain Murray. Ever spiteful, Brown returns to the Holcombe home, Rose Hill, and burns it to the ground, killing Margaret's two-year-old baby. Although the results are tragic, the Holcombe sisters require no further proof that they acted prudently in rejecting the unsuitable suitors. Such cowardly and vindictive men surely are unworthy of two southern belles.

Magill detailed the motives and intent that compelled her to write her novel. Like Whittlesey, Magill believed that with each passing year, the memory of the war faded from the South's consciousness. Magill wished to "wake" this memory from the chambers into which it had fallen in its "first slumber." Unlike Whittlesey, however, Magill publicly acknowledged the "delicacy and difficulty" in writing a "story of the 'Lost Cause.'" Rather than exacerbate the almost excruciating tension between the North and the South by writing an inflammatory war novel, Magill professed to write "the story of WOMAN in her proper sphere, by the firesides, in her household duties, and by the side of the sick and dying." In short, *Women; or, Chronicles of the Late War* was to be "the simple unexagger-

ated narrative of what non-combatants are forced to endure in a country torn"
by internecine strife.[43]

Magill held a rather uncircumscribed view of women's "proper sphere." In her
book, women review troops; discuss policy and plans of attack with Confederate
officers, including Stonewall Jackson; and venture forth onto the battlefields. "If
you really want to be of use," George Holcombe taunts the females of his family,
"get your bonnets and go out to the battlefields; that is if you think you have the
nerve to stand the sad sights which will meet you there." Mary, Margaret, and
the rest of the female Holcombes accept his challenge, presumably to minister
to the wounded, and confront the ghastly sights and sounds on the field. The
women soon appreciate that on the front line "life and death are fighting it out
. . . the one triumphing by groans, shrieks, prayers and imprecations, the other
by a silence more dreadful still."[44]

Magill stated her intention to write about women and not about war, but in
so doing, she demonstrated the inextricable ties among women, war, and war
narratives. Never finely drawn, the line distinguishing the home front from the
battlefield was especially hazy in the Civil War South, where troops fought in
backyards and the Federal army burned private homes that stood in its way.
As feminist theorist Margaret R. Higonnet argues, civil wars, more than other
wars, offer greater potential for women to transgress traditional expectations.
The Holcombe women could therefore visit the battlefield, an area traditionally off-limits as a male domain. That the women make the visit at a man's behest does not lessen this action's radical potential. Although the women perform
"traditional" womanly services — ministering to the sick — caring for soldiers on
battlefields is extremely unusual.[45] Moreover, Mary and Margaret's refusals to
marry the cravenly Confederate and the reprobate Yankee are political as much
as private decisions. Magill could not separate her story of "WOMAN" and the
home front from the story of the war any more than southern women could
remove themselves from the fighting that surrounded them.

If Magill did not wish to foment tensions between the two sections, Mrs. L. D.
Whitson made no such pretensions. Whitson did not wish southerners to forget northern atrocities, but more than Whittlesey and others who bid the South
to remember the horrors of the war, Whitson encouraged the hatred southerners bore toward their erstwhile foe. "We cannot — we have no wish to — forget,"
she proclaimed in her 1874 novel, *Gilbert St. Maurice*, "and if there be any sin
in hating, let it lie at our own door." Lest any of her readers feel pangs of guilt
for sharing in this deep, abiding hatred, Whitson explained that this loathing,

which began as "wrath" against the North, had developed into a "holy, righteous" revulsion.[46] This seemingly pathological emotion was thus justified and even divinely sanctioned.

Like other southern women authors of the Reconstruction period, Whitson painstakingly delineated the differences between the North and the South, explaining not only why the war was inevitable but also why reconciliation was impossible. "It will take two more generations to eradicate the bitter feeling and prejudices generated in our minds by the result of the war," Whitson predicted. Indeed, how could the South "clasp hands in fraternal greeting" with the North, pondered Whitson, when "rivers of blood" separated the two? "The mutilated forms of slain Confederate soldiers will rise before any southerner attempting to bridge the gap," argued Whitson, rendering useless the entire process of reconciliation.[47] Readers could be sure that when the hero, Gilbert St. Maurice, died on the battlefield, his fiancée, Marion, did not betray his memory or repudiate the Confederacy by marrying a Yankee soldier. Symbolic reconciliation was as abhorrent and absurd to Whitson as was the notion of its political reality.

The Weary Burden of a Wounded Heart

In 1867, Mary Ann Cruse of Huntsville, Alabama, published *Cameron Hall*, one of the most successful Reconstruction-era southern novels of the war (rivaled perhaps by only John Esten Cooke's 1866 *Surry of Eagle's Nest*). *Cameron Hall* unmistakably had strong roots in the antebellum sentimental, melodramatic school of women's fiction, with romantic subplots, lost relatives, mistaken identities, and a perfect little girl named Agnes. Cruse nevertheless contended that her work "belong[s] rather to truth than to fiction."[48] Despite Cruse's classification of the novel, *Cameron Hall* exemplifies the war stories penned by southern white women during Reconstruction, pointing in the direction that later novelists would follow.

More than any other southern white female novelist of this period, Cruse offered a sustained and clearly articulated explication of the inherent differences between the North and the South and the ways in which those differences precipitated the inevitable war. "This war can all be traced," explained Mr. Cameron, "to that bigotry and fanaticism [Puritanism] which would bind the galley chains of its own notions and prejudices upon the hearts and conscience of the whole world." The characters who populate Cruse's Cameron Hall and environs agree. Uncle John, a staunch Confederate from the beginning of the war, defines the issue more specifically, arguing that the North's wholesale attack on the Constitution, "because it does not square with that higher law [abolitionism], which [the North] professes to have found," necessitated a violent severing of South from North. More forcefully than other novelists, Cruse emphatically denied that slavery caused the war. To argue such a position, according to Cruse, was tantamount to claiming that the tea floating in Boston Harbor started the Revolutionary War.[49]

Like Spencer, who infused her history of North Carolina with contempt for the North's conduct during the war, Cruse derided the villainous Yankee raids, which surprise none of Cruse's characters because they see the attacks as mere symptoms of the North's fanatical nature. Uncle John warns his family at the outset of the war that the South should expect such beastly behavior. The same blind intensity with which the Puritans persecuted witches in colonial New England would guide the North to inflict pain and misery on the South, he implies. As Mr. Cameron explains to his daughter, Julia, the North engaged in such conduct simply "to destroy as much of what sustains life."[50] Cruse depicted numerous Federal raids to prove Mr. Cameron's point.

The prospect of lost life and property daunts Julia Cameron. But she believes, however, that the oath of allegiance that the Yankees force their victims to swear is far more heinous. Attempting to persuade her father to abandon Cameron Hall before a raiding party arrives, Julia warns him neither of the wanton destruction of property nor of the possibility of death: "Think of the oath of allegiance, that fearful oath," she screams, "you cannot subscribe to that." Despite Julia's protestations, Mr. Cameron remains with the house, although he refuses to take the oath both after the raid and at the end of the war. "Were I a soldier," Mr. Cameron self-righteously proclaims, "sacrificing health and perhaps even life itself, no defeat in battle, no privations in camp, no suffering that I might endure, would so effectually paralyze my arm, and weaken my energies, and discourage my heart, as to know that the men for whom I was fighting so little valued the precious boon which I was purchasing at so tremendous a price, that like Esau, they were willing to barter the costly birthright for a mess of pottage."[51] The Yankees banish Mr. Cameron for his defiance.

Although Cruse claimed to have finished *Cameron Hall* before the war ended, she included in her novel an interpretation of the Lost Cause myth that was completely absent from Civil War novels written during the conflict. Uncle John articulates the myth in *Cameron Hall*, arguing that although defeat was inevitable, at least the South had not quietly succumbed to "objectivity, servility, and submissiveness." Like General St. Clair in Chapin's *Fitz-Hugh St. Clair*, Uncle John predicts with uncanny prescience Virginia's "desolated homes, her soil, not sprinkled, but literally drenched with the blood not only of her sons, but with that of the noblest and best of the land; of her ravaged fields, her ruined farms, her homeless, wandering children, her exiled fathers, her unprotected wives and daughters." Echoing Pollard's history of southern defeat, Mr. Derby, a fellow plantation owner and friend of the Camerons, attributes the South's impending loss to the North's overwhelming manpower, superior war matériel, and foreign assistance.[52] Later writers would infuse their novels with readings of the Lost Cause myth, but writers during Reconstruction rarely employed this tactic. Although the Lost Cause assuredly resonated with southerners during Reconstruction, it had yet to dominate the postbellum southern consciousness as it would by the turn of the twentieth century.

Unlike Pollard, however, Cruse refrained from crediting the North entirely for its victory. Like Ives, who ascribed a great deal of power to a divine force in *The Goddess of the Moon*, Cruse maintained that the same vengeful God who smote the Israelites punished the South for its errant ways. Unlike Ives, however, Cruse named the South's sins. Mr. Derby expresses what he believes to be the most egregious sin committed by southerners. "When I hear the self-confident boasting that talks of an invincible people, a nation that cannot be conquered, a proud, high-spirited, chivalrous race my be exterminated but never subdued, I tremble," he confides to Mr. Cameron, "not for the final result, but for fear that, like rebellious Israel, it may be decreed that none of this generation shall enter into the promised rest of freedom and independence." The North, however, was guilty of crimes far worse than hubris. In addition to fanaticism, explains Mr. Derby, the North has "now added the inauguration and persecution of a war, which for cruelty, oppression, and vindictiveness, and malignity, has scarcely its counterparts in modern times." Although unpardonable crimes tainted the North's record, God had chosen to punish the South. "Our retribution for our portion of iniquity has come first, and for some mysterious purpose of His own, God has allowed us to be chastened by those who were once our brethren." The South need only wait, however, for the North's day of judgment would come. According to Mr. Derby, that day would "be so awful, so tremendous, that the most revengeful of those over whom they have tyrannized will be moved to pity and cry 'Forbear!'"[53] Unlike in Ives's fairy tale, however, the South had yet to witness its deliverance.

Four years of hard warfare had rendered white southerners bedraggled. Not even the most severe battle fatigue, however, could prepare them for the torpor and malaise that ensued. Cruse feared the worst for Confederate men. "Woman, born to endure, can long drag the weary burden of a wounded heart," she explained, "but when once the strong, self-reliant man is broken in spirit, he sinks at once beneath the load." Even Cooke suggested that women would bear up under the pressures of defeat better than their menfolk: "As the sorrowful survivors of the great army came back, as they reached their old homes, dragging their weary feet after them, or urging on their jaded horses, suddenly the sunshine burst forth for them, and lit up their rags with a sort of glory," wrote Cooke. "Those angels of the home loved the poor prisoners better in their dark days than in their bright. The found eyes melted to tears, the white arms held them close; and the old soldiers, who had only laughed at the roar of the enemy's guns, dropped tears on the faces of their wives and little children!"[54] Cooke imagined that the indefatigable spirit of southern white women would sustain their defeated soldiers. Cruse remained skeptical. Unlike Spencer, Cruse bore no contempt for the defeated southern men and did not even pity them. Rather, Cruse resigned herself to the fate of the conquered. More than any other southern white woman novelist of this period, Cruse realized that Reconstruction, not merely defeat, was the South's cross to bear.

Cameron Hall espoused similar rhetoric to other novels written during Reconstruction but also pointed in new directions. Later writers would cast entire works in Lost Cause molds, with the Confederacy always doomed before it had even been formed. Cruse's early supposition that the war followed a divine plan that rested outside the realm of human action would become a familiar part of the Lost Cause formula. The Lost Cause myth and conception of a divine retribution certainly did not originate with *Cameron Hall*. Indeed, earlier writers used these tropes, at least to a degree. Cruse, however, fleshed out these tropes more fully, a tactic that later writers would almost universally employ.

Never More Be Shermanized

In addition to biographies, histories, and novels, southern women during Reconstruction composed poetry to glorify the achievements of the Old South and to mourn the loss of the Confederacy. Regional magazines such as *The Land We Love* and *Our Living and Our Dead* swelled with the regular contributions of

Margaret J. Preston, Mary B. Clark, I. M. Porter, and others. Local newspapers, too, published these works occasioned by the Confederacy's demise. Anthologies, although rarer, reprinted poems that appeared elsewhere, ensuring the wide circulation and readership of selected poems.[55]

This poetry of southern defeat exposed themes similar to those found in histories, biographies, and novels, but the genre afforded its authors a way to encapsulate their meaning and intent in a form that was much more accessible than other, longer works. With the exception of anthologies, which required special purchase, these poems appeared alongside news and business articles in newspapers and magazines to which southerners already subscribed. In a short poem published in the first issue of *The Land We Love*, Preston underscored the South's fear and distrust of northern plans for reunification. Although southerners welcomed a respite from the bloody war, Preston argued, they did not embrace the terms of peace:

> We do not accept thee, Heavenly Peace!
> Albeit thou comest in a guise
> Unlooked for, undesired, our eyes
> Welcome, through tears, the sweet release
> From War, and woe, and want — surcease
> For which we bless thee, holy Peace![56]

In six lines, Preston rejected the North's peace in a manner that was unmistakable to her readers.

Other poems also possessed familiar and comforting elements. Fanny Downing's "They Are Not Dead" and Lou Belle Custiss's "Hallow'd Ground" must have held special meaning for those southern women concerned with memorializing fallen soldiers. "Each grave an altar shall remain," wrote Downing, confirming the importance of the work undertaken by the numerous Ladies' Memorial Associations. Catherine M. Warfield's poem, "Manassas," reminded southerners that they had once held the position of victors, encouraging them to revel in the knowledge that

> Long shall Northmen rue the day,
> When they met our stern array,
> And shrunk from battle's wild affray
> At Manassas!

L. Virginia French's poem, "Shermanized," incited southerners to throw off the shackles of northern occupation:

May her daughters aid that effort to rebuild and restore,
Working on for *Southern freedom* as they never worked before!
May Georgia as a laggard never once be stigmatized
And her PEOPLE, PRESS, or PULPIT, never more be Shermanized![57]

These poems and hundreds of others offered readers the most expedient and most direct interpretation of a southern understanding of the war.

This poetry of defeat certainly resonated with southern women, for they crammed their diaries with cherished lines from favorite poems and with their own compositions. Loula Kendall Rogers maintained a copying book for this purpose, filling it with poetry and passages from novels. Grace Elmore partly vented her frustrations about defeat by writing poetry alongside her recordings of daily events.[58] Poetry lent itself to transcription and easy memorization and proved to be a convenient medium for reflection and meditation. This genre remained one of the most utilized forms for imparting an appreciation of southern history and an understanding of Confederate defeat.

Southern white women had vociferously championed the Confederacy. Defeat and the realities of Reconstruction forced them to push beyond their roles as propagandists to become the builders of a new southern consciousness. Crucial to this new postwar consciousness was a reconciliation not between the North and the South but between defeat and southerners' conception of themselves as divinely chosen. Their writings challenge Gaines M. Foster's assertion that by the end of Reconstruction "white southerners had begun to come to terms with defeat." Foster's analysis of the "electoral crisis of 1876–1877" compelled him to conclude that white southerners saw their "political future within the Union." Although "a few remained irreconcilable," their influence in southern society "declined rapidly" by the mid-1880s. Foster's world of the Reconstruction South, however, was overwhelmingly male. His conclusion that southerners "abandon[ed] the past as a guide" failed to account for the writings of white southern women.[59] Southern white women's first postwar literary efforts encouraged southerners to understand their history without repudiating it. Moreover, their writings held greater cultural significance than Foster's formulation would allow.

For some women, this responsibility of constructing a new southern consciousness proved too great, at least initially. Although Augusta Jane Evans recognized the pressing need for a history of the Confederacy, she abandoned the project, on at least one occasion citing postwar malaise as the reason. Some writers only tentatively picked up the gauntlet. Sarah Dorsey hesitatingly wrote a quasi-history of the war but disguised it as biography. She later honed her arguments in her novel, *Lucia Dare*. Other authors, however, enthusiastically accepted the challenge—for example, Cornelia Phillips Spencer, who immediately wrote an unequivocal, unapologetic history of North Carolina's role in the war.

The business of creating a postwar southern consciousness remained new during Reconstruction. Writers had yet to solidify elements of the Lost Cause myth that would later dominate the South's understanding of the war. Certain plotlines and literary conventions were becoming familiar but had yet to become standardized. The myth of the Lost Cause was most malleable during Reconstruction, as writers attempted to establish the myth's boundaries. Moreover, southern white women were writing in isolation. The network among women authors and readers and especially among members of the United Daughters of the Confederacy, which was critical to the formation of a uniquely southern understanding of the war, did not develop until the end of the nineteenth century and the beginning of the twentieth. Nevertheless, southern women made their initial attempts at creating a new southern consciousness during Reconstruction.

Sallie A. Brock may well have captured the concerns of all southern women who wrote about the war. Near the end of her 1867 poem, "The Fall of Richmond," she asked,

And am I done? and is my story told?—
   Told quite, in all its varied, saddened phrases
Of hopes that rose as Titans rose of old
   To war with Fate and powers in highest places?[60]

Even though Brock had "told her story," both in poetry and in history, she doubted that she had completed her narrative. There must be more to tell, she reasoned. Others would have agreed. The ever-increasing amount of literature generated by southerners fascinated with the Civil War never daunted aspiring novelists, poets, historians, biographers, and autobiographers. Indeed, the late-nineteenth-century surge in the publication of Civil War narratives encouraged southern women to believe that the literary market would accommodate yet another story. As more and more women wrote, they soon came to appreciate the expansiveness of the literary market and the southern reading public.

Little more than a month since the war ended and the country had sprung into new life; everywhere was busy activity, fences being made, sawmills cutting the air with the prolonged whiz-z-z and a sight seldom seen in that state. Pater-familias guiding the plow, while sons and delicate daughters planted or hoed.
—EMMA LYON BRYAN, 1860–1865: A Romance of the Valley of Virginia

By wintry daylight the battlefield is still more ghastly. Gray with the pallid crab-grass, which so eagerly usurps the place of last summer's crops, it stretches out on every side to meet the bending sky. The armies that successively encamped upon it did not leave a tree for miles, but here and there thickets have sprung up since the war and bare and black they intensify the gloom of the landscape. The turf in these segregated spots is never turned. Beneath the branches are rows of empty, yawning graves where the bodies of soldiers were temporarily buried. Here, most often, their spirits walk, and no hire can induce the hardiest ploughman to break the ground. Thus the owner of the land is fain to concede these acres to his ghostly tenants, who pay no rent.
—MARY NOAILLES MURFREE, Where the Battle Was Fought

3

A View from the Mountain, 1877–1895

The Great Compromise of 1877 brought an end to Reconstruction in the South. For most white southerners, the related tasks of rebuilding their land and reclaiming their past took precedence in the post-Reconstruction era. Reunification in any real sense did not follow Rutherford B. Hayes's 1876 election to the presidency. White southerners merely experienced what they perceived as a lull in the worst horrors of Reconstruction. Coupled with the devastating effects of the war, Reconstruction left white southerners with remarkably little to claim in the present. Many could, however, see hope for the future, and they could at least take comfort in a resplendent antebellum past that white southerners were constantly creating and revising. Southern white women's post-Reconstruction literature reflects their desire to cast their glances back into a familiar, comfortable past and forward toward the future, which certainly had to be better than the present. These novels, biographies, and reminiscences suggest that the conditions of the post-Reconstruction period afforded authors a great deal of interpretive latitude in penning their narratives about the South.

A singular devotion to the task of writing epic tales links together these seemingly disparate narratives. There is little or no discussion in any of these works about the "real" reasons for Federal victory—the expansion of the nation-state, northern industrialization, the role of manufacturing, and the resupplying of goods, materials, and soldiers, all of which gave the North the crucial advantage. Instead, southern white women cast their narratives in heroic terms. Their tales described gods fighting on mountaintops, not the conditions that conspired against the Confederacy.[1] Despite these women's varying interpretations of the Civil War, all imagined the Confederates as the protagonists, transformed humiliating defeat into justified warfare, and fought to control the establishment of "historical truth."

Reflecting on the profound changes that shaped the southern landscape during and after Reconstruction, Alabama author and New South booster Kate Cumming cataloged southerners' tremendous postwar achievements. Despite military defeat and twelve years of occupation, the South had miraculously rebounded and forged ahead to a leading position in industry, urban and suburban beautification, tourism, education, and agriculture. Testifying to its indomitable will and the righteousness of its cause, the South cast off the remnants of defeat and strove to make its people "happy and prosperous." From Cumming's position in 1892, "God [was] indeed showering his blessings and energy upon this sunny land."[2]

Others were not quite as sanguine. Georgia lecturer and columnist Rebecca Latimer Felton apparently did not see divine benediction on the sunny South, for after the war she could peer only "down into the valley of the shadow of death." Whatever brilliant feats southern industry might have achieved in the post-Reconstruction years did not remedy the poverty, racial tension, ineffectual leadership, and woefully inadequate educational system. Nor did the achievements of the postwar era redeem the "sacrifice of young white men—the cries of children for dead fathers, and the wail of widowhood," from which the South could never recover. While Cumming believed that she and her fellow southerners were marching down the path to great prosperity, Felton maintained that the South was heading down a different road. Beset by both sectional hatred and war prejudices and lacking the "statesmanship" to maneuver its way clear, the South faced at best continued social and economic hardships and at worst a bloody race war.[3]

Both women's visions of the South's future contained a measure of truth. And most students of post-1877 southern society have recognized these conflicting patterns of development, innovation, and redefinition. Metaphors of the South's standing at a crossroads or junction dominate much of the historiography of this period, and with good reason. Populism briefly threatened the politics of "redemption," for example. Tom Watson, in arguing for the establishment of a third political party, wrote in 1892 that "the future happiness of the two races will never be assured until the political motives which drive them asunder, into two distinct and hostile factions, can be removed. There must be a new policy inaugurated," he continued, "whose purpose is to ally the passions and prejudices of race conflict, and which makes its appeal to the sober sense and honest judgment of the citizen regardless of color." The Wilmington race riot of 1898 suggested to most people, however, that Populism had failed to deliver on its promise.[4]

Other promises proved equally hollow. Cumming's depiction of southern urban growth, for example, failed to materialize in any large measure. The population of towns and villages unquestionably increased dramatically in the post-Reconstruction era, but the rate of urbanization still lagged behind that of the North. Furthermore, the growth of southern cities was, as noted scholar Edward L. Ayers points out, "not a sign of urban opportunities but of rural sickness."[5] With a growing share of the countryside's economy undiversified and tied to cotton, cotton's distinctive problems of tenancy, crop liens, debt peonage, and absentee ownership increasingly plagued the rural South. The southern city offered no panacea for those fleeing the poverty of the countryside, however. Southerners faced a different set of problems in the city, not the least of which was social dislocation and class confusion. Although African-Americans might have encountered greater opportunities in the cities than in rural areas, unfulfilled promises from northerners and former owners continued to thwart blacks' full integration into southern society.

Cities and towns did not develop in isolation from rural backwaters. Banks and railroads created complex and interdependent networks of trade and commerce, facilitating the flow of capital, commodities, and influence throughout the South. Yet this contact magnified the problems endemic to both urban and rural areas. The countryside's demand for goods highlighted its provinciality and encouraged consumers to go into debt. The movement of people to towns and cities exacerbated the breakdown of the household structure and social hierarchy.[6]

The seemingly equivocal, fractured narratives of the post-Reconstruction South are not solely the creation of postmodernist historians. These conflicting images of the South—that of a phoenix rising from the ashes or conversely of the land irreparably damaged by the war—shaped the literature written by southern women between 1877 and 1895. While the war still clearly dominated their historical and literary imaginations, the exigencies of the post-Reconstruction South influenced the ways in which these women represented its course and consequences. Thus in 1895 Cumming reissued her tale of the war as *Gleanings from the Southland* by combining a summary of the wartime journal she had originally published in 1866 with an introduction on the marvelous achievements of Birmingham, Alabama, the "epitome of the New South." Similarly, Fannie Beers, who published *Memories: A Record of Personal Experience and Adventure during Four Years of War* in 1888, included a section at the end of her reminiscences on the twenty years since the war had ended. Novelists were not immune to the present's pervasive influences on stories of the past. The destruction of the southern landscape and civilization plagued Mary Noailles Murfree's literary imagination as much as it did the characters in her 1882 novel, *Where the Battle Was Fought*. Constance Cary Harrison's *Flower de Hundred* was as much a response to the reconciliation literature of northerners as a defense of southern antebellum society and the Confederacy. Just as these women could not understand the war without filtering it through the realities of the post-Reconstruction South, they could not comprehend their present condition without considering the past.

Although these diarists and novelists approached their narratives of the war from varying positions, all of these writers were part of the growing group of white southern women who entered the public discourse about the meanings of the Civil War. Women who had not been born during the war or who were very young children at the time began to pen their narratives, culling bits and pieces from narratives already a part of the public discourse. Older women continued to write and publish their tales or entered the literary market for the first time after a period of silence. The ties of formal and organized networks would come later, with the founding of the United Daughters of the Confederacy (UDC), but an examination of this post-Reconstruction literature points to the authors' continuing interest in competing and complementary narratives. Although they lacked the structure the UDC provided its members, who with great frequency and intensity commented on, revised, recommended, and reviled literature on the war, these earlier women kept apace of the current literature and had it in mind when fashioning their tales.

The Human Side of Affairs

The same financial and commercial networks that linked newly industrializing southern towns and cities with the countryside also eased the South's reintegration into the rest of the nation. With the end of Reconstruction came political reunification. But an American nationalism, devoid of sectional rancor, did not necessarily ensue. Historian Paul Buck heralded a "union of sentiment" that the regions had achieved within one generation after the close of the war, claiming that the defeated southerners, wearied and resigned to their fate, had made the first overtures at reconciliation. Joyce Appleby and Nina Silber concur that a "conciliatory culture" did indeed dominate the late-nineteenth-century American scene, but they argue that the North introduced the reconciliation theme and that the South, "susceptible to the sentimental appeal of reunion culture," followed the North's lead. Of course, not all northerners embraced this theory of reconciliation. Former Union soldier and carpetbagger Albion Tourgée, for example, suggested in his 1879 novel of Reconstruction, *A Fool's Errand*, that the North and the South remained incompatible despite the outcome of the war. As Edmund Wilson notes, *A Fool's Errand* depicted the North and the South as "virtually two different countries, almost as unsympathetic toward one another and incapable of understanding one another as those other two quarrelsome neighbors France and Germany, and . . . the outcome of the Civil War had settled their differences as little as the subjugation of Ireland by England or of Poland by Russia."[7] According to Appleby and Silber, however, Tourgée's notions remained on the cultural fringes of a nation swept up in the fervor of reconciliation.

Historiographers of the Civil War have pointed out that by the late nineteenth century, a pronorthern interpretation of the war "gained rather general acceptance, thus seemingly confirming Jefferson Davis's fears that this might become the South's greatest war loss." As plantation romancer and sentimentalist Thomas Nelson Page noted in 1893, "There is no true history of the South. . . . By the world at large we are held to have been an ignorant, illiterate, cruel, semi-barbarous section of the American people, sunk in brutality and vice, who have contributed nothing to the advancement of mankind: a race of slave-drivers, who, to perpetuate human slavery, conspired to destroy the Union, and plunged the country into war." And although much northern literature promoted this "devil theory" of the coming of the Civil War, these writings also articulated the theme of reconciliation. Thus, Herbert George, who published *The Popular History of the Civil War* in 1884, claimed that "the causes of the Civil War . . . had their origin in but one Hydra-headed element, commonly known as States' Rights" but also pushed reconciliation. "Even the hoarse echoes of the cannon's thunder and the clash of steel have sunk to sleep," wrote George, "the fretful murmurs of semi-satiated passion and prejudice which succeeded the savage frenzy of murderous hate have even been hushed, and the timid tenders of reconciliation have been supplanted by an eager anxiety to proffer and respond warmly to fraternal greetings among citizens of all sections throughout the now happily re-United States." To be sure, some pronorthern interpreters of the Civil War cast doubt on the success of this purported national reconciliation. John A. Logan, for example, suggested that the South had failed to recognize the enormity of its crime. In a passage many white southerners would have regarded as a patent falsehood, Logan claimed, "When the Rebellion was quelled, the evil spirit which brought it about should have been utterly crushed out, and none of the questions involved in it should have been permitted to be raised again. But the Republican Party acted from its heart, instead of its head. It was merciful, forgiving, and magnanimous." The result of the Republican Party's generosity during Reconstruction, according to Logan, was the South's attempt to regain control of the federal government. "Already the spirit of the former aggressiveness is defiantly bestirring itself," Logan wrote in 1885. "The old chieftains intend to take no more chances. The feel that their Great Conspiracy is now assured of success, inside the union."[8] As with Tourgée's iconoclastic views of Reconstruction, Logan's sentiments seem to counter the prevailing northern trend toward reconciliation.

Metaphors and cultural images of reunion may well have abounded in postwar northern culture, but they remained scarce in the South. True, by the 1880s former Confederates participated in national veterans' reunions, but while northerners were interested in forgetting the past, white southerners sought to perpetuate their heroic struggle for an independent nation. If the mentality that the past was dead governed the northern imagination, the need to remember and honor all that was great and noble about the Confederacy drove southerners to tell their tales of the war. Although Silber maintains that Americans created myths about the Civil War because the event had "faded" from their collective memory, southerners generated tales precisely because the war dominated their consciousnesses. "If the South, as a matter of policy, were to ignore the past," explained Cumming, "she would gain the contempt" of northerners and southerners alike.[9] To abandon the principles for which the Confederacy had sacrificed its existence would imply that the South had repudiated its past and signal to the North that the bloody conflict was merely a farce.

For those southerners who chose to participate in this "conciliatory culture," however, the *Century Illustrated Monthly Magazine* proved an important forum. The magazine had its roots in *Scribner's Monthly*, a popular late-nineteenth-century journal. On 4 April 1881 the enterprising Roswell Smith, a major stockholder in the Scribner's and Company publishing firm, bought out the firm's shares owned by its parent company, Charles Scribner's and Sons, for two million dollars and renamed the subsidiary after the Century Club in New York City. The newly established Century Company immediately began publishing the *Century Illustrated Monthly Magazine*, which thrived under the editorial leadership of many of the men who had made Scribner's and Company so successful, including Alexander W. Drake, Richard Watson Gilder, Josiah Gilbert Holland, and Robert Underwood Johnson. Smith soon gave Gilder, a noted mugwump, complete editorial control, and under his guidance the magazine became an important outlet for southern writers.[10]

Gilder explained to a fellow journalist that because the magazine was "national and antislavery in its views," it provided an invaluable service to southern writers. "It is of no particular utility to the South to have a Southern periodical manifest hospitality to Southern ideas," he reasoned. "But it is of great use that a Northern periodical should be so hospitable to Southern writers and Southern opinion, and should insist upon giving a fair show to Southern views even when they are not altogether palatable to our Northern readers, among whom, of course is our greatest audience." The *Century* exposed its southern authors to a wider readership than they would have received had they published solely in southern journals, thereby ensuring that their versions of "facts and opinions" circulated beyond the boundaries of Dixie.[11]

Beginning in 1884 the *Century* began a three-year project that one historian refers to as a "triumph of journalistic enterprise." Noting the favorable reader response to the few articles that other magazines had published on the Civil War, Gilder and his staff set out to capitalize on this popularity and planned a series of eight to ten articles on the war's major battles. The scheme grew, especially after formerly reluctant generals, many of whom faced financial hardship because of the economic panic of the 1880s, agreed to provide pieces.[12]

Robert Johnson averred that he and the other series editors were determined to present a "nonpolitical" account of the war. More accurately, the editors cultivated the politics of reconciliation, eschewing the rancor of sectional rhetoric. They therefore chose to publish nonpolemical articles from both northerners and southerners, hoping that the series would result in a comprehensive history of the war. Announcing the series, the editors stated that they aimed to "clear up cloudy questions with new knowledge and the wisdom of cool reflection; and to soften controversy with that better understanding of each other, which comes to comrades in arms when personal feeling is dissipated." The introduction of the series could not have been more fortuitous, the editors reasoned, because the passions of the war had disappeared from politics with the end of Reconstruction. The time had come for sectional motives to be "weighed without malice, and valor praised without distinction of uniform."[13]

The editors were more than satisfied with their efforts. "On the whole 'Battles and Leaders' is a monument to American bravery, persistence, and resourcefulness," boasted Johnson. More importantly, it fostered the sectional reconciliation that the editors so coveted. Through their skillful editorial management, the series "struck the keynote of national unity through tolerance and the promotion of good-will." By judiciously selecting articles that "celebrated the skill and valor of both sides," the editors hastened the "elimination of sectional prejudices" and contributed to national reunification "by the cultivation of mutual respect." Johnson and his fellow editors had every reason to be proud of their pet project. "Battles and Leaders of the Civil War" ran through 1887; nearly doubled the magazine's sales during the first year of the series' publication; prompted the Century Company to issue a four-volume companion set, which sold more than seventy-five thousand copies; and ultimately garnered more than one million dollars.[14]

The "Battles and Leaders" series did more than merely pique readers' intellectual curiosity about the Civil War: it prompted many of them to pen their own experiences and market them aggressively. White southern women were no strangers to this literary enterprise and peddled their articles with great fervor. The lure of financial compensation for their efforts was incentive enough for some. Mrs. E. J. Beale of Suffolk, Virginia, explained to the editors of the *Century* that she wrote her recollections "not for notoriety, nor for pleasure, but as a poor widow struggling with poverty, and endeavoring to take care of her children." Similarly, Susie Bishop sent the magazine "a sketch of an occurrence which took place . . . at the end of the war which I have narrated with the strictest regard to the truth, and being unmarried, delicate, penniless, and almost alone in the world I have written it with the hope that [I] might dispose of it to you or some other, and I thus would help relieve my most pressing needs." These unknown women could not hope to receive the same sums as the former generals were paid for their contributions: Joseph E. Johnston received $500 for two articles, Ulysses S. Grant $4,000 for four articles, and James Longstreet $2,715 for his article on the battle of Gettysburg. But if the *Century* chose a woman's article for either the magazine series or the supplemental four-volume set, she could expect to be paid $40–$100.[15]

Other women were less concerned with the terms of remuneration than with having their tales of the war told. Mrs. Herbert Ellerbe of Atlanta, Georgia, confessed to the editors that she was "exceedingly anxious to become a contributor" to the *Century* and was therefore enclosing an "authentic" account of the inauguration of Jefferson Davis. Lucy R. Mayo of Hague, Virginia, informed the editors that her recollections of the war were "strictly true [and] the incidents in themselves are romantic and interesting" and thus worthy of publication. Mary Bedinger Mitchell, upon reading that the *Century* was about to publish an article by General George B. McClellan on the battle of Antietam, offered the magazine her "short description" and "personal experiences" of the battle. Mitchell concluded that the article would be valuable to the magazine not only because of its veracity but also because "it may not be without interest to your readers." Despite her equivocating language, Mitchell had confidence in her work and was willing to subject it to the scrutiny of a major New York publishing house. The *Century* concurred with Mitchell's opinion of her work and paid her sixty dollars to publish the piece in the supplement. Despite the risk of rejection, other women expressed the same confidence in their literary efforts and informed the editors of the *Century*, as did Mrs. Jonathan Coleman, that if the work "is rejected, or if the piece offered is deemed insufficient; will you return it as I would like to distribute it to other companies?"[16]

Some women chose not to attempt to publish their recollections of the war but instead offered corrections to other writers' accounts published in the *Century*. Varina Davis, the widow of ex-Confederate President Jefferson Davis, chastised the magazine for a statement it had printed about the former president "which is so remarkable for the utter absence of the slightest foundation in fact that I am impelled to inquire how you came to make it and if you have been unwittingly imposed upon by others destitute of truth." Davis later admitted that she hoped that the editors "had been deceived by some malicious falsifier," for if they had "uttered this libel in good faith," then they definitely owed her space in their magazine for a rebuttal. Fannie Conigland Farinholt was less vituperative in her request to the editors of the *Century* for a correction to one of their articles on the Union prison at Johnson's Island. Contrary to the author's statement that no one had ever escaped from the prison, Farinholt believed that she knew of an escapee and was willing to furnish the editors with the address of the daring Confederate soldier. In both of these cases and in countless others, women challenged printed wartime accounts and presented alternate versions they believed to be true.[17]

The *Century* not only received unsolicited manuscripts from southern women but often actively sought out war narratives. After publishing a biographical sketch of General Stonewall Jackson written by his sister-in-law, noted author and poet Margaret Junkin Preston, the editors of the magazine requested that she write a similar sketch of General Robert E. Lee. Preston promised to submit to the magazine her biography, which "will consist of just such illustrative anecdotes and reminiscences as I myself have personal knowledge of from living beside the General for five years."[18] The *Century*'s editors recognized authors who pleased the magazine's audience and therefore eagerly encouraged such writers to churn out narratives of the war.

Despite the solicitation of the *Century*'s editors and the attempts of unrecognized authors, the magazine published few articles written by white southern women. Those articles selected were generally of a lighter nature than the formal and stilted prose of the former combatants. Although the editors recognized the importance of publishing statistics and official records, they encouraged stories that told of the "human side of affairs, avoiding the dry bones of history." One of the *Century*'s favorite authors was Virginia native Constance Cary Harrison, a descendant of Thomas Jefferson and the wife of Burton Norvell Harrison, private secretary to Jefferson Davis. Harrison opened her wartime reminiscences not with the details of a battle but with a description of a walk through the woods: "My first vivid impression of war-days," she recollected, "was during a ramble in the neighboring woods on Sunday afternoon in spring, when the young people in a happy band set out in search of wild flowers." The sound of a train carrying volunteers to Manassas broke in on the young Harrison's sylvan romp, confronting her with the reality of the war. "It was the beginning of the end too soon to come," she concluded. Contrasted with the martial language of the former soldiers' reports, the sentimentality of Harrison's prose glares especially bright. Her editors, however, apparently believed that "Virginia Scenes in '61" offered a representation of the war that the more official recollections failed to produce. Many of the *Century*'s readers concurred. Not surprisingly, Page believed that he owed Harrison "a debt of gratitude for perpetuating such an exquisitely tender picture of the sorrowful days of the war." Only a "great artist," praised Page, could create a story so "absolutely real."[19] Page believed that he was eminently qualified to comment on Harrison's work on antebellum and wartime Virginia. Born into a plantation family shortly before the war began, Page was well versed in the stories of the Old South as well as a creator of its legends. Immeasurably gratifying to both Harris and Page was their obvious agreement on the character of the South. The *Century* series' editors were keenly aware of the mass appeal of a well-written personal recollection of the war and thus juxtaposed Harrison's "social" history with the strategic and military accounts to satisfy the magazine's reading public.

Indeed, Harrison so impressed Johnson that he sought to print a second article by her. Despite the severe space limitations in both the magazine and the proposed four-volume supplement, Johnson assured Harrison that the *Century* was committed to publishing her manuscript on Richmond. The publishing company had received such favorable comments on the "charm" and "graphic descriptiveness" of Harrison's previous writing that Johnson concluded, "if the war were to be now, what a capital 'Woman's History of the War' you could write, — for men to read, equally." Johnson and his fellow editors at the *Century* hoped to cash in on the projected success of Harrison's work and included "Richmond Scenes in '62" in the second volume of the supplement. As with her first piece, Harrison established that she did not intend to chronicle the movements of the armies during the Battle of Richmond: "It is not my purpose to deal with the history of those awful Seven Days," she admitted. "Mine only to speak of the other side of that canvas in which heroes of two armies were passing and repassing, as on some huge Homeric frieze, in the manoeuvres of a strife that hung our land in mourning." Despite her veiled apology, however, Harrison knew that she had written a strong article. She attached a note to the revised manuscript she sent to her editor in which she acknowledged that she was so pleased with her work that she could "breathe free after it."[20] The *Century* editors shared in Harrison's relief and confidence and continued to publish her work for the next fifteen years.

Although the *Century* was probably the single most important vehicle through which southerners voiced their desire for national reconciliation, it was not the only one. Private and published reminiscences provided southern women with another such outlet for expressing their hope for reunification. Despite the emotional turmoil Annie Broidrick experienced during the siege of Vicksburg in 1863, she confessed in her recollections that thirty years later, she "hardly realized or understood" the "fierce vindictive hate" with which the Civil War had been fought. Although Broidrick first deferred to "wiser heads" to render judgments on the inevitability of the war, she later stated that not only the war but its outcome was predetermined. Yet from the "ruined homes, poverty, distress and death" of the war sprung the New South, which "in loving reconciliation," according to Broidrick, "holds fast the hand of her Northern brother, and feels that though reconstructed they are now stronger in affection and more united in thought."[21] Broidrick acknowledged that the South had experienced its trial by fire, to be sure, but the region escaped permanent damage and, much to her satisfaction, quickly and openly returned to the folds of the Union.

Parthenia Antoinette Hague, writing twenty years after the war, expressed sentiments similar to Broidrick's. Hague also detailed the hardships endured by her family during the war and declared that despite the devastation suffered by the South, her region had reconciled itself to its fate. "Accepting all the decisions of the war," she explained, "we have built and planted anew amid the ruins left by the army who were the conquerors." Moreover, the South had developed a loyalty to the Union so profound that it "pierces like a sword, our ever being taunted and distrusted." Through this reverence and by its own industry, according to Hague, the South would fulfill its glorious and prosperous destiny.[22]

A Literature for Remembering

Most white southerners found Hague's conciliatory position politically and psychologically untenable. Unless they repudiated their Confederate past, they could not embrace northerners in brotherhood, having considered them mortal enemies. Unlike the pieces published in the *Century*, which the editors chose more for their lack of vitriolic sectional rhetoric than for their explicit pronouncements in favor of reconciliation, and the occasional utterances in reminiscences by women such as Broidrick and Hague, then, most southern narratives made little mention of reunification. Although a "conciliatory culture" might have dominated the late-nineteenth-century North, such an attitude merely brushed the South. In a memoir cum history of the Civil War, former Confederate soldier Richard Taylor, for example, described northerners and the federal government as the "enemies" of the South, bent on sowing "seeds of a pestilence more deadly" than that rising from disease-infested marshes. Of the still besieged South, Taylor wrote, "now that Federal bayonets have been turned from her bosom, the influence of three-fourths of a million negro votes, will speedily sap her vigor and intelligence." Moreover, the *Southern Historical Society Papers* ran a number of post-Reconstruction articles that spoke to the white south's need to remain skeptical of the northern cultural trend of reconciliation. To be sure, the society did publish some character sketches of Union officers, thereby participating, perhaps cautiously, in the spirit of reunion. General Dabney H. Maury's piece, "Grant as Soldier and Civilian," argued that "there are indications of a returning sense of justice in the factions so lately arrayed against each other in the bloodiest drama of modern times, and as the era of peace and fraternity, of which we of the South have heard so much and seen so little, is near at hand, a discussion of the military conduct of the great Captains who led the opposing hosts may now be conducted in a spirit of fairness—and in such manner as may conserve the interests of history." More common in the pages of the *Papers*, however, were stories that vindicated the Confederate past. Indeed, Rev. R. L. Dabney excoriated George Washington Cable, who, in a reconciliation-style article published in the *Century*, suggested that Confederates "went to war in 1861 without justly knowing what we did it for." Cable, argued Dabney, "like a good child thanks our conquerors for whipping the folly and naughtiness out of him, although with whips dipped in hell-fire." Judge J. A. P. Campbell warned readers, "we cannot and must not in anywise in the least sympathize with that spirit of seeming apology we sometimes meet."[23] Thus, many white southerners recognized but categorically rejected the northern impetus for reconciliation.

In spite of cultural pressure, white southern women novelists and short story writers continued to eschew the northern literary convention of marriage between a reconstructed southern belle and a sympathetic Federal soldier, the metaphoric representation for national reunification. Page, a Virginian who began publishing short stories in the *Century* in 1884, advised Louisiana author Grace King, who was having trouble getting her novel published, to refashion her tale. "Now I will tell you what to do," he told her. "It is the easiest thing to do in the world. Get a pretty girl and name her Jeanne, that name always takes! Make her fall in love with a Federal officer and your story will be printed at once!" Page predicted. "The publishers are right; the public wants love stories. Nothing easier than to write them."[24] Although King held Page in great esteem, she apparently rejected his advice.

Sherwood Bonner, whose 1878 Reconstruction novel *Like unto Like* offered readers a potential reconciliation-romance plot, nonetheless ultimately shied away from marrying the southern belle, Blythe Herndon, to the former Union soldier and abolitionist, Roger Ellis. In the end, Blythe finds that she cannot marry Roger because his position is too radical, too far removed from all that she had been taught to cherish. And although Blythe tries to break free from what novelist Ellen Glasgow would later term "the South's stranglehold on the intellect," the heroine fails, limply declaring that she did not sever her engagement to Roger because he was a radical "or because of his politics, or because of his being a northern man. It is simply that we don't suit each other—that's all there is about it." The couple's unsuitability, however, stems as much from Roger's politics as from their contrary personalities. However stifling Blythe finds southern convention, Roger's comments on the North's halfhearted prosecution of the war and its lenient Reconstruction policies are even more troubling. In the end, Blythe cannot marry a man who "despises what I feel dimly I ought to revere, and who was always turning a tilt against things that a giant could not shake."[25]

Similarly, novelist Emma Lyon Bryan had little patience for southern women who temporarily fell under the sway of Union soldiers. Mina, the female protagonist in Bryan's 1892 novel, *1860–1865: A Romance of the Valley of Virginia*, chastised a "fallen" Confederate woman who had been entertaining Yankee soldiers. "What an elegant silk flag, while ours, poor ours, is trailing in the dust tattered and torn, our starving boys, shoeless, ragged and hatless, while these fat villains are basking in gold and broadcloth—oh, my poor country . . . our dear boys." Harrison's scenario between a Federal soldier and a southern belle, sketched out in an 1892 short story, "Crow's Nest," typified scenes found in white southern women's fiction of the post-Reconstruction era. When Newbold, the Union soldier, confesses his love for Pink, the daughter of a Virginia plantation owner, his friend chastises him: "Why can't you have the common sense to know that . . . she would never look at you? These Southern girls are the very devil!"[26] Indeed, Newbold never stands a chance with Pink and spends his remaining years alone.

Virginia novelist Mary G. McClelland also refused to offer her readers a reconciliation romance of the Civil War. In her 1893 novel, *Broadoaks*, for example, she told the story of Julian Kennedy, a once-proud Virginia aristocrat of the Old South who loses his family fortune, his youthful vigor, and his two sons in the Civil War. Because the Kennedy sons died in battle, Julian's daughters alone carry the burden of perpetuating the Kennedy lineage and by extension the heritage of the antebellum South. But the Kennedy girls cannot entirely be trusted with such a heavy load because they were too young during the war to understand fully the meaning of defeat. "Looking backward through the years," McClelland explained, "the episode of the war was to the girls like some shadowy, far away dream, filled with distorted images, and known rather from hearsay than from tangible, individual memories. Of the vital excitement which had permeated all things and caused life to seem as though lived amid an atmosphere surcharged with electricity they, of course, knew nothing." Because the Kennedy daughters neither appreciate the "charms" of the Confederate South nor understand the legacy of its defeat, they are susceptible to the advances of unscrupulous carpetbaggers. Rebecca (Rebie) seems particularly vulnerable and eventually falls under the sway of Stuart Redwood, who "had been sent south by a New York syndicate to take charge of a mining venture in the mineral belt of Piedmont, Virginia."[27]

Only Julian Kennedy, armed with memories of the past, recognizes Stuart as a scheming, acquisitive speculator, and Julian is suitably horrified at Rebie's growing infatuation with the northerner. Julian had considered Geoffrey Bruce, a family friend and Confederate veteran, a more appropriate suitor. Only Stuart's timely death saves Rebie from making a disastrous choice in marriage partners, releasing her from her infatuation and freeing her to love Geoffrey. McClelland ended her novel before Rebie and Geoffrey developed a loving relationship. But if McClelland did not fully imagine a postwar South reinvigorated by the marriage of the southern belle and the Confederate veteran, she nonetheless left the possibility open. She had quite effectively (and literally) killed off the possibility of a reconciliation romance. Stuart Redwood's death prevents any such reunion from taking place in *Broadoaks*.

According to McClelland, the town of Piedmont suffers, in many ways, from a cultural amnesia that makes it as vulnerable as Rebie is to Stuart's predatory machinations: "Redwood had been well received by the people of the neighborhood and made himself, on the whole, fairly popular." Indeed, so smitten are the townspeople with Stuart that, despite all evidence pointing to his deeply flawed character, they mourn his death more than is warranted. Most of the locals fail to realize that Stuart died while trying to plunder the grave of a Kennedy ancestor. "In their ignorance of the true state of the case they had reached conclusions tender and more human than would have been possible could they have known. And reverently, regretfully, one phase of the omnipresent sentiment entombed in honor the man on whom another phase had ruthlessly trampled down to earth not many hours before."[28] McClelland's message was clear: failure to appreciate the virtues of the Old South, the Confederacy, and the meaning of defeat rendered one vulnerable to Yankee onslaught. And although the Virginia town was saved by a deus ex machina, divine intervention was not guaranteed. Better to gird oneself with proper and accurate accounts of the past to fend off a possible future.

Perhaps no Southern narrative so dramatically altered the reunification plotline as Elizabeth Avery Meriwether's *The Master of Red Leaf*. Born in Tennessee in 1824 to Quaker parents, Meriwether purported to have always been uncomfortable with the institution of slavery. Although she and her husband, Minor Meriwether, freed their slaves before the start of the Civil War, Minor fought for the Confederacy and later joined the Ku Klux Klan, and both Elizabeth and Minor remained unreconstructed southerners. Her uneasiness with slavery combined with her firm conviction in the Confederate cause to heavily influence her first novel, *The Master of Red Leaf*. Published in 1879 by a London firm because northern houses shied away from its explicit political content, the novel tells the story of Hester Stanhope, the daughter of a rabid New England abolitionist. A missionary society sends Hester to Louisiana to foment rebellion among the slaves. During her tenure as governess on the Devaseurs' Red Leaf plantation, the Civil War erupts and the plantation is besieged by the Federal army. The protracted scenes of Union raids afford Hester, the Devaseurs, and readers ample opportunity to encounter and judge the actions of the Federal officers, who are potential suitors for Hester; Clara Devaseur; and her cousin, Gertrude Gordon. Rather than falling prey to the murderous, thieving, and rapacious Union soldiers, however, the women are horrified at the unrestricted warfare that these men wage against noncombatants and consequently spurn the soldiers' professions of love. Only Lieutenant Reese, who resigns his commission in the Federal army after discovering that "restoring the Union meant the utter subjugation of a proud people long accustomed to the usages of freedom, meant seating an inferior and ignorant race over a superior," stands a chance with the women of Red Leaf. Reese's former superior, Captain Pym, however, so alienates the Devaseur household with his lascivious behavior that Gertrude, the object of his lust and greed, repels his advances. Unable to accept Gertrude's marriage to the master of Red Leaf, Lynn Devaseur, Captain Pym murders her rather than face her rejection. Meriwether hardly presented her readers with a portrait of symbolic reunification. Only by repudiating the northern position in favor of the Confederate stance can Reese marry the southern belle. But just as Gertrude could never embrace Pym, Meriwether suggested, the South could never return to the folds of the Union.[29]

Many of the stock characters that populated northern reconciliation narratives also appeared in southern narratives. Thus, the southern belle; the infirm, ineffectual Confederate veteran; and the loyal freedman appeared in narratives from both regions. These characters, who were politically powerless, proved to be especially attractive to northern writers because they suggested that no one could oppose national reintegration.[30] Many southern authors, however, added the determined, healthy, politically viable Confederate veteran to this cast of characters. In these southern versions of the postwar era, the southern belle married this young, dashing, gallant Confederate soldier rather than a Federal officer. Instead of a symbolic reunification, southerners depicted a reinvigorated South, represented by the young southern couple. The South might have lost the war, the unreconstructed southerners argued, but through its own ingenious and enterprising efforts, it could withstand this second Yankee onslaught and perhaps establish the independent South promised by the Confederacy.

In *Like unto Like*, for example, Bonner described a vibrant southern town that, although impoverished, had not been enervated by the war and Reconstruction. "As to the people of Yariba," Bonner wrote, "they were worthy of their town: could higher praise be given them? They lived up pretty well to the obligations imposed by the possession of shadowy ancestral portraits hung on their walls along with wide-branched genealogical trees done in India ink by lovely fingers that had long ago crumbled to dust." The ancestors have long since faded away, but their blood continues to nourish the town of Yariba: "They were handsome, healthy, full of physical force, as all people must be who ride horseback, climb mountains, and do not lie awake at night to wonder why they were born. . . . That they were Southerners was, of course, their first cause of congratulation. . . . They felt their Southern air and accent a grace and distinction, separating them from a people who walked fast, talked through their noses, and built railroads."[31]

The First to Rebel . . . and the Last to Succumb

Far more common than the theme of reconciliation was either glorification of the Confederacy or promotion of the New South. Both positions stressed southern distinctiveness and superiority. Harrison's *Flower de Hundred*, which first appeared in serialized form in the *Century* in 1890, was "a fascinating story and one that is bound to live as a picture of the old times, or by gone-never-to-return times in the South." Jeannette L. Gilder, an editor with *The Critic* and the sister of Richard Gilder, concluded that "if the public is not a fool the book is bound to be a success."[32] Judging from the favorable reader response and critical reviews Harrison and her editors at the *Century* received, Gilder's prediction was not far off target.

Many of the accolades heaped on Harrison praised her accurate portrayal of southern life before and during the war. The *Boston Transcript*, for example, informed its readers that *Flower de Hundred* offered "a most enticing picture of an ideal family in an ideal home" in antebellum Virginia. So real were the war scenes, cautioned the reviewer, "that it is not easy to realize the chronicler was not an eye-witness and participant." Jonathan Hubert Claiborne, a transplanted southerner living in New York City, was not alone when he confided to Harrison that she had "touched me to the bottom of my heart and I rejoice that you have dipped your pen and your memory and preserved for your children and the children of all time and loyal Virginians a picture of that splendid race of men and women of which, you, madame, are a notable example." Comments such as this one gratified Harrison, who explicitly set out to offer an authentic social history of Virginia in *Flower de Hundred*. On the day she began writing her "long planned, eagerly intended, hopelessly halting Southern novel," Harrison recorded in her diary that she had filled her study room with colonial literature and "innumerable old letters and diaries," which she had amassed to aid her in her writing. She later declared, rather dramatically, that should her novel succeed, she could die a happy woman: "If I can tell the story simply, unaffectedly of things as I remembered them and have seen of them in childhood and yet preserve a thread of dramatic interest I'll ask no more," Harrison promised.[33]

Although clouded by popular yet tangential plotlines of mistaken identities, scheming relatives, and a misallocated inheritance, *Flower de Hundred* at its heart defends slavery and the South's attempt to form an independent nation. The novel centers on Colonel Throckmorton, an "indulgent master" of a "large, clamorous, and unreasoning train" of slaves. Harrison carefully avoided advocating a return to slavery and claimed instead that the system stymied the South by withholding it "from the progress with which the modern world was advancing to general enlightenment." Such observations aside, she nevertheless intimated that even with the guiding hand of their benevolent southern masters, slaves sat precariously on the edge of a precipice, ever ready to descend into a life of barbarism, debauchery, and heathenism. Only the kindness of owners such as Colonel Throckmorton prevented slaves from "relapsing into the . . . habits and beliefs of their African ancestors." Harrison also averred that "it must be owned that these black-skinned peasants, laughing, singing, dancing . . . when their work was done on the grassy slopes of a fertile land of which each had his little share, was [sic] better off than the teeming throngs of whites in the London slums, or of abject Orientals under European heels." In a direct barb at northern abolitionists, Harrison declared that the condition of southern slaves was "certainly far in advance of that of African negroes any where else in subjugation."[34] Harrison thus satisfied postwar readers on the issue of slavery without repudiating her slaveholding past. She glorified the antebellum southern civilization while acknowledging the impossibility of its return.

Despite her defense of slavery, Harrison steadfastly denied that the Civil War was fought to perpetuate the peculiar institution, and she castigated those who maintained the myth that slavery caused the war. Colonel Throckmorton chides the fire-eating Peyton Willis for making "slavery the matter of contention between the States. If to fight we are finally driven," Throckmorton warns Willis, "let it be for the right of self-government, for liberty, but not for slavery."[35]

Harrison was by no means alone in locating the cause of the war in the North's infringement of southern rights. Flora McDonald Williams underscored this point in her 1886 novel, *Who's the Patriot?* by having a nonslaveholder defend the southern position. Explaining to his father his reasons for fighting for the Confederacy, Jacob Wilder states, "the more I turn it over in my mind, the more I think the State had got the first right. The State is older than the Union; she gave the Union her power at first, and they made a bargain. The Federal Government breaks the bargain — that frees the State from her part also, and naturally throws it back to the first condition." So faultless is his own reasoning, "I can't see how anybody can look at it any other way," Jacob muses.[36] Williams thus explained the motivation of nonslaveholders who fought for the Confederacy. Because the conflict centered on constitutional interpretations rather than on slavery, all southerners, not just plantation owners, had a stake in the South's claim to independence.

The tactics of these southern white women authors differed considerably from those of Cable, a former Confederate soldier. In his 1883 war novel, *Dr. Sevier*, Cable suggested that the Confederacy fought for little more than "pomp," "giddy rounds," "banners," "ladies' favors," and "balls." For Cable, few southerners had a stake in independence. As Daniel Aaron notes, "nothing Cable wrote during or after the War indicates he was ever an enthusiastic partisan of secession." By the

"'Allow me,' said Captain Thomas, 'to suggest that we crown a queen of this Gypsy-like scene.'" Illustration from Flora McDonald Williams's 1886 novel, *Who's the Patriot?: A Story of the Southern Confederacy.*

1880s, he had transformed "from a dutiful if lukewarm secessionist into a disbeliever of the Confederate cause and a civil libertarian." Of the southern soldiers headed off into battle, Cable wrote,

Farewell, Byronic youth! You are not of so frail a stuff as you have seemed. You shall thirst by day and hunger by night. You shall keep vigil on the sands of the Gulf and on the banks of the Potomac. You shall grow brown, but prettier. You shall shiver in loathsome tatters, yet keep your grace, your courtesy, your joyousness. You shall ditch and lie down in ditches, and shall sing your saucy songs in defiance in the face of the foe, so blackened with powder and dust and smoke that your mother in heaven would not know her child. And you shall borrow to your hearts' content chickens, hogs, rails, milk, buttermilk, sweet potatoes, what not. . . . And there shall be blood on your sword, and blood — twice — thrice — on your brow. Your captain shall die in your arms; and you shall lead charge after charge, and shall step up from rank to rank; and all at once, one day, just in the final onset, with the cheer on your lips, and your red sword waving high, with but one lightning stroke of agony, down, down, down you shall go in the death of your dearest choice.[37]

Absent from this passage—and, indeed, from the novel—was any talk of self-government, states' rights, or liberty. Cable apparently found little justification for the Confederate cause or had any sense that the carnage somehow ennobled the South.

The white southern women writers who denied southern responsibility for the start of the war, however, asserted the superiority of southern civilization. Some, like South Carolinian Grace Elmore, implied that because southerners maintained the revolutionary generation's belief in state supremacy, the northerners had strayed from the original vision of the Founding Fathers. In Elmore's unpublished autobiographical novel, "Light and Shadows," she wrote that to the framers of the Constitution, "their state was the centre from which all light radiated." They might have respected their country, but "their love for their own State [was] Supreme." The Confederates upheld this sentiment. Bryan's *1860–1865: A Romance of the Valley of Virginia* also championed southern supremacy and castigated the North for both straying from the intent of the Founding Fathers and for starting the Civil War. "The ominous cloud, that for years had been lowering over the political sky," wrote Bryan, "had now gathered in one black mass to explode in the presidential election of 1860, electrifying the country with the momentous questions of State Sovereignty and Slavery." Moreover, Lincoln's election demonstrated "how useless were all efforts on the part of the Southern people" to avoid a bloody conflagration. Williams rhetorically asked her readers if, given its love of the Union, the South could have seceded without the firm conviction that the North endangered liberty. "Her guaranteed rights were threatened," Williams responded, "and the South rose as a man to defend them, and in a manner which she interpreted to be a lawful and just one."[38] For these women, the South's correct interpretation of the Constitution assured the region its rightful inheritance of the revolution's legacy and demonstrated the corruption and waywardness of northern civilization.

For other women, the proof of southern superiority lay not with ideological parallels between the Confederacy and the revolutionary generation but with southern soldiers' wartime conduct, and the genre of biography proved especially useful for the task of glorifying these men. Although southern women did not publish biographies on Confederate leaders in earnest until the turn of the twentieth century—despite Sarah Dorsey's claim that women were well suited to the genre—women slowly entered this market during the 1880s. Thus, in a little piece on Jefferson Davis, Loula Kendall Rogers, a poet and columnist from Barnesville, Georgia, cited the former president as the symbol of the entire Confederacy. His "christian purity, . . . upright principles, . . . and unsullied integrity" shone like a beacon to guide the South through its ordeal. Writing in 1886, Rogers implored southerners to continue to follow Davis's lead to resist the temptations of "worldly ambition, selfish greed, and cruel avarice"—in other words, the sins of the North.[39]

Also in 1886, Margaret Junkin Preston published "Personal Reminiscences of Stonewall Jackson" in the *Century*. As Jackson's sister-in-law, Preston believed that she "held a key to his character" and was thus eminently qualified for the task of biographer. Rather than focusing on Jackson's military career, Preston chose to highlight his religiosity, compassion, morality, and devotion to the state of Virginia, claiming that these principles fueled the man who "to the end was the popular idol of the South."[40]

Preston's essay undoubtedly captured the imagination of many of her readers, perhaps none more than Jackson's second wife, Mary Anna, who plagiarized much of Preston's work in a biography of the general. Anna Jackson's *Life and Letters of General Thomas J. Jackson*, published by Harper and Brothers five years after Preston's essay appeared, borrowed heavily from Preston's discussion of Jackson's military career and character development, for which Preston was present but Mary Anna Jackson was not. Prevailing practice allowed for the absorption of public discourse into personal narratives, but Preston did not feel so generous. Incensed, she informed her editors at the *Century* of Anna Jackson's intellectual dishonesty and vehemently expressed disgust at this act. "I was . . . very much surprised," she wrote to Richard Gilder, "to find some of [the article's] most illustrative anecdotes and as many as fourteen partial pages in Mrs. Jackson's book copied from this Century article, without any credit given to author or Edition. . . . This is an inadmissible appropriation of another person's literary property." Preston fully expected the Century Company to challenge Harper and Brothers and Anna Jackson on this matter, if not to protect one of the magazine's favorite contributors then surely to guard its own interests as publishers of the original article. The circulation of Jackson's biography "will be immense in the south," Preston predicted, and she wished to be acknowledged as the creator of the narrative as well as to be guaranteed a portion of the profits.[41]

Although mere carelessness might explain Anna Jackson's omission of the proper reference to Preston's essay, it is equally likely that Jackson, as the general's widow, believed she held a proprietary claim to his life and life story, even the part that did not include her. Although Anna Jackson cited other sources from which she lifted long, descriptive passages, she was unquestionably unwilling to share her husband's life story with another of his intimates. Anna alluded to Preston as a "lady who was a relative, with whom [Jackson] lived under the same roof [for] several years," but never named her. Preston voiced her frustrations with Anna Jackson's affront to the editors of the *Century*, noting, "as Acknowledgment is given everywhere throughout the book, even when the extracts are slight, it is a most unaccountable thing that it is invariably omitted where I am concerned. Almost everywhere you read of what a 'friend' or 'person' has said or done," she continued, "you may credit it to me." Moreover, Preston was hardly a "mere lady who was a relative," and Anna's failure to acknowledge Preston as an authority on Stonewall Jackson mightily insulted the general's former confidant. By lifting portions on the formation of Jackson's character from one of his contemporaries and intimates and presenting the material as her own, Anna Jackson was, in effect, writing herself into a critical stage in the general's career. In lionizing her late husband, she also gave herself a more prominent role in his history.[42]

Anna, of course, made no such admission. Rather, she claimed that she wrote her version of the late general's life so that her grandchildren could appreciate "that tender and exquisite phase of his inner life, which was never revealed to the world." She explained her long-held public silence by noting that "for many years after the death of my husband the shadow over my life was so deep, and all that concerned him was so sacred, that I could not consent to lift the veil to the public gaze." She later contended that she had intended to "keep myself in the background as much as possible" when discussing the general's early life. In explaining her account of their married life, however, Anna wrote that "in what follows, my own life is so bound up with that of my husband that the reader will have to pardon so much of self as must necessarily be introduced to continue the story of his domestic life and to explain the letters that follow."[43] This statement appears directly following the passages lifted from Preston's essay. Jackson could now easily explain her "intrusion" into the narrative.

Anna Jackson's biography of her late husband is broader in scope than Preston's essay, however, and the widow provided her own interpretation of Stonewall Jackson's career. Believing that his Shenandoah Valley campaign of 1862 best represented his military prowess, Anna Jackson ascribed biblical imagery to the event. For forty days and forty nights the mighty Stonewall battled the powerful

Federal forces. Chronicling his seemingly miraculous achievements, Anna wrote that Stonewall had "marched 400 miles; fought four pitched battles, defeating four separate armies, with numerous combats and skirmishes; sent to the rear 3,500 prisoners; killed and wounded a still larger number of the enemy, and defeated or neutralized forces three times as numerous as his upon his proper theatre of war, besides keeping the corps of [General Irvin] McDowell inactive at Fredericksburg." In addition to using familiar biblical constructions to describe her husband's battles, she underscored his profound piety, leading her readers to understand the war in terms of good and evil. With Stonewall Jackson and his men cast as Christian heroes, their foes could be seen only as the forces of darkness. While Anna Jackson was by no means the first to confer Christian-hero status on Confederate soldiers, she was one of the most vocal hero makers in the post-Reconstruction South.[44]

Anna also used the occasion to counter unflattering reports of her husband's military acumen. Reports of Jackson's ill-fated 1862 Bath-Romney campaign particularly irked his widow. The general, determined to shore up western Virginia's support for the Confederacy, had devised a plan to take the strategically important town of Romney. On New Year's Day, which was unusually warm, Jackson's men, reinforced by six thousand of General William W. Loring's troops, set out to march. By the end of the day, the weather had turned brutally cold. The supply wagons lagged far behind the marching men, leaving the solders cold and hungry. Jackson pressed his men onward, despite their obvious fatigue, and on January 14, 1862, they finally reached Romney. Only then does Jackson appear to have realized that many of his men were openly complaining about his strategy, earning him the name "Fool Tom Jackson." Anna Jackson suggested that Stonewall's men completely trusted him, however. She recounted the story, for example, of a conversation she had overheard between a Confederate officer and a woman from Winchester. When asked for his opinion of General Jackson, the man replied, "I have *the most implicit confidence in him*, madam. At first I did not know what to think of his bold and aggressive mode of warfare; but since I *know* the man, and have witnessed his ability and his patriotic devotion, *I would follow him anywhere*." Anna also suggested that the rumored discontent of the men on the Romney expedition came not from Jackson's troops but from those of General Loring. Although the severe weather made the campaign difficult, she admitted, Jackson's "command bore up with great fortitude and without murmuring, but the adverse weather had the effect of greatly intensifying the discontent of Loring and his men." She intimated that the discontent stemmed less from the severe weather and Jackson's insistence on pressing forward, however, than from Loring's opposition to a winter campaign. Moreover, "an unfortunate jealousy" developed between the two commands, causing "an immense amount of trouble and disappointment to Jackson, and frustrated much of the success for which he had reason to hope." To shore up her version, she included in the second edition of the biography a series of reminiscences by men who had served with Jackson, testimonials to his military genius.[45]

Varina Davis, too, entered the literary market in the 1890s, publishing a two-volume biography of her late husband, Jefferson Davis. Jefferson Davis had penned a cumbersome, two-volume defense of states' rights theory, *The Rise and Fall of the Confederate Government*, in 1881, writing with the assistance of the recently widowed Dorsey, author of the *Recollections of Henry Watkins Allen* and the novel *Lucia Dare*. For the former president of the Confederacy, reunification meant an increase in state debt, fraud, and crime as well as the dissolution of the supremacy of law and an abridgment of the sovereignty of the people. Restoration demanded, according to Davis, a "complete revolution in the principle of the government of the United States, the subversion of the State governments, the subjugation of the people, and the destruction of the fraternal Union." The question remained, though, whether the reunification would last or whether the people would "come forth 'redeemed, disenthralled, regenerated'" and "rally . . . to shout in thunderous tones for the sovereignty of the people and the unalienable rights of man." According to biographer Bertram Wyatt-Brown, Dorsey offered valuable direction to Davis, corresponding "with sundry politicians and generals to enlist their memory of specific events to be treated" in his manuscript. In addition, "she transcribed notes, took dictation, corrected prose, and offered advice about style and organization—most if it, unfortunately, not taken." Dorsey viewed Davis as a "generous-hearted, much abused leader, who deserved the gratitude and acclaim of Southerners and the respect of gentlemen everywhere."[46]

Not surprisingly, Varina Howell Davis, away in Europe at the time, suspected Dorsey's motives, worrying not only that the relationship between the former president and Dorsey might develop into an intimate one but also that Dorsey sought to "claim co-authorship of the memoirs." According to Wyatt-Brown, "Dorsey's editorial help galled" Varina Davis because "that had once been [her] privilege."[47] It is therefore not surprising that despite the risks of conjuring up painful memories of defeat and of antagonizing the North, Varina Davis penned a biography of her husband shortly after his death. Rather than allowing

Dorsey's imprimatur on Jefferson Davis's account of the Confederacy to stand, Varina Davis asserted her authority as his widow to in effect write herself back into his life.

Varina Davis noted that she felt compelled to combat the northern characterization of her husband as a "monster of ambition and cruelty." She admitted to her readers that although she was inconsolably bitter about the defeat of the Confederacy, she sought neither recrimination nor revenge but wished only to present evidence to convince her readers that her husband was "one of the most patriotic, humane, and benevolent of men." Above all, she asserted, he "honorably and religiously lived, and fearlessly died." The criticism leveled against her husband did not surprise her: "If Moses found, in the theocratic government he served, a golden calf lifted on high under the blaze of the 'pillar of fire by night,'" she reasoned, "one cannot wonder at my husband's fate." The comparison to Moses certainly did more than explain Davis's unfavorable reputation as the fate of all misunderstood leaders. It posited him as the leader of a weary, downtrodden people, who, like Moses, had to guide his followers on an exodus to freedom. And like Moses, who died on Mount Nebo before reaching the promised land with the Israelites, Jefferson Davis died before white southerners could redeem their downfall at Appomattox. The efforts of Varina Davis, however, and the countless other southern women who chose to memorialize his life would ensure that "posterity is the just and generous judge" who recorded Jefferson Davis's name "high on the shining lists of brave and self-sacrificing heroes."[48]

Both Varina Davis and Anna Jackson found themselves in the curious position of lionizing losers. Although novelists and diarists defended a defeated southern culture, they did not face the singular task of naming one figure as the source of all that was right with the Confederacy. No matter how firmly Davis, Jackson, and other biographers believed in the cause of the South and the virtue of their subjects, they could not forget the frustration, humiliation, and pain suffered at Appomattox. Both Jackson and Davis expressed the trepidation they felt as they began their projects. "The task of relating my husband's life in the Confederacy is approached with anxious diffidence," conceded Davis. Jackson confessed her hesitancy to reveal her husband's life to "the public gaze."[49] Issues of authority and authorship might explain this reluctance to record their husbands' lives, but it is also possible that Jackson and Davis recognized the problems inherent in aggrandizing losers.

Varina Davis and Anna Jackson relied heavily on official records of the war, and Davis referred to her husband's account as well. At times, the words of men comprised entire chapters of both women's works, with little original writing by way of introduction or transition. In one instance, Davis deferred completely to men, claiming, "the details of the great battles of the war I will not attempt to describe, leaving that duty to the participants, and refer my readers to the many able historians who have depicted them, and to official reports now being published by the Government." She later rescinded her vow and included her own descriptions of war scenes, but even then, she depended on the words of men, apparently distrusting her own voice, as she did when countering accounts that disparaged her husband's character or slandered the Confederacy. Responding to the allegations that Jefferson Davis had failed to duplicate the Confederate victory at Manassas in the later months of 1861, Varina Davis drew on other sources to instruct "otherwise . . . impartial historians" who might have missed the refutations of such charges. "I have quoted enough," she believed, "to enable the reader to see the gross injustice of the accusation that he was responsible for the non-action of our armies."[50] Although Davis felt qualified to enter the literary market on the war, she did not completely trust her ability to tell her husband's story without assistance.

Varina Davis's and Anna Jackson's reliance on men's words to tell tales of war raises interesting questions about women's access to political discourse. As non-combatants, women are "immunized" from political action. Feminist theorist Margaret R. Higonnet asks, "Can words without acts have authority?"[51] Both Jackson and Davis seized on one strategy for eluding this conundrum: quoting extensively from combatants. Jackson and Davis recognized that they were intimately connected to the Civil War and that they could legitimately write their versions of it. Their claims to authorship could not be challenged. Issues that have traditionally fallen into "women's sphere," such as home, family, virtue, piety, and patriotism, are inextricably tied to the waging of war and the creation of war narratives. Furthermore, legacies of defeat did not discriminate by gender. The annihilation of the Confederacy transformed Davis's and Jackson's experiences, as it did for all southerners. The widows' assertions of authority on battles, however, were more specious. The marshaling of lengthy passages from war records and accounts of former Confederates, then, served to bolster their claims of authority.

Varina Davis did rely on her own words, however, when discussing the women of the Confederacy. Although her work was ostensibly a biography of her late husband, Davis never missed an opportunity to comment on the devotion, sincerity, and industry of southern women: "As I revert to the heroic, sincere, Christian women of that self-sacrificing community," she wrote of the women of Richmond, "it is impossible to specify those who excelled in all that makes a woman's children praise her in the gates and rise up and call her blessed, and this tribute is paid to them out of a heart full of tender reminiscences of the years we dealt with them in mutual labor, sympathy, confidence, and affection." Although Davis offered only tentative comments on battles themselves, she unhesitatingly interpreted the actions of southern women. Moreover, she believed the entire narrative to be her own creation. When the Belford Publishing Company allegedly failed to live up to its contract with Davis, she sued to recover possession of the manuscript.[52]

Phoebe Yates Pember, a Confederate nurse from Richmond, similarly upheld the Confederate cause by praising the nobility of southern white women. In her memoirs, *A Southern Woman's Story*, published in 1879, Pember noted that "the women of the South had been openly and violently rebellious from the moment they thought their states' rights touched. . . . They were the first to rebel," she explained, and "the last to succumb. Taking an active part in all that came within their sphere, and often compelled to go beyond this when the field demanded as many soldiers as could be raised; feeling a passion of interest in every man in gray uniform of the Confederate service; they were doubly anxious to give comfort and assistance to the sick and wounded." Even when confidence in the South's efforts waned, according to Pember, Confederate women stood steadfastly behind their men and their cause. "In the course of a long and harassing war . . . no appeal was ever made to the women of the South, individually or collectively, that did not meet with a ready response." Moreover, Confederate women gave generously and unostentatiously, according to Pember. Like Varina Davis, then, Pember commented on the devotion and industry of Confederate women as a means of valorizing the Confederate cause in general.[53]

According to many white southern women, the baseness and amorality of the Federal soldiers underscored the nobility and virtuousness of the Confederates. In sharp contrast to Jefferson Davis and his devotees, for example, were the soldiers of General William T. Sherman's army, who ransacked the southern countryside during the last year of the war. Clara D. Maclean published her reminiscences of a Federal raid in the *Southern Historical Society Papers*, telling of one Union soldier who tore "open the dress-neck of the dignified old mother, and drawing thence a silk handkerchief in which was wrapped sixteen gold dollars." Grace Pierson Beard of Fairfield County, South Carolina, witnessed the wholesale destruction of her home at the hands of Federal soldiers, whom she likened to the locusts of Egypt. Of all the northerners' violent and disrespectful acts, none was more outrageous to Beard than their directive to her slaves, who "were told . . . that if white women refused to give up all their private possessions the rule was to strip and search them."[54] The waging of war against noncombatants was heinous, she believed; the encouragement of slaves to harass their white women owners was contemptible.

Pember's narrative stands in marked contrast to such contemptuous descriptions of Federal raids. Of the Union invasion of Richmond in the spring of 1865, Pember wrote, "There was hardly a spot in Richmond not occupied by a blue coat, but they were orderly, quiet, and respectful. Thoroughly disciplined, warned not to give offense by look or act, they did not speak to anyone unless first addressed; and though the women of the South contrasted with sickness of heart the differences between this splendidly equipped army, and the war-torn, wasted aspect of their own defenders, they were grateful for the considerations shown them; and if they remained in their sad homes, with closed doors and windows, or walked the streets with averted eyes and veiled faces, it was that they could not bear the presence of invaders, even under the most favorable circumstances." But even Pember noted that "there was no assimilation between the invaders and the invaded."[55]

Elizabeth Avery Meriwether described Union raids that rivaled those recorded in women's diaries or recounted in their reminiscences. A victim of Sherman's raids, Meriwether fictionalized her experience in *The Master of Red Leaf*. Unlike Meriwether's home, which stood in the way of Sherman's advancing army, Red Leaf plantation was targeted by General Benjamin Butler's troops. Like Beard and countless other southern women, Meriwether was outraged by the Federal army's policy of waging war on women and children. Captain Pym, the leader of the raid on Red Leaf, justifies his murderous activity by deferring to the policy of Butler, "who believed it as much to the interest of the Union Army to crush the spirit of secession in women as in men." In this same vein, Pym conducts the raid with calculated efficiency, invading "every place, closet, and corner" and torching the Devaseur property in less than twenty minutes.[56] The invaders were no longer external, removed from the Devaseur family. Frequent visitors to the Louisiana plantation, the Federal soldiers soon became familiar, if not welcomed, "guests" of the Devaseur household. Red Leaf housed the forces of its own destruction.

Through fiction and increasingly through biography and reminiscences, then, southern women lionized the actions of the Confederates while casting moral aspersions against the Federals. Both tactics underscored the superiority of ante-bellum southern civilization. Significantly, these authors made few references to the postwar South. For some, the future offered little solace after the Confederacy's demise. Meriwether, for example, believed that by exciting the passions of southerners, the war had completely corrupted their society. She therefore restricted the majority of her writing to the antebellum and war years, largely avoiding the painful postwar era. The biographers centered their works on the moral development and subsequent military careers of their subjects. Because Stonewall Jackson had died at the battle of Chancellorsville in May 1863, Anna Jackson had little reason to carry her narrative beyond the war. Because Varina Davis was intent on vindicating her husband's somewhat tarnished political reputation, she also restricted her biography to the pre-Reconstruction era. Women writers such as Constance Cary Harrison and Flora McDonald Williams linked the South's superiority with its fidelity to the Founding Fathers' vision and consequently had little need to extend narratives into the postwar period: they had redeemed the Confederacy's downfall at Appomattox. By divorcing the outcome of the war from issues of righteousness and justice, Harrison, Williams, and others of their ilk demonstrated the nobility of the Confederates and, by extrapolation, of their descendants. All of these authors of the immediate post-Reconstruction era, however, shared the belief that southern majesty and grandeur rested with Confederacy.

The Grim Tragedies of Existence

Some southern women never identified with the Confederacy. Unlike Kate Cumming and others who glimpsed the promises of the post-Reconstruction South, however, these women saw only the desolation of the countryside. Local-color novelist Mary Noailles Murfree, writing about her native Tennessee, painted a bleak picture of the land in *Where the Battle Was Fought*. The war had ended, the South had been "redeemed," yet "black waste" and a "pallid horizon" surrounded the inhabitants of Chattalla. The lives of the townspeople were as bleak as the landscape. "The pulses of life throbbed languidly," Murfree wrote. Little interested the citizens save the tragic and hopeless events of the war. "They looked upon the future as only capable of furnishing a series of meagre and supplemental episodes," she observed. Chattalla failed to realize the spectacular developments promised by New South boosters.[57] The dizzying achievements of the New South had altogether bypassed Murfree's Tennessee town, and its in-

Mary Noailles Murfree. (Courtesy Special Collections Department, Robert W. Woodruff Library, Emory University)

habitants were left without a future on which to pin their hopes and without a past to sustain them.

The inadequacy of the past—specifically, the Confederate past—to nurture the residents of Chattalla is most acutely felt by General Vayne, the bitter and unreconstructed main character of Murfree's novel. His house overlooks the barren plain "where the battle was fought," and from the windows the general can see the ruins of Fort Despair, where he lost his arm fighting the Federal army. Confronted by the physical reality of his loss as well his memories of the battle,

Vayne at times surrenders to "those distraught questions . . . which involved the righteousness of the Lost Cause." Reviewing his life, "doubts thickened about him. Doubts! And his right arm was gone, and his future lay waste, and his children's lot was blighted. And he had flung away the rich treasure of his blood, and the exaltation of his courage, and his potent enthusiasms, and the lives of his noble comrades, who had followed him till they could no longer." Indeed, memories of the Confederacy so plague Vayne that he is "glad when the screws of the usurers [come] down again, and the present [bears] so heavily upon him that he [grows] dulled in the suffering of the past."[58] For the general, the only guarantee fulfilled by the post-Reconstruction South is that the pain of the present can surpass that of the past.

The past does not haunt only General Vayne, however; it literally haunts the land "where the battle was fought." The residents of Chattalla believe that the ghosts of dead soldiers roam the ravaged former battlefield. The shattered mirror in Vayne's home faces the world outside and offers "bizarre reflections" and "distorted glimpses," casting an eerie pall over the household. Coupled with the weird sights is the fantastic noise that emanates from the field—"a hollow roar through the vastness of the night and the plain," explained Murfree. To the inhabitants of the Vayne household, the noise resembles the sound of the battle. "The tramp of feet, that long ago finished their marches, rose and fell in dull iteration in the distance." The wind contributes to the unearthly noise: "The gusts were hurled through the bomb-riven cupola, which swayed and groaned and crashed as it had done on the day when even more impetuous forces tore through its walls. Far—far and faint—a bugle was fitfully sounding the recall."[59] The war—indeed, the entire southern Confederacy—offers little to the Vayne family or to the town of Chattalla. The hollow, ghostlike memories are fleeting, distant, and disembodied, incapable of providing for residents of the post-Reconstruction South.

Not even the Vayne home can sustain the family. From the parapet at Fort Despair, "the shattered old house was visible in the distance, its upper windows still aflame with the sunset, as with some great inward conflagration." The house certainly fits in with the surrounding ruin, yet "the whole place was grimly incongruous with the idea of home." Here, as in other local-color fiction of the late nineteenth century, "home" is a realized and fixed yet infertile and uncreative place. Unlike the sentimental writers who conceived of the home as a metaphor for woman's nurturing influence, Murfree represented the home as an existential, concrete spot that not only was destroyed by the war but itself constituted a source of decay and death. Before the novel's action begins, Federal raiders have destroyed the Vayne home, as they did Red Leaf plantation in Meriwether's novel. Murfree's image of the "inward conflagration" suggests that the forces of destruction came from inside. The family itself, still living within the ransacked house, is incapable of guaranteeing survival. Living with the old, crippled General Vayne is his widowed sister, Mrs. Kirby, and his daughter, Marcia, who has become hardened by the war: "She derived a commensurate idea of the grim tragedies of existence from the sight of the same crack of troops before the sun went down, decimated and demoralized, mangled and rooted."[60] Unable to protect Marcia from the harsh realities of war or from its radical changes to the surrounding countryside, the Vayne home could not offer Marcia or her dying family any solace regarding the future.

Given Murfree's gloomy predictions for the South's future, it is not surprising that her publisher, James R. Osgood, expressed reservations about the novel's success. Although the book was published during the same year that the *Century* began its Civil War series, Osgood experienced none of the heady optimism about his company's financial return in which Robert Johnson and Richard Gilder reveled. While Johnson and Gilder hoped to ride the wave of popularity that Civil War narratives were enjoying in the late nineteenth century, Osgood delayed the publication of *Where the Battle Was Fought*. Although the editor professed that the country exhibited a "prevailing dulness [*sic*] in business, and general lack of interest in things literary," to explain the changes in the novel's production schedule, the publication of Civil War literature waxed in the post-Reconstruction years. Osgood never explicitly expressed a lack of confidence in Murfree's writing, yet his hesitancy to release *Where the Battle Was Fought* suggests doubts about the ability of Murfree's reading public to accept her bleak picture of the South.[61]

Despite Osgood's reservations about the likely reception of Murfree's novel, other southern women shared the writer's vision of a desolate South. Georgia lecturer and columnist Rebecca Latimer Felton maintained that the war increased the general level of southern poverty while creating a new underclass of poor whites. Worse, the abolition of slavery engendered a scarcity of field labor, which, according to Felton, forced poor white "unprotected" southern women "to go to the roughest and hardest work, unfit for the delicate and peculiar conditions of the sex." The transplantation of poor white southern women out of their "sphere" seemed especially pathetic to Felton because they were the descendents of brave soldiers who had given their lives to defend the Confederacy although they had never owned slaves. The South, in other words, was incapable of taking care of the daughters of the war generation, who were also — and more importantly — "the mothers of the coming generations of whites."[62]

Another inescapably tragic result of the war was the prevalence of "race antipathy" in the South. According to Felton, the federal government forced on a resentful South a society "with black and white races combined" that the North would never tolerate. The inevitable outcome of this racial tension, Felton predicted, was a race war, "the most bitter and irreconcilable of all conflicts." This "revolutionary uprising will either exterminate the blacks," she warned, "or force the white citizens to leave the country." Although antebellum southern politicians had made a "fatal mistake" by not recognizing the global abhorrence of slavery, northern abolitionists and politicians had precipitated this "irrepressible" race war by convincing the freed slaves that they were the "white man's equal." One generation after the Civil War, another war would soon be fought, again on southern soil, and again white southerners would be the losers. Soon after Felton expressed these views, the town of Wilmington, North Carolina, erupted in a bloody racial massacre. Here, however, the losers were equity and a vision for racial justice, not the white south.[63]

Felton certainly was not the only white southerner who commented on the "Negro problem" in the post-Reconstruction era. Cable, for example, published a series of essays in the 1880s on African-Americans' position in the reconstructed Union. As a Confederate soldier, Cable did not "question slavery as an institution," as Aaron notes, "and believed in a 'White Man's Government.'" Two decades of social unrest, however, had caused Cable to rethink his position, and by the mid-1880s he was championing civil and political rights for the former slaves. Cable believed that he spoke for "the silent South" and hoped that his essays would convince southerners to "settle" the Negro problem without outside intervention. In 1885, Cable published "The Freedman's Case in Equity" in the Century. Cable quickly detailed the fate of the newly freed slaves in the twenty years since emancipation. Although legislation and constitutional amendments had afforded certain protections to African-Americans, Cable noted, recent decisions by the Supreme Court — probably the Civil Rights Cases of 1883, which gutted the Civil Rights Act of 1875 and the Fourteenth Amendment — made those achievements "void." Moreover, "the popular mind in the old free states, weary of strife at arm's length, bewildered by its complications, vexed by many a blunder, eager to turn to the cure of other evils, and even tinctured by that race feeling whose grosser excesses it would so gladly see suppressed, has retreated from its uncomfortable dictational attitude and thrown the whole matter over to the states of the South." The North's abandonment of African-Americans thus afforded the South an unprecedented opportunity to ensure justice for the newly freed men and women. Cable argued that continued oppression stemmed from "the surviving sentiments of an extinct and now universally execrated institution; sentiments which no intelligent or moral people should harbor a moment after the admission that slavery was a moral mistake." The South must act swiftly, Cable warned, standing "on her honor before the clean equities of the issue." Defying the Constitution, "the withholding of simple rights," is expensive, Cable noted; "it has cost much blood." Concessions, he argued, "have never cost a drop." More to the point, morality and justice could not be deferred, he suggested, perhaps a bit naively. It is "every people's duty before God to see" universal justice and equity "until the whole people of every once slaveholding state can stand up as one man, saying 'Is the Freedman a free man?' and the whole world shall answer, 'Yes.'"[64]

Not surprisingly, the *Century* received a flurry of angry letters in response to Cable's article. As Arlin Turner explained in his edition of Cable's essays, the editors at the *Century* decided to have Henry Grady, a New South booster and editor of the *Atlanta Constitution*, summarize the opposition. Grady's essay, "In Plain Black and White," argued for the continuation of white supremacy, noting that whites had to rule because they have "intelligence, character, and property." Turner observed that the distance between Cable's and Grady's positions was most acutely realized in Grady's declaration, "Nowhere on earth is there kindlier feeling, closer sympathy, or less friction between two classes of society than between the whites and the blacks of the South today."[65] Cable's rebuttal, a seventeen-page article titled "The Silent South," appeared in the April 1885 issue of the *Century*.

In this article, perhaps more than in his earlier writings, Cable stressed the urgency with which the South needed to act. "We occupy a ground . . . on which we cannot remain," he wrote. Nor could the South "go backward." Cable believed that "the best men of the South are coming daily into convictions that condemn their own beliefs of yesterday as the antiquated artillery of an outgrown past." According to Aaron, "Cable badly misjudged the audience, or at least underestimated the durability of time-tested Southern dogmas immune to logic and unaffected by even his brand of tactful argumentation." If Cable spoke for the "silent South," then surely the "silent contingent must have held their tongues after the public outcry provoked by Cable's published lectures and articles." Few came to defend him publicly. Indeed, Louisiana author Grace King believed that Cable, through his writings, especially his fiction about New Orleans, had "'stabbed the city in the back . . . to please the Northern press,' proclaiming 'his preference for colored people over white' and 'quadroons over the Creoles.'" King set out to write a story, later published as *Monsieur Motte*, as a corrective to Cable's writings.[66]

Few of the southern white women writers considered in this volume questioned the white supremacy of the Jim Crow era. Bonner, for example, decried "Negro rule" in *Like unto Like*. As the female protagonist, Blythe Herndon, contemplates her relationship with former abolitionist and Union soldier Roger Ellis, she seeks a lesson in politics from Van Tolliver, a staunch supporter of the Democratic Party. Blythe finds Van's position compelling, for "equally free from rant or coldness, firm in opinion but modest of utterance, his words had a manly ring that could not fail of impressing the listener." Tolliver does not advocate the return of slavery or wish to abridge the rights of free men. "But as for having [blacks] rule over us, that is a different thing. [They are] the tool of these miserable carpet-baggers, who have plundered the country steadily since the war, and who must be driven out, root and branch. The very essence of the Constitution is violated by their presence among us. . . . We have been taxed and robbed and insulted long enough. We must get in a Democrat President next fall, who will free our country of its incubus, and then an era of prosperity will set in for the South." Even Colonel Dexter, a Republican, agrees with Tolliver's assessment of "negro rule." "The Democrats," offers the colonel, "committed a political crime in the South; the Republicans, a political blunder. Both ruined their party. But our blunder—negro rule—is likely to be more disastrous to us than your crime—armed secession; because you've turned about, and we can't. It will ruin the North as well as the South." Bonner later emphasized African-Americans' incapacity and northerners' inability to shepherd the freedmen and -women by killing off Civil Rights Bill, a young former slave left in Roger's care. Realizing that he is about to die, Bill longingly looks at Ellis and says wistfully, "You was goin' to make a man of me." Bill had imagined a life that was not to be. "I could see myself tall an' straight as Mars' Van Tolliver," the proud southern Democrat, but Roger could not save his charge.[67]

Some white southern women described additional problems confronting the postwar South. Like Felton, Meriwether saw little in the postwar south to sustain hope. Although Meriwether extolled the virtues of antebellum southern society, she did not believe that they had survived to carry southerners through the postwar years. Instead, she described the irreparable losses suffered by the South during the war. Like Murfree, Meriwether underscored the damage done to the land. Through the voice of the heroine of *The Master of Red Leaf*, Meriwether catalogs the destruction she witnessed "almost every day" during the war: "I saw—fields laid waste, and dead cattle on the wayside rotting. I saw—ten thousand homes in ashes, and over the ruins charred chimneys stood sentinel. I saw—desolation, and woe, and despair spread over the South. And I saw—battlefields and bleeding men, and dogs of WAR lapping human blood." Meriwether, like Felton, argued that women were the greatest sufferers of the war. After the hostilities had ceased, "whither went the wretched women, once happy mothers in those homes left in ashes?" she asked. In response to her own question, she offered, "Alas! they went wandering to and fro over a desolate land, houseless, homeless, husbandless, 'hollow-eyed with hunger, their children cried for bread, and there was none to give them.'" Moreover, Reconstruction did not relieve the South of any of its ills. Captain Pym, the marauding, murdering Federal officer, becomes a prominent member of the Louisiana state government. His two illiterate slave accomplices, Preacher Jim and One-Eyed Sampson, are rewarded for their efforts by being appointed to the board of education and the New Orleans police force, respectively. Under this carpetbagger and scalawag despotic rule, the South continues to suffer the indignities and injuries that began during the war.[68]

Of all of these tragic results of the Civil War, the most disturbing for Meriwether was its effect on her soul. She was not immune to the passions engendered by sectional politics and the war, and her "un-Christian" emotions surprised and troubled her: "I, like all people in the Union, went mad, and was possessed by the spirit of war," she confessed. "It drove me like a demon; it made itself an ally of my passion; it egged on the envy and jealousy of my nature, and there united and goaded me to crime." The crisis in morality did not end with the war but continued through Reconstruction, and again, Meriwether found herself susceptible to bitterness and resentfulness. Meriwether defended her crisis of faith: "when the monster [war] stalks over the land, from his blood-stained hands he scatters every evil possible to humanity. He breaks all bonds, strikes down law, tramples order under his feet. He makes a moral chaos and sets despotism to rule over it." Ultimately, however, Meriwether found this explanation unsatisfactory. Her soul, along with forty million others, had been corrupted, and there was no chance for redemption. If war embodied all that was evil in humanity, then the future was bleak for those tainted by war's poisonous influence. There could be no recovery for those who fell from grace. Meriwether, in the voice of Hester Stanhope, the narrator of *The Master of Red Leaf*, concluded her tale by stating that although many years had passed since the action of the novel took place, time had "brought no change for the better." "My skies are still ashen," Hester wearily admits, "and the sun's light is not light for me; and all nature yet wears a sombre hue, and the pale faces of the dead I saw buried in the old sarcophagus, with the grey bones of a past age, still flit and float before my eyes." Like the townspeople of Chattalla in Murfree's novel, Hester is haunted by the past and inconsolable about the prospects for the future.[69]

Other white southern women may not have been as publicly pessimistic as Murfree, Felton, and Meriwether but nevertheless confided their fear for the South's future in their unpublished writings. Jane Cronly of Wilmington, North Carolina, for example, complained in the early 1880s that northerners "have been our judges, our Post-masters, the collectors of our ports, the officers of our courts and National Governments, and at the same time had not a thought or feeling in unison with our people, only the desire to grow rich at our expense." Under such a heavy yoke, reasoned Cronly, the South could never develop its indigenous resources or talents. Also writing twenty years after the war, Flora K. Overman of South Carolina dwelt on the horrors of the immediate postwar period. While New South boosters praised the splendid achievements of southern industry and memorialists romanticized the grandeur of the Confederacy, Overman apparently failed to connect the war with a viable past or a promising future for the South. Instead, she linked only "grief, sorrow, mourning, and trouble" with the war and its legacy.[70] Overman, Cronly, and many other southern women had a much more limited audience than Meriwether and other published writers, but these lesser-known authors recoiled with equal disdain, lamented with equal despair, and criticized with equal vigor the disastrous implications of the war and the hollow praise of the New South boosters.

The post-Reconstruction literature of southern women confirms their growing preoccupation with the war. Publication figures for Civil War novels, which had waned during Reconstruction, began to soar during the 1880s and 1890s.[71] The works of southern women certainly contributed to this surge. Increasingly breaking free from the confines of the purely imaginative realm, women began in earnest to publish biographies, diaries, histories, and reminiscences. Whether reveling in the accomplishments of southern industry, celebrating the resurgence of the Democratic Party, or mourning the devastation of the landscape and the destruction of the individual soul, these women could not escape the war's profound and lasting legacies. With consciousnesses ever consumed by the exigencies of the war, southern white women increasingly turned to writing as a way to exorcise their demons.

Countless southern white women, most of them complete neophytes in the literary world, unabashedly peddled their stories to the major New York publishing houses. While these women might otherwise have refrained from such public behavior, relegating the rest of their lives to the interests of their local communities, they confidently entered the very public world of the national debate on the war. For some women, like Mary Noailles Murfree, this entrance marked the beginning of a long and distinguished literary career. Others published only during this period and only on the Civil War. Still others, like Varina Davis and Mary Anna Jackson, were public figures who chose to shore up their reputations by writing about the Civil War. Although the number of women who published their accounts of the war increased throughout the post-Reconstruction era, the majority of white southern women may never have intended their works to be seen by a national reading public. But if their stories were personal, they were not meant to be private. Grace Pierson James Beard's "A Series of True Incidents Connected with Sherman's March to the Sea" remained unpublished, but she nevertheless expected others to peruse her account, writing, "Dear readers, I am now old and long since a widow but I notice there exists in the minds of so many erroneous ideas of those troubled times that I felt it incumbent upon me to make public the real experiences through which I then passed."[72] Beard's intended audience might have been only her immediate family, but even if her readership were so circumscribed, she believed that her narrative could remedy the ills to southern society caused by untrue accounts of the war. Regardless of the size of her audience, Beard entered the public debate on the Civil War. She, along with many other women, both published and unpublished, could no longer remain outside the national dialogue. Just as the war itself profoundly affected white southern women, so too did the postwar dialogue, and these women increasingly participated in the discussion.

Throughout the post-Reconstruction period, southern women offered only isolated accounts of the war. Their works demonstrate their familiarity with other versions of war stories, but as a group these writers did not respond to these other accounts. By the mid-1890s, however, southern women had banded together and formed one of the largest organizations for the collective mobilization of southern accounts of the war, the United Daughters of the Confederacy.

The UDC attracted thousands of members, who soon found themselves mandated by their new organization to write their accounts of the war. The number of stories in circulation skyrocketed, but the variation in interpretations lessened. Although the UDC did not dictate how its members had to write, it did uphold certain works as models and offer guidelines to be followed. One single narrative of the war never existed, and of course women who were not members of the UDC continued to pen accounts, which frequently differed from the organization's agenda, but the variety of interpretations that had characterized the immediate post-Reconstruction era ended.

The Confederate war should be classed with those world-wide movements which do not begin or end with themselves, which do not remain within boundaries, which become universal thrill. All the patriotisms of all the peoples of the earth were vital-ized in that civilization which called men, women, and children to the work of 1860. Confederates should know where, when, and how began that superb war, which was a poetic prophecy. That war means heroic senti-ment and just thought, bound into active, willing sacrifice by a people.

—MRS. THOMAS TAYLOR, *Address to the United Daughters of the Confederacy*

To men like Pinetop, slavery, stern or mild, could be but an equal menace, and yet these were the men who, when Virginia called, came from their little cabins in the mountains, who tied the flint-locks upon their muskets and fought uncomplainingly until the end. Not the need to protect a decaying institution, but the instinct in every free man to defend the soil, had brought Pinetop, as it had brought Dan, into the army of the South.

—ELLEN GLASGOW, The Battle-Ground

The Imperative of Historical Inquiry, 1895–1905

"Some twenty years after the overthrow of the slaveholding gentry," the blind Mrs. Blake, a tragic and pathetic character in Ellen Glasgow's 1904 novel, *The Deliverance: A Romance of the Virginia Tobacco Fields*, sat in what had once been her overseer's decrepit hovel but was now her home, tenaciously clinging to the false belief that the Confederacy had won the war. "She lived upon lies," Glas-gow wrote, "and thrilled upon the sweetness she extracted from them." For Mrs. Blake, the Confederacy had never fallen, "the quiet of her dreamland had been disrupted by no invading army, and 300 slaves, who had in reality scattered like chaff before the wind, she still saw in her cheerful visions tilling her familiar fields. . . . In her memory there was no Appomattox, news of the death of Lin-coln never reached her ears, and president had peacefully succeeded president in the secure Confederacy in which she lived." Glasgow intended for Mrs. Blake to stand for much more than one old southern woman "blind and nourished

"In a massive Elizabethan chair of blackened oak a stately old lady was sitting straight and stiff." Illustration from Ellen Glasgow's 1904 novel, *The Deliverance: A Romance of the Virginia Tobacco Fields.*

by illusions." Rather, Mrs. Blake symbolized the postbellum South, paralyzed by an inability to grapple with the tremendous economic, political, and cultural upheavals that occurred because of the Civil War. Just as Mrs. Blake clung to her former way of life, so too did the South cling "with passionate fidelity to the ceremonial forms of tradition."[1]

Augusta Jane Evans Wilson's characterization of the Confederate widow in her 1902 novel, *A Speckled Bird*, resembled Glasgow's characterization. Although not blind to the changes in southern society, like Mrs. Blake, the unreconstructed Mrs. Maurice nonetheless "shut her doors to them" and secreted herself away in a "darkened chamber" in her home where she had constructed a shrine to her slain husband and to all the Confederacy. "Over the old-fashioned marble mantel hung a portrait of General Egbert Maurice," Wilson wrote, "clad in uniform wearing three stars and a wreath on his collar, and holding his plumed hat in his right hand. At one corner of the mantel a furled Confederate flag leaned until it touched the frame of the picture, and from the marble shelf, where lay the General's sash and sword, hung the stained and torn guidon of his favorite regiment."[2] Throughout the novel, Mrs. Maurice refuses to accept the realities of postwar society. Instead, she prefers her predictable and solitary world of dead hopes and embalmed memories to the disturbing reality raging outside her door.

By the time Glasgow and Evans had described their visions of the southern widow who dedicated her life to the memory of the Confederacy, white women across the South, mostly from the middle class and mostly from cities and towns, had banded together to form the United Daughters of the Confederacy (UDC), one of the largest organizations devoted to the creation and mobilization of memories of the Civil War. By the early 1890s, women who had belonged to auxiliaries of United Confederate Veterans (UCV) camps splintered off, setting a separate agenda and beginning separate work. The relationship between the UCV and UDC remained friendly, however. Even after the UDC's formation, the UCV maintained its interest in praising the work of Confederate women, frequently setting aside time at its reunion meetings for women to address the aging veterans. For its part, the UDC's objectives were at once philanthropic, educational, historical, and memorial. The driving force behind its creation was the divinely commanded imperative its members felt to tell the "true" story of the Civil War. Kate Noland Garnett, a founding member of the Virginia Division of the UDC, summarized the organization's mission at its 1905 annual convention, held in San Francisco: "We have met together to pledge anew our undying fidelity to the memory of the Confederate soldier, to teach our children, to remote generations, the true history of the South; the deeds of bravery, of heroism, of patriotism and of self-sacrifice that distinguished 'the men who wore the grey.'" In an era of progressive reform, the UDC's "function was to celebrate the past, not to reform the present."[3]

Although the exact moment and location of the UDC's origin remain a matter of debate, its tremendous growth and popularity are indisputable. In 1896, the UDC had 87 chapters nationally and a total membership of 4,612. Two years later, the figures had swelled to 245 chapters and 14,124 members, and by 1905, the organization boasted nearly 850 chapters and more than 40,000 members across the country. Not surprisingly, its stronghold lay in the Deep and Upper South, with Virginia and Texas the states with the most chapters and members. Southern women who had left the former Confederacy after the war also were inclined to band together to form chapters of the UDC, which thus exerted its influence in places as unsouthern as New York, California, and Montana.[4]

Pitted against the Daughters in this epic battle over the narrative of the Civil War were those northerners who continually "falsified" the historical record by publishing erroneous, contemptible accounts of the war. The heart of the debate turned on the war's origins. While northern historians insisted that the South had precipitated the war to protect slavery, the region's most cherished institution, the UDC argued that the North had instigated the conflict, seeking to strip the South of its constitutionally guaranteed liberties. The task was clear, pointed out Garnett in her 1905 address: the South "must not only write, but she must use her own histories, or she will be judged by those written from a Northern standpoint, which place the South wholly in the wrong."[5]

Two years after Garnett's speech, Cornelia Branch Stone of Texas elaborated on the UDC's mission. "For do not fail to realize that we are no accidental thing," she admonished the organization in her 1907 presidential address. "God has brought us into existence for specific purposes . . . which no other people on the face of the earth can do or will do." The consequences would be dire should the Daughters of the Confederacy fail to tell the true history of the Civil War. "God will hold us accountable for this work which He means for us to do," Stone informed her audience, suggesting the critical nature of the task. Not only did each new generation of southerners depend on the UDC for accurate accounts of the war, but an exacting and demanding God mandated that the Daughters obey his will. Louise Wigfall Wright, president of the Maryland Division of the UDC, thanked God that he had given the women of the South the strength to do his work. Speaking to the Maryland Division's 1907 convention, Wright exhorted, "Shall we not thank God that we were given the strength and means to make this memorial to him?" Moreover, she suggested, UDC members should give thanks for knowing "that as long as time shall last, the grief of the women who loved him, there portrayed, shall follow him, and the glory, which the false enemy shall wrest from him, shall fold him forever to her breast, while the light of the Divine patience of his sacrifice of self shall shine ever round and about him, and more and more shall illumine our path from the dark mysteries here of pain and earth to the heaven where we shall know the reason of it all."[6]

UDC members relied on a variety of outlets to advance their message. In an 1895 article published in the Nashville-based *Confederate Veteran*, which began publication in 1893 and by late 1895 advertised itself as the official UDC organ, "A Nashville Daughter" appealed to the women of the South: "There is a great and holy task devolving upon you," she informed her readers. This task required them to join the UDC, standing "shoulder to shoulder as a bulwark of truth against the assaults of every calumny" designed to mislead the new generation of southerners about the war. "A Nashville Daughter" believed women to be "the books, the arts, the academes" that nourish the world and therefore to be particularly suited to this mission.[7] And, in her view, the UDC offered the best way for women to fulfill this mission.

Confederate Veteran offered scores of women like "A Nashville Daughter" an opportunity to praise the UDC's efforts to champion a true history of the South. According to its banner, the *Veteran* was "published monthly in the interest of Confederate veterans and kindred topics." Editor Sumner A. Cunningham therefore chose to print notices, updates, and reports about the national and state divisions of the UDC as well as short reminiscences and articles by UDC members. Mrs. Thomas Taylor of the Wade Hampton Chapter, South Carolina Division, explained her organization's mission at a local meeting, for example, and *Confederate Veteran* published a short excerpt from her address. "We are not working for what is unattainable," she noted. "The Daughters are honest and vigorous in their effort to cherish the immortal spirit which will keep working those activities, which will have to work perhaps as nature does dark work — the secret growing of power below the surface of the earth — until the fullness of time comes for it to burst out, meet the sunlight and strengthen life." Lest readers grow concerned that the Daughters were overstepping the bounds of southern propriety, Taylor cautioned, "it is good for women to do their part; the part we are now doing as nourishers, and there we stop. We cannot make healthy manhood by standing in its place and assuming its obligations." The UDC, she assured her readers, concentrated on "collecting relics and records" to reach the "spirit" contained therein. "If we do no reach" that spirit and "bind it to our uses," she warned, "we will have bread without salt."[8]

This sense of a divine imperative was not merely a rhetorical device, used only in public addresses and printed articles. Members of the organization infused their private correspondence with a sense of accountability and urgency with which they must undertake their work. Rebecca Cameron, North Carolina Division state historian, advised Elvira Evelyna Moffit, a newly elected chapter historian, on the importance of the UDC's work: properly written and preserved, history "lives" well after "the dust of the men who made it has been resolved into its primal elements." Thus, Cameron reasoned, the UDC should treat its task as a sacred debt to future generations, "a trust and a responsibility for which we must be held to account." Cameron later emphasized the importance of expeditiously carrying out this work. "Let your chapter realize that right now is the time to do this work," she counseled Moffitt. Both the critical need to inform the new generation of southerners about the exploits of the Confederacy and Cameron's conviction that only her aging generation could accurately record the events of the war fueled her sense of urgency: "We, who have lived thro' the war, are the ones who know what happened and how we lived;—we might just as well write."[9] Accountability and urgency, then, not only made good speech and press copy but also guided the UDC's daily organizational work.

The UDC believed that a divine power did much more than compel the organization to tell the true history of the war: this divine power organized the realm of historical action. According to at least one historian, the Civil War caused most Americans to abandon a millennial, providential conception of history in favor of a secularized understanding of it.[10] This secular view emphasized historicism, or the idea that each event in history can be explained by prior events in historical time. The UDC and many other southerners, however, maintained that the direction of historical events exceeded the realm of human action, instead obeying divine guidance. Much in the same way as colonial New Englanders deciphered their jeremiad, the UDC interpreted the Confederacy's downfall as a sign that God had selected his people to endure this travail. Defeat did not signal that the South was wrong in its intentions but rather confirmed southerners' chosen status.

While a new generation of historians flocked to the newly established graduate schools, modeled after German universities, to learn about the application of scientific objectivity to the discipline of history, UDC members contented themselves with the conviction that divinely mandated events of history resisted the ordering and manipulation of a secular branch of knowledge. The Civil War may not have proven an especially popular subject of inquiry with these northern historians. As Civil War historiographer Thomas J. Pressly notes, a new generation of historians came of age during the 1890s, "and that decade was marked by any number of incidents which demonstrated that the primary issues and alignments in American life were no longer those of 1861." Universities offered professional historians interested in the Civil War more than just training, however. Graduate schools and the historical profession "reflected and probably stimulated among historians the contemporary spirit of nationalism and of sectional reconciliation, for both the graduate schools and the historical profession quickly became national in scope and sentiment, and apparently militated against intellectual sectionalism." Even southern scholars who trained at the nation's premier universities, such as Woodrow Wilson, William P. Trent, John Spencer Bassett, Edwin Mims, William Garrott Brown, and William E. Dodd, abandoned traditional Confederate explanations of the coming of the war. Dodd especially decried the censorship of history textbooks by the history committees of Confederate memorial organizations and compared the advocates of pro-Confederate history to Union veterans who defrauded national coffers by drawing exceptionally large pensions. "The Confederate Veteran," he wrote in 1904, "works almost as great havoc in the field of history . . . as does the Union Veteran in the neighborhood of the United States Treasury."[11] UDC members thus understood that the war continued to hold interest and stood ready to counter methodological threats and incorrect interpretations.

The scientific method was, according the UDC, a wholly inappropriate analytical tool for the understanding of the forces of history. Addressing the Daughters' 1898 national convention in Hot Springs, Arkansas, Adelia Dunovant asked her colleagues, "How then, can [science] be applied to the attributes of the soul?" Northern historians' fundamental flaw lay in their attempts to grasp and regulate the divinely ordered universe in human or "earthly" terms. Science and mathematical formulas, she informed her audience, could not explain "God-given attributes—truth, justice, mercy." The pathos of southern defeat could not be justified by accounts of so many hundreds of northern troops, so many thousands of Confederate dead, so many battles won and lost. "Ah, can Arabic numerals measure injustice, anguish, desolation, heartbreaks?" queried Dunovant.[12] For the Daughters of the Confederacy, the answer was a resounding no.

If science did not provide an adequate model for writing history, the humanities did. In an 1896 address of welcome to the Georgia Division convention, Eliza F. Andrews claimed that historians had traditionally ignored "the hero of the 'Lost Cause,'" relegating his story to the poet and the artist. Andrews did not bemoan the fate of the story of the Lost Cause hero, however: "I, for one, am well content," she confessed to her colleagues, "that . . . it is better to live in the ballads and legends and cherished traditions that are so near to the hearts of the people than to fill a cold niche in the archives of history." But Andrews was not completely sanguine about the ability of "modern literature" to tell the Confederate hero's story. "Paltry realism enthralls" literature, and, according to Andrews, this condition was caused by the same phenomena that confined history to the grip of science. When writers and artists rose above this current state of literary affairs, they would once again cherish the lofty, noble, and heroic. "Then, when the great epic or drama or novel, or whatever form the favorite literary product of the future may assume comes to be written," Andrews concluded, "the artist will turn for his theme to the South, the land of legend and romance, the land of brave men and noble deeds, the land that has had its baptism of blood and its purification by fire."[13]

Andrews had good reason to be concerned about the fate of the Civil War in realist literature. As David Shi notes, "underneath the Civil War's romantic veneer lurked grim realities: mass killing, maiming, and civilian travails that sobered many participants and onlookers. In this sense, the war served as a double-edged sword. For some the wrenching event reinforced romantic and sentimental tendencies. For others, it provoked—or heightened—a more realistic outlook toward life and culture." Those whom the Civil War sobered countered the sentimentality of the romanticists with narratives that suggested that warfare was less the stuff of legend than of nightmares. Stephen Crane's *The Red Badge of Courage*, published in 1895, hardly conforms to a sentimental view of war, for example. Of this novel, Daniel Aaron wrote, "A picture of war that resembles a religious revival in hell, all sound and fury, seems to place Stephen Crane on the side of the debunkers and against the participants who saw it as a holy crusade. His war is cruel and purposeless, especially for the foot soldier." At the turn of the century, white southerners like Andrews who engaged in interpreting the Civil War could hardly have argued that the war was purposeless, for to do so would have been tantamount to repudiating the Confederate past, a treasonous action in the Jim Crow South. As Virginia novelist Glasgow bemoaned in a 1928 article, few realists resided in the South. Those who did were "as lonely as sincerity in any field, who dwell outside the Land of Fable inhabited by fairies and goblins."[14]

Sentimentalism and romanticism thus remained popular modes of expression in the late-nineteenth-century white South. UDC historian-general Adelia Dunovant echoed Andrews's assessment of the poetic nature of the Lost Cause narrative. Speaking before the 1898 national convention, Dunovant agreed with John Milton's assessment that history was a heroic poem. Only historians with "epic souls," not those with professional, scientific training, could write true history: "What a grand panorama of epics is offered by our Civil War to the historian with an epic soul, to him who could enter into the soul of the great South, 'who could follow the footsteps of her heroic sons.'" Having an epic soul required "valor, truth, and integrity" — in other words, only a hero could truthfully portray heroes.[15]

White southerners generally shared the UDC's view of history. B. B. Munford, writing in the *Southern Historical Society Papers*, explained, "the very pathos of our story will enlist the interest of the world. Calvaries and Crucifixions take deepest hold upon humanity. The truth will be found," he continued, "and proclaimed just so sure as sacrifice and devotion appeal most strongly to the hearts and minds of men." Elizabeth Preston Allan noted in her introduction to Margaret Junkin Preston's Civil War diary, published posthumously in 1903, that the famed North Carolina poet had disdained telling merely cold hard facts: "As this little volume claims to be history, it is perhaps necessary to say that our poet could never be trusted to tell an unvarnished tale! True, she used only facts in her narrations; but the poor bare facts would have found it hard to recognize themselves when she was done with them! It was neither history nor romance," Allan concluded, "but the romance of history." Caroline Merrick, a former plantation mistress from East Feliciana, Louisiana, prefaced her 1901 memoirs by noting the merits of historical endeavors. She hoped to elicit her readers' interest and sympathy through her honest efforts "to tell the truth . . . for, after all, truth is the chief virtue of history."[16]

The UDC claimed to prize truth above all else and translated its theory of history into tangible works and deeds. Members of the 1901 Historical Committee distributed a circular to the state historians that detailed the suggested format for UDC meetings. Significantly, the committee did not see its organization's engagement in serious, rigorous study as a betrayal of the commitment to providential history. Rather, such study would reinforce the UDC's interpretation. Each chapter meeting should begin with a reading, the committee suggested, "with a due regard for connected, methodical thought," followed by a discussion of the chosen passage. The circular later offered the goals of proper "considerations in historic study." Diligent attention to accurate histories should immediately lead UDC members to realize that "History is the Mother of Literature." The Historical Committee, then, clearly placed history within the realm of the humanities rather than the sciences. Daughters should also quickly discern that while history elucidates "human action," it also embraces certain "principles" on government and war. The objects of this rigorous course of study were fourfold:

- Vindication of the men of the South
- Proof that they were patriots; and martyrs to Constitutional Liberty
- Fulfillment of an obligation which we owe to the memory of our Brave Defenders
- The discharge of a duty to future generations, throughout the universe, to present in clear outline the Federative System of Government established by our fore-fathers; for upon the preservation of those Principles the destiny of mankind will, sooner or later, depend.

Finally, an "effective study of history" would lead UDC members to comprehend the "hopes and purposes" of their ancestors, "the founders of the Government of the United States." In other words, southerners would gain the appreciation that they were the true inheritors of the generation that created the Constitution.[17]

State divisions and local chapters evidently followed the Historical Committee's outlines for meetings. The recording secretary of the Secessionville Chapter, James Island, South Carolina, noted that the chapter "decided to take an appropriate subject for each month, and in this way make a study of local Confederate History." The group began with papers on Generals P. G. T. Beauregard, Robert Anderson, and Wade Hampton and proceeded to the bombing of Fort Sumter, the Battle of Shiloh, and readings from Mary Chesnut's 1905 *Diary from Dixie*. Cameron's Hillsboro, North Carolina, chapter followed the guidelines drawn up by South Carolina Division Historian Mary Poppenheim for chapters in her state. Poppenheim "respectfully and earnestly" requested that the Daughters devote meetings to the study of "nullification in all its phases in American History," breaking the assignment into manageable sections with appropriate readings. The West Virginia Division drafted a twenty-four-month study plan for its local chapters that singled out specific battles and delineated general topics, such as the history of slavery and the doctrine of states' rights.[18] Countless other divisions and chapters followed these outlines, ensuring that members received adequate guidance in their academic pursuits.

The UDC's historian-generals and state historians also prescribed the proper format for papers that members read at local meetings. These guidelines included information on the physical presentation of the material. For those chapter historians who endeavored to compile historical volumes, historian-general Mildred Lewis Rutherford of Athens, Georgia, advised the use of 7"×9.25" paper, with a 1" left margin. She also suggested that the women write on one side of the paper, construct an index, paste (not copy) newspaper clippings, and send the completed volumes of four to five hundred pages to the state historians for statewide use. Each UDC local chapter, according to Rutherford, should complete volumes of muster rolls, reminiscences, sketches of women, Confederate relics, the Daughters of the Confederacy, stories of faithful servants, Confederate history, naval heroes, Confederate flags, and books by southern authors. Rutherford made a number of proscriptions as well: "Don't allow the *War between the States* to be called a Civil War." By following that incorrect convention, she warned, "we own that we were *one* state, not many as we contend." Daughters should refrain from calling themselves "rebel," even in jest, for although "there was a rebellion . . . it was north of the Mason and Dixon line." Finally, "Don't procrastinate," she advised, urging the women "to do the work you have pledged yoursel[ves] to do when you accepted the honor conferred upon you." Rutherford promised a silk banner to the state division that most carefully and thoroughly followed her guidelines.[19]

More important than the UDC's guidelines on the presentation and organization of historical papers, however, were its directives on content. Rutherford and other UDC historians suggested topics for historical inquiry, such as the different systems of labor in the North and South, the Missouri Compromise, the Nullification Acts, the Kansas-Nebraska Act, the Dred Scott decision, biographies of Confederate soldiers and statesmen, women's work during the war, and major battles. Critical to any narrative on the war, however, was a discussion of its causes. Addressing the Georgia Division's 1899 convention, Rutherford asserted that differing interpretations of the Constitution had led directly to the war. The South maintained that "the friends of that instrument were those who confined the Federal Government within the limits prescribed by it; the enemies were those who were willing to sacrifice the rights that belong to each State in order to subserve personal or political ends."[20] This overriding conviction must, according to Rutherford, guide every paper written by UDC members.

With each Daughter compelled to write a narrative of the war according to specific, detailed guidelines, the UDC generated thousands of papers, each presenting one woman's interpretation of the war. Taken together, these papers offer a single, collective metanarrative that reflects the UDC's understanding of history. Not surprisingly, the numerous papers written by Rutherford during her long tenure as the organization's Georgia Division historian and as national historian-general ably demonstrate the UDC's position on the Civil War. Non-officeholding members contributed to the corpus of UDC work as well. Harriet Cobb Lane's "Some War Reminiscences" supports the UDC's assertion that the South fought the war to preserve constitutionally guaranteed liberties and stresses the urgent need for the UDC to set straight the historical record. "There are children in the South who have been taught to believe that the war of the sixties was a war of humanity, waged to set free a cruelly oppressed people, and there are some who have been taught that the war was precipitated to save the Union and preserve the United States flag," claimed an indignant Lane. "But when the truth is known it proves that no flag on earth waved over darker crimes than did this same stars and stripes when it was perverted to coerce nearly one half of the United States." Similarly, Mrs. George Reid's paper on Kershaw's Brigade of Virginia reiterated the UDC's position that true history did not merely offer "a skeleton consisting of an enumeration of the battles, and skirmishes and marches . . . with the names of the commanding officers." Rather, history should illuminate the purposes and principles for which the Confederates had fought the war.[21] Individual members demonstrated their respect for the UDC's theoretical musings on history by infusing them into these historical papers.

UDC members also recognized that multiple accounts of one event could form a single collective narrative that offered a common interpretation of the war. Addressing a South Carolina local chapter, Harriott Horry Ravenel somewhat hesitatingly gave her personal recollection of the burning of Columbia. The numerous versions of the event "by abler pens than mine" initially troubled Ravenel. She then remembered that a photographer had once told her that to take a perfect picture, it was necessary to take many photos, "each from its own focus," and to place the negatives together. The result would be one picture that "unites them all and gives a real and correct picture in true and perfect proportions." Ravenel believed that the same could be done with stories of the war and hoped that "by combining these various accounts, each given from its own standpoint, our Confederate History may come to be written with the force of sincerity and truth."[22] The UDC compelled its members to tell their accounts of the war not only out of an interest in letting every woman be heard but also because the group wanted to present a single collective narrative supported by many accounts.

A Deeper, Surer, and More Permanent Mode of Vindicating the South

Not content merely to compel its members to write their stories of the war, the UDC established a Textbook Committee to select meritorious works for southerners to study. The UDC was not the first or only southern organization to recommend and condemn works on the Civil War to its members. Beginning in 1892 the UCV's Historical Committee, for example, generated impressive reading lists for its members. Omitted from these lists, of course, were works "written by northern historians in the first ten or fifteen years following the close of the war, dictated by prejudice and promoted by the evil passions of that period, [which] are unfit for use, and lack all the breadth, liberality, and sympathy so essential to true history." The UCV recommended organizing subcommittees at the state level, "a deeper surer, and more permanent mode of vindicating the South than relying upon the employment of one or more writers to act as special attorneys to plead the cause at the bar of history." In evaluating Civil War histories, the UCV's History Committee recommended that its members ask, for example, "in giving a truthful narration of the events of the civil war, [do the works offer] the unparalleled patriotism manifested by the southern people in accepting its results, and the courage and perseverance displayed by them in building up their shattered homes and ruined estates." The UDC took its cue from the UCV, formulating rather sizable reading lists, continually updating them, and distributing them at local, state, and national meetings. The UDC banned northern histories that praised Abraham Lincoln, asserted that the South fought to preserve slavery, or omitted discussions of the North's early attempts at nullification. Most insidious, however, were histories that suggested that the colonies were a compact nation at the time of the revolution. By imposing a false unity on the colonies, the UDC argued, these histories glossed over the very real differences between the two sections of the country.[23] According to the UDC, this reading signaled northern historians' incorrect interpretation of the Constitution, which in actuality gave primacy to the individual states rather than to the nation.

Not surprisingly, the UDC placed a high premium on works written by southern white women. Thus, works deemed worthy of serious study by the UDC during the first years of its existence included Myrta Lockett Avary's *A Virginia Girl in the Civil War*, Virginia Clay-Clopton's *A Belle of the Fifties*, Judith McGuire's *Diary of a Refugee* (written under the pseudonym A Lady of Virginia), Sara Pryor's *Reminiscences of Peace and War*, and Louise Wigfall (Mrs. D. Giraud) Wright's *A Southern Girl in '61*. The UDC did not limit its focus to women's personal recollections of the war but also sanctioned the *Charleston Courier's* collection of documents, *"Our Women in the War,"* Emily Mason's *Popular Life of Gen. Robert Edward Lee*, and Mrs. S. Fox Sea's *A Brief Review of Slavery in the United States*.

The works of Clay-Clopton, Pryor, Avary, and Wright departed significantly from earlier writings by prominent Confederate women. Both Varina Davis and Mary Anna Jackson had chosen biography as the genre best suited to deliver their interpretations of the Civil War. No longer constrained by the shackles of that genre, however, early-twentieth-century women wrote about themselves and, in so doing, contributed to the public discourse about the war. Like Davis and Jackson, these later women's status as wives of Confederate statesmen and soldiers ensured legitimacy and authority to write on the war. The UDC, in turn, bolstered this authority, avowing that any southern woman's personal story of the war deserved to be told. As an organization that asserted its influence in local communities, state governments, and national dialogues, the UDC forcibly demonstrated that southern women possessed a great deal of cultural power by encouraging its members to wield their pens. As white southern women grew more confident in telling their tales, and with the backing of a national association, they increasingly abandoned the task of writing strict biographies, shifting the focus of their narratives to themselves.

Although these women boldly entered the literary market, they still needed an introduction to the reading world to justify their projects. Oddly enough, Roger A. Pryor prefaced his wife's *Reminiscences of War and Peace* with a slight to Sara's talents as a writer: "It will be obvious to the reader," he began, "that this book affects neither the 'dignity of history' nor the authority of political instruction." More competent pens than Sara Pryor's, skilled in the art of war narrative, had already completed those weighty tasks. "But," he continued, "descriptions of battles and civil convulsions do not exhibit the full condition of the South in the crisis." A complete narrative of the war depends on "social characteristics and incidents of private life" as well as on descriptions of battles. Although Sara Pryor was neither a statesman nor a philosopher, concluded her husband, she was nonetheless eminently qualified to comment on the antebellum and wartime South.[24]

Similarly, Avary, editor of *A Virginia Girl in the Civil War*, introduced her volume by proclaiming its ability to bring readers "close to the human soul." She explained, "Memoirs and journals written not because of their historical or political significance, but because they are to the writer the natural of expression of . . . life . . . have a value entirely apart from literary quality." Avary believed that *A Virginia Girl* portrayed events and emotions unexplored in standard histories and novels yet captured the "veracity" and "charm" of both genres. The reviewer for the *Confederate Veteran* agreed with Avary, writing, "Strictly speaking, the book cannot be called a novel, and yet it abounds in many of those elements without which a novel would prove a failure. It is animated with incidents that follow in happy sequence," the reviewer continued, "and it throbs with the anguish of war and thrills with the joy of loving its heroes." Perhaps most noteworthy to the reviewer, however, was that "the hideous automatons of second-rate fiction are relegated to the shades where they belong, and their grim specters do not cross the pages to haunt the reader." The reviewer felt compelled to offer such a glowing review, "lest perchance the other half of the reading world that has not yet seen the splendid book may fail to reap the harvest of pleasure which it affords."[25]

These volumes afforded new generations of southerners firsthand glimpses of antebellum civilization. Avary described opulent New Year's celebrations that were unknown to the impoverished, weary postwar generation. "Pretty girls fluttering in laces and ribbons and feathers and sparkling with jewels and smiles . . . and gallant men young and old, ready to die for them or live for them," populated these parties but were strangers to Avary's postwar readers. Wright, the daughter of a Confederate senator, peppered her reminiscences with gossipy tales about Miss Pegram's "fashionable school" for girls. "Richmond has always been famed for its lovely women," she boasted, "but I venture to assert that there has never been a larger assembly of beauties than that collected at Miss Pegram's School during the war." Wright and the other fashionable girls found it quite difficult to maintain their studies when "such 'beaux soldats' were marching, with drums beating, and banners flying by our very doors."[26] Just as the editors of the *Century* had chosen women's accounts of the war for the "Battles and Leaders" series because of the belief that women offered perspectives different from those of former soldiers and veterans, publishing firms capitalized on these narratives' contributions to a fuller understanding of the war.

Yet Avary, Clay-Clopton, Pryor, and Wright by no means refrained from entering political and military discussions in these "social" reminiscences. Clay-Clopton offered her assessment of the origins of the war early in her account: "There was, on the part of the North, a palpable envy of the hold the South retained so long upon the Federal City [Washington, D.C.], whether in politics or society, and the resolution to quell us, by physical force, was everywhere obvious," she claimed. For forty years, Clay-Clopton contended, the North had seethed with animosity and jealousy regarding the South, until armed conflict remained the only outlet for these emotions. In full accord with the UDC's position on the justification of the southern cause, Pryor outlined the "common soldier's" motivation for enlisting in the Confederate army: "Not to establish the right of secession, not for the love of the slave—he had no slaves," but the determination "simply to resist the invasion of the South by the North, simply to prevent subjugation," compelled the average southern soldier. "His quarrel was a sectional one," she concluded, "and he fought for his section."[27] Ostensibly centering narratives on fashion and the social activities of prominent southerners, these women utilized every opportunity to defend the Confederacy.

With so many white women publishing their narratives of the war, the literary market became saturated by the turn of the twentieth century. Clay-Clopton's editor, Ada Sterling, immediately developed a strategy designed to make her client's work stand out. "I perceived long ago, and very clearly," she advised Clay-Clopton, "that your memoirs must be . . . light and gay, and incautiously put together, so that they would serve as a summer's reading, and so please or at least be taken by publishers who provide popular reading." Despite this strategy, Sterling nevertheless experienced difficulty in convincing publishing houses of the financial viability of still another southern woman's memoirs introduced in the 1904 literary season. Sterling bitterly informed Clay-Clopton, "Our work has now been turned down by three houses, to wit, the Century people, the A. S. Barnes Co., and, serially, Harpers [sic]." Significantly, "the Barnes people" had contacted presidents of local UDC chapters about their willingness to purchase and market the book. "The answers to the letter sent out seem to have been unsatisfactory," Sterling surmised. Much to Sterling's excitement, however, Doubleday, Page, and Company subsequently agreed to publish the work, targeting the fall of 1904 as its release date. Sterling and the publishers adopted an aggressive marketing plan designed to blanket the South with copies and favorable critical notices. Although close to a dozen southern women's reminiscences of the war came out at the turn of the century, Sterling's confidence in her client's work was bolstered when she passed a secondhand book store on Twenty-third Street in Manhattan and saw shelves of remaindered copies of Pryor's *Reminiscences of War and Peace*. Sterling expected a more dignified end for *Belle of the Fifties*.[28]

Such reservations about oversaturating the literary market proved unfounded. Southerners apparently read these accounts voraciously and with great pleasure. Henry Watterson of the *Louisville Courier-Journal* wrote to Clay-Clopton, informing her that he had recently read *Belle of the Fifties*, *Reminiscences of War and Peace*, and *A Southern Girl in '61*, "which have quite filled me with memories of the old times." Not surprisingly, most readers favored one account over the others. Emily Ritchie McLean singled out Avary's *A Virginia Girl in the Civil War*: "Of all the multitudinous 'war stories,'" McLean wrote to the author, "none has proven so attractive to me as this 'Virginia Girl.'" The narrative so impressed McLean that she regarded it as "a little classic" and predicted that the general public would soon share her view, guaranteeing *A Virginia Girl*'s place among the invaluable works on the war. Similarly, Letitia Dowdell Ross of Auburn, Alabama, praised *A Belle of the Fifties*, confessing to Clay-Clopton that southerners owed her for what "you have done, for what you endured, for your devotion and work for the South, and we will owe you more love and homage for the pleasure and profit we must gain from these true and patriotic glimpses of our dear homeland through your reminiscences."[29]

The UDC undoubtedly contributed to the popular and critical success of these reminiscences. With each of the organization's thousands of members directed to read works singled out by the national executive board, a wide audience was guaranteed for the selected reading list. Publishers were acutely aware of the UDC's power, as Sterling's letter to Clay-Clopton suggests. Without the organization's explicit pledge to promote vigorously *A Belle of the Fifties*, a major firm refused to handle Clay-Clopton's manuscript. The UDC not only guaranteed a work's success but in some cases dictated whether a manuscript would be published.

The White Light of Truth

Many works fell within the UDC's guidelines but were not specifically singled out for study. Helen Dortch Longstreet's and La Salle Corbell Pickett's biographies of their husbands both conformed to the organization's ideas of a millennial and heroic history.[30] Like Davis and Jackson decades earlier, Pickett and Longstreet aggrandized Confederate "heroes." Although these later writers followed Davis's and Jackson's method of relying heavily on previously published sources, both Longstreet and Pickett were much more willing to trust their own voices. Although Davis and Jackson offered interpretations of the meaning of Confederate defeat, Longstreet and Pickett pushed beyond these limits and described battles and strategy. These works differed from those turn-of-the-century reminiscences by Avary, Clay-Clopton, Pryor, and Wright, however. Longstreet and Pickett still clung to the genre of biography. More significantly, they deferred to recognized authorities on especially troublesome events, ensuring that their narratives contained accepted elements. By telling their tales in familiar ways and supporting popular conceptions of history, Longstreet and Pickett elevated to idol status two of the Confederacy's most controversial figures.

Helen Dortch Longstreet opened *Lee and Longstreet at High Tide*, her 1904 biography of her deceased husband, General James Longstreet, with a declaration of her life's mission: "This hour . . . clamor[s] for the white light of truth which I reverently undertake to throw upon the deeds of the commander, who, from Manassas to Appomattox, was the strong right arm of the Confederate States Army." From the time the young Dortch married the aging general in 1897 until her death in 1962, she strove to relate "the truth" of her husband's prominent and highly controversial role at Gettysburg, "unwarped and·undistorted by passion." Throughout this work and in other writings, Helen Longstreet painstakingly and repeatedly emphasized that her narration of the events of that pivotal battle were based solely on cold, hard facts. Indeed, she relied heavily on her husband's memoirs, *From Manassas to Appomattox*, published in 1895. The general offered his work in much more of a conciliatory spirit than his widow later offered, prefacing his memoirs with the statement, "I believe there is to-day, *because of the war*, a broader and deeper patriotism in all Americans; that patriotism throbs the heart and pulses the being as ardently of the South Carolinian as of the Massachusetts Puritan." His memoirs, he believed, contributed to the passing of "the materials of history to those who may give them place in the records of the nation,—not of the South nor of the North,—but in the history of the United Nation." His charity did not extend to those who blamed him for the Confederates' loss at Gettysburg, however. Because "it does not look like generalship to lose a battle and a cause," argued Longstreet, General Robert E. Lee's supporters had needed to find a scapegoat for Gettysburg. That role fell to General Longstreet, who spilled a lot of ink defending his name.[31] In part because Helen Longstreet's work relied so heavily on her late husband's memoirs,

General James and Helen Dortch Longstreet, 1901. (Courtesy
Special Collections Department, Robert W. Woodruff Library,
Emory University)

her claims of objectivity are spurious: *Lee and Longstreet at High Tide* is a work
of passion and subjectivity. Her representation of the battle sought to recast her
husband's image from that of the traitor of Gettysburg to that of a hero of the
Confederacy.

Helen Longstreet's work was very much a part of the tradition of southern
women's biographies lionizing "patriotic" Confederates, a tradition that Davis
and Jackson had begun in the 1880s and 1890s. But more than these other
women, who faced the tensions inherent in glorifying losers, Longstreet found it
difficult to fit her narrative within the parameters of the Lost Cause myth. General Longstreet did not face accusations of merely losing a battle in a war that,

by the turn of the twentieth century, most southerners deemed unwinnable by the Confederacy. Indeed, had that alone been the case, Helen Dortch Longstreet could easily have told of her husband's valiant efforts to fend off an unstoppable enemy in the face of sure defeat. But General Longstreet's fellow officers charged him with disobeying orders, with betraying General Lee—in short, with forsaking the cause of southern independence.[32] Although competing discourses continually caused the myth of the Lost Cause to evolve, it had yet to reach the stage of embracing a traitor to the Confederacy. Thus, Helen Longstreet's narrative instructively delineates the ways in which white southerners sought to expand the myth's boundaries in the early twentieth century.

The controversy surrounding General Longstreet's actions at Gettysburg started well before he married Helen Dortch, a former classmate of his daughter by a previous marriage. While some observers questioned his behavior immediately following the Confederate debacle, the dispute did not begin in earnest until late 1872 and early 1873, when General William Pendleton launched a speaking tour devoted to denouncing Longstreet and aggrandizing Lee. Helen Dortch Longstreet made much of the timing of this campaign against her husband, claiming that his detractors could only have vilified Longstreet after Lee's death: Lee, she felt certain, would have defended Longstreet. Helen Longstreet correctly noted the delay in the tarnishing of her husband's reputation. "When James Longstreet rode away from Appomattox in April 1865," historian Jeffry D. Wert wrote, "few, if any, would have predicted that in time he would become the scapegoat for the Confederate defeat." Longstreet had advanced in the Army of the Confederacy and had been Lee's senior subordinate. "Like other high-ranking generals in the army, [Longstreet] had had his failings, but his performance had ranked him with 'Stonewall' Jackson as Lee's finest officers." Once Lee was effectively silenced—and, perhaps equally significant, once Longstreet had accepted a political post from Republican President U. S. Grant—"the storm broke." Generals Pendleton, John Gordon, Fitzhugh Lee, and other ranking members of the former Confederacy accused Longstreet of disobeying Lee's orders to attack the U.S. Army at sunrise and of being "culpably slow" in his attack on July 3. From the time of Pendleton's defamation of Longstreet in 1872, charged his widow, until she began her crusading efforts to "reconstruct" her husband's image more than twenty years later, "the south was seditiously taught to believe that the Federal victory was wholly the fortuitous outcome of the culpable disobedience of General Longstreet."[33]

The timing of Helen Longstreet's response to her husband's critics was no less opportune than that of the detractors' themselves. *Lee and Longstreet at High Tide* appeared one year after General John B. Gordon, one of Longstreet's harshest critics, published his memoirs, *Reminiscences of the Civil War*. Not surprisingly, Gordon used his memoirs as a vehicle for defending Lee's strategy at Gettysburg and for criticizing Longstreet's inaction at this crucial battle. According to Gordon, "Lee died believing (the testimony on this point is overwhelming) that he lost Gettysburg at last by Longstreet's disobedience of orders." Gordon had leveled his most severe criticisms at a fellow Confederate officer. Moreover, he had claimed to offer his memoirs in the spirit of conciliation. He prefaced his account by stating, "It will be found, I trust, that no injustice has been done to either section, to any army, or to any of the great leaders, but that the substance and spirit of the following pages will tend rather to lift to a higher plane the estimate placed by victors and vanquished upon their countrymen of the opposing section, and thus strengthen the sentiment of intersectional fraternity which is essential to complete national unity." Despite the memoir's conciliatory tone, however, the UDC's Historical Committee endorsed Gordon's account at its 1903 national convention in Charleston, South Carolina.[34]

Helen Dortch Longstreet wanted her biography to counter Gordon's most recent attack on her husband's reputation and to challenge the UDC's recommendation of Gordon's account. She faced a difficult task. Both Gordon and Longstreet died in 1904. Not only did Gordon's account of Gettysburg bear the imprimatur of the UDC, but his death was mourned by countless chapters of the organization. Scores of tributes to the former general appeared in the *Confederate Veteran* during 1904. With the exception of a brief obituary, no such tribute appeared for General Longstreet. "Now that the old fighter is dead," the obituary read, "it is better to forget his mistakes, if he made any, and to remember only the great things of his life, which, indeed, were many, and to honor him for their sake."[35] This "defense" of General Longstreet would hardly satisfy his young widow.

Fortunately for Helen Longstreet, she wrote when the myth of the Lost Cause was the dominant discourse in southern narratology. If southern audiences were unaccustomed to accounts that posited "traitors" as "heroes," such readers were certainly familiar with the formula Longstreet used to tell her tale. Like Davis and Jackson, Longstreet quoted extensively from official records, ex-Confederates' accounts, and her husband's descriptions of the battle. *Lee and Longstreet at High Tide*, she asserted, "is the carefully sifted story of the records and contemporaneous witnesses." Although she admitted that for clarity she introduced "here and there" General Longstreet's account of the disputed story, she vehemently insisted that in the end hers was "the story of the records."[36] This method gave her, like Davis and Jackson, the authority to write on war despite her status as a noncombatant. Although the myth of the Lost Cause sheltered Longstreet, a Confederate officer's widow, from attack by suspecting southerners, her claims of authority were nevertheless specious. Unlike Davis and Jackson, who had at least lived through the 1850s and 1860s and were intimately connected with their husbands' careers during the Civil War, Longstreet was of a different generation and did not meet the general until long after his controversial participation in the Battle of Gettysburg. Moreover, although she had married a Confederate, he was to most southerners a traitor and had yet to be enshrined by the Lost Cause. Helen Longstreet thus sought to gain legitimacy with her audience by mimicking the way in which Davis and Jackson wrote their biographies. The familiar formula, Longstreet hoped, would compensate for the unfamiliar text.

La Salle Corbell Pickett, General George E. Pickett's third wife, also followed the biographical form established by Davis and Jackson and did so for similar reasons. "In the compilation of this record," Pickett admitted in her preface, "the reader must know that I could not bring personal witness to the events described." To compensate for her role as a noncombatant, then, she "based her own narrative upon the original material," quoting extensively from official records and personal reminiscences. Indeed, according to a recent biographer of General George Pickett, Lesley J. Gordon, Sallie Pickett plagiarized long passages describing military movements from Walter Harrison's *Pickett's Men*. More forcefully than Davis, Jackson, or even Helen Longstreet, Sallie Pickett justified her biography and her inclusion within the narrative: "My story has been so closely allied with that of Pickett and his division," she reasoned, "that it does not seem quite an intrusive interpolation for me to appear in the record of that warrior band." Fending off any potential criticism for offering her particular version of the war, she rhetorically asked, "How could I tell the story, and the way in which that story was written, and not be a part of it?"[37] Believing that she played a critical role in her husband's military career, La Salle Corbell Pickett was more willing to trust her own voice than were the other biographers discussed here. In addition to quoting from official sources and plagiarizing from other biographies, then, she supplemented her account with her analyses of battles and Confederate policy. To avoid alienating readers, however, Pickett followed the basic biographical methods established by Varina Davis and Anna Jackson.

Sallie Pickett's biography of her husband resonated with white southerners not only because it mimicked traditional works on Confederate leaders, however. Pickett also espoused a millennial, preordained conception of history that complemented the UDC's understanding of the discipline. Explaining General Pickett's ill-fated charge at Gettysburg, his widow suggested the ways in which Nature prepared for the battle. "Looking down the far slope of time," wrote Pickett, Nature "saw a great battle in which questions that had heretofore weakened the unity of the nation should be settled at countless cost of blood and treasure, and prepared for that mighty conflict a fitting field." Elsewhere, Pickett transferred the course of events out of the realm of human action and placed it within a divine mission. "By his untrammeled will," she explained, "does the god of war choose the stage for the unfolding of each scene in his blood-red drama. Having made his selection, he leads hither his followers by some slight incident in which his hand is unseen." Sallie Pickett had previously employed this strategy in an article that appeared in the *Southern Historical Society Papers* in 1896. Describing the battle, she wrote that her husband had "led the immortal charge over those sacred heights, on through the passage of the Valley of Death." In both instances, La Salle Pickett located General Pickett's charge within a larger scheme, incomprehensible to mere mortals, and thereby removed all blame from her husband for his crushing and decisive defeat. Indeed, she removed all blame from any Confederate soldier. Many strategists and writers had attempted to assign responsibility for the defeat of the Army of Northern Virginia at Gettysburg, but in Sallie Pickett's view, they wasted their time. "I cannot find it in my heart, nor do I think it reasonable," she asserted, "to believe that any man or officer of that grand army, led by the peerless hero, did aught but what the most profound sense of duty and patriotism, controlled by the emergencies which surrounded him, suggested that he should do."[38] For Pickett, this millennial view of history made defeat much easier to accept than did believing that the events of Gettysburg fell within the realm of human action. She cast her husband and his compatriots as players in a drama in which they had no control over the ending. She thus supported the UDC's view of a divinely ordained history while vindicating her husband.

Finally, La Salle Corbell Pickett offered an interpretation of the Civil War that was palatable to most white southerners. Like most of her contemporaries, Pickett located the cause of the war not with the institution of slavery but with the principle of states' rights. Because the Confederacy upheld the vision outlined by the framers of the Constitution, southerners were blameless for the war. "Under the Southern flag there were no traitors, no rebels," she proclaimed.

"To state the reverse of this proposition is to falsify history; to charge it is a crime." Moreover, Pickett argued that traditions of the Old South maintained their resonance in the postwar era. Although the Union might have obliterated the Confederacy, the North had not eradicated the roots of southern culture, which "dwell deep in the hearts of the people, where they give light and glory to life, as the sunlight of the ages, locked up in the depths of earth, transmuted its glow into the sparkle of the glittering gem."[39] Not only was the Confederate cause justified, but its defeat signaled only its political demise. The roots of the antebellum civilization, according to Pickett, remained to nourish the following generation.

This vision also helps to account for Helen Dortch Longstreet's strategy for resuscitating her husband's image. She did not depend solely on a familiar formula to tell her tale. She hoped that white southerners would embrace her narrative because she shared their vision of history as an epic, heroic poem. Like the UDC, which saw no contradiction between writing "dispassionate" history based on facts and offering moral judgments, Longstreet professed objectivity yet infused her work with sentiment and emotion. In the preface to her biography, Longstreet announced that she was writing this work out of love for the general. Furthermore, her contempt for her husband's detractors matched the reverence she felt for him. "I cannot forget," she confessed, that Longstreet "poured out his heroic blood in defense of the southern people, and when there was not a flag left for him to fight for many of them turned against him and persecuted him with a bitterness that saddened his left years." Indeed, she so intently loathed her husband's critics that she claimed emotional paralysis when asked to write about the general's personal life: "I must not write about him," she stated, "until I can write bravely, sweetly, cheerfully, and in this hour it is, perhaps, more than my human nature can do." She later declared, "I cannot take the public into my confidence about the man I loved. The subject is too sacred."[40] But Longstreet clearly overstated her reluctance to share with her readers the "personal" Longstreet, for the biography continues for another 250 pages. But more important, she negated her own expressed intentions of writing a dispassionate account of the Battle of Gettysburg and offered instead an epic narrative of good versus evil.

If Helen Dortch Longstreet was cognizant of the tension between her quest for historical truth and her method as a practicing historian, she did not publicly acknowledge this awareness. She expected her readers to discern the truth about her husband's role at Gettysburg through her narrative style. Longstreet did not perceive herself as being misleading when she presented events out of chronological order, when she peppered her historical narrative with accounts from official records and personal reminiscences, or when she idolized General Longstreet. In fact, her truth depended on the passionate and epic grandeur of her tale. Without the presence of both, she would not have been able to tell her story. She believed not only that she had written the definitive account of Longstreet at Gettysburg but that she alone could have done so. As his loving wife and trusted confidant, she felt that she knew his story as no one else did. More important, she believed that it was her duty to share this knowledge, bound up with emotion, with the world.

Helen Longstreet depended on the shifting boundaries of the Lost Cause myth. Although its proponents and adherents still demanded an unflagging loyalty to the memory of the Confederacy, the ways in which followers could express this loyalty changed greatly during the first fifty years after Appomattox. Ironically, as the pleas for greater adherence to a particularly southern interpretation of the war grew more intense, the myth's boundaries expanded to include those who had been left out by the first generation of writers. In other words, as southerners were encouraged to participate in an increasingly heated and bitter sectional debate over the origins, meanings, and results of the Civil War, they were also encouraged to glorify those who had previously been at best formally ignored or at worst vilified. Rather than hone and tighten their arguments or whittle their list of canonized heroes, Lost Cause writers broadened their defenses to combat the onslaught of northern accounts of the war. La Salle Corbell Pickett could therefore burnish the image of her husband, commander of the ill-fated charge at Gettysburg. Seemingly even more bizarre, Helen Dortch Longstreet could attempt to change her husband's image as a traitor into that of a Confederate hero, with the possibility of a modicum of success. Even authors who privately expressed their disregard for certain Confederate "heroes" did not publicly tarnish their images. Helen Longstreet believed Generals George Pickett and Stonewall Jackson to be "two of the most overrated men on the southern side of the Civil War," yet she vowed never "to take away from [Pickett] any prestige history has given him, however much undeserved." As southerners called upon themselves to fight a "powerful, but silent battle, that of opinion," they marshaled all available material, no matter how altered or even distorted, to serve as part of the bulwark against northern interpretations of the Civil War.[41]

Many white southerners willingly expanded the parameters of the Lost Cause myth because the stakes were greater than the telling of personal stories. These writers understood fully that their individual narratives contributed to a larger discourse on the Civil War. They did not believe that northern accounts attacked personal stories but rather perceived that the southern version of the war — the totality of narratives that comprised the metanarrative — faced annihilation by the pens of northern writers. By broadening the myth's boundaries, southerners presented the North with a united front. By embracing those who were susceptible to criticism, white southerners strengthened the weak links in their defense of the Confederacy. The more inclusive the discourse, the more resistant it was to outside attack. La Salle Corbell Pickett and Helen Dortch Longstreet did much more than resuscitate their husbands' waning reputations: they propped up the Lost Cause by placing more "heroes" within its fold.

Longstreet believed that her faith in her readers' willingness to accept her version of history was well placed, for some white southerners had come to sanctify her husband. By the time she published her biography, the James Longstreet Chapter of the Georgia Division of the UDC had warned, "perish the hand and strike down the pen that would rob him of a people's gratitude to a brave and loyal son." Similarly, the Sidney Lanier Chapter of Macon, Georgia, promised to "do all in our power to teach the children of our dear Southland the story of [Longstreet's] sublime courage, his devotion to duty, of the willingness of his men to follow wherever he led." The Troy chapter of the Alabama Division proclaimed, "The memory of the Confederacy is a sacred trust, for the men who made its history we entertain an unalterable veneration. For General Longstreet, one of its distinguished heroes, we feel an abiding affection." Helen Longstreet hoped that these proclamations evidenced General James Longstreet's secure place in the Lost Cause myth. These statements defended the formerly controversial figure and protected him as other worshipers of the Confederate pantheon guarded the memories of Lee, Jefferson Davis, and other Confederate heroes. History has not borne out Helen Longstreet's faith, however. As Wert notes, "With the war's end [Longstreet] belonged to history, and it would not be kind. . . . By the time of his death, his opponents had created a history of the conflict that continues to this day. Undoubtedly," Wert concluded, "James Longstreet was the greatest victim of the Lost Cause interpretation."[42]

The Safest Antidote to Sentimental Decay

Fiction remained a popular genre for white southern women who wished to tell their stories of the Civil War. Augusta Jane Evans Wilson, who had remained largely silent on the meaning and legacy of the war and Reconstruction in the

fiction she published after *Macaria*, returned to southern history as the catalyst for the action in her 1902 novel, *A Speckled Bird*. The novel tells the story of
the Maurice family, headed by the widow of slain Confederate General Egbert
Maurice. Shortly after the war, General and Mrs. Maurice's daughter, Marcia,
had disgraced the family name as well as the memory of the southern cause by
marrying a Yankee carpetbagger and federally appointed judge, Allison Kent.
Her traitorous deed did not go unpunished, however, for she died tragically. The
novel opens with Mrs. Maurice trying to cope with raising her detested granddaughter, Elgah, a bitter and constant reminder of Marcia's marriage. The literary convention of a union between a southern belle and a Yankee soldier did
not symbolize sectional reconciliation in *A Speckled Bird* but rather underscored
many white southerners' anger and resentment about the North's presence in the
South during Reconstruction. "To the truly typical southern woman who survived the loss of family idols and of her country's freedom, for which she had surrendered them," Wilson explained, "'reconstruction,' political and social, was
no more possible than the physical resurrection and return of slain thousands
lying in Confederate graves all over the trampled and ruined south." In a passage that could have described the author as well as her character, Mrs. Maurice,
Wilson noted, "no mourning Southern matron indulged more intensely an inexorable, passionate hatred of Northern invaders than did Mrs. Maurice, who
refused to accept the inevitable and shut her doors against the agents of 'Union
and reconstruction' as promptly as she barred out leprosy or smallpox." For
white southerners of her generation, Wilson later explained, time was not an
"emollient panacea" for "political rancor": "Section hatred bites hard on memory, as acid into copper."[43]

Although time did not soothe Wilson's soul regarding the defeat of the Confederacy, the passing years did afford her the ability to unleash publicly the bitterness that had remained unexpressed for almost forty years. Wilson assailed
all that was wrong with northern society: socialism, trade unionism, feminism,
religious fanaticism, unscrupulous acquisitiveness, and general amorality. Wilson's description of Mrs. Dane, a New Yorker, underscores this suspicion of all
things northern: "She is avowedly a socialist of the extreme type: belongs to
labor organizations, attends their meetings, makes impassioned addresses, and
. . . is a female Ishmael. . . . She is reported as possessing some education, advocates 'single tax' and all the communistic vagaries that appeal to the great mass
of toiling poor, the discontented, and the morose. . . . She frequents a hall down
on the East side, where at night the clans of disgruntled assemble, and long-

haired men and short-haired women—who absolutely believe that the only real 'devil is private property'—denounce wealth and preach their gospel of covetousness." Wilson contrasted Mrs. Dane with Elgah, who, despite her suspect parentage, embraces the values of southern civilization. "I am not in rebellion," Elgah declares to one of her northern companions, "against legal statutes, nor the canons of well-established decency and refinement in feminine usage, and finally, I am so inordinately proud of being a well-born southern women, with a full complement of honorable great-grandfathers and blue-blooded, stainless great grandmothers, that I have neither pretext nor inclination to revolt against mankind."[44] Even Elgah resonated with Wilson's southern readers.

The novel did not fare as well as her previous novels had with critics, many of whom saw the tale as a decidedly old-fashioned story merely brought up to date. The critic for the *Dial* wrote rather flippantly that "unquestionably 'A Speckled Bird' will be widely read, and that by those to whom books in a later manner make no appeal whatever." Wilson's audience, however, apparently did not object to the conventions of the domestic novel or to the author's obtrusive politics, and although not as successful as her earlier novels, this book pleased enough readers to satisfy Wilson.[45]

Virginia novelist Ellen Glasgow was perhaps the harshest southern critic of the UDC's interpretation of southern history and its manner of telling that history. Born in the early 1870s to a father who worked in manufacturing and a mother from the Tidewater aristocracy, Glasgow inherited important legacies from both the Old South and the New. She published her first novel anonymously in 1897 and by the end of her literary career in the 1940s had published nineteen novels, including many best-sellers and one winner of the Pulitzer Prize, and was hailed by critics and readers as one of America's most important authors.

With the exception of *Virginia*, published in 1913, critics and readers have tended to dismiss Glasgow's early novels, reserving praise primarily for her later work, notably *Barren Ground* (1925), *The Sheltered Life* (1932), and *Vein of Iron* (1935). Many of the slighted works, however, reveal Glasgow's early attempts to counter the dominant theme in late-nineteenth- and early-twentieth-century southern literature, sentimentalism, which she felt eroded civilization. In a celebrated passage, Glasgow prescribed "blood and irony" to cure a rotting southern culture. The South needed blood because "it had grown thin and pale: it was satisfied to exist on borrowed ideas; to copy instead of create. And irony is an indispensable ingredient of the critical vision; it is the safest antidote to senti-

Ellen Glasgow. (Courtesy Special Collections Department, Manuscript Division, University of Virginia Library, Charlottesville)

mental decay."[46] Although not always successful in these early novels, Glasgow began to apply this prescription in her "social histories" published at the turn of the twentieth century.

Glasgow began the first of her six social histories of the state of Virginia in the fall of 1898, when she was in her mid-twenties. She had already published two moderately successful novels and was beginning to make a name for herself in the literary world. *The Voice of the People*, however, represented a departure from her previous novels. "It is not historical in the conventional sense," she explained to her agent, "and it is not romantically exciting." Recognizing that she might lose some of her followers, she hoped that she would attract new readers. "It is a good, sound, solid, true-to-life kind of novel," she proudly admitted, and she projected that this work would stand as the "literary base" for her subsequent Virginia novels.[47]

The novel explicitly criticizes southern society after the war and Reconstruction, implicitly arguing that Populism was the south's only remaining salvation. Indeed, if the Civil War represented a "people's war," as Glasgow argued elsewhere, then this war was not complete until the final phase of the agrarian reform movement of the 1890s. Glasgow believed that *The Voice of the People* documented "a social revolution in the moment of triumph." The key to the Populists' success, according to Glasgow, lay in their use of the "orderly forces of government." Rather than advocating armed rebellion, Populists chose to use the political system to their advantage. Nicholas Burr, the hero of the novel, represents the quintessential populist politician, the son of an impecunious farmer "who was always working with nothing to show for it—whose planting was never on time, and whose implements were never in place." Nick knows that he will never be like his father, having decided early in life to rise above his station and effect social and economic change through the law. His parents take an active interest in politics. Marty Burr, Nick's mother, contends that "if this here government ain't got nothin' better to do than to drive poor women till they drop I reckon we'd as well stop payin' taxes to keep it goin'." Amos Burr, Nick's father, complains bitterly that since the Civil War, the government has promised to ease the plight of the farmer but has failed to do so. "Ain't it been lookin' arter the labourer, black an' white?" Amos queried. "Ain't it time for it to keep its word to the farmer?" He later demands, "I want my rights, an' I want my country to give them to me."[48] Marty and Amos Burr, however, are in no position to do more than complain.

"There ain't nothin' in peanut-raisin'," a youthful Nick declares in the novel's

"There was a niche in a small alcove, where he spent the spare hours of many a day." Illustration from Ellen Glasgow's 1900 novel, *Voice of the People.*

opening scene, and so he studies law. By always keeping "the agricultural interests at heart," he soon becomes chairman of the Virginia Democratic Party. In the final triumph of the "voice of the people," Nick is elected the state's governor. "At that moment he was the people's man," wrote Glasgow. "His name was cheered by the general voice. As he passed along the street bootblacks hurrahed! him. He had determined that the governor should cease to represent a figurehead, and for right or wrong, he was the man of the hour."[49]

The Voice of the People was, however, a cautionary tale. Two years after the Wilmington race riot, the "people" of Glasgow's novel, in the form of a faceless mob, set out to lynch a black man accused of some unnamed heinous crime. Nick goes to the jail to calm his "constituents" and is gunned down in the cross fire, after which the sheriff callously remarks, "and he died for a damned brute."[50] As soon as the "people" deviate from the political system and turn to overt violence, the chaos of the Reconstruction period returns. For Glasgow, then, Populism represented the culmination of the people's war as well as the potential risks of abandoning civilized government.

The Voice of the People, "conceived and written in an impassioned revolt" against the Victorian tradition in nineteenth-century fiction, constituted part of Glasgow's larger attempt to abandon the pervasive "sentimental elegiac tone" in southern literature. To this end, she chose not merely to write on "southern themes" but to "record" southern society from the Civil War to the time in which she lived. Glasgow declared herself to be "a rebel, . . . in search of truth, not sensation." Shrewdly, she began not with her Civil War book but with one whose subject matter was contemporary. "My subject matter seemed to be fresh," Glasgow later admitted, "and most certainly it remained untouched; for Southern novelists heretofore had been content to celebrate a dying culture."[51] Her treatment of discontented farmers, Populist politicians, and local and state government suggests that Glasgow resisted the sentimentality she so abhorred.

Determined as she was, however, Glasgow alone could not stage a literary revolution. The southern tradition in letters was too great for her to overcome. Reflecting on her failed attempt to cast sentimentality back to the Victorians, Glasgow admitted that she had neither the emotional maturity nor the technical proficiency to complete her mission. She could not divorce herself from the tradition she most detested. "The background was too close," she confessed, "the setting was too much a part of my entire world." Elsewhere, she explained her inability to throw off the mantel of sentimentality: "I had grown up in the yet lingering fragrance of the Old South; and I loved its imperishable charm even while I revolted from its stranglehold on the intellect." Like the New South, Glasgow suggested, she too "inherited the tragic conflict of types."[52]

In addition to discontented farmers and Populist politicians, then, stock characters that had populated southern Civil War literature from its beginnings crept into *The Voice of the People*. Uncle Ish, a "picturesque and pathetic" former slave, longs for the social hierarchy and order of antebellum days. An aging judge continues to toast the Confederacy. Delphy, the former mammy, not only remains devoted to her former master, Dudley, but refuses to let a "new-come nigger" raise his infant child. A former Confederate general articulates the South's states' rights position well into the 1890s. Even Governor Nicholas Burr, the embodiment of the New South's salvation, displays a portrait of a Confederate soldier after Appomattox above his office mantel. Finally, Jane Dudley Webb, the widow of a slain Confederate officer, wears a button cut from a Confederate uniform as a testament that "the women of the South have never surrendered!" Despite the poverty to which she had been reduced, "she had once been heard to remark that if she had not something to look back upon she could not live."[53] In an effort to keep the past very much a part of her present, she proudly displays among her meager possessions her husband's sword and a tattered Confederate battle flag. All of these characters testify to Glasgow's inability to complete her revolt against sentimentality.

The Voice of the People received favorable reviews. "With her latest work," heralded the Louisville Courier-Journal, "Miss Glasgow places herself in the front rank of American writers and shows herself worthy of a place among the greatly gifted." Ironically, the review later praised Glasgow for the novel's sentimentality: "It is no shattering of sentimentalities that has been wrought in this book, even if it is a story of new Virginia." National journals also praised Glasgow's work. Both the Dial and Bookman compared Nicholas Burr to Abraham Lincoln. Lauding Glasgow's hero, the Dial informed its readers that Nick "illustrates that type of American manhood of which Lincoln is the great, historical exemplar . . . the type of sturdy honesty and downright manliness which our country is still capable of illustrating from time to time, and without which our prospects would indeed be hopeless." Critics thus not only celebrated the novel for its sentimentality but also matched Glasgow's representative New South politician with the former U.S. president and bane to the Confederacy. These favorable reviews nonetheless pleased Glasgow. Writing to Walter Hines Page about the success of The Voice of the People, she swore that she would never pander to a "sensation loving public for any amount of money" but admitted that she did want her work "to be widely recognized."[54]

If Glasgow found it difficult to revolt against sentimentalism in The Voice of the People, she faced her toughest challenge in her second novel on the social history of Virginia, The Battle-Ground. Published two years after The Voice of the People, this novel offered Glasgow's version of the Civil War. Born in the 1870s, Glasgow was painfully aware of the stories of the war, recalling, "The adventures of my mother, as a young wife during the war, were as vivid to me as my own memories." Fictional narratives "supported" her mother's stories, yet

Glasgow remained dissatisfied. The northern reconciliation romances that presented a "gallant" northern invader rescuing the "clinging" southern belle did not mesh with Glasgow's ideas of the war: "I could not believe that the late invasion had been a romantic conflict between handsome soldiers in blue uniforms and southern ladies in crinolines," admitted an exasperated Glasgow. But she found heroic legends of the Lost Cause no more artistically or intellectually fulfilling. "I may say just here," she confessed to Page, her confidant and a fellow southern writer, "that the usual war novel of our country is detestable to me." Although she later maintained that heroic legends are the "noblest creation" of a culture, she firmly believed that for them to be a "blessing [they] must be recreated not in funeral wreaths but in dynamic tradition and the living character of a race." "I want to do something different," she stated about her war novel, "to make . . . a picture of varied characters who lived and loved and suffered during those years, and to show the effects of the times upon the development of their natures."[55] With *The Battle-Ground*, Glasgow attempted to correct the glaring faults she found with the Lost Cause myth.

To create the critical distance that permitted an unsentimental portrayal of the war, Glasgow further developed her argument, first articulated in *The Voice of the People*, that the Civil War was a people's war. In her novel, not only did the wealthy planters' sons fight for the southern cause, but so did the yeomanry. Although many southern novelists argued the Confederate position through their nonslaveholding characters as a strategy for divorcing slavery from the debate on the causes of the war, Glasgow fleshed out her yeoman character to a degree unparalleled elsewhere in southern fiction. Pinetop, a nonslaveholding farmer from the mountains of Tennessee, fights in the same unit as Dandridge Montjoy, an aristocratic planter's son. After their first battle, Pinetop states that while standing "out thar with them bullets sizzlin' like frying pans round my head," he questioned the viability of the institution of slavery. "Look here, what's all this fuss about anyhow?" Pinetop rhetorically asked. "If these folks have come arter the niggers, let 'em take 'em off and welcome! I ain't never owned a nigger in my life and, what's more, I ain't never seen one that's worth owning."[56]

Pinetop's motivation for fighting was nonetheless clear. "Not the need to protect a decaying institution," explained Glasgow, "but the instinct in every free man to defend the soil had brought Pinetop, as it had brought Dan, into the army of the South."[57] Pinetop hardly conformed to the Lost Cause's heroic, romantic figure of the noble Confederate soldier dashing off to defend the South. Yet through him Glasgow most forcefully articulated the Confederate cause. Thus, according to Glasgow, the Civil War was fought not exclusively by great men over great ideas but also by common farmers defending their land.

Pinetop did not carry the weight of Glasgow's argument, however. She supplemented his humble defenses of his actions in the war with protracted discussions of Confederate ideology between Major Lightfoot, a fire-eating Democrat, and Governor Ambler, a moderate Whig. For the first 275 pages of the novel, the governor calmly stresses the similarities in politics and sentiment between the North and the South, while the major spews invectives against the North. Ambler advocates a peaceful settlement between the two regions, while Lightfoot begs the South to live up to its revolutionary heritage and to secede to protect its guaranteed liberties. The two men continue their amicable disagreements until the governor receives word that President Lincoln has sent troops to South Carolina to defend Fort Sumter. Governor Ambler then abandons his pacifist stance in favor of secession and, if necessary, war. "There slowly came to him," Glasgow wrote "as he recognized the portentous gravity in the air about him, something of the significance of that ringing call [to arms]; and as he stood there he saw before him the vision of an army led by strangers against the people of his blood — of an army wasting the soil it loved, warring for an alien right against the convictions it clung to and the faith it cherished." Betrayed by his Unionist position, Ambler actively fights for the Confederacy after learning of the Federal invasion of southern soil. "There are some things that are worth fighting for," the dying governor tells Dan, "and the sight of home is one of them."[58] The governor comes to share Major Lightfoot's convictions and begins to articulate a much more eloquent defense of the Confederacy than Pinetop ever could have uttered. Although Glasgow used Pinetop to advance her belief that the Civil War was a people's war, she fell back on the established literary convention of using two aristocratic southern gentlemen to carry the defense of the Confederacy. She ultimately collapsed the yeomen's and the slaveholders' arguments into a common position. Moreover, she employed stock characters, familiar to any reader of Lost Cause romances, to lend credence to Pinetop's argument.

To complicate further the standard Lost Cause plot, Glasgow offered a deeply unsentimental portrait of battle. In this respect, *The Battle-Ground* reads more like *The Red Badge of Courage* than like a standard Thomas Nelson Page novel. Dandridge Montjoy has always understood his patriotism in terms of "romance rather than as a religion." The call of the bugle, the colors of the battle flag, "the flash of hot steel in the sunlight" stir Dan's soul, compelling him to join the fight. Not Dan's soul but his stomach stirred at the site of his first battle, however. The sight and smell of blood turn Dan faint: "I didn't know it was like this," he re-peats to himself, surveying the scorched land and scattered bodies. Abandoned by his former sense of patriotism, only the absurdity of battle grips Dan after his first engagement with the Union army.[59] Like the governor and the major, Montjoy is a stock character of Lost Cause fiction, familiar to most of Glasgow's readers. She complicated his character, however, by giving this very romantic hero very unsentimental reactions to battle.

Glasgow succeeded only in adding texture to Dan's character. Glasgow plucked most of her characters of *The Battle-Ground* straight from those novels against which she was ostensibly rebelling. Mrs. Ambler, the governor's wife, is the quintessential plantation mistress of southern fiction. Early in the novel, Mrs. Ambler ministers to the souls of her "family." While the master rides through his fields, Mrs. Ambler cares for her "home and children, and the black people that had been given into her hands."[60] On the Ambler plantation, she alone never rests from her labors. Mrs. Ambler is merely a variation on the countless plantation mistresses who populated Lost Cause romances.

In this scene and elsewhere in the novel, Glasgow perpetuated a critical component of the Lost Cause myth, maintaining that southern slaveholders were benevolent, paternalistic masters who genuinely cared for their slaves' corporal and spiritual well-being. The slaves of the novel reward their kindly masters with unflagging loyalty and devotion. Big Abel, one of the Lightfoots' slaves, follows Dan to the University of Virginia and later into battle and finally chooses to remain with Dan and his family after the war. Returning home from the war beleaguered and despondent, Dan and Big Abel are met by Congo, another of the Lightfoots' slaves, who happily informs them, "We all's hyer, Marse Dan. We all's hyer."[61] Despite the defeat of the slaveholding South, Dan's former slaves continue to work at their traditional tasks. Big Abel, Congo, and the rest of the Lightfoots' slaves were all familiar characters to Glasgow's readers, for the "faithful darky" made an appearance in almost every Lost Cause novel. No matter how firmly Glasgow insisted that she eschewed the traditional elements in sentimental southern literature, she could not write a Civil War novel without them.

Finally, Mrs. Ambler's daughter, Betty, represents the celebrated southern belle of plantation fiction. Decades after publishing the novel, Glasgow admitted that Betty Ambler personified "the spirit that fought with gallantry and gaiety, and that in defeat remained undefeated." Like all the women of the Confederacy, Betty "told herself that no endurance was too great, no hope too large with which to serve the cause." Only Betty's unswerving devotion saves south-

"Betty." Illustration from Ellen Glasgow's 1902 novel, *The Battle-Ground*.

ern civilization from sinking into the abyss. Soothing Dan's war-weary soul, she hopefully promises, "We will begin again . . . and this time, my dear, we will begin together."[62] Here, as in similar scenes from countless southern-authored Civil War tales, the future of the postbellum South is guaranteed by the union of a healthy, albeit ragged, Confederate veteran and a southern belle. In a passage that surely appealed to the sentiments of the UDC, Betty pledges her love to a defeated Confederate soldier and vows to rebuild the war-ravaged land on the principles of the Old South. In the end, Glasgow created a southern belle who very much resembled the sentimental heroines that the author derided.

Critical praise for *The Battle-Ground* was not as forthcoming as it had been for *The Voice of the People*. "The book is simply a war-time story, like many others," reported one reviewer for the *Critic*. "A good novel though not a great one," claimed Benjamin Wells in the *Forum*. "Striking and forceful," admitted the reviewer for the *Louisville Courier-Journal*, but it "falls short of *The Voice of the People* in scope and brilliancy." Carl Hovey stood virtually alone in his un-equivocal praise for *The Battle-Ground*, claiming that it "is something new and different from the common run of novels, fire-eating, ponderous, or simply me-diocre." And as with *The Voice of the People*, critics lauded the novel's sentimen-talism: *The Battle-Ground* contains "all the infinite pathos of the Lost Cause and the return of the shattered, but proud hosts in glory," wrote the Louisville re-viewer, citing the novel's one redeeming feature. Perhaps even more of an affront to Glasgow was the criticism levied by Benjamin Wells, who faulted Glasgow for the novel's inadequate character development, a task for which Glasgow felt eminently qualified. "A writer of such talent should not be content with work that does catch and reflect admirably what lies on the surface, the much abused 'local color,'" wrote Wells, "but fails to lay firm hold on the deeper qualities of human character." Glasgow's ability to transcend the dominant theme of south-ern literature remained limited, and her critics recognized this fault. Despite her intent to write "something different," Glasgow could not escape the romance of the Lost Cause.[63]

Glasgow followed her war story with a tale of Reconstruction. Published two years after *The Battle-Ground*, the third novel in Glasgow's social history of Vir-ginia, *The Deliverance: A Romance of the Virginia Tobacco Fields*, represented her most successful attempt to date to resist the sentimental trend in southern lit-erature. This novel stands in stark contrast to other white southerners' novels of Reconstruction. Thomas Nelson Page, for example, offered a version of Re-construction that emphasized the inevitable doom to the plantation and all that it represented. Dr. Cary, the patrician hero of Page's 1898 novel, *Red Rock: A Chronicle of Reconstruction*, recognizes in the heady days "before the great ex-plosion in the beginning of the Sixties" that the impending war threatened the world of the plantation South with imminent collapse. "War is the most terrible of all disasters, except Dishonor," he warns a group of secessionists. "I do not speak of the dangers. For every brave man must face danger as it comes, and should court glory; and death for one's country is glorious. I speak merely of the change that War inevitably brings," Cary continues. "War is the destruction of everything that exists. You may fail or you may win, but what exists passes, and something different takes its place." The slaveholding South would assuredly suffer because of war. "No people who enter a war wealthy and content ever come out of war so," Cary observes. The righteousness of the Confederate cause might compel white southerners to fight, he reasons, but the Old South's defenders should recognize the costs that war would surely bring.[64]

For Page, Reconstruction bore out Dr. Cary's fears. Indeed, Page's interpretation of Reconstruction suggested that the era represented the worst abuses heaped on a righteous civilization. White southerners had been "subjected to the greatest humiliation of modern times," he wrote in the preface to *Red Rock*. "Their slaves were put over them." Redemption signaled, however, the ultimate triumph of white southerners. "They reconquered their section and preserved the civilization of the Anglo-Saxon." As Fred Hobson notes, "the year of *Red Rock*'s publication, 1898, was a time of great racial and unrest and social upheaval in the South." The 1898 Wilmington race riot destroyed the possibility of an interracial political union under the auspices of the Populist Party, as once imagined by Tom Watson and even Ellen Glasgow in *The Voice of the People*. Historians David S. Cecelski and Timothy B. Tyson observe that "few communities escaped racial terrorism—if only one city became an enduring reminder of the dangers of democratic politics and interracial cooperation." No one, "black or white, could deny that the racial massacre signaled a sea change in how white Americans would regard civil rights for African Americans." The message was clear: "White people in Wilmington had violently seized their government, and no one had acted to stop them." The aftermath of the riot ensured the emergence of "the Jim Crow social order, the end of black voting rights, and the rise of a one-party political system in the South that strangled the aspirations of generations of blacks and whites." The appearance of Page's novel, then, at the same moment that white supremacists violently regained control of politics in Wilmington, North Carolina, shored up the ideology of the Jim Crow South. Not surprisingly, many southern readers praised Page's interpretation of Reconstruction. "I honestly believe you have done more to set the South right in the eyes of the world and to correct the misrepresentation of fanatics, fools & scoundrels," one reader wrote to Page, "than all the other stories put together."[65] Glasgow, however, had a different reading of Reconstruction.

For Glasgow, the confusion that followed in the wake of the war mocked the apparent stability of the Old South. Indeed, the war had exposed the antebellum South's false sense of security and forced southerners to acknowledge that their region had been "condemned to stand alone because it had been forsaken by time." In *The Deliverance*, Glasgow constructed an inversion plot of aristocratic decline. In this respect, as literary critic Richard Gray notes, Glasgow's work does not diverge significantly from Page's novels of Reconstruction, *Red Rock* and *Gordon Keith*. But whereas Page emphasized the tragic plight of the fallen aristocracy, Glasgow used her novel to criticize the mythic version of the Old South. At the center of *The Deliverance* stands Blake Hall, a once gracious two-hundred-year-old planter's mansion with Doric columns and a "cheerful spaciousness" that has been claimed by the vulgar overseer and his family. "What remained was but the outer husk, the disfigured frame, upon which the newer imprint seemed only a passing insult." A war-related reversal of fortune forces the once aristocratic but now impecunious Blake family to move to the overseer's shack. Through this reversal of fortunes, Glasgow condemned the notion of inherited gentility, at once debunking claims both to white superiority and, implicitly, to black inferiority.[66]

The pathetic figure of old Mrs. Blake may best illuminate the confusion and anxiety of Reconstruction while exposing Glasgow's revulsion at the myth of the Lost Cause. Convinced that the Confederacy had won the war, Mrs. Blake proudly states at the beginning of the novel, "I am almost seventy years old, I'm half dead, and stone blind into the bargain, but I can say to you that this is a cheerful world in spite of the darkness in which I linger on." Mrs. Blake firmly believes that "the present is very little part of life . . . it's the past in which we store our treasures."[67] Glasgow explicitly rejected Mrs. Blake's claim. Time had forsaken Mrs. Blake, just as it had the old South, and like the world she cherished, Mrs. Blake was doomed.

Glasgow did not reserve her critical judgment solely for Mrs. Blake, however. Through Mrs. Blake's son, Christopher, the antihero of the novel, Glasgow tested "the strength of hereditary fibre when it has long been subjected to the power of malignant circumstances." Although Christopher is descended from aristocratic stock and possesses proper breeding, the war has destroyed any sense of humanity in him, reducing him to the basest elements. Christopher acknowledges that environment, not inheritance, has determined his character. Early in the novel, he recognizes "that about himself there was a coarseness, a brutality even, that made him shrink from contact with . . . others." Bent on revenge against the overseer, Christopher spends his days conspiring to bring

"[Christopher] stood, bareheaded, gazing over the broad field." Illustration from Ellen Glasgow's 1904 novel, *The Deliverance: A Romance of the Virginia Tobacco Fields.*

down the overseer's son, Will Fletcher, seducing the boy into drinking, gambling, and murder. Christopher feels absolutely no compassion for his enemy. As Glasgow explained, Christopher's "god was a pagan god, terrible rather than tender, and there had always been within him the old pagan scorn of everlasting mercy." Convinced that he and his family have been victims of "heroic crimes," Christopher devises "heroic tortures" and often imagines the overseer amid the flames of a lighted stake. For Glasgow, this tale of the Lost Cause would be one of hatred, not love. "The tone would be harsh," she admitted, "the illumination would never be softened or diffused."[68]

In Glasgow's novel, the heroine needs protection not from the lusty former slave but from the white son of the former plantation owner. Maria Fletcher leaves the Virginia tobacco fields to escape Christopher Blake rather than some caricature of the African beast. For Glasgow, the Civil War did not emancipate millions of base and rapacious animals, incapable of self-rule, but instead reduced southern aristocrats to uncivilized thugs. Here, Glasgow offered a stunning challenge to a southern literary convention whose most notable proponent, Thomas Dixon, had published *The Leopard's Spots* in 1902. According to Dixon, southern white men needed to protect from freed slaves both white women and white voting rights. In a note to the reader that prefaces *The Clansman*, the 1905 sequel to *The Leopard's Spots*, Dixon wrote, "In the darkest hour of the life of the South, when her wounded people lay helpless amid rags and ashes under the beak and talon of the Vulture, suddenly from the mists of the mountains appeared a white cloud the size of a man's hand. It grew until its mantle of mystery enfolded the stricken earth and sky. An 'Invisible Empire' had risen from the field of Death and challenged the Visible to mortal combat." Like Page, Dixon saw the white South's vindication with "Redemption" and the Supreme Court's decisions in *Plessy v. Ferguson* (1896) and *Williams v. Mississippi* (1898). Dixon's work fared well with readers: within a few months of publication, *The Clansman* had sold more than one million copies.[69]

Given the reception Dixon's work received, Glasgow was acutely aware of her novel's potential unpopularity with readers and critics. She nevertheless persevered. Just as the UDC felt a divine imperative to tell a certain history of the war, Glasgow was driven to counter that history: "I could no more help writing it than I could live and not breathe the air about me," she informed Walter Hines Page as she began penning *The Deliverance*. There will always be "happy souls who will turn out popular romances," she asserted. But there would also be others, like her, "who have never been able to forget our Gethsemane and our cross, will continue to inflict upon our publishers the books that go down into the heart of things and appeal to those few that have been there before us." Her newest novel, she believed, was "another, big, deep, human document which no one will understand because it is wrung from life itself—and not from sugared romance." Despite its uncertain reception, Glasgow boldly put forth her most critical novel about the South and about the Confederacy's legacy.[70]

Glasgow evidently did not give her readers due credit. Although not a universal success, the novel received a number of important favorable reviews. Writing for the *Dial*, William Morton Payne proclaimed *The Deliverance* "a masterpiece of conscientious workmanship, vivid in its portrayal of a half-tragic situation, and powerful in its appeal to our human sympathies." Not only was this novel Glasgow's "most important" to date, but it represented "one of the strongest and most vital productions" by any author in recent years. The reviewer for the *Louisville Courier-Journal* was even more effusive: "Like a great thunder storm on a peaceful summer day comes . . . *The Deliverance*, mighty in proportion, great in promise, magnificent in the fulfillment." Archibald Henderson of the *Sewanee Review* believed *The Deliverance* to be the first southern novel to exhibit a "masterly grasp of mental and moral problems." Although some critics might have become "weary" of the novel's "decayed southern gentility," *The Deliverance* managed to capture some praise, countering Glasgow's lack of faith in her reading public.[71]

These first three "social histories" of Virginia represented Glasgow's earliest attempts to offer an alternative to the dominant theme of southern literature, a task that would occupy her for the rest of her literary career. But these early attempts failed. As repulsed as she was by the artificiality of the Lost Cause myth, she could not break free from its grasp on southern literature. She could not devise another way of telling the southern story of the Civil War. Only *The Deliverance*, a story of inversions, countered the myth. By creating antiheroes instead of heroes, developing hatred rather than reverence for the Old South, and refusing to provide a base on which the defeated South could build anew, Glasgow told a seemingly unfamiliar story of the war. All of the elements of the Lost Cause myth were still present, however; they had just been turned on their heads. Glasgow had yet to create a southern story of the war devoid of the Lost Cause.

The formation of the UDC had a profound impact on southern women's narratives of the Civil War. No longer writing in isolation, southern women now had the strength of a major organization both supporting and directing their efforts. The UDC's sense of a divine imperative to write the true story of the war compelled its members to pen their personal accounts. The group's convictions regarding a providential history provided the tone for the larger collective narrative and even allowed for lionizing of individual Confederate soldiers who had previously been vilified. The guidelines issued by the UDC's Historical Committee organized the members' papers into uniform, familiar accounts. Finally, the organization's Textbook Committee compiled reading lists, offering models of works for the Daughters to follow. Although the UDC never dictated the specific content to be included in members' accounts, the firm rules guaranteed that these women wrote in similar ways and told similar stories.

The UDC's impact extended far beyond its members, however. Recognizing the economic power the Daughters represented, publishers were unwilling to issue war stories without advance, explicit endorsements from the UDC. Women writers who were not organization members found themselves succumbing to its guidelines on historical narrative. Even Ellen Glasgow, who was so doggedly determined to revolt against the sentimentality of southern literature, needed three tries before coming close to offering an alternative to the Lost Cause myth. The UDC continued to wield its considerable influence throughout the early twentieth century, aiding the South's attempt to win the battle over the authoritative war narrative.

*We look back with loving memory upon our past,
as we look upon the grave of the beloved dead whom
we mourn but would not recall. We glorify the men
and the memories of those days and would have the
coming generation draw inspiration from them. We
teach the children of the South to honor and revere the
civilization of their fathers, which we believe has
perished not because it was evil or vicious in itself, but
because, like a good and useful man who has lived out
his allotted time and gone the way of all the earth, it
too has served its turn and must now lie in the grave
of the dead past.*
—ELIZA ANDREWS, The War-Time Journal of a
Georgia Girl

*Who is responsible for the South's unwritten history?
Surely we cannot blame the northern historian. His
duty is and was to record the facts as they are given to
him; and if we of the South have not given him these
facts, how can we hold the historian of the North
responsible. . . . The fault we find with the northern
historian (of course there are a few exceptions) is not
so much what he has said against us as what he has
omitted to say.*
—MILDRED LEWIS RUTHERFORD, *"The South
in the Building of the Nation"*

Righting
the Wrongs
of History,
1905–1915

When Mrs. Alexander B. White, president-general of the United Daughters of
the Confederacy (UDC), convened her organization's nineteenth annual convention in 1912, she did so in the Union's capital city, Washington, D.C. The arrange-
ments committee had chosen the place ostensibly to dedicate a monument at
Arlington National Cemetery to the fallen of the Confederacy, but the location
marked a turning point in the organization's efforts to legitimize the southern
story of the war. To be sure, the UDC had met outside of the Confederacy twice
before this historic meeting. In 1904, the organization held its national convention in St. Louis, and the following year, it met in San Francisco. Neither of these
meetings, however, carried quite the significance of the Washington meeting.
For the first time, the UDC, one of the largest organizations devoted to the preservation and mobilization of southern memories of the Civil War, met in the
capital of its former enemy. The convention's location did not represent the orga-

nization's reconciliation with the North, however. Instead, it signaled the UDC's ability to turn a southern story into a national one.

In an effort to ensure the presence of prominent Confederate dignitaries at this "great event," Florence F. Butler, 1911–12 president of the UDC's Washington, D.C., chapter, wrote to Stonewall Jackson's widow, expressing enthusiasm about the upcoming convention. The leadership of the UDC considered the convention's location significant, Butler told Mary Anna Jackson, "not only in the history of our great organization, but in the history of our country, and . . . the mothers, wives, and daughters of the bravest body of soldiers that ever answered the call of duty are to meet in Washington to lay the cornerstone of this monument that is to commemorate the deeds of our men as well as the noble sacrifices of our splendid women." Future generations surely would regard the 1912 meeting as "a milestone in the history of our country," Butler promised Jackson, suggesting that the widow of one of the South's most revered generals would be foolish to decline this personal invitation to attend.[1]

Jackson turned down this "gracious offer," insisting that she was too old and too weak to attend. First, however, Jackson praised Butler and the UDC's "noble work in their efforts to perpetuate the history of the men and women who made such sacrifices for this beloved Southland." Despite Jackson's inability to come, Butler and other organizers had every reason to believe that the 1912 convention would be a success. "I think every body in the South wants to write a paper or make a speech," Butler told Jackson, suggesting the difficulty Butler was facing in trying to juggle the numerous requests she had received for stage time. Similarly, Mildred Lewis Rutherford, historian-general of the UDC, complained to Butler that the number of requests she had received for placement on the historical program far exceeded the time allotted. The number of women who wished to participate in the Arlington monument dedication ceremony apparently so overwhelmed Butler that, although a "disagreeable job," she refused every woman's request.[2] Although convention organizers had to turn away willing participants, they nonetheless faced an onslaught of delegates, all of whom descended on Washington, D.C., in November 1912.

Convention attendees heard ample evidence that the UDC and its supporters had begun the process of transforming the southern story of the war into a national one. Mrs. L. Eustace Williams, chairman of the newly formed Committee on the War between the States, reported on her efforts: "In the interest of correct history," the UDC had pressured Congress to "make the official title of the war of '61 and '65 'The War Between the States' instead of using the various incorrect and misleading terms which are now applied to it." Southerners had long balked at the term "Civil War," arguing that because the South had in fact seceded from the Union and formed an independent nation, the descriptive term "civil" was grossly inaccurate. Among other tactics, Williams's committee beseeched members of Congress, finding the New York senators particularly courteous and amenable to the project. At the time of Williams's report, Congress had yet to pass a resolution condemning the common usage of the phrase "Civil War." The committee nevertheless reported increased sympathy from northern editors and teachers.[3]

More telling than Williams's self-aggrandizing report, however, was the address delivered by President William Howard Taft at the monument dedication ceremony. Although he never conceded the legitimacy of secession as a course of action, he agreed with the UDC's position that the institution of slavery did not cause the Civil War: "The historian no longer repeats the falsehood that the men who lie here before us, and their comrades who sleep on a thousand battlefields, died that slavery might live," Taft proclaimed, "or that the soldiers who rest in those graves over there enlisted to set the negroes free." Northerners fought for the Union, Taft asserted, while southerners fought for independence. "All were freemen, fighting for the perpetuity of free institutions."[4] From its beginning, the UDC had insisted that the Confederacy had not fought to preserve slavery. And although the UDC and its supporters might have ascribed more sinister motives to the Union's involvement in the war, these southerners could rest assured that the president of the United States well understood the Confederacy's position in the war.

Taft's "general address of welcome" to the organization went even further in embracing the southern interpretation of history than did his address at the monument ceremony. Speaking on the postwar tensions between the North and South, Taft placed the blame squarely on the shoulders of his own party: "For years after the war, the Republican party . . . was in control of the administration of the government, and it was impossible for the Southerner to escape the feeling that he was linked in his allegiance to an alien nation and one with whose destiny he found difficult to identify himself." Southern redemption and the Democratic Cleveland administrations, however, had eased the national hostility toward the South. "Southerners were called to Federal offices, they came to have more and more influence in the Halls of Congress and in the Senate, and the responsibility of the government brought with it a sence [sic] of closer relationship to it." Taft believed that the recent election, which had just brought Democrat and Virginia native Woodrow Wilson to the White House, would ensure that "Southern opinion will naturally have greater influence, and the South greater proportionate representation in the Cabinet, in Congress, and in other high official stations." Although Taft boasted of his administration's achievements, he conceded that he could not "deny that my worthy and distinguished successor has a greater opportunity, and I doubt not that he will use it for the benefit of the nation at large."[5]

Isabell Worbell Ball, an unsympathetic local reporter, captured the significance of the UDC's meeting in general and of President Taft's participation in particular. Ball found the presentation of a "large silk flag emblem of the defeated South" over the head of the U.S. president especially treasonous. Nearly as scandalous, however, members of the UDC invaded the U.S. capital, "carrying rebel flags, a thing the whole rebel army failed to accomplish in four years of fighting."[6] Although some northerners may not have been receptive to the UDC's efforts to inflict its interpretation of the war on the nation, they nevertheless had to come to terms with the growing cultural resonance of the southern story.

A Silent Battle of Public Opinion

The UDC worked tirelessly and diligently to ensure that the nation sanctioned the group's representation of the past. Convinced that the Daughters must be well versed in the catechisms of the Confederacy to better educate the nation at large, the organization relentlessly pushed its members to continue their studies. The indefatigable Mildred Lewis Rutherford, longtime historian-general and a veritable institution within the UDC, vehemently admonished the women to engage in historical inquiry lest the stories of the Confederacy perish forever. Mounting evidence, however, suggested that the southern interpretation of the war was gaining national cultural currency. Although northern historian James Ford Rhodes viewed slavery, not the protection of states' rights, as the sole cause of the Civil War, for example, he nevertheless refused to blame southerners personally for the institution. Moreover, Rhodes asserted that if blame were to be levied for the institution of slavery, England and the northern states could not escape scrutiny. As Thomas J. Pressly notes, "Rhodes made a distinction between slavery and individual slaveholders, and the slaveholders were absolved, for the most part, of the blame for slavery which they customarily received." Rhodes was convinced that the verdict of history "would be that slavery was the calamity of Southern men, not their crime; they deserved sympathy rather than censure."

Furthermore, Rhodes rejected the dominant northern view that a handful of treasonous men had started the war. Rather, Rhodes believed that secession was a popular movement supported by the majority of white southerners. Finally, Rhodes opposed the Fifteenth Amendment and believed that white southerners should dictate the tenor of the region's race relations.[7]

Professor William A. Dunning interpreted Reconstruction as a national tragedy, a view that most white southerners could find sympathetic. According to Dunning, "Few episodes of recorded history more urgently invite thorough analysis and extended reflection than the struggle through which the southern whites, subjugated by adversities of their own race, thwarted the scheme which threatened permanent subjugation to another race." Dunning saw the Radical Republican rule foisted on the southern states as corrupt, inefficient, extravagant, and, in some instances, a "travesty of civilized government." Dunning had little sympathy for the newly freed slaves. "The negro had not pride of race and no aspirations or ideals," Dunning wrote, "save to be like whites. . . . A more intimate association with the other race than that which business and politics involved was the end towards which the ambition of the blacks tended consciously or unconsciously to direct itself." This unnatural ambition, according to Dunning, manifested itself in the "demand for mixed schools, in the legislative prohibition of discrimination between the races in hotels and theatres, and even in the hideous crime against white womanhood which now assumed new meaning in the annals of outrage."[8] For Dunning, Reconstruction was a glaring failure, righted only by the overthrow of the Radical Republicans and "redemption" in the South.

Despite modifications to the northern story of the war, however, Rutherford continually feared that white southerners were not endeavoring earnestly enough to correct "the wrongs of history." "When sons and daughters of Veterans write articles," she declared, "condemning the principles for which their Confederate fathers fought, and even stand for a changed Constitution that will overthrow the very bulwark of the South — state sovereignty — it is full time for the Daughters of the Confederacy . . . to become insistent that the truths of history shall be written, and that those truths shall be correctly taught in our schools and colleges." Rutherford frequently chastised the UDC, claiming that its mission went unfulfilled. To the same convention that listened to President Taft's remarks on the growing influence of southern opinion, Rutherford professed her "keen disappointment" in the work of the historical committees. "Now I know that you would much prefer that I should throw beautiful bouquets tonight and tell you of the things that you have done well," she snipped. Unwilling to lavish praise, however, Rutherford pronounced the Daughters "guilty, and if the historical work does not measure up to the full requirement each Daughter of the Confederacy should be blamed." Two years later, she pleaded with the Daughters to compile historical data, "for the time is fast coming when much of our history will be lost forever because of our inactivity." As a final piece of advice, Rutherford suggested, "Put the historical work in the hands of the most capable member of your chapter."[9]

Some UDC officers did not share Rutherford's pessimism. Mrs. J. Enders Robinson, Rutherford's immediate predecessor as historian-general, had praised the UDC's efforts to compile historical data and write accurate narratives. "The results from the History Department during the past year," she boasted to the 1911 convention, "have more firmly than ever convinced me that the Divisions and Chapters . . . are gradually developing a body of women of high intellect, excellent methods, and historical intuition." Indeed, "their earnest effort to secure accurate facts seems to be the controlling influence in their work." Mrs. L. H. Watson, historian-general of the Texas Division of the UDC, had addressed the 1909 convention, encouraging her listeners to fight for a correct history of the war: "Everything we accomplish that is worth doing is from a successful battle fought with our fellow man for supremacy in excellence, or against the forces of nature." The UDC engaged itself in a "silent battle" of public opinion armed with its "battle flag of Right"—the principles for which the Confederacy had fought. "We will ever tell the story," Watson proclaimed, "and if, in the great conflict, victory comes to our Southland—it will be from the teachings of our Veterans and the UDC."[10] Convinced that victory was within their grasp, the Daughters of the Confederacy hunkered down and geared themselves for the final battle for truth.

The national organization continued to provide its local chapters with materials to aid members' study of the true history of the war. Rutherford devised a catechism titled "The Wrongs of History Righted" in which she encouraged Daughters to memorize what she deemed pertinent facts about U.S. and Confederate history. "Why did Massachusetts threaten to secede in 1803?" she asked. "Give the order of secession of the first six seceding states," she demanded. "Name the War Governors." For answers to these questions, Rutherford referred the Daughters to her 1914 pamphlet, *The Wrongs of History Righted*, and her 1907 work, *The South in History and Literature*. She also listed Carl Holliday's *History of Southern Literature*, J. L. M. Curry's *Civil History*, and Thomas Nelson

Page's *The Old South*, among other works, as suitable sources. Concerned with the proper edification of its members, in 1914 the UDC formed the Committee on Southern Literature and Endorsement of Books. Marshaling the resources of the UDC's history, education, and literature departments, which "deal specifically with the higher intellectual development of our people," this the new committee advocated the adoption of "a uniform use of terms" as well as of southern works that "enlarge the ideas, shape the tastes, and stimulate the aspirations." Members certainly did not always find the tasks outlined by the national committee easy to execute. For example, to state division historian Mary Calvert Stribling, Rosa H. Mullins of the John C. Breckinridge Chapter in Clay, West Virginia, confessed that although she found the historical work of the UDC the most interesting, she wondered "sometimes if those of the UDC living in Southern communities can realize just what it means to a handful of timid Southerners surrounded in every hand by a Northern element to get out and work for a change of histories and things of like nature."[11]

As part of the UDC's efforts to properly educate the citizenry, it continued to condemn and block the use of "scurrilous" histories of the war. The Daughters found Henry William Elson's *A History of the United States of America* particularly loathsome and drafted a resolution recommending that high schools and colleges not use the work. At the 1911 national convention, the UDC agreed that "no university could use this history as a text-book or in any way that gives it prominence without creating in the mind of the student a distrust of all that pertains to the South, its institutions and statesmen, [students] will in time become ashamed of the noble, self-sacrificing actions of their fathers in the terrible days of the 'War between the States.'" The authors of the resolution offered Colonel Hilary A. Herbert's *The Abolition Crusade and Its Consequences*, Susan P. Lee's *The New Primary History of the United States*, and Riley, Chandler, and Hamilton's *Our Republic* as more suitable texts. The Historical Commission of South Carolina engaged Louisa B. Poppenheim, a founding member of the South Carolina Division of the UDC, to draft a response to a volume of the *Publications of the Southern History Association* that contained an article on Sarah and Angelina Grimké, abolitionists from South Carolina, designed "for the delectation of fanatics and South-haters of like tendencies." According to the Historical Commission, the Grimké sisters were "unbalanced mentally, morally and socially, and the capable historical or literary critic of to-day would anywhere regard it as a case of histeria [*sic*] to see them put down as exponents of the best in the South." Southerners should celebrate Elizabeth Pinckney, Louisa McCord,

Augusta J. Evans, and Varina Davis rather than the Grimkés, "whose efforts to violate the laws of the land and the laws of decency and good behavior" scandalized their fellow South Carolinians. "Kill the myth if you can and stick a steel pen charged with your brightest sarcasm into its carcass if you cannot kill it," the commission advised Poppenheim. "Let the patriotic daughters of the Abolitionists resolute on you if they want to, but hit the lick in the interest of history anyway."[12] By banning "offensive" material such as Elson's history and challenging "erroneous works" like the article on the Grimké sisters, the UDC strove to ensure that only certain narratives of the war would be told.

The UDC also continued to encourage its members to write and publish stories of the war. Rutherford concretely outlined the proper and useful qualifications for historians, who first needed to be truthful, for "history is truth." Second, historians should be "*bold* and *fearless*, daring to tell the truth even if adverse criticism comes to you for doing it." Third, historians should possess a philosopher's temperament. Finally, "you must be a *patriot*—because the Confederate soldier was the highest type of patriot."[13] Rutherford then sent forth thousands of white southern women determined to correct the sins of historical fallacy perpetrated by the North and to redress the sins of silence by the South.

Armed with this special training, some local chapters, including the John K. McIver Chapter of Columbia, South Carolina, collected biographies of local war heroes. These sketches often served as vehicles to promulgate the author's interpretations of the war. In an article ostensibly about her father's postwar activities, one woman railed against Reconstruction: "A white man had no rights that a negro was bound to respect," she explained. "Instead of the stars and stripes we had the bloody shirt waved in our faces." Lucy Davis King, author of a biographical sketch on the chapter's namesake, John K. McIver, described the fallen soldier with words that countless other southern women had used to describe Confederate soldiers: "No truer patriot shed his blood for his country's rights," she claimed, "no fonder heart was ever torn from loved ones and home than his." Like thousands of others, "he laid down his life to maintain the rights in which he believed."[14] Just as Varina Davis, La Salle Corbell Pickett, Mary Anna Jackson, and Helen Dortch Longstreet had previously used their biographies of their famous husbands to enter the national dialogue on the Civil War, these twentieth-century women contributed to the public discourse on the war by sketching the lives of local heroes.

By the early 1900s, however, most UDC members had turned away from biographies, instead writing historical sketches. Although Daughters had written these types of narratives from the organization's inception, the prodding of UDC historians such as Robinson and Rutherford encouraged women to cast wider nets. Kate Mason Rowland of Virginia, for example, honored the Confederacy's English sympathizers, a little-explored avenue of research. To a crowd assembled in Richmond, Virginia, Rowland singled out a number of noteworthy supporters, beseeching her listeners to "string these names on our rosary for remembrance . . . those champions tried and true of the Confederate South 'when the whole world watched with bated breath and hushed / as close the great Constrictor wound its coil / around us, as we struggled, fought till crushed.'" Mary Johnson Posey wished to expand her audience beyond the members of the UDC and sent her manuscript, "The Fight between the First Ironclads," to the editors at *Confederate Veteran*. "To be able to lift the veil from the years that are gone, and recall the wonderful incidents of history for the present generation," Posey believed, "must be the most pleasant things possible." She indeed must have enjoyed historical narratives, for she sent many manuscripts to *Confederate Veteran*. Mrs. George B. Russell, a member of the A. H. Carrington Chapter of the UDC in Charlotte Courthouse, Virginia, also sent a manuscript to the editors of *Confederate Veteran*. Rather than write about the causes that led to the Civil War, the righteousness of the Confederacy, or battles, Russell chose instead for her "subject one which relates to the patriotic, heroic and self-sacrificing part which our Mothers took in the great war which devastated the Southland, and claimed as its toll the lives of nearly one hundred and fifty thousand of the flower of her manhood; to what their daughters of this generation have done and are doing to continue the great and good work begun by them."[15] Russell went on to catalog the heroic deeds of the women of the Confederacy in a manner that undoubtedly pleased the officers of her local UDC chapter. No longer confined to writing biographical sketches of local heroes, southern women continued to expand their contributions to the public discourse on the Civil War.

UDC member Lillie V. Archbell of Kinston, North Carolina, published her own magazine, *Carolina and the Southern Cross*, to ensure adequate distribution of southern women's war narratives. She printed the first issue in November 1912, dedicating it to "our busy people who always have time to make history but never time for research." Archbell promised to devote her magazine to "a simple truthful account of all battles that have taken place in North Carolina, the personal experiences of reliable people who came in contact with those battles, home life in the state during the Confederacy, what people did to make a living, and how they helped the soldiers in field." Targeting a popular reading audience rather than scholars, Archbell believed that the straightforward articles in *Carolina and the Southern Cross* must surely "make people better and stronger for knowing such things." Concerned with oversaturating the market for southern magazines, Archbell assured her readers that her magazine did not duplicate the efforts of *Confederate Veteran* or of the Poppenheim sisters' magazine dedicated to southern women, *The Keystone*. According to Archbell, *Carolina and the Southern Cross* sought "to preserve the history that is so rapidly becoming mere tradition, by publishing it now, and to use the publication by planting it in the minds of the people instead of laying it away in the archives for the dim and distant future." Although Archbell and her contributors believed that a true and accurate portrayal of the war was crucial for the South, they contended that the North need not fear the truth, which could not "pluck" away their political victory. The Union might have won on the battlefield, but the Confederacy would win the battles over memory and history.[16]

Archbell apparently took quite seriously her promises to publish historically accurate material. And while she consistently published articles that celebrated the Confederacy, she did not advocate gratuitous glorification. In at least one case, Archbell challenged La Salle Corbell Pickett's defense of her late husband's infamous charge at the Battle of Gettysburg. Although Sallie Pickett "doubtless records what she believes to be true," Archbell contended that the widow "claims too much for her husband's service and she accentuates his admiration and friendship for his country's enemies at a time when such friendship was disloyal to the cause that he espoused." Moreover, Archbell pointed out, Pickett was not an eyewitness to the charge and thus could not substantiate her claims. Archbell might have been sympathetic to Pickett's need to render her husband a hero and might even have felt pangs of guilt for disparaging the narratives of such a devoted Daughter of the Confederacy, but Archbell firmly averred that "it is a great mistake to sacrifice the truth for any cause, for, in the end, it injures the Cause." Those who had lived through the Civil War and Reconstruction had sacrificed their blood; they must not "sacrifice honor for peace nor gain," Archbell proclaimed. "God forbid that we should be dishonest among ourselves."[17]

Some people did not accept the growth of the UDC with equanimity. Nashville author Corra Harris ridiculed the organization's efforts to memorialize the Confederate dead, for example. Of one such effort, "The truth was," Harris explained in her 1912 novel, *The Recording Angel*, "the figure of the soldier on the pedestal was of extremely short stature. This was due to the fact that the 'Daughters of the Confederacy,' who had erected the monument, had not been able to afford the price demanded, and the skinflint sculptor shortened the legs of the hero make up the difference. It was a sacred defect about which Ruckersville was so sensitive that it was never mentioned." For Harris, the statue represented "that element of the grotesque which is so characteristic of the South when it exalteth itself either in oratory or in any other form of exaggeration. The visible facts never warranted the proclamation." Moreover, "Once you erect a statue, you have belittled and defeated yourself. You cannot compete with it. The thing outlasts you. This is one reason why in those countries where there are the greatest number of monuments to the memory of men and deeds there is to be found the poorest quality of living manhood." Although at least one reading group expressed disappointment in Harris's portrayal of small-town southern life, others congratulated her on her abiding "realism." One reader explained her attraction to the novel: "I am a southerner myself, 'Alabama-born,' and that in a small town, too. Perhaps that is one reason why I am enjoying 'The Recording Angel' so highly, because it describes life with which I am acquainted." Apparently missing the message Harris wished to convey, the reader continued, "My experience with Yankee life and customs has been brief, but long enough to make me prefer our sleepy little old Southern towns with all their 'duck-legged Confederate statues' and other peculiarities."[18]

Despite Harris's unflattering portrayal of the UDC, the organization matured during the second decade of its existence. It recruited new members, enlisting more women in its battle to tell the true history of the war. It formed new chapters in northern states, ensuring that its message reached a broader audience.[19] The office of the historian-general wielded more power in the organization, providing local groups with firmer direction in historical writing. The formation of new committees dedicated to educational and historical work shored up the position of the historian-general and her committee. With an increasingly powerful organization behind them, southern white women continued to tell their stories of the war.

Matter Frankly Southern in Flavor

For those southern white women who chose to publish their Civil War narratives, the literary market proved especially accommodating. The frenzied publication of diaries and memoirs that began in earnest in the 1890s continued during the first decades of the twentieth century, with scores of women taking blue pencils to their manuscripts, rendering their stories suitable for a postwar audience. The most famous Civil War diarist who emerged in this period was Mary Boykin Miller Chesnut, whose posthumously published *A Diary from Dixie* (1905) immediately captured the imaginations of readers and critics alike. In addition, revised narratives by Eliza Frances Andrews, Nancy De Saussure, Laura Elizabeth Lee Battle, and Sarah Morgan Dawson, among others, crowded the bookshelves of readers still fascinated with the Civil War decades after Lee surrendered at Appomattox Courthouse. Taken together, these decidedly twentieth-century publications of nineteenth-century diaries demonstrate the Civil War's powerful hold on the postwar consciousnesses of southern women in particular and the American public in general.

As Elisabeth Muhlenfeld notes, "It is for the work she did during three of the last five years of her life that Mary Boykin Chesnut is remembered at all, for between late 1881 and 1884 she substantially completed an expansion and revision of her Civil War journals—twenty years after they had been written." She did so with a heavy editorial hand. Chesnut applied the techniques of dialogue, characterization, and narration, honed in her failed attempts at fiction writing, to her Civil War manuscript. In the process of revision, she removed "trivialities, irrelevancies, and indiscretions." But she added more material to her diary than she omitted or condensed. As C. Vann Woodward notes in the introduction to his edition of the Chesnut diaries, in the end, "the integrity of the author's experience is maintained . . . but not the literal record of events expected of the diarist."[20]

Before Chesnut died in 1886, she entrusted her journals to Isabella Martin, a Columbia, South Carolina, schoolteacher whom Chesnut had met during the war. When Martin failed to find a publisher for the journals, she stashed them until 1904, when she met fellow southerner Myrta Lockett Avary, whose *A Virginia Girl in the Civil War* had sold well the previous year. Convincing Martin of the marketability and profitability of Chesnut's diary, Avary set out at once to publish the journals, contacting D. Appleton and Company, the firm that had handled *A Virginia Girl*.[21] Within a year, Avary and Martin had published *A Diary from Dixie*, purging nearly three-quarters of Chesnut's revised text. The work that emerged in 1905 bore little resemblance to Chesnut's original journals.

While Avary handled business affairs, Martin began preparing the introduction to the Chesnut journals. A dispute among Avary, Martin, and Appleton's Francis W. Halsey arose almost immediately regarding the introduction the publishing firm had intended. Anticipating criticism from southern readers, Avary and Martin cataloged the inaccuracies in the introduction Halsey had provided:

"First," Avary and Martin informed him, "Mrs. Chesnut can not be strictly described as a typical woman of the Old South, or the 'personification of the soul of the Old South.'" Avary and Martin felt Chesnut too cosmopolitan to be described in such provincial terms, ascribing her "breadth of vision" and her "satire" not merely to her southern heritage but to human nature. "It is . . . in this dual character that the South would accept best her criticism of persons and happenings," Avary and Martin believed. Equally egregious, the introduction painted the two editors as literary mercenaries, bent solely on turning a large profit. "Isabella Martin is represented as sending Myrta Lockett Avary North 'with a commission' 'to seek a Publisher' for Mrs. Chesnut's Diary, thus putting a commercial frame around a gilt-edged picture." The potential reaction of Chesnut's family especially troubled the two women, who did not want the diarist's relatives to think that "the Diary was being 'hawked around.'" Avary and Martin told Halsey that they would reluctantly work with the proposed introduction, although their attorney had "counseled us to reject it altogether."[22]

The matter of the introduction settled, Appleton moved forward with the publication of A Diary from Dixie, even though "there are several other similar books announced by other houses." The length of the original manuscript concerned Halsey, however, and he explained that publishing an unexpurgated version would be "fateful to its sale." Halsey counseled Avary to include only those selections that related directly to the Civil War and illustrated "the social and domestic conditions of the South." Moreover, "there are passages also which we forsee [sic] that Miss Martin might prefer to have omitted, because the feelings of persons still living might be wounded." Martin undoubtedly would wish to "safeguard the memory of Mrs. Chesnut," Halsey suggested, advising Avary and Martin to cut even more from the manuscript. Avary balked at the suggestion of further editing the manuscript, offering instead to bring the work out in two volumes. "There is more to it than war history—there is psychological interest, social development, the woman's personality, her keen criticism of people and things, her bon mots. Women's tales of the war between the states are plentiful," Avary informed Halsey, "but such wit, such esprit as this, NO!"[23] Halsey did not find Avary's arguments persuasive.

Avary and Halsey next tangled over the issue of a second introduction to be penned by a northern historian. Although Avary conceded that there are "some things which a northern man might say which Miss Martin and I do not say and can not say gracefully, but which might add to the books [sic] uniqueness and interest at the North," she did not want to "overburden" the text. "To me, the

book seems too beautiful and self-sufficient" to be weighted down with an introduction, preface, index, and copious footnotes. "I fear, sometimes, that its wings
will be so freighted that it may not fly so swift or far as it might have gone with
a word from any of us 'explainer generals,'" she professed. Appleton's editors
were unrelenting. "We expect the largest sale will come from the North," W. W.
Appleton wrote to Martin, threatening that the diary "would fail of a proper
reception unless it were authenticated by the fullest explanations." Indeed, so
determined were Halsey and Appleton to cater to the northern reading audience that Halsey suggested dedicating the volume "to the men and women of
the North who would understand."[24]

Neither Avary nor Martin initially approved of the proposed index. When the
finished list arrived in South Carolina, however, the two women were aghast.
"Had it been a snake, it could not have startled us more," Avary told Halsey,
"as it unwound its interminable lengths from envelopes." In addition to their
original objections, Avary and Lockett cringed at many of the terms listed, including "Civil War," knowing that they would offend southern readers: "If we
can get around wounding or offending them by changing a few words . . . into
forms acceptable to everybody, it will be good policy," Avary believed. The two
women found Appleton's use of northern terms for battles even more objection-
able than the use of "Civil War": according to Avary, "In Index, I see 'Fair Oaks,'
no 'Seven Pines': Southerners hardly recognize the battle under that title. 'Fair
Oaks' stamps the book as a Northern product or Northern interpretation of the
Diary." Avary suggested "Seven Pines or Fair Oaks" to appease both sections.[25]

Despite this wrangling between Avary and Martin and the publishing firm, *A
Diary from Dixie* was released in 1905 to considerable popular and critical success. "The 'Diary is quaint, picturesque and beautiful beyond description," one
admirer wrote to Martin. "The world owes you a debt for bringing the Diary
to light," the reader continued. "It is more interesting than any love story, and
excites in my mind an interest and admiration for Mrs. Chesnut that is little
less than idolatry." Similarly, Selene Ayer Armstrong praised Avary in *Southern
Woman's Magazine*: "The genius for discovery is of quite as much value to the
world as the creative faculty and for bringing to light the Chesnut Diary Mrs.
Avary deserves the credit of having made a notable contribution to the literature which has grown up around the war." Armstrong recognized the Chesnuts
as well, professing that *A Diary from Dixie* "reflects more faithfully than any previous book perhaps, the spirit with which Southerners bore their triumphs and

reverses, and . . . gives an uninterrupted account of the progress of the entire war."[26]

A *Diary from Dixie* did not, of course, provide readers with the only "uninterrupted" account of the war. Both Martin and Avary realized, as did the editorial staff at Appleton, that scores of white southern women had penned their Civil War narratives during the early decades following the conflict, threatening to swamp the postwar literary market. Chesnut's position as the wife of a prominent South Carolina politician gave her access to many of the Confederacy's most influential statesmen and officers, lending a certain air of importance to her diary. Moreover, Chesnut believed that education, position, and intelligence had eminently qualified her to comment on the world around her. Chesnut's consummate skill as a diarist and as her own editor, therefore, distinguished Chesnut's diary from the pack of others. As historian Woodward notes, "the importance of Mary Chesnut's work . . . lies not in autobiography, fortuitous self-revelations, or opportunities for editorial detective work [but] with the life and reality with which it endows people and events and with which it evokes the chaos and complexity of a society at war."[27]

Mary Chesnut left no record of her thoughts on revising her diary, but Eliza Frances Andrews, a UDC member and author of a 1908 narrative, *The War-Time Journal of a Georgia Girl*, appended a prologue to her journal of Sherman's March in which she commented extensively on her revisions: "To edit oneself after the lapse of nearly half a century," Andrews noted, "is like taking an appeal from Philip drunk to Philip sober. The changes of thought and feeling between the middle of the nineteenth century and beginning of the twentieth century are so great," she continued, "that the impulsive young person who penned the following record and the white-haired woman who edits it, are no more the same than were Philip drunk with wine of youth and passion and Philip sobered by the lessons of age and experience." Because diary keeping prevented the author's "self-conceit" by chronicling precisely "what a full-blown idiot he or she is capable of being," Andrews begged her readers' forgiveness for expunging "anything that would too emphatically 'write me down as an ass.'" Although Andrews edited liberally, she assured her readers that her changes had "not been allowed to interfere in any way with the fidelity of the narrative."[28]

Andrews believed her diary to be typical of that of any southern woman from the planter class. Moreover, she averred that "the feelings, beliefs, and prejudices expressed reflect the general sentiment of the Southern people of that generation." Firmly convinced that her journal shed light on the "inner life" of the unique society of the Old South, she offered her "private" journal—a record she had maintained with "absolutely no thought of it meeting other eyes than the author"—to the reading public. Andrews never pretended that her journal substituted for "history," claiming instead that it offered "a mere series of crude pen-sketches, faulty, inaccurate, and out of perspective," but a true representation of events as she saw them.[29] Her journal also was not impartial but rather was infused with an ardent patriotism for the Confederacy. And while time might have tempered her ardor, Andrews neither repudiated her passion for the southern cause nor excused her hatred for the North.

Although Andrews never rewrote her wartime opinion of the institution of slavery, her views clearly differed from those of most white southerners in the early twentieth century. Andrews believed slavery to be a benevolent institution, with paternalistic masters caring for their charges. Early in April 1865, Andrews ranted against the Federal officers who had invaded her town of Washington, Georgia, writing, "To have a gang of meddlesome Yankees down here and take [the slaves] away from us by force—I would never submit to that, not even if slavery were as bad as they pretend." But, even though Andrews consistently maintained that slavery "was not the monstrosity that some would have us believe," she also argued that the institution had become anachronistic by the mid-nineteenth century. Slavery had "served the purposes of the race," according to Andrews, "since the days when man first emerged from his prehuman state until the rise of the modern industrial system made wage slavery a more efficient agent of production than chattel slavery." Pure "economic determinism" had engendered the end of slavery, "which means that our great moral conflict reduces itself, in the last analysis, to a question of dollars and cents, though the real issue was so obscured by other considerations that we of the South honestly believe to this day that we were fighting for States' Rights, while the North is equally honest in the conviction that it was engaged in a magnanimous struggle to free the slave."[30]

Andrews's theory of economic determinism offered a new twist on the myth of the Lost Cause but did not supplant it. With the same rhetoric that other members of the UDC had infused into their writings on the Civil War, Andrews explained the demise of the Confederacy. Of the southern soldier, Andrews wrote, "His cause was doomed from the first by a law as inexorable as the one pronounced by the fates against Troy, but he fought with a valor and heroism that have made a lost cause forever glorious." Although the Confederacy had gone "down in a mighty cataclysm of blood and fire," it had been a glorious end, better "than to have perished by slow decay through the ages of sloth and rottenness, as so many other great civilizations have done, leaving only a debased and a degenerate race."[31] Andrews's economic interpretation of the war might have been heterodox to her fellow southerners, but the larger framework in which she wrote remained consistent with other Lost Cause narratives of the Civil War.

If Andrews's explication of the institution of slavery was iconoclastic, Nancy Bostick De Saussure, who published *Old Plantation Days* in 1909, offered a more orthodox interpretation. De Saussure wrote her memoirs so that her granddaughter, who knew only the New South, might learn of the fallen Confederacy. De Saussure's reminiscences and those of all southerners of the older generation "are a legacy to the new generation. . . . it behooves the old to hand them down to the new." De Saussure felt it especially incumbent on her to explain slavery to those born into the New South. Determined to counter the portrait offered by Harriet Beecher Stowe in *Uncle Tom's Cabin*, a novel that De Saussure believed continued to shape public opinion about slavery, she offered personal recollections about the master-slave relationship. Members of a wealthy South Carolina family, her parents had "inherited most of their negroes," De Saussure wrote, implying that her father had not participated in the domestic slave trade. "There was such an attachment existing between master and mistress and their slaves," De Saussure wrote of her black and white "family," "which one who had never borne such a relation could never understand." So beneficent was the institution that De Saussure's former slaves repeatedly told her, "I'd never known what it was to suffer till freedom came, and we lost our master."[32] De Saussure's interpretation of slavery certainly fit more closely with others circulating around the South during the early twentieth century than did Andrews's Marxian theories.

De Saussure subtitled her reminiscences *Being Recollections of Southern Life before the Civil War*, yet she devoted as much ink to the horrors of Reconstruction as she did to her blissful antebellum days. For De Saussure, the war had been a glorious and exciting period that did not equal the devastation she and her defeated region felt under Republican rule. Moreover, a new relationship between the races based on fear, hatred, and distrust had eclipsed the once harmonious and intimate balance that had existed between master and slave. Worried that she inadequately painted the postwar picture, De Saussure advised her audience, and specifically her granddaughter, to read Thomas Dixon Jr.'s *The Leopard's Spots*, "which gives a better description of what we endured than I can ever write."[33] De Saussure might have felt unequal to the task of substantively adding to the tales of Reconstruction, but she was keenly aware of those narratives that circulated throughout the South. By referring her readers to Dixon, she endorsed the dominant southern interpretation of Reconstruction, which in 1909 assuredly included Dixon's story.

Unlike Chesnut, Andrews, and De Saussure, who had come of age before the Civil War, Laura Elizabeth Lee Battle was only six years old when the first shots were fired on Fort Sumter. She nevertheless published her wartime memoir, *Forget-Me-Nots of the Civil War*, in 1909. Battle, like other southern writers of her generation, tried to divorce the South's defense of its homeland from its dedication to the institution of slavery. She established her father's abolitionist convictions early in her narrative, for example: Charles Lee "was a typical southern gentleman," she informed her readers, "with a courtly, dignified bearing." Moreover, "he was a descendant from that illustrious Virginia family, whose lives have been recorded on the pages of American history since the colony of Virginia first had a Secretary of the State." Despite his heritage and education, however, Charles Lee was an abolitionist. His convictions "made him a target for the slave owners," who feared "that he might be a disturbing element if left alone." Their threats failed to intimidate her father, however, and he remained firmly in his place as a southern farmer. Lee's abolitionism did not prevent his two sons, Walter and George, from fighting for the Confederacy. Indeed, when news reached the Lee family that Fort Sumter had been attacked, "George threw up his cap and howled, 'Hurrah for South Carolina, I am going to be a soldier now.'" Battle suggested that George and Walter had enlisted in the Fourth North Carolina Regiment not because they wished to defend slavery but because they wished to defend the South's liberty. When the troops marched off to war, they heard a band playing and a crowd singing, "Shout the joyous notes of freedom."[34]

If Battle deemphasized the South's commitment to slavery, she did not suggest that slaves desired their freedom. The Lee family owned one slave, Aunt Pallas, who had belonged to Charles Lee's first wife. Aunt Pallas "was so devoted . . . that she was no more a slave than the wife, and was permitted to do exactly as she pleased." When Lee made out his will, he asked Aunt Pallas if she had any objection to being set free. Echoing the works of Thomas Nelson Page, Battle claimed that Aunt Pallas refused her freedom. "Lawsa massey Mars Charlie I ain't got no notion of bein' a free niggah," Aunt Pallas explained. "No sah I ain't, don't put dat down in black and white, cause I shore don't want no more freedom den I has already got. I thankee, Mars Charlie, just de same," she added.[35] Significantly, Battle did not ascribe her father's abolitionism to Aunt Pallas. And because Battle did not give voice to a slave-owning fire-eater or a rebellious slave who desired freedom, Lee and Aunt Pallas must stand in as representatives of their types. Battle's postbellum readers might have found her father's position iconoclastic, but they could take comfort in reading about a slave who wished to remain loyal to her white family.

Battle confessed that she remembered little of the early years of the war: "The year eighteen sixty-one was ushered in with loud mutterings of war, and among my earliest recollections were those of seeing a body of men drilling in front of our home." Because she had few memories of the war, she supplemented her account by reprinting letters home written by Walter and George. Because she could not comment directly on the front line and scarcely remembered the home front, Battle needed to shore up her legitimacy as a Civil War memoirist. The letters, she hoped, would bring interest to her narrative. "It may be interesting to publish them for future generations," she explained, "to know exactly what two young Southern boys thought of war in the beginning, and how one, at least, throughout those terrible battles at Spottsylvania [sic] Court House, etc., lasted to give us such a vivid description of them."[36] Battle devoted nearly a third of her book to the publication of these letters, using them to fill in her narrative gaps.

Battle remembered much of the postwar era, however. She recalled, with great amusement, the day Aunt Pallas burst in to tell the family of the formation of the "Red Strings," a "sassiety" of newly freed slaves. "Laws a massey," Pallas began, "I wish . . . you . . . could see dem 'Red things' a trying to drill, he! he! he!" Mr. Roby, the organizer, wanted to "make a 'provement on us," she explained, by imposing military-style discipline. Aunt Pallas could hardly contain her laughter as she recounted the sight of "all de free niggahs in de county a marchin'." To Aunt Pallas, they resembled "chicken on a hot griddle." Battle made it clear that Aunt Pallas had no desire to exercise her right to join an organization of freedmen and -women.[37] Battle used this episode to support her contention that Aunt Pallas wished to remain with the Lee family even after emancipation. In this sense, Battle's narrative resembles the writings of Page, one of the most forceful articulators of the plantation myth.

Battle also remembered the formation of the Ku Klux Klan. She opened her chapter on the Klan by recounting Aunt Pallas's fear at seeing "hants." One night, when Aunt Pallas and "Brother Dannyell" were sitting on the porch "talkin' about Mars Charles and de good old days," a group of "ghosts" appeared: "Dey was so tall . . . dey just riz plum up to de sky and laik a skeleton wid a fire a burning in its head, an it was all wrapped in something like white sheets, reachin' clear to the ground. I jest raised my voice and said 'Praise de Lawd, Brother Dannyell, dis ole niggah's time have come." The "ghosts" told Pallas and Daniel to tell their "'Red String' friends to look out, for de Ku Klux Klan are out riding dis country up and down to catch niggahs dat are in mischief." Battle's family doubted Pallas's story but later learned of a freeman who "had been found, killed and quartered and hung from the Neuse river bridge, with a notice of warning to the other negroes in the 'Red Stringers.'" The murder "cured our country of such lawlessness": the Red Strings "disbanded and never drilled again." Battle later told of a young white girl who was assaulted and murdered by a "young negro." While he was in jail awaiting trial, "lynch law took him in hand." The attack on the young girl was so reprehensible, Battle recalled, that "I can still see a good reason, why the 'Ku Klux Klan' was organized."[38] In this sense, Battle's account resembles the writings of Dixon, who glorified the Klan as the protector of white womanhood. *Forget-Me-Nots of the Civil War* reminded Battle's readers of the lawlessness and violence wrought by Reconstruction.

If some southern white women published their memoirs of the Civil War to offer a new generation of readers a southern interpretation of ante- and post-bellum race relations, Louisiana's Sarah Morgan Dawson published her Civil War journal, *A Confederate Girl's Diary* (1913), to settle the historical record on the war itself. Unlike Chesnut and Andrews, who had edited and revised their diaries, and unlike De Saussure and Battle, who had constructed their narratives decades after the Confederacy's defeat, Dawson claimed that she left her manuscript untouched by the blue pencil. She therefore believed her diary to be a more accurate narrative of the war. According Dawson's son, Francis Warrington Dawson II, who wrote the diary's introduction, Dawson decided to publish her diary after a chance encounter in the 1890s with a northerner. The two had argued over the events surrounding a battle between the *Essex* and the *Arkansas*, and Dawson mentioned that she had recorded the incident in her diary. The Philadelphian, eager to see the account, implored Dawson to publish her diary, claiming, "We Northerners are sincerely anxious to know what Southern women did and thought at that time, but the difficulty is to find contemporaneous evidence. All that I, for one, have seen has been marred by improvement in light of subsequent events."[39] Dawson assured her companion that the diaries remained in a tall, cedar-lined wardrobe, untouched and fading from age.

Encouraged by this meeting, Dawson set to transcribe her diary in preparation for sending it north. Francis Warrington Dawson II claimed that after receiving the manuscript, the northerner returned it "with cold regrets that the temptation to rearrange it had not been resisted. No southerner at that time," the man continued, "could possibly have had opinions so just or foresight so clear as those here attributed to a young girl." Keenly disappointed, Dawson returned the manuscript to its resting place, never to see it again. With curiosity piqued and with a determination to vindicate his mother's reputation, Francis Warrington Dawson II undertook the publication of his mother's Civil War diaries, pledging himself "to the assertion that I have taken no liberties, have made no alterations, but have strictly adhered to my task of transcription, merely omitting here and there passages which deal with matters too personal to merit the interest of the public."[40]

Like Sarah Morgan Dawson, Francis Warrington Dawson II wished to assure the diary's readers that it was an authentic document of the war and had not been created thereafter. Dawson believed that his mother was particularly susceptible to charges of revision because her diary displayed such a rare degree of prescience and judicious temperament. In May 1863, for example, Sarah Morgan had noted that should the North conquer the South, "it will be a barren victory over a desolate land." Indeed, the Union "will find herself burdened with an unparalleled debt, with nothing to show for it except deserted towns, burning homes, a standing army and an impoverished land." And while Morgan disparaged Benjamin F. Butler, she did not equate all Federal officers with the Beast of New Orleans.[41] Morgan had been a young woman of great maturity when she began her diary of the war, and her son believed that her work should be duly praised, not besmirched by those who doubted its authenticity.

Francis Warrington Dawson II's concerns apparently were ill founded, for *A Confederate Girl's Diary* met with great popular and critical success. R. E. Blackwell, president of Randolph-Macon College in Virginia, praised the work, proclaiming it "a valuable contribution to history in that it gives a vivid picture of the daily lives of our people at a critical time." Blackwell also called the work an even more valuable piece of literature, providing "the picture of a beautiful soul." Blackwell finished the diary eager to read more, and he assiduously hoped that Sarah Morgan Dawson had left a "manuscript that will do for the Reconstruction period what this has done for the war." Elise Ripley Noyes, whose mother, Eliza Ripley, was another Louisianan who had published her reminiscences, found the volume "most absorbing." That Dawson's diary contained descriptions of people and events that resembled those in Ripley's account especially pleased Noyes, who professed her gratification that the work had "become part of that little library of valuable Southern Chronicles." Noyes wrote that she had undertaken the posthumous publication of another manuscript by her mother, "Social Life in Old New Orleans," and that she believed that had the two women lived, they "would have read each other's books with a keen enjoyment." Noyes closed her letter by stating that although the Old South had fallen, "every new bit that can be recorded of it is very precious."[42]

The critical reviews were equally favorable. "Among the many books dealing with the Civil War," stated the reviewer for the *Philadelphia Enquirer*, "few surpass in interest 'A Confederate Girl's Diary.'" Although women's civil war diaries were commonplace, most authors were "seldom logical enough to look calmly at things which concern them vitally." Sarah Morgan Dawson, however, had to be congratulated for her even, well-tempered work. Similarly, the *Springfield (Illinois) Republican* praised Morgan's "fairness of judgment and balance of treatment, . . . although, on a few pages, [the diary] is marred by bitterness." That "the great publishing house" of Houghton Mifflin supported such a project suggested to the reviewer at the *Charleston (South Carolina) Sunday News* the "special value" of *A Confederate Girl's Diary*: "It is no easy matter nowadays to get the larger publishing houses to undertake the publication of war material," let alone to print "matter frankly Southern in flavor." The reviewer for the *Milwaukee Free Press* also noted the publisher, comparing the diary with Mary Johnston's Civil War novel, *Cease Firing!* also published by Houghton Mifflin. "The contrast is great," according to the reviewer, "between the temperance and reasonableness with which Miss Morgan expresses herself, she who had lived through the most poignant sorrow and loss, and the rankling bitterness in 'Cease Firing,' written by one who had personally suffered nothing, having been born after the last echoes of the conflict had died away."[43]

These published accounts represent but a small handful of the reminiscences and revised diaries that southern women penned during the early twentieth century. Most women did not seek publication, choosing instead to write for their families or perhaps for their local UDC chapters. Some published shorter works in their local papers—in 1905, for example, the *Atlanta Journal* ran a special feature on women in the war—or in *Confederate Veteran* or *Carolina and the Southern Cross*. Although not all southern women published, scores of them wrote, and this act of writing is remarkable. That the Civil War still consumed the consciousnesses of southern women to such a degree that they felt compelled to write about it forty years after Appomattox suggests the war's transformative role in southern white women's lives. Moreover, the profusion of writing demonstrates that despite the degree to which southern women supported the region's dominant interpretation of the war and to which they believed that this interpretation was incomplete until they had contributed their personal narratives.

This Little Story of Olden Days

The same impulse that compelled countless women to write their reminiscences and to revise their diaries drove other women to publish quasi-fictional accounts of the war. These authors believed that their stories would contribute to the well-established public discourse on the war, with which they were intimately familiar. "At the beginning of an omnivorous reading," wrote Lucy Meacham Thruston, author of the 1906 novel *Called to the Field: A Story of Virginia in the Civil War*, "the writer recalls striking upon a sentence which tersely and dramatically demanded why had not some women told the women's side of the war." Thruston knew well the stories of the battlefield, the "adventurous, man's side of the question," but these tales failed to capture "the dominant note." Thruston centered her novel, therefore, on the "days and months and years of the women left behind when the men were 'Called to the Field.'" Similarly, Rose Harlow Warren never intended to tell of battles in her 1914 novel, *A Southern Home in War Times*, for "that is the man's side of the war." Instead, Warren told "of the women's point" of the crisis. "If these were 'times which tried men's souls,'" she offered, "then what must it have been for the women at home?" Perhaps the most direct, South Carolina author Phoebe Hamilton Seabrook informed the readers of her 1906 novel, *A Daughter of the Confederacy*, "in this little book the writer has endeavored to portray some of the features of Southern life during war time as it really was in her memory."[44] Although Seabrook did not question the veracity or the validity of others' tales, she did question their inclusiveness. Believing that her story had yet to be told, she—and others like her—felt it incumbent on them to contribute to the public discourse on the war.

Although convinced that they had new stories to tell, these women penned familiar novels that surely resonated with their readers. Thruston's aristocratic planter, Mr. Yancey, defends secession as a constitutionally guaranteed right, arguing that the South had no desire to protect the institution of slavery. Although he calls slavery a curse, Yancey nevertheless refrains from repudiating the South's slaveholding history, arguing instead that "wise care and good government are the Negro's only salvation." Warren infused her narrative with the Lost Cause myth from the opening pages, inserting the authorial voice to shore up her argument. "There are those who will tell you that the men who fought under the Stars and Bars were all optimists and deluded themselves with visions of the ultimate success of the Southern army," Warren wrote, "but if we are to believe the testimony of some of the bravest of our fighters, were are assured that the majority of them felt it was a forlorn hope from the first."[45] Despite their claims to originality, both Thruston and Warren embraced common elements of the southern discourse on the war, arguing that the Confederacy was at once justified and doomed.

Most early-twentieth-century Civil War novels penned by white southern women praised the heroic efforts of Confederate women, a tactic that the UDC and other memorializing organizations supported. Texas, the heroine of Fannie Selph's 1905 novel *Texas*, smuggles contraband medicine across enemy lines to aid her wounded father. Dr. Pendleton, the physician in charge of her father's case, praises Texas, claiming that when the love of a "pure daughter" is "exercised in a mission of such a grand conception as in this case, its fruits cover a broad field and bring in a harvest of a hundred fold." Cicely, the heroine of Sara Beaumont Kennedy's 1911 novel, *Cicely: A Tale of the Georgia March*, confronted a Union soldier on the eve of Sherman's march through Georgia: "Go back to your commander and tell him this from the women of Atlanta," she orders. "If General Sherman persists in making exiles of these homeless defenseless people, he will earn for himself the abiding bitterness of the South. No number of years will ever win him forgiveness," she predicts. Indeed, memories of "the serpent's tail that Sherman left across the pulsing heart" of Georgia "rankle[d] in the hearts of two generations of gentle, peace-loving women and . . . stirred the bitterness of the South." Not surprisingly, the UDC's Committee on Southern Literature and the Endorsement of Books singled out *Cicely* as an especially worthy novel. At the sound of distant gunfire, Lucy, the heroine of Thruston's *Called to the Field*, echoes the sentiments recorded by Confederate women in their diaries forty years earlier, telling her father that "to fight, to die—it is easy . . . it is the uncertainty which kills." While the menfolk could sacrifice their lives for the good of the southern cause, women had to sit at home, knowing "that battles rage, that the one being whose life is more than life to her is in the midst of them, that any second may end it—and she not even know for days, for weeks." Thruston's readers undoubtedly identified with Lucy's fate—to "sit and suffer."[46] Praising women's roles and acknowledging their hardships in the war, these novels reinforced the dominant early-twentieth-century southern discourse on the war. Moreover, despite their professed claims to separate the home front and the front line, these women discovered that the Civil War narrative resisted such easy dichotomization.

Not surprisingly, these novels also glorified the Confederate soldier, perhaps no work more so than *The Bugles of Gettysburg*, by General George Pickett's widow, La Salle Corbell Pickett. Thirteen years after publishing a biography of her husband, Pickett turned to fiction so that she might "tell this little story of olden days," woven from the "threads" spun from "memory." Despite the South's devastating loss at Gettysburg, she asserted, bugles would "forever carry around the world the fame" of the Confederacy.[47] Her novel would ensure that the bugles would continue to sound.

Pickett rendered her late husband the hero of Gettysburg. "The soldier who thrills me as no other," writes one soldier home to his cousin, "is the Commander of our Division, General Pickett. It is an inspiration to seem him ride along our lines." Recovering from near-fatal wounds suffered at Gettysburg, the soldier maintains, "You can never know what General Pickett has been to me; a strong arm to support, a steady hand to guide, a wise head to counsel, a gentle heart to sympathize in joy and sorrow." But Sallie Pickett also lionized the once-vilified General James Longstreet. The same soldier writes, "Longstreet . . . seems to have all the attributes of a great soldier — not the dash perhaps of him who fell at Chancellorsville [Stonewall Jackson], but he has care, caution, and bull-doggedness, which are equally necessary, and all the country knows how brave he is." Both Pickett and Longstreet recognize the folly of Lee's plan to invade Pennsylvania yet obediently follow their commander. "I like not to strike at other men's homes," Pickett tells Longstreet. "To choose our ground and let the enemy attack us is the way to win," responds Longstreet, citing the Confederate success at Fredericksburg, "I dream nights of the glory of that day."[48] The generals nevertheless follow their orders to attack, believing that Lee must have some grander vision.

La Salle Corbell Pickett had romanticized warfare in her biography of her husband, and she employed the same tactic in her novel. Once again, the "God of Battles" directs the action. Describing the battle, Pickett wrote, "A cannon-shot shivered the awful silence. While it echoed from the hills another shot thundered out and a cloud of smoke hung over the plain. Then came a crash of artillery and between the two ridges was a blazing sea over which a heavy curtain of smoke waved and tossed tumultuously like a wrack of storm-clouds in a raging wind. The hills trembled with the roar of battle. It was if warring worlds had meshed together in one stupendous conflict. Through a rolling ocean of smoke and dust flaming arrows darted across the field." By the time Pickett penned her novel, she had accepted that Providence, which had directed the battle's action, had ordained a northern victory. "The God of Battles knew that the safety of the Union was the safety of the States," she acknowledged. But all glory went to the Confederates, the true defenders of liberty. As the southern soldiers met their fate on that third day at Gettysburg, "the glory of the battle [swept] around them, enfolding them in a mantle of flame, urging them forward with exultant feet and hearts on fire."[49]

Sallie Pickett's greatest work of fiction, however, was not *The Bugles of Gettysburg* but *The Heart of a Soldier: As Revealed in the Intimate Letters of General George E. Pickett, C.S.A.*, which she released on the golden anniversary of the Battle of Gettysburg. Ostensibly a collection of forty-four letters written by the general to his wife between 1861 and the postwar years, the book instead represented Sallie's work. As historian Carol Reardon notes, Sallie Pickett was quite adept at keeping "the spotlight on her husband." Her collection of letters served, as did most of her other writings, to sentimentalize her husband's part in Gettysburg. As Gary Gallagher points out, *The Heart of a Soldier* engendered controversy almost from the moment of its publication, "accepted by some writers, rejected by others, and questioned, at least in part, by most." Douglas Southall Freeman, for one, declared that historians "should never believe anything that La Salle Corbell Pickett had written about her husband." Gallagher offers a reasoned and careful discussion of the letters, demonstrating convincingly that the correspondence "is worthless as a source on the general's Confederate career." Gallagher also notes that Pickett "systematically plagiarized" from Walter H. Harrison's *Pickett's Men: A Fragment of War History* (1870) and borrowed heavily from Longstreet's account of Gettysburg published in the *Southern Historical Society Papers* and *Annals of the War* and from Edward Porter Alexander's "long letter on the cannonade preceding Pickett's Charge," also published in the Southern Historical Society Papers. Gallagher also offers further evidence to bolster his assessment of the reliability of the letters as historical documents, noting, for example, that the letters' "overpowering sentimentality and gushy prose" do not match George Pickett's style. Moreover, Sallie's fondness for black dialect becomes apparent in that many of the published letters but none of George's originals contain passages about his body servant. Gallagher speculates that a need for financial security, coupled with a desire to bolster "the intensely romantic portrait" of her husband that she had painted elsewhere, might have compelled

Sallie to forge the letters. On the second score, Reardon believes that Sallie's strategy succeeded: "In the war for popular memory, in 1913 as surely as in 1863, Pickett and his men decisively won." Gallagher takes a more jaundiced view: "Instead of honoring George Pickett, the letters cast a shadow on him that will be lifted only if [an additional] cache of genuine letters comes to light."[50]

Regardless of the success of Sallie Pickett's strategy, her Gettysburg novel and her forged letters belong to a class of writings that romanticized war and the southern cause. "There is never history without its romance," Selph explained. Although the excitement of the battle might overshadow its romance, "the spirit . . . rises like an echo, and enjoys its season of recognition."[51] For these novelists, the story of the Civil War remained one of good versus evil, of Lost Cause gods fighting the forces of darkness.

Some white southern women novelists broached the theme of national reconciliation through the trope of the intersectional marriage, but even in the early twentieth century, these writers failed to embrace completely the "conciliatory culture" that northern novelists had sketched out decades earlier. In an early scene in *Cicely*, Kennedy introduces a sympathetic Federal soldier whose exemplary behavior shines among a troop of brutes. Captain Fairlee fights for the United States because he genuinely believes "that as broad as this land is, it is too narrow to hold two separate governments." When the Union army invades Georgia, Fairlee judiciously exercises his power, never sinking to the level of his rapacious, mercenary fellow soldiers. By the end of the war, he possesses a greater understanding of the South and the cause for which it fought: "He realized the absolute faith the Southern people held in their right to secede, and understood the passionate devotion they had carried to their cause." Indeed, his musings on the Confederacy's bid for independence became, in a very real sense, the southern defense of secession. "With everything to lose and scarcely a chance of success," Fairlee reasons, "they went into that fight, picking up their rifles at the call of the state." He continues, "Set aside from the rest of the country by the pastoral and agricultural nature of their pursuits, by training and by the act that the original blood of the section had been but little diluted by immigration, they were Americans; but first, above all, they were Southerners. Against a foreign foe they would have stood shoulder to shoulder with the North, no outside hand should have plucked a feather from the eagle that was their country's emblem; but if they themselves wished to withdraw from the shadow of those brooding wings and set up a banner of their own, they held it was their inalienable right."[52]

By the time Cicely, the heroine of the novel, declares her love for Fairlee, readers can rest assured that he is now sufficiently "southern" to deserve the love of the belle of Pinehurst plantation. Although the union between Fairlee and Cicely might have represented intersectional healing, the South did not need to confess its sins before the ceremony. Instead, the North, symbolized by Fairlee, had to appreciate the legality of the Confederacy's claim to independence.

In *A Daughter of the Confederacy*, Seabrook railed against the possibility of intersectional marriage. In an unfamiliar twist, she opened her novel with a southern planter married to a young northerner. "Her air and deportment," Hamilton explained of the new plantation mistress, "were of a middle-class New Englander, who had no conception of the dignity of her position. It would be casting pearls before swine to try to correct her," the author added. Universally despised by the planter's family and his slaves and unable to adjust to southern life, Minnie's presence demonstrates the incompatibility of the two regions. When at the end of the war Admiral Bee, a Federal commandant, attempts to court May, the planter's daughter, she has already witnessed the disastrous intersectional union between her father and stepmother. The Union army's devastation of the southern landscape only intensifies May's hatred of northerners. When her sister, Di, asks May if she could ever love Admiral Bee, May's response is resounding: "If a woman marries, she should choose a man she could 'love, honor and obey.' I could never love a Yankee, for the blood of my murdered brother would ever rise between us, and cry out against the unholy union. I could never honor one," she continues, "for all the ruin of my home and native land lies at his door." Northerners have nary a quality to recommend them, May asserts, pledging that she will never put "such trust in the enemy of my country, and family, and all that a woman holds dear."[53] For Seabrook, the symbolic reunification of North and South made a mockery of the values for which the Confederacy had stood. Although northerners might have participated in a conciliatory culture, the characters in Seabrook's novel, at least, found such participation unpalatable.

Seabrook, Kennedy, and other such authors did not tell vastly different or terribly original stories: these authors' tales fit the mold used by scores of earlier southern writers. But these early-twentieth-century novels nonetheless demonstrate the cultural resonance of the southern war narrative. Indeed, southern women's continued efforts to tell familiar war stories and the degree to which the public read each new tale suggest the viability of the dominant southern interpretation of the war.

Between 1905 and 1915, Ellen Glasgow continued to reflect on the changes to southern society wrought by the Civil War, themes she had first explored in her early social histories of Virginia. Although she did not return to the Civil War as a catalyst for the action of her novels, she did offer explicit commentary on the conflict. Glasgow set out "to define and to embalm the southern lady of the 1880s" in her 1913 novel *Virginia*. Virginia Pendleton, the story's heroine, "embodied the feminine ideal of the ages." Indeed, "to look at her was to think inevitably of love," Glasgow wrote. "For that end obedient to the powers of Life, the centuries had formed and coloured her as they had formed and coloured the wild rose with its whorl of delicate petals." Glasgow suggested that in many ways, Virginia had inherited many of the qualities of her former teacher, Priscilla Batte, the headmistress at the Dinwiddie Academy for Young Ladies. Miss Priscilla is a relic of the antebellum South for whom Confederate defeat ultimately means little. Of her, Glasgow scathingly wrote, "Just as the town had battled for a principle without understanding it, so she was capable of dying for an idea, but not of conceiving one. She had suffered everything from the war except the necessity of thinking independently about it, and though in her later years memory had become so sacred to her that she rarely indulged in it, she still clung passionately to the habits of her ancestors under the impression that she was clinging to their ideals." Virginia had been a "docile pupil" of Miss Priscilla's "who deferentially submitted her opinions to her superiors" and who remained content "to go through life perpetually submitting her opinions," "the divinely appointed task of woman."[54]

These lessons failed to provide Virginia with the tools necessary to negotiate the postwar South, however. Her charms are sufficient to bewitch the dashing Oliver Treadwell, an aspiring playwright, but she is unable to keep him interested in her after the first few months of their marriage. Treadwell wishes to write "great" plays that will inspire his audience: "I've got something to say to the world," he tells his cousin, "and I'll go out and make my bed in the gutter before I'll forfeit the opportunity of saying it." Yet Treadwell tempers his youthful idealism with a dose of cynicism. Commenting on the theatergoing public, Oliver remarks, "Why, that box over there in the corner is full of plays that would start a national drama if the fool public had sense enough to see what they were about. The trouble is that they don't want life on the stage; they want a kind of theatrical wedding-cake. Any dramatist who tries to force people to eat bread and meat when they are dying for sugar plums may as well prepare to starve until the public begins to suffer from acute indigestion." Heady optimism prevails, however, and Treadwell takes a play to the New York stage, where the work fails. Virginia is unable to understand Treadwell's consequent misery: according to Glasgow, "Introspection, which had lain under a moral ban in a society that assumed the existence of an unholy alliance between the secret and the evil, could not help her because she had never indulged in it." Because of her upbringing, Virginia "shared the ingrained Southern distrust of any state of mind which could not cheerfully support the observation of the neighbors." Treadwell eventually chooses commercial viability over art and writes plays that satisfy the vapid playgoing public. He also chooses the actress who plays the lead in his latest hit play over his wife. Virginia leaves New York "speechless, inert, and unseeing" and returns to "death in life" in Dinwiddie.[55]

Like Virginia, the town of Dinwiddie is ill equipped to handle the demands of the postwar South. The old order had a fond regard for Dinwiddie, "with its intrepid faith in itself, with its militant enthusiasm, with its courageous battle against industrial evolution, with its strength, its narrowness, its nobility, its blindness." "Of the world beyond the borders of Virginia," Glasgow wrote, "Dinwiddians knew merely that it was either Yankee or foreign, and therefore to be pitied or condemned, according to the Evangelical or the Calvinistic convictions of the observer. . . . It was a quarter of a century since 'The Origin of Species' had changed the course of the world's thought, yet it had never reached them." The most troubling aspect of Dinwiddie's provinciality, however, is its inability to cope with the "Problem of the South." When Virginia and her mother, the wife of a preacher, go to the "bad" section of town, they notice that "the scent of honeysuckle did not reach here." Instead, the "sharp acrid odour of huddled negroes" float out to greet them. In Tin Pot Alley, "where the lamps burned at longer distances, the more primitive forms of life appeared to swarm like distorted images under the transparent civilization of the town." Virginia's mother looked at the "'Problem of the South' as Southern women had looked down on it for generations and would continue to look down on it for generations still to come—without seeing that it was a problem."[56]

Virginia's father, Gabriel Pendleton, is no more enlightened on matters of race than is his wife. "The terrible thing for us about the negroes," he comments to a fellow Dinwiddian, "is that they are so grave a responsibility—so grave a responsibility. . . . We stand for civilization to them; we stand even—or at least we used to stand—for Christianity," he continued. "They haven't learned yet to look above or beyond us, and the example we set them is one that they are condemned, for sheer lack of any finer vision, to follow." Pendleton reminds his neighbor that "the majority of them are hardly still more than uneducated children, and that very fact makes an appeal to one's compassion which becomes at times almost unbearable." Indeed, Gabriel's "compassion" costs him his life. When a mob threatens to lynch the grandson of one of Gabriel's favorite former slaves, who had smiled at a white woman, Gabriel defends the grandson: "Spinning round on the three of [the attackers] he struck out with all his strength, while there floated before him the face of a man he had killed at his first charge at Manassas. The old fury, the old triumph, the old blood-stained splendour returned to him." Unfortunately, his luck in battle did not hold, and he died defending Mehitable's grandson. Even more tragic, the town of Dinwiddie had yet to find a solution to the "Problem of the South."[57]

Virginia met with a favorable critical reception at the time of its publication. "The power of the book is undeniable," proclaimed Lewis Parke Chamberlayne in the *Sewanee Review*. "Conservative people" might find Glasgow's indictment of "old fashioned feminine ideals" "harsh, sweeping and bitterly unjust, but to those Southerners . . . who hope for radical change, the book is to be recommended as one of startling modernness and extraordinary timeliness." The reviewer for the *Nation* remarked that in Glasgow's novel, "a belated specimen of the old-fashioned Southern lady lingers on into the era of feminine self-assertion—the fine flower of a vanished social order, by a miracle of spiritual force sustaining itself in a hopelessly altered habitat, only to fade at last among the encroaching ranks of a lustier, more aggressive womanhood." The *North American Review*'s critic saw *Virginia* as an antidote to the "sentimental tenderness" the state of Virginia had received from its historians.[58]

But, as many literary critics have pointed out, however, although Glasgow had intended the tone of her novel to be ironic, as her sympathies for Virginia grew, the tone became more compassionate. As with her earlier social histories, Glasgow seemed incapable of creating the critical distance from her subject matter that she so desired. Glasgow imagined a circumspect world for white southern women, but "although Glasgow as realist sees such narrowness of vision to be false and dangerous, she refuses to condemn it utterly. Instead," according to literary critic Anne Goodwyn Jones, "she grants to such narrowness an intensity, a concentration, that can under great pressure permit insight, the growth of character, heroic actions, and the birth of genuine symbols rather than illusory fictions." Instead of embalming the southern lady, then, Glasgow nearly "enshrined her."[59]

Perhaps no other writer challenged the prevailing turn-of-the-century pomp and ceremony surrounding the "late war" more than Virginia novelist Mary Johnston. The daughter of a Confederate officer and the cousin of celebrated Confederate General Joseph E. Johnston, she had seemed naturally well suited to write a novel on the Civil War. Indeed, she had frequently mentioned the thrill she had experienced when listening to the older generations' stories of the war. She recalled in her unpublished autobiography the tales told to her by her grandfather regarding the relic-filled "hiding place" behind his house. During her childhood, she and her siblings embellished those stories and reenacted local battles "on dark days." "We yet lived in a veritable battle cloud, an atmosphere of war stories, of continual reference to the men and to the deeds of that gigantic struggle." As a young woman, while riding on a train with her father, she sat across the aisle from Virginia novelist Thomas Nelson Page, entranced as the two men swapped stories about the war. Her plan to embark on "a war story," which she formulated in the summer of 1908, therefore surprised no one.[60]

Johnston was part of the group of "post-Victorian" southerners who, as Daniel Singal notes, endeavored "to break with the Victorian (or New South) mentality that they felt was so inadequate to the task of rebuilding southern society and culture. They wished above all to free themselves from the romantic and chauvinistic view of southern history they identified with their predecessors." Johnston sought to break from the romantic, even celebratory nature of the southern Civil War novel and fought a three-year battle with her editor over the iconoclastic content of her work. But however sincere her quest for realism, she failed to loosen the "stranglehold on the intellect." Johnston, like others of her cohort, remained bound by the cavalier myth, "with its notion of the South's essential innocence from evil or guilt."[61] Johnston critically examined war, but her ultimate failure as a novelist stemmed from her inability to discuss—let alone probe—southern civilization. Johnston had no interest in entering such a discussion—her "battles" rested elsewhere. By refusing to absolve, chastise, or reject a priori the notion of the South's responsibility for the war, she let the stranglehold remain.

Johnston's plan for her novel initially pleased Ferris Greenslet, her editor at Houghton Mifflin, who recognized not only her consummate skill as a storyteller but, perhaps more important, the potential profitability of her newest en-

Mary Johnston (Courtesy Special Collections Department, Manuscript
Division, University of Virginia Library, Charlottesville)

deavor. Indeed, Greenslet had every reason to believe that Johnston's project
would reap both her and his firm a substantial sum. Johnston had already
proven her financial worth to the editors at the prestigious Boston publishing
house, writing best-sellers, gaining critical accolades, and establishing herself
as a prominent writer of historical romances. Her three most successful novels,
Prisoners of Hope (1899), *To Have and to Hold* (1900), and *Audrey* (1902), had
sold nearly three-quarters of a million copies combined and had earned Johnston well over $150,000 in U.S. royalties alone. One theater company immedi-
ately adapted *Audrey* for the stage, and the Famous Players Film Company later
adapted both *Audrey* and *To Have and to Hold* for the silent screen, with each
production increasing Johnston's earnings and reputation. Her two most re-

cent projects, a five-hundred-page free-verse poem on the French Revolution, *The Goddess of Reason* (1907), and a historical romance on the Jeffersonian period, *Lewis Rand* (1908), had not fared as well as her earlier works, but she had emerged from these literary experiments with her reputation unscathed.[62] Greenslet thus unhesitatingly took on her war project, convinced that it would rival her previous achievements.

Greenslet also recognized that the literary market was particularly accommodating to stories of the Civil War. His firm had handled the reprint of Mary Noailles Murfree's *Where the Battle Was Fought* (1884) and would later publish her 1905 war novel, *The Storm Centre*, as well as Sarah Morgan Dawson's 1913 *A Confederate Girl's Diary*.[63] If Greenslet doubted the market's ability to absorb yet another tale of the war, he did not publicly express his misgivings but instead enthusiastically embraced his latest assignment.

During the next three years, Johnston diligently worked on her projected three-volume manuscript, reading military histories, honing her prose, and forwarding drafts to her editor. Greenslet quickly learned that his client's vision of the project differed significantly from his. The editor had hoped that Johnston would generate another commercial success patterned after her historical romances. Johnston had other plans. Although she initially considered the book a paean to her father, she soon discovered that she abhorred war and predicted that she would "be weary and disheartened enough before the two years' piece of work is done." She later admitted to an obsession with wounded soldiers, imagining their fallen bodies strewn across the Virginia countryside.[64] If Greenslet anxiously awaited another romantic best-seller, Johnston's drafts quickly tempered his enthusiasm.

The bulk of Johnston's manuscripts signaled to Greenslet that Johnston's newest project would resemble no other. "My plan now is not one war volume but three — a trilogy," she reasoned first in her diary. "It is impossible to put everything into one book. The first would close with Chancellorsville — and Stonewall Jackson the dominant historical figure. The second would be the struggle further South, — Chickamauga, Vicksburg, Dalton to Atlanta, etc, and cousin Joe Johnston the leader. The third back to Virginia, the Wilderness, Petersburg, etc. Appomattox, Lee the dominant." Even Johnston acknowledged the magnitude of her undertaking. "Four years work," she conceded, "and I don't enter on it with a light heart." Greenslet initially agreed with the projected length of the "war story," reassuring Johnston that "if it is as fine as we expect it to be, it ought to be something of which American fiction has not hitherto seen the like." Greenslet went on to warn Johnston, however, that "a great deal of the commercial success of the undertaking will depend on the first volume." He recommended that she design each volume to contain a complete substory, better still "if this first volume could have a reasonably happy ending." Greenslet angled for a traditional marriage plot between Richard Cleave and Judith Cary, hero and heroine, thereby providing readers a ray of hope in the midst of war. Perhaps even the second volume might end happily for Richard and Judith, he excitedly mused, "though we recognize of course," he added as an afterthought, "that naturally there would be rather ominous clouds upon the horizon."[65]

Both the length and the content of Johnston's manuscript threatened Greenslet's vision of a commercially viable historical romance. An uncompleted first draft of the first volume of the war story ran 356,000 words. A exasperated Greenslet told Johnston that no volume in "modern times" had run that long, noting that the book would be "physically unattractive," with "tiny print on tissue paper." "I am disposed to think that it might be possible for you to omit certain chapters," he tactfully suggested, "letting the reader read the story of certain campaigns by title, as it were,—without serious artistic loss,—possibly indeed, with an artistic, if not historic, gain." Johnston agreed to cut 75,000 words, although not without initial reservations. After the purge, however, she acquiesced that the book had been "condensed, knit together, and improved."[66]

The conflict between author and editor soon expanded to cover the manuscript's content as well as its length. Greenslet had initially praised Johnston's skill, singling out her ability to describe battles: "The Bull [Run] chapters are, it seems to me, a masterpiece of imaginative description." He admitted his shock at finding "the battle scene described . . . through the eyes of the Muse of History, rather than through those of some of your characters," but agreed that her tactic was effective. But six months later, the battle scenes wearied him: "I had a feeling throughout the Kernstown chapter that there was coming to be a little monotony in the descriptions of battles—that there wasn't quite the upward curve of interest which there perhaps ought to be at this point." Johnston had switched the point of view, letting her characters describe the battles without providing historical exposition. Greenslet offered a suggestion: "I wondered whether perhaps the effect of sameness which seems to run along through here would both be obviated if you could take the occasion somewhere to point out a little more clearly what was going on in other fields, and the relation of one to another."[67] Johnston apparently disagreed.

Johnston had become more interested in providing her readers with a sense of immediacy than in maintaining her authorial, omniscient voice. She endeavored to eclipse the distance that separated the reader from the events of the novel. The members of the Stonewall Brigade had had little sense of "what was going on in other fields" and certainly had no way of intuiting Kernstown's relationship to other events in the war. In fact, few fighting men understood the war in terms of epic struggle, but they certainly grasped the realities of warfare with grim fatalism. "What's the use of ducking?" one Confederate soldier asked another. "If a bullet is going to hit you it's going to hit you, and if it isn't going to hit you it isn't—." Johnston's soldiers rarely experienced the glory of battle but rather felt the endless repetition of their tasks. "Long ago they had fought in a great, bright, glaring daytime," Johnston wrote. "Then again, long ago they had begun to fight in a period of dusk, an age of dusk. The men loaded, fired, loaded, rammed, fired quite automatically. They had been doing this for a long, long time. Probably they would do it for a long time to come."[68]

More egregious than the monotony, however, was Johnston's refusal to provide a happy ending for the first volume. "Perhaps you will forgive me if I say bluntly," Greenslet tersely wrote, "that I don't like the proposed treatment of the affairs of the fictitious characters in the book, and that I am as fully persuaded as I can be that it might be followed by a very disastrous consequence commercially." Greenslet invited Johnston to put herself "in the place of a hypothetical buyer and reader of the book." He hoped that she would realize the disappointment that was sure to greet readers of the manuscript as it stood. According the Greenslet, readers "had every reason to expect a story of the first two years of the Civil War given coherence and unity not only by its chief historical character, but also by a certain amount of completed design involving its fictitious characters." Instead, readers found no resolution, no happy ending, and no hint about the number of volumes to come. Greenslet opined that publishing the existing manuscript of the first volume would greatly "handicap" the success of future volumes and urged Johnston to make immediate and necessary corrections. "Forgive me," he pleaded, "and think it over."[69]

Johnston did not need to think over Greenslet's request. She sent him an immediate response, declaring that his plan was "quite impossible." "I speak as an artist," she informed her editor. "I must tell my story in my own way, and the consequences must take care of themselves." To add an artificially happy ending to the first volume would ring false. "I write for the intelligent reader," Johnston proclaimed, noting that just as the war did not end with the Battle of Chancellorsville, the book's last scene, the affairs of her characters also could not end

"The Lovers." Illustration from Mary Johnston's 1911 novel, *The Long Roll*.

there. Moreover, "it is now too late to alter, nor indeed should I care to make the attempt." She concluded emphatically, "Like all the rest of us, I want money but I have never wanted it t[h]at badly." Greenslet clarified his position and made one last attempt to persuade Johnston but in the end respected her position as the "artist."[70]

Houghton Mifflin published *The Long Roll*, the first volume of Johnston's war story, in the summer of 1911, reaping twenty-five thousand dollars in revenues during the first few months after the novel's release. Although this success made Greenslet's fears about the novel's viability seem unwarranted, Johnston had not written a conventional novel of the war, designed to appeal to the mass of southern readers. She drew heavily on the dominant trope of southern fiction—the myth of the Lost Cause—and, even before she began the story of the war's action, she provided her readers with an explanation of the Confederacy's demise. Early in the novel, before the bombing of Fort Sumter, Warwick Cary, one of the heroes, explains to his family the impossibility of southern victory: "We are utterly unprepared. We are seven million against twenty million, an agricultural country against a manufacturing one. The odds are greatly against us," he calculates. "We have struggled for peace, apparently we cannot have it, now we will fight for the conviction that is in us. It will be for us a war of defense, with the North for the invader, and Virginia will prove the battleground."[71] Johnston's audience could thus read on, secure in the knowledge that the story of the Confederacy's downfall would be told in acceptable terms: the South, however peace loving and reluctant to fight against the Union, would do so under dire circumstances, but with complete conviction and valor. Johnston not only glorified the southern cause but, more importantly, expressed what she believed to be the futility of war. These two aims might have seemed paradoxical to Greenslet and to many readers, but in the author's mind, they reinforced each other while demonstrating the power of the Lost Cause myth over southern consciousness. No matter how noble, virtuous, and loyal to the Constitution were the Confederates, they were doomed to failure.

Johnston further sought to justify the righteousness of southern secession. Born into a prominent Virginia family, she was proud of her southern lineage and of the South's history in the formation of the American nation. She devoted the first chapter of *The Long Roll* to a careful delineation of Virginia's role in settling the colonies, fighting in the American Revolution, drafting the *Constitution*, and developing republican thought. While the South remained true to the ideals of the Founding Fathers, theorized Johnston, the North quickly deviated, seeking to impose its tyrannical will on the South. For Johnston's characters, the Union was the "golden thread" that linked the sovereign states, "not the monster that Frankenstein made, not this minotaur swallowing States!" Although "war is a word that means agony to many and a set-back to all," the North had violated the terms of the Union and the South could not remain yet preserve its integrity.[72] War not only was inevitable but also served as the South's only recourse for preserving its constitutionally guaranteed rights.

Johnston noted in her diary before she began writing *The Long Roll*, however, that she planned "to state the case for the South at once and definitely, and then through all the remaining chapters to leave alone . . . all [discussions] of abstract right and wrongs." Johnston did not intend her war story to defend the South but rather to demonstrate the horrors of the Civil War and, by extension, of war in general. A future member of Jane Addams's Woman's Peace Party, Johnston was a pacifist and sought to counter the South's glorification of the Civil War. In a very early scene, Margaret Cleave warns her children about the horrors of war: "As for you two who've always been sheltered and fed, who've never had a blow struck you, you've grown like tended plants in a garden—you don't know what war is!" Cleave ranted. "It's a great and deep cup of Trembling. It's a scourge that reaches the backs of all. It's universal destruction—and the gift that the world should pray for is to build in peace." Johnston directed her message at the new generation of southerners who had been raised on romantic war stories. Lest there be any confusion, Johnston described the Confederates' bleak march through Bath and Romney. "Was this war?" she asked, "War, heroic and glorious, with banners, trumpets and rewarded enterprise?" Manassas might have fit this conception of war, "but ever since there was only marching, tenting, suffering, and fatigue—and fatigue—and fatigue."[73]

"What I was after," Johnston later explained to one of her readers, "was to show what war could do." She confessed, however, that "in writing these . . . books, the emphasis in my own mind shifted after a while from the tragedy of that war to the tragic absurdity of all wars." To her reader's complaint that Johnston spared the life of the novel's traitorous coward but killed off gallant and brave Confederates, Johnston retorted, "I wished to show that war takes these of the richest promise proportionally speaking, it is the Edward Cary's who are slain and the Steven Dagg's who are spared." In a final declaration, she asserted, "War is altogether stupid as hell is horrible."[74] Although Johnston's pacifism might have seemed to undermine her vindication of the South, it also allowed her to come to terms with southern defeat. By locating absurdity in war itself rather than in the Confederacy, Johnston imaginatively liberated the South from the burden of its past and, no less important, relieved herself of the obligation to examine critically the Old South. On this basis, Johnston could assert categorically that the South had not lost the war because of any putative sins: it had lost because war is an inherently evil and ultimately destructive force that knows neither good nor evil.

Most reviewers pronounced *The Long Roll* a literary triumph, even if they did find the battle scenes a bit grim. The reviewer for the *Baltimore Sun* heaped the most praise on Johnston, claiming that "a daughter of the Southland has written the prose epic of the Civil War—written it worthily—nay, more, written it splendidly, written it with the vigor of a man, the vision of a poet, the sympathy of a woman, and the accuracy of a scientist." The same reviewer confessed his surprise that a woman had written such a powerful war story: "That any woman should have so complete a grasp upon a prolonged military campaign, should hold the thread of military narrative so firmly in hand as never to confuse the reader and to unroll before the mind's eye a great war panorama with the clearness of a map is remarkable." The entire project seemed to be "outside the possibility of a woman's genius," according to the reviewer, ascribing Johnston's success to the tales she had heard as a young child.[75]

While all reviewers did not offer such unqualified praise of Johnston, most agreed that the novel set new standards for southern war fiction. If Greenslet and some other readers balked at the graphic depictions of war, reviewers cited as Johnston's greatest achievement her ability to paint a realistic picture of war. "The whole book is a series of . . . graphic pictures," explained the reviewer from Charleston, South Carolina. "It is not always coherent. Indeed, much of it is distinctly scrappy," the reviewer noted. But through this incoherence and scrappiness, Johnston ably captured the "verisimilitude" of war. "The military observations and analyses would do credit to an experienced soldier," proclaimed the *Dallas News*, and the battle scenes were described with the "virility and dramatic effect one would expect from an experienced war correspondent." The *New York Evening Globe* stated simply, "'The Long Roll' is not a novel—it is history; it is not history—it is war itself."[76]

Johnston's readers did not revolt against her grim depictions of battles, but some readers publicly decried the book's "slanderous" portrayal of General Stonewall Jackson. In a particularly offensive passage, Johnston wrote of a unit, "Just when they were happy at last in winter quarters, [they had to] pull up stakes and hurry down the Valley to join 'Fool' Tom Jackson." Although Jackson might have understood the purpose of his march to Romney, "to the majority his course seemed sprung from a certain cold willfulness, a harshness without object, unless his object were to wear out flesh and bone." Johnston purposefully and effectively drew out the scene of Jackson's march through the Valley of Virginia, inviting the reader to identify with the foot soldiers under Jackson's command. Several pages into her description of the march, Johnston wrote, "This day they made four miles. The grey trees were draped with ice, the grey zigzag of the fences was gliding ice under the hands that caught it, the hands of the sick and weak. Motion resolved itself into a Dead March, few notes and slow, with rests. The army moved and halted, moved and halted with a weird stateliness. Couriers came back from the man riding ahead, cadet cap drawn over eyes that say only what a giant and iron race might do under a giant and iron dictatorship. General Jackson says, 'Press Forward!' General Jackson says, 'Press Forward, men!'"[77] The unit did not reach its destination that night, Johnston reported. It would have to continue to press forward.

As depicted by Johnston, General Jackson's men have little confidence in "the damned clown," Fool Tom Jackson. "The individual at the head of this army is not a general," says one soldier to his compatriots, "he's a pedagogue—by God, he's the Falerian pedagogue who sold his pupils to the Romans." Finishing his analogy, the soldier continues, "Oh, the lamb-like pupils, trooping after him through flowers and sunshine—straight into the hands of Kelly at Romney, with Rosecrans and twenty thousand just beyond." At the protestations of a cadet from the Virginia Military Institute, the soldier concludes, "Stiff, fanatic, inhuman, callous, cold, half mad and wholly rash, without military capacity, ambitious as Lucifer and absurd as Hudibras—I ask again what is this person doing at the head of this army?"[78] Although Jackson garners the support and confidence of his men over the course of the novel, some readers saw Johnston's initial characterization of the general as tantamount to blasphemy and deserving of serious rebuke.

Mary Anna Jackson, no stranger to literary scandal, published a scathing review of The Long Roll in the New York Times, claiming that although she would have preferred to remain silent as a result of her opposition to "publicity and newspaper controversy," she felt that she had to set straight the historical record. "Pity 'tis but true that fiction is more read by the young than history," Jackson lamented, "and it would be a great injustice to General Jackson that such a delineation of his character and personality go down to future generations." According to Jackson, Johnston had rendered the general "rough, uncouth, boorish, slovenly, and unbalanced." Even worse, "Miss Johnston acknowledges that she never saw or knew General Jackson, which fact is very evident from the hideous caricature she uses as her frontispiece [by artist N. C. Wyeth] representing him and his little sorrel and which alone is enough to condemn the book." And though Johnston's "presumptuousness" might be dismissed as the folly of a young mind, literary success, which acted like a "fine wine," had dulled her senses to the detriment of history. "Will not all true Confederate soldiers who followed Stonewall

"Stonewall Jackson." Illustration from Mary Johnston's 1911 novel, *The Long Roll*.

Jackson," Anna Jackson pleaded at the end of the review, "give an expression of their opinion of 'The Long Roll,' and if they approve of it let them say so candidly but if not will they unite in such a protest against this false and damaging portraiture of their commander as will settle the question for all time."[79]

Former soldiers willingly picked up the gauntlet thrown down by Stonewall Jackson's widow. Captain J. P. Smith, who had served on General Jackson's staff, resented Johnston's characterization of Jackson, finding fault with the "exaggerated" accounts of his profanity, which were historically inaccurate and should be "regretted in a book to be read by many of our boys as it is not just to the characters of their fathers." According to Smith's assessment, published in *Confederate Veteran*, Confederate officers had "repressed" all profane behavior "whenever they came into the army." Moreover, the noble and pious commanding officers had quickly checked those soldiers who maintained their boorish habits.[80]

Like Anna Jackson, Smith found the "uncouth, misshapen, [and] monstrous" frontispiece insulting to all who knew the general. In addition to including this "ungainly" caricature, Smith charged Johnston with unjustly painting Jackson as "harsh, hostile, pedantic, awkward, hypochondriacal, literal, and strict." Worse than these sins of commission, according to Smith, however, were Johnston's sins of omission. Johnston provided "no adequate conception of the religious character of Stonewall Jackson," Smith fumed. And although Johnston described the general as obsessive, bordering on fanatical, and unfit for duty, he was, according to Smith, "devout and reverent, humble, steadfast, prayerful in spirit and faithful in duty." Smith doubted that Johnston had consulted any historical or biographical source. "It will be an unmeasured loss to generations to come," he believed, "if a picture so marred be retained in the thought and memory of our people." Although the editors of *Confederate Veteran* distanced themselves from the Smith's views, they nevertheless urged Johnston to eliminate the novel's profanity and to revise Jackson's "picture and character." "While the book is a novel," they conceded, "it is also a wonderful history of the people to whom Miss Mary Johnston desires to give full credit."[81]

Despite taking this position, the editors allowed Johnston to defend her work. The author challenged her detractors to support their claims regarding the novel's historical inaccuracies. To levy their complaints, her critics "must really strike out of existence the hundred and odd volumes of the official records, the whole series of Southern Historical Society papers, all the newspapers of '61–'65, the articles contributed by Southern officers to 'Battles and Leaders,' as well as those contributed to Mrs. Jackson's life of her husband, Henderson's biography, histories, memoirs, and diaries without number, forms of record too numerous to mention." Although Johnston later addressed specific charges, such as the issue of profanity, her defense of the novel's historical accuracy is most telling. Because southerners were engaged in a raging debate over the Civil War, Johnston felt particularly slandered by the criticisms of her countrymen and -women. Although she might have intended to debunk the prevailing glorification of war in general, she certainly never sought to disparage the Confederate cause or any of its leaders. While Johnston's detractors believed her characterization of Jackson rendered him an uncouth boor, she felt it made him human. Her novel, she proclaimed, "has done a service to Virginia and the South." Convinced of her book's importance, Johnston noted finally, "Jerusalem is not the only city that stones her prophets, nor antiquity the only time that preoccupies itself with some blemish—it may be reality, may be fancied only—on the forehead of a great and real service."[82]

The debate regarding Johnston's portrayal of Stonewall Jackson provided her readers with ample topics for discussion. The Secessionville Chapter of the South Carolina Division of the UDC, for example, tabled its historical program for October 1911 so that the chapter's historian could read aloud Smith's criticism and Johnston's defense. And although this chapter did not devote its entire November 1911 meeting to The Long Roll, the members did discuss a favorable review of the novel "in which the narrative of the book is described as being true to life and a faithful reproduction of the scenes of that time." Indeed, some readers did not take offense at Johnston's characterization of Stonewall Jackson. After reading Anna Jackson's attack, Joseph Ames, the future president of the University of Chicago, dashed off a letter to Johnston. Although he realized that she probably never wanted "to see the name Jackson again," Ames felt "as if I must write to tell you how much I—a Yankee and an ignorant one—enjoyed your picture of the great General." He later thanked Johnston for delivering to those "who never knew the war, an *impression* which we shall never forget." William Terrence published his spirited defense of Johnston in the *Richmond Times-Dispatch*, citing "an embarrassment of riches" to support her portrait of Jackson. Moreover, "as an artist, it is Miss Johnston's right to take what ever she knows to have been true of the man and use it to the advantage of her characterization." Those who accused Johnston of "poison[ing] the minds of the young" had failed to prove that she falsified any public record. Even Greenslet, who continually worried about the novel's public reception, reassured Johnston: "It is a pity that the writer of fiction should have the trouble of the biographer. . . . I think you will find, however, that in the long run even Mrs. Jackson will take a different view."[83]

Undeterred by the controversy, Johnston immediately launched herself into the second and final volume of her war story, *Cease Firing!* If Johnston harbored any lingering doubts regarding her ability to write a war narrative, Greenslet put them to rest. The quibbling that had characterized their working relationship on *The Long Roll* was held in check while they worked on the second volume. "I have read chapters XII, XIII, and XIV and time fails me to tell you of the many things in them that have powerfully impressed me," Greenslet wrote, "but I must say at least that the passage dealing with the married lovers in their cave in the besieged city stands out in my mind as one of the unforgettable pictures in fiction." Greenslet was referring to a scene in which two minor characters, the recently married Edward and Desiree Cary, discuss love and death while trapped in a cave during the bombing of Vicksburg, Mississippi. Greenslet envisioned a heralded place in the field of southern literature for *Cease Firing!* proclaiming, "The book promises, I think, to be unique in its field in its union of the elevated with the tranquilizing, I have a notion that this is just what is needed at the moment."[84]

Johnston had abandoned her plan to feature General Robert E. Lee in this volume, a decision that relieved Greenslet. Anxious to avoid the disputes that had surrounded *The Long Roll*, Greenslet wholeheartedly supported the change: "I think the fact that you have not made any one historic character so conspicuous as Jackson in 'The Long Roll' is an advantage." Greenslet hoped that *Cease Firing!* would smooth the feathers ruffled by *The Long Roll*, providing readers with a "general unity of impression." If the two works taken as a whole "don't eventually become 'classics,'" swore Greenslet, "I shall lose what vestige of faith in my judgment I have managed to keep through ten years of the compromise which is publishing."[85]

Johnston might have steered clear of any wrangling involving Confederate leaders, but Greenslet felt that she was heading into troubled waters near the end of the second book, and he advised her to leave out "that bit of historical controversy toward the end of Chapter 39 in the passage dealing with the burning of Columbia." Although Greenslet did not doubt that General William T. Sherman possessed a "medieval mind," he did not want *Cease Firing!* mired in a literary scandal. Calling the scene "controversy imperfectly imbedded in an imaginative context," the editor urged the author to switch the point of view of Sherman's march through Columbia to those of her fictitious characters, refraining from authorial commentary and intertextual references — for example, a Federal officer who says, "As for the wholesale burnings, pillage, devastation, committed in South Carolina, magnify all I have said of Georgia some fifty-fold, and then throw in an occasional murder, 'just to bring an old hardfisted cuss to his senses,' and you have a pretty good idea of the whole thing." Greenslet urged Johnston to cut all of the chapter's historical references: "It seems to me that if you describe the burning of the city as part of the texture of the chapter," Greenslet firmly advised, "you bring the wrong of the act home to the reader much more impressively than you do if you drop from the imaginative plane to the strictly historic, and go into the argument as to responsibility." Although Johnston was unwilling to cut the "historical" from the manuscript, she placed the burning of the city on the imaginative plane, ending the scene with Sherman's men torching a convent. Huddled in the churchyard, the nuns and their young female charges watched as "the convent burned, with a roaring and crackling of flames and a shouting of men."[86]

More important than the artistic integrity of the novel, however, was its reception by readers. "Speaking as a publisher," Greenslet warned that the passage as originally written would "hurt the book with Northern readers, and . . . hamper the permanent work the two books together ought to do in bringing about a better understanding in the North of what the war meant to the South." Greenslet took this opportunity to broaden his discussion of reader reception of the novel, urging Johnston once again to provide a "happy ending" for her fictional characters. "After the . . . almost unbearable tragedy of Chapter 40 I hope you will find it possible to end the book on a different note." And once again, Johnston failed to acquiesce. Mortally wounded in Sherman's attack on Columbia, Desiree lies dying beneath the ruins. Her husband, also mortally wounded, drags himself on his knees to join her. Desiree dies first, but not before telling him of the death of their child in the attack. "With a last effort he moved so that his arms were around her body and his head upon her breast, and then, as the sun came up, his spirit followed hers."[87]

Indeed, a sense of grim reality permeated the entire novel. Unwilling to paint a romantic picture of war, Johnston focused on the monotony of battle that had so troubled Greenslet during the writing of *The Long Roll*. "There was growing in this war," she wrote, "as in all wars, a sense of endless repetition. The gamut was not extensive, the spectrum held but few colours. Over and over and over again sounded the notes, old as the ages, monotonous as the desert wind. War was still war, and all music was military." To counter the efforts of those who endeavored to elevate the Civil War to a noble and just battle, worthy of glorification and celebration, Johnston honed in on the brutality of all war, including the Civil War. In her view, war devastated all, and the wanton destruction rendered sanity nearly impossible. "And so at last . . . from the general to the drummer-boy, from the civil ruler to the woman scraping lint, no one looks very closely

"The Bloody Angle." Illustration from Mary Johnston's 1912 novel,
Cease Firing!

at what falls beneath the harrow," Johnston explained. "Madness lies that way,
and in war one must be very sane."[88]

Johnston's readers and critics praised her starkness. Ames again wrote to
Johnston, telling her that he had read and enjoyed *Cease Firing!* "but what a
tragedy." The novel, he believed, transcended other war stories and, taken with

The Long Roll, served as "what theologians would call an apology." The force of Johnston's prose compelled readers on "in spite of the awful horror that one knows awaits one." Johnston wrote "in a manner that has justified critics in comparing [her] with Tolstoy, Hugo, and Sienkiewicz," proclaimed a Wilmington, Delaware, reviewer, "in the vigor, vividness, and terrible reality of her descriptions of war and its havoc, its destruction, its fearful sacrifice of human life, the devastation it spreads over the land, and the misery and woe it inflicts upon those who perforce must remain at home and suffer in silence and agonizing waiting." The reviewer for the *Minneapolis Journal* was similarly effusive, claiming that the novel, unlike any historical text, could "acquaint us . . . with the human tragedy of war." "Read *Cease Firing!*" the *Journal* urged, "the reading will make you better Americans."[89]

Although Johnston offered the most sustained early-twentieth-century commentary on the bleakness of the Civil War, others shared her vision. Mary Noailles Murfree, author of the 1884 novel *Where the Battle Was Fought*, returned to the Civil War as a catalyst for the action in her 1905 novel, *The Storm Centre*, and her 1912 collection of short stories, *The Raid of the Guerilla and Other Stories*. Unlike the earlier novel, in which the ghosts of the Civil War dead haunt the characters and the landscape, the characters and towns in these two later works are haunted by warfare itself.

Mimicking the postwar disarray that had crippled much of the South, Murfree described the unnamed, occupied Tennessee town in *The Storm Centre* as "an ever-shifting kaleidoscope of confused humanity," filled with Federal officers and their "wild" daughters, ragged freedmen, soldiers, hospital nurses—in short, everyone but the "old townsmen" who belonged there. For those non-combatants who remain—women, children, and old men—warfare makes little sense. The picket lines, driven by "some vague rumor of danger," continually move against the enemy, but "apparently in pursuance of no definite plan of aggression." These skirmishes "seemed a sort of game of tag—a grim game, for the loss of life in these futile maneuvers amounted to far more in the long run than the few casualties in each skirmish might indicate." Equally incomprehensible, however, are the "intervals of absolute inaction," at times lasting so long that the townspeople begin to question "why the two lines were there at all, with so vague a similitude of war." Although the war's efficacy and purpose remain unclear in the townspeople's minds, its destructive power is obvious. All could see the former home of the Roscoes, the family on which this novel centers, now reduced to a mass of "charred timbers" between two gaunt chimneys. "The scene was an epitome of desolation," Murfree explained, "despite the sunshine which indeed here was but a lonely splendor."[90]

The inhabitants of Tanglefoot Cove, "a feeble community of non-combatants" in Murfree's short story "The Raid of the Guerilla," fare no better than the confused residents of The Storm Centre. Although "the volunteering spirit" had swept through Tanglefoot Cove during the war's early days, the systematic decimation of its healthy male population in battle, coupled with the town's change of hands during the war, cripples its support for the Confederacy. When news comes that a Confederate raider plans to liberate Tanglefoot Cove, there is little celebration. Moreover, "there was no splendor of pageant in the raid of the guerilla into the Cove. . . . The dull thud of hoofs made itself felt as a continuous undertone to the clatter of stirrups and sabre." The raider's fate is no more distinguished once he reaches the town. "In lieu of the materialization of the stalwart ambition of distinction that had come to dominate his life," Murfree explained, "his destiny was chronicled in scarce a line of the printed details of a day freighted with the monstrous disaster of a great battle; in common with others of the 'missing' his bones were picked by the vultures till shoved into a trench, where a monument rises to-day to commemorate an event and not a commander."[91] His fate inextricably tied to the downfall of the Confederacy, the raider's plans remain unrealized, his courage unrewarded, his accomplishments uncelebrated.

In addition to chronicling the physical destruction caused by the war, Murfree echoed Johnston's sentiment that war destroys the sanity of those involved. In Murfree's short story "The Lost Guidon," published in the same collection as "The Raid of the Guerilla," a young soldier suffers from dementia after witnessing the decimation of his comrades in battle. Casper "had no physical hurt that might appeal to the professional sympathies of the senior surgeon," Murfree wrote. After Casper is found wandering among the dead, trying to rally them for action, the surgeon laughingly dismisses the soldier, exclaiming, "He can't rally Dovinger's Rangers this side of the river Styx." Casper leaves the war still obsessed with his fallen comrades and the guidon he has lost on the field. "Change ran riot in the ordering of the world," according to Murfree, "and its aspect was utterly transformed when Casper Girard, no longer bearing the guidon of Dovinger's Rangers, came out of the war." Years later, his returned battle flag in hand, Casper cries out, "I'll rally on the reserves," condemned to live in the past, his mind forever shattered by the war.[92]

That Johnston and Murfree could write such grim stories of the Civil War while maintaining their decidedly southern perspective demonstrates the malleability of the southern narrative of the Civil War. To be sure, Johnston and to a lesser extent Murfree celebrated the South's role in America's history, championed the South's distinct civilization, and professed the South's right to secede. In this respect, neither author broke with the past. But these women also did not glorify the Civil War: the war brought only destruction, and a Confederate triumph would in no way have mitigated the devastation of the southern landscape. No matter how compelling postwar white southerners found the Confederacy's claim to independence, no matter how seductive the idea of secession, the war qua war had been a disaster for the South. And while some readers cringed at Johnston's and Murfree's interpretations of the war, southerners bought and read these works, incorporating them into the southern metanarrative on the war.

The early-twentieth-century literary market proved very accommodating to southern women's war narratives. Although editors and agents expressed some concern about a seemingly saturated market, few ever refused to undertake a project for fear that one more southern women's tale would drive readers away, causing sales to plummet. Rather, publishers and authors recognized the public demand for these stories. Moreover, the UDC's largely successful campaign to tell the "true" history of the war fueled this demand for a southern story, and this southern story increasingly became a national story. Southern narratives received favorable reviews in national and northern journals and periodicals, suggesting that these tales had cultural resonance outside of the former Confederacy. Even U.S. President William Howard Taft endorsed the UDC's explications of the war and suggested that southern interpretations would gain greater national currency in ensuing years. By 1915, southern women felt secure in the knowledge that they had authored a culturally sanctioned representation of the past. Through their struggles to secure that authorship for themselves, southern women helped to fashion a new cultural identity for the postbellum South and increasingly the nation as a whole. By the debut of *Birth of a Nation* and, especially, the appearance of the book and film versions of *Gone with the Wind* in the late 1930s, the southern women's version had largely prevailed. And its triumph owed much to changing U.S. patterns of cultural production and dissemination, most notably the advent of radio and film. Ironically, as the audience for these narratives increased in size and social and cultural diversity, southern women's distinct interpretation of the war attained growing "official" cultural hegemony.

We are justly proud of our boys who went forth [to the European field] with as chivalrous spirits as any knight of old, to fight and suffer and die, if need be, that small countries as well as great might exercise their right to control themselves without interference from without. That men and women everywhere might stand forth free to keep their homes inviolate. Might pursue their daily occupations unafraid and happy. Our boys went gladly and promptly, because they had drawn in the whole idea of States' rights with their mothers' milk, had listened all their lives to talk of how their sires and grandsires had fought and suffered and died for the selfsame principle, which beckoned them on to service now.

—LIZZIE GEORGE HENDERSON, *Report to the United Daughters of the Confederacy*

War is dirty business and I do not like dirt. I am not a soldier and I have no desire to seek the bubble reputation even in the cannon's mouth. Yet, here I am at the wars—whom God never intended to be other than a studious country gentleman. For, Melanie, bugles do not stir my blood nor drums entice my feet and I see too clearly that we have been betrayed, betrayed by our arrogant Southern selves, believing that one of us could whip a dozen Yankees, believing that King Cotton could rule the world. Betrayed, too, by words and catch phrases, prejudices and hatreds coming from the mouths of those highly placed, those men whom we respected and revered— "King Cotton, Slavery, States' Rights, Damn Yankees."

—MARGARET MITCHELL, Gone with the Wind

Moderns Confront the Civil War, 1916–1936

In the late summer of 1934, Helen Dortch Longstreet received word that Charles Scribner's Sons would soon publish a biography of General Robert E. Lee. General James Longstreet's widow dashed off a letter to Scribner's, noting her pleasure at its latest literary venture. She also observed that Scribner's decision to publish what would be Douglas Southall Freeman's Pulitzer Prize–winning biography of Lee confirmed her conclusion that "the World War caused a great revival of interest in the military leaders of our American Civil War." Because her late husband's "republican politics brought him under the ban of the south during the reconstruction period," she explained, "less has been written of him than any other Corps Commander on either side of the civil war." Helen Dortch Longstreet believed, however, that Americans' participation in the Spanish-American War and World War I had abated those sectional tensions. "The new generations are ready to receive the truth of history and to honor both Union and

Confederate leaders as Americans who fought with American skill and courage," she proclaimed. In this new spirit of Americanism, she encouraged Scribner's to publish her story of General Longstreet, tentatively titled *Longstreet, the Gallant Southron*. If Scribner's found that title unsuitable, perhaps it would consider *In the Path of Lee's Old War Horse*. Helen Longstreet eagerly awaited word from Scribner's.[1]

Two weeks later, Longstreet received a short note from Scribner's, which was declining to publish her manuscript. "The biography of Robert E. Lee, which we are publishing this year, is a very comprehensive work in four volumes," explained an agent for the publisher, "and we hope it will take its place, not only as the definitive life of Lee, but incidentally in a way the final history of the Civil War." Because Scribner's planned to devote considerable time, energy, and expense to Freeman's biography of Lee, the agent continued, "we do not feel that we can confidently issue another life of a Civil War leader at the same time."[2] Despite the agent's explanation, Scribner's probably worried less about saturating the market with Civil War narratives than about the commercial viability of Longstreet's story. Indeed, Helen Longstreet's assertion that the nation's recent experience with World War I encouraged retelling of the Civil War proved true. And Scribner's certainly did not restrict its Civil War catalog to Freeman's biography of Lee. The same year that *R. E. Lee* appeared, for example, Scribner's also published Stark Young's wonderfully successful Civil War novel, *So Red the Rose*, and three years later the firm published Caroline Gordon's *None Shall Look Back*. Scribner's probably recognized that Longstreet's decidedly "old-fashioned" narrative did not conform to the prevailing literary trends of the 1930s.

Drafts of "The Gallant Southron" and "In the Path of Lee's Old War Horse" suggest that little had changed in Longstreet's conception of war or her late husband since she had published her 1904 biography of the general. As evident from her correspondence with Scribner's, she did recognize the ways in which World War I had bolstered Americans' interest in the Civil War. "To this generation," she prefaced a draft of "The Gallant Southron," "the story of the deeds of either side has the same wide human appeal. We are proud of these great leaders as Americans who fought with American skill and American courage." But the language she used to describe James Longstreet, Civil War battles, and the Confederacy echoes that of *Lee and Longstreet at High Tide*: "Across the pages of deathless history," she wrote, "the Confederate victory at the Second Manassas, is limned as a brilliant prelude to the bloodiest day of the War between the States, Antietam." For Helen Dortch Longstreet, Antietam's significance rested not with its carnage but with Lee's bestowal of the accolade "my Old War Horse" on General Longstreet. "To Longstreet that touching greeting made up for any slight that was put on his judgment" when Lee dispatched Stonewall Jackson to Harper's Ferry despite Longstreet's objections. Ever eager to champion her husband's reputation as a brilliant tactician, Helen Longstreet noted that Lee "must have realized that Longstreet was right" by the time of Antietam and that Lee also had come to recognize that Longstreet "had been right in advising retreat across the Potomac without battle, instead of making the stand at Sharpsburg."[3] As with her earlier publication, Helen Longstreet saw her "biographies" as a vehicle for advancing her husband's reputation.

Freeman agreed with Helen Longstreet on at least one point. He, too, believed that World War I had fostered renewed interest in the American Civil War. Explaining the reasons for the length of his 1934 biography of Lee, Freeman noted, "Had not the world war demonstrated the importance of the careful study of the campaigns of great strategists, I should feel disposed to apologize for such an elaborate presentation." But because G. F. R. Henderson's 1900 biography of Stonewall Jackson had influenced British strategy during the Great War, Freeman had cause to believe that "the professional soldier who will follow, step by step, the unfolding of Lee's strategic plans will, I think, learn much and perhaps equally from the leader of the Army of Northern Virginia." But unlike Helen Dortch Longstreet, for whom World War I had not tempered a romantic vision of war, Freeman had become increasingly horrified at the carnage. "For more than twenty years the study of military history has been my chief avocation," he explained. "Whether the operations have been those of 1914–1918, on which I happened to be a daily commentator, or those of the conflict between the states, each new inquiry has made the monstrous horror of war more unintelligible to me." Reminiscent of Mary Johnston rather than Helen Longstreet, Freeman continued, "It has seemed incredible to me that human beings, endowed with any of the powers of reason, should hypnotize themselves with doctrines of 'national honor' or 'sacred right' and pursue mass murder to exhaustion or ruin." As a caveat to his readers, Freeman warned, "If, in this opinion, I have let my abhorrence of war appear in my description of Malvern Hill after the battle, and in a few indignant adjectives elsewhere, I trust the reader will understand that in these instances I have momentarily stepped back on the stage only because I am not willing to have this study of a man who loved peace interpreted as glorification of war."[4] Both Helen Longstreet and Freeman wrote during the high tide of American isolationism, but that cultural impulse influenced them differently. Longstreet continued to glorify her late husband and the Confederacy; Freeman, however, came to view war — any war — as a national tragedy. Much of the literature of the period between World War I and World War II reflects this tension.

The literary record of the interwar period suggests that white southern women offered a new perspective on the Civil War. The recent experience with World War I gave a new impetus to southerners' preoccupation with reconstructing the memory of the Civil War for themselves and for the entire nation. The papers of the United Daughters of the Confederacy (UDC), for example, reflect the intersection of southerners' interest in both the Civil War and World War I. During the war, UDC members worked tirelessly for the Red Cross, sewing and mending clothes, fashioning bandages and other medical supplies, and raising war bonds to aid American men stationed overseas. This wartime work in many ways emulated that of Confederate women during the Civil War, and the Daughters made that connection clear in their official records and private correspondence. Moreover, World War I continued to influence the UDC's work in the immediate postwar years. Southern veterans of World War I, for example, sponsored essay contests for the UDC, offering cash prizes to the Daughter who penned the best narrative on southern support for the Allied war effort. Throughout the 1920s and 1930s, then, the UDC contemplated the meaning and legacy of the Civil War through the prism of America's experience in World War I.

Southern white women continued to write for a national audience during the interwar period. Their renewed focus on Civil War battles, military leaders, and Confederate statesmen reflected in part the Great War's influence in shaping Civil War narratives. Although some southern women continued to publish personal accounts — for example, La Salle Corbell Pickett released *What Happened to Me* in 1917 — others returned to the battlefield or the halls of the Confederate congress as the field of action. To be sure, demographics influenced subject matter — the number of southern women who lived through the Civil War and who penned their personal narratives declined through the 1920s and 1930s. But southern women published general accounts of Confederate women less frequently than works on Confederate soldiers and statesmen, suggesting that a certain fascination with World War I directed, at least to some extent, the ways in which southern women told their tales of the Civil War.

White southern novelists also grappled with the meaning and legacy of the Civil War in light of recent experiences in World War I. Evelyn Scott's *The Wave* (1929) and Margaret Mitchell's *Gone with the Wind* (1936) represent white southern women's diverse fictional accounts of the Civil War written during the inter-war period. Scott's panoramic novel attempts to tell a national story of the war, detailing the ways in which fictional and historical characters deal with the un-controllable forces wrought by the Civil War. Although *The Wave* received gen-erally favorable reviews from national magazines, Mitchell's *Gone with the Wind* eclipsed Scott's novel in popularity and sales, setting the mark for those tales of the Civil War that followed.

The Eyes of the World Are upon Us

The UDC endeavored mightily to demonstrate that it was a patriotic organi-zation, loyal to the U.S. government during the Great War. When President Woodrow Wilson proclaimed America's official neutrality in the war, the UDC scrambled to support the policy. By 1916 the UDC had established a Peace Com-mittee, designed above all to promote American neutrality. Mrs. Dunbar Row-land, chairman of the committee, admitted that her work was difficult. "I am confronted by a paradoxical situation," she reported to the UDC national con-vention, "in as much as we have won, during the past year, one of the most mag-nificent victories that has ever marked the annals of any civilization—that of maintaining peace for America at a time of universal war—and at the same time have witnessed one of the profoundest manifestations of the spirit of militarism that has stirred the American people for decades." There were times, Rowland confessed, when she thought that "our stainless white flag would go down in defeat before the red ensign of war." But the cause of peace prevailed and, to demonstrate its thanks to President Wilson for keeping the United States out of war, the UDC sent "numerous telegrams and messages" to the White House, testifying "how nobly we upheld his hands in the greatest test to which our civili-zation has ever been subjected." The organization's actions may seem odd, given all of the ink spilled and energy spent glorifying the Confederate cause in the Civil War. The women of the UDC had certainly not previously shied away from militarism. The UDC's loyalty to Wilson may have stemmed from two sources. First, as President William Howard Taft intimated to the Daughters when he addressed their 1912 national convention, the presence of a southern Democrat in the White House might prove beneficial to their agenda, and Wilson's efforts to segregate Washington, D.C., certainly bore out Taft's assumption. The UDC, therefore, had reason to believe that it had a friend in the White House and was therefore willing to support the president's policies. As Birdie A. Owen, president of the group's Tennessee Division, stated, "The greatest glory that the South can claim is the giving to the world of Woodrow Wilson. . . . He is the South's."[5] Second, the UDC's pacifist stand might have shored up its claim that southerners were peace-loving people who resorted to war only when provoked. In other words, the organization's dedication to peace during the initial years of the Great War might have supported its claims about the South during the crisis that preceded the Civil War.

President Wilson's request for a congressional declaration of war caused the UDC to alter its pacifist position. "Immediately following the declaration of hostilities by President Wilson," UDC President-General Cordelia Powell Odenheimer explained to members meeting at the 1917 national convention, "I offered him the services of our members in what ever capacity they might be available. This action on my part was given wide publicity by the Associated Press, and individuals, chapters, and divisions proceeded to demonstrate their patriotism by efforts which have not been surpassed by any other organization," she further noted. "Without sacrificing a single principle for which we have contended since our organization . . . became a National patriotic society," she concluded, the UDC had "enthusiastically responded to the country's call, with results in which we may well take pride." The Mississippi Division agreed. One month after Congress declared war, the Mississippi Division passed a resolution stating,

Whereas the United States government is at war with a foreign foe and needs the united efforts of all citizens in every part of every State, and the United Daughters of the Confederacy, of which the Mississippi Division is a component part, feels proud of its descent from patriots, men and women who gave all they had for the blessed privilege of being governed only by their own consent, the great States' right principle of our government; and whereas these United States have entered this great world war that the peoples of the earth may enjoy the privilege of being governed by their own consent, thus making the world safe for democracy; and whereas we believe it right and just that President Woodrow Wilson should be assured that he has the whole of every part of this country back of him in these days of stress and trial; therefore be it resolved that the Mississippi Division, U.D.C., in convention assembled, wishes to go on record as approving the course its country has pursued in staying out of the struggle as long as it consistently could and preserve its ideals of peace and democracy and then enters only to preserve those ideals and rights which our "fathers fought for."[6]

The Mississippi Division apparently saw the Confederacy's fight for states' rights as compatible with U.S. efforts "to make the world safe for democracy," thus allowing Daughters of the Confederacy to be loyal to both causes.

Odenheimer and other UDC officers used *Confederate Veteran* to direct Daughters on useful war work. "Chapters, and Divisions, can participate, as they may desire," Odenheimer suggested in May 1917, "in the work inaugurated by the Red Cross, the Council of Women, and the Women's Section of the Navy League, and others." Furthermore, she stated that "the patriotism of the South is second to that of no other section of the country." Mrs. J. Norment Powell, registrar-general of the UDC, called for members to register for wartime service as stenographers and nurses. She recognized that not all women were able to leave their homes and serve U.S. war efforts but pointed out that other avenues for participating existed: "Southern women face an opportunity for enormous usefulness," she offered. "With the South rests the duty of feeding the nation during this war, and the eyes of the world are upon us, expecting us to do our part. There should not be wasted one bean," she warned, "one tomato, or one particle of food. In no other way," she advised, "can our women be of better service than by increasing and conserving the food supply. The canning industry is of immense importance," she argued. "Bulletins giving the latest scientific knowledge on this subject can be obtained free of cost from the Department of Agriculture; and it is of utmost value to your country that you obtain this information and not only register a vow against any waste, but instruct the children in this industry." Odenheimer recommended that the Women's Committee of the Council of National Defense be given "all data in connection with the recent tabulation of woman power available for war service." In an unprecedented spirit of cooperation, Odenheimer cautioned Daughters "to subordinate the glory of their own group to the State."[7] Once again, Daughters found accord between the glorification the Confederacy and supporting centralization of a national war effort.

By 1918, the UDC listed "war relief work" among its "five great efforts to develop our Association to its full power and opportunity for usefulness." The UDC's Committee on War Relief drew up guidelines to be distributed to state divisions, assuring Daughters that "all your energies and sympathies in behalf of the youth of America who are giving up their all at their country's call will be directed, systematized, recorded as UDC work." State divisions seem to have complied willingly and enthusiastically with the guidelines. Mary Calvert Stribling, historian-general of the West Virginia Division, followed specific directions on the making of surgical dressings and patterns and counted among her achievements the making of "two hundred irrigation pads in one week." The Georgia Division proudly reported that it had "measured up to the tremendous demands of the awful war struggle" and noted that it was "our privilege to honor and preserve the memory of our heroic past while we gave magnificently of time, talent and money to the war calls of our heroic President." The division then tabulated the number of articles knitted and surgical dressings made for the Red Cross, liberty bonds and war savings stamps bought, items donated to French and Belgian orphans, and hospital beds endowed. The Virginia Division recorded that in 1918 "the relief work accomplished is unprecedented and seems to suffer no decrease, even though the Red Cross work occupies all hearts and hands. A bed for tuberculosis patients will be supported at the Catawber Sanatar Sanitarium ... and money has been given for the brass plates for the bed ... at the American military hospital in France." The Arkansas Division noted that its Confederate Council would "take charge of the registration of the soldiers who are descendants of Confederate Veterans."[8]

Of course, the war did not necessitate a suspension of the UDC's regular work. Indeed, Daughters felt increasingly compelled to carry out their mission as time continued to distance them from the Civil War. As Louise Ayer Vandiver, president of the South Carolina Division, noted in her report on the 1917 state convention, "the objects for which the UDC was organized were by no means forgotten nor overlooked." The study of proper Confederate history seemed especially important as the ranks in the war generation rapidly dwindled. Historian-General Anne Bachman Hyde expressed surprised pleasure that the historical work of the UDC continued despite the exigencies of the Great War. "Amid the clash of arms art is neglected and literature suffers," she exclaimed. "When history is being rapidly made historical chronicles languish and the fingers deftly rolling Red Cross bandages cannot readily grasp the pen." Nevertheless, the UDC had accomplished a great deal of "historical work" during a year of "sorrow, turmoil, and unrest." Hyde continued to use the pages of Confederate Veteran to advise divisions and chapters on topics for historical programs. In addition to working for war relief, Daughters were to study General Patrick Ronayne Cleburne, the "Stonewall of the West"; Jefferson Davis; and General Winfield Scott Featherston, "Old Swet." Moreover, Daughters were to aid aging Confederate veterans, care for needy Confederate women, sponsor essay contests and scholarships for worthy descendants of loyal Confederates, provide direction for the future generation by directing the Children of the Confederacy, and maintain various committees.[9]

The Great War influenced the UDC's regular work in many ways. In addition to the to the usual prizes awarded by the organization, such as the Mildred Rutherford Medal "for the best historical work done by small Divisions numbering less than ten chapters," the UDC began offering the Soldier's Prize, which recognized the best essay written by a Daughter on southern-born staff officers in the world war. It also awarded the Youree Prize to the division that filed the largest number of world war records. The World War Record Committee endeavored to record "every lineal descendant of a Confederate Veteran who served in the World War." Mrs. J. A. Rountree, chairwoman of the committee, noted that "there is a lofty inspiration derived from work connected with records of Confederate Veterans — our gray-clad heroes — which, when linked with our own personal experiences of the sacrifices made for patriotism, high ideals and true democracy by the heroes of the World War, bring to us a full realization of what our work really means — the compiling of records of two generations of soldiers — the bravest heroes the world has ever known." Mrs. John W. Goodwin explained that this work convinced Daughters that the Great War "was not a war against a nation but a struggle for the supremacy of right. It was," therefore, "a war for the establishment in all the world of those principles upon which our government was founded by our forebears." As an outgrowth of the War Records Committee, the Hero Scholarship was established to aid World War I veterans who were descended from Confederate soldiers.[10]

The Great War also influenced the Textbook and Education Committees, which continued to advocate works that offered a particularly southern interpretation of the Civil War. The Committee of Southern Literature and Endorsement of Books found it particularly unfortunate that, during a time of national unity, some accounts still perpetrated "slanderous allusions to our great heroes." Mrs. Alexander White warned southerners against being seduced by rhetoric of national unity and harmony: "The South is still a 'section' to the rest of country," she argued, "despite its work in the World War. Things said and written during the World War and comparisons made detrimental to the South show we are still drifting and are letting errors stand unchallenged as truth." She suggested that Daughters renew their interest in southern and Confederate history as a means of combating the complacent attitude with which Daughters had been accepting unfavorable accounts.[11]

The UDC had long bestowed the Cross of Honor on Confederate veterans. Beginning in the 1920s, the group offered similar medals to veterans of the Great War "as a testimonial to the patriotic devotion and loyalty" of the lineal descendants of Confederate soldiers and sailors. This latest project seemed a logical outgrowth of the group's memorial work, hardly worthy of controversy. A delegate to the 1923 convention, however, inquired about whether "descendants" could include women as well as men who were honorably discharged, stating, "Nurses served in France and were exposed to the same dangers as the men"; therefore, "the crosses should not be denied them." A Georgia delegate opposed awarding the Cross of Honor to women, interjecting that "women of the Sixties did noble work and the Confederate women were not asking for Crosses of Honor." Rountree, chairwoman of the Insignia Committee, then moved to add the modifier "male" to describe "descendants." The motion carried, but it did not end discussion of the matter. The minutes of the 1924 meeting of the Executive Board of the UDC's Georgia Division, for example, demonstrate that the efforts to limit the Cross of Honor had yet to be settled. Mrs. W. D. Lamar, past president of the division, recommended the elimination of the word "male." The motion carried seventeen to five and was later referred to the state convention. The UDC ultimately refused to award the Cross of Honor to women, regardless of their service in the Great War or their Confederate lineage, thus further shoring up the organization's reputation for conservatism.[12]

World War I surely influenced the ways in which the UDC compiled its historical work. The Georgia State Historical Program for 1920, for example, included "Georgians in the World War" as one of its topics. Appropriate avenues of inquiry included "Woodrow Wilson and His Life in Georgia," and "War Relief Work in Your Chapter." During December, the program encouraged Georgia's Daughters to investigate "'Red Cross' work during the War between the States." Women's wartime work was now cast in terms understandable only in light of World War I. A Georgia daughter, asked to write a history of "Women of the South in War Times," proclaimed her enthusiasm, noting that as a woman, she found "great pleasure in telling of some of the wonderful deeds that have been done by the women of the sixties, and by their daughters in the great World War of 1914." She argued that her investigation should not be limited to the War between the States because, although conditions differed, "and our fair land was not molested by invading troops" in World War I, "still the women bravely sent their sons and husbands across the seas, into the trenches, and 'kept their home fires burning,' as they bowed in submission to God's will."[13]

The state reports included in national convention minutes and in *Confederate Veteran* testify to the continued importance the UDC accorded the writing of "proper" histories of the Civil War as well as the stressing of the South's

contribution to the Great War. Moreover, Daughters came to view each conflict through the prism of the other. Confederate women's wartime work undoubtedly inspired those southern women who worked for the Red Cross during World War I. In turn, white southern women began to regard all women's
wartime work as "Red Cross" work. Daughters interpreted World War I as a vindication of the Confederate cause. As drawn by the deft pens of the UDC, World
War I centered on states' rights. Finally, World War I renewed interest in the
Civil War, encouraging UDC members to study diligently and write unceasingly,
thereby fulfilling the organization's original goals.

A Cross of Political Expedience

The sense of nationalism and sectional reconciliation that had marked Civil War
historiography at the turn of the century continued to guide writings regarding
the war throughout the 1920s, and this trend influenced the work of amateur
historians. For example, Fannie Eoline Selph's 1928 book, *The South in American
Life and History*, published under the auspices of the UDC, stressed the South's
"part in building up our great nation, the United States of America." Selph traced
the history of national development through the lens of southern history, always
highlighting the region's contribution and continued loyalty to the vision of the
Founding Fathers. Selph unabashedly defended the institution of slavery, which
she contended was misnamed: "The relation of master and slave in the South
held so much beneficence, so much responsive affection with wholesome results," she argued, "that the term slave was a misnomer." She also defended the
actions of the fire-eaters, who advocated secession when it became clear that the
provisions of the Compromise of 1850 were no longer tenable. But her defense
stemmed from a belief that these men acted out of a sense of loyalty to the intent
of the Constitution. "These men," she wrote, were of "solid character, of education, refinement, and [were] well-versed in government." More to the point,
"their object was not to tear down, but to build up with greater permanence and
security." Although Selph was clearly a partisan of the South, she nevertheless
sought to ground her study in the South's contribution to the nation.[14]

The publication of Twelve Southerners' *I'll Take My Stand* in 1930, however,
signaled a shift in the historiography of the war. The Agrarians' spirited defense
of the "southern way of life" reflected the arguments of white southerners who
penned histories of the "irrepressible conflict" during the 1930s. Historiographers of the Civil War C. E. Cauthen and Lewis P. Jones note that "between 1900

and 1930, historians had generally been credited with objectivity." Of course, objectivity did not guarantee an absence of debate, but criticisms "were usually in good spirit." The debates of the 1930s became much more vitriolic, however, and "historians sometimes became so acrimonious as to engage in name-calling." The defensive posture of the Agrarians and others of their ilk certainly suggested the ways in which many white southerners understood and wrote about the war. Interpretations of the Civil War obviously reflected changes in the intellectual climate and thus, as David Potter demonstrates, the literature of the 1930s reflected "the impact of Marxist thought, the post-Versailles disillusionment with war in general, the declining influence of moral and legal absolutes, and the changing emphasis upon economic determinism."[15] In addition, however, conservative white southerners who were dissatisfied with federalist approach of the New Deal turned to an idealized version of the history of the Old South and the "lessons" of the Civil War to vent their frustrations.

Helen Dortch Longstreet, clearly struggling under the weight of the Great Depression, hoped to capitalize on the growing interest in the Civil War during the interwar years by writing, almost unceasingly, stories of her late husband and his exploits. "Recent days witness a great revival of interest in our American Civil War," she explained to the editor of the Washington (D.C.) Star. "This inspires me to offer a series of humanly interesting war stories. . . . I can supply an almost endless chain of stories," she offered, "which illustrate the romance and humor of the war." She sent similar letters to other publications. On the same day that she wrote to the Star, she also wrote to the editor of the Washington (D.C.) Herald, confessing that "ever since the country went off the gold standard the depression has been growing ever hard and harder for me to bear up under." Her "brilliant" solution to her poverty included "selling the Herald an endless chain of humanly interesting war stories." Displaying a remarkable degree of candor, Longstreet admitted, "I am selling them to the highest bidder. Let me know your offer quick. I would rather have the Herald print them because it has more readers." Longstreet evidently took no chances, also sending letters of inquiry to the Washington (D.C.) Post and Liberty magazine.[16]

Longstreet met with some degree of success. Her coverage of the celebration of the seventy-fifth anniversary of the Battle of Antietam proved especially popular. Once again, she promoted her connection to General Longstreet and claimed that she would be better able than anyone else to tell the story. "Being the only surviving widow of a Corps Commander on either side of the war between the States," she informed the editor of the Burlington (Vermont) Free Press, "I feel

Helen Dortch Longstreet at the seventy-fifth anniversary of the Battle of Gettysburg, 1938. (Courtesy Atlanta History Center)

sure that my story will be of historic value and picturesque interest to Americans." On this occasion, she credited increased interest in the Civil War not to World War I but to President Franklin D. Roosevelt's attack on the southern politicians who had refused to support his New Deal programs. Once a Roosevelt supporter, Helen Longstreet had broken with the president after his court-packing scheme, forming Defenders of the Republic, an anti-Roosevelt organization. "In this strange day when southern statesmen are crucifying on a cross of political expedience, the imperishable principle of States' Rights so gloriously upheld at Antietam by Lee's ragged, hungry army of 40,000 against McClellan's well-fed, splendidly equipped 90,000," should prove especially compelling, according to Longstreet. Whether editors were motivated by political considerations or by Helen Longstreet's connection to the late commander, her coverage of the celebration was syndicated in scores of publications, including the *New York Times*.[17]

Helen Dortch Longstreet met with less success when trying to peddle her full-length history of the Civil War. She collaborated with Sears W. Cabell on "Glory's Bivouac on High Fields," a manuscript of some eighty-six thousand words. The introduction to the manuscript suggests that Longstreet's conception of the Civil War had changed little since she published *Lee and Longstreet at High Tide*, noting, "The battle that raged on the field of Antietam, on a September day, seventy-five years ago lives again in the vivid picture drawn by Helen Dortch Longstreet." The introduction pointed out that Helen was "not yet born when the gray line of the Confederate army put up its unequaled fight against McClellan's force of double size," but in her years with the general "her husband's memories became her memories, and to her own life-time she has added his life-time, carrying it on through the present and doubtless projecting it into years to come." She had written herself into her husband's past, with all the romance and sentimentality that had characterized her writing.[18]

The manuscript displays the same lack of attention to organization that undermined *Lee and Longstreet at High Tide*. In a note to Cabell appended to the finished manuscript, Longstreet confessed, "I have no idea about the preferable arrangement of chapters," although she did at least intuit that "the descriptions of battles should be according to dates on which fought." "The dedication comes first, of course," she added. The bulk of the text consisted of pieces Longstreet had cobbled together from previous writings. She wrote the last chapter, "Bugles Are Calling," for this particular project, however, and used it to emphasize her hatred of the Roosevelt administration. She seems to have abandoned her fascination with World War I's influence on Civil War narratives and instead to have focused on implicating the "menace of totalitarianism . . . at America's gates." In a specific indictment leveled against Roosevelt, Longstreet wrote, "Under a lash, wielded from the seat of economic and political power, descendants of men who followed the banners of Lee, are piloting States' Rights to the guillotine!"

In red ink, designed to stand out from the rest of the text, Longstreet begged, "Father, we implore, save us from the infamy of slaughtering self-government, a people whose forbears fought, falling and starving, through four terrible years, for the stars and bars!" As she noted at the end of the chapter, the paragraphs in red ink needed to remain distinct from the rest of the text "to bring out the meaning more startlingly. This chapter," she wrote, "is the excuse of the book and gives it its whole value and meaning!" Longstreet thus hoped to use her narrative of the Civil War to warn Americans of the dangers of Roosevelt rule. "If the phool [*sic*] publishers don't publish it," she exclaimed in a fit of histrionics, "I'm gonna commit suicide . . . drown my fair head under the briny waves of the Atlantic."[19]

America's participation in the World War I engendered certain tensions that strained various segments of American culture and society: agricultural depression, increasing industrialization of the South, and the role of the federal government in "local concerns." As Thomas J. Pressly notes, these strains compromised the spirit of reconciliation and nationalism that had guided an earlier generation of Civil War historians. "Under the pressure of these tensions," Pressly explains, "some Southerners came to consider their problems in terms of the South *versus* the nation."[20] For Helen Longstreet, the expansion of the federal government under the Roosevelt administration proved especially troublesome. She believed that as a white southerner, she best understood the threats posed by an "aggressive" federal government. She used her "history" of the Civil War as a vehicle for reminding readers that the threat to "local rule" was by no means stifled at Appomattox. For Longstreet and many other white southerners, the 1930s resembled the 1850s. The South had to gear itself for battle once more, Longstreet warned, lest the region perish altogether.

We Will Take Up the Pen Again

Although the number of memoirs published by white southern women declined during the interwar years, a number of such works appeared on the literary market, sustaining the tradition begun by Confederate women generations earlier. Few women explicitly mentioned the Great War, but the recent U.S. overseas involvement unquestionably influenced their narratives. Indeed, the timing of their entry into the literary market had as much to do with World War I as with a need to tell a story of the Civil War. The fighting looms large in each of these memoirs, relegating a secondary place to nonmilitary events—extended commentary on antebellum life remained conspicuously absent from most of these narratives, for example. But time did not temper these women's enthusiasm for the Confederacy or professed support for the war effort. In that sense, American isolationism had failed to influence these memoirists.

In 1917, La Salle Corbell Pickett published *What Happened to Me*, an account that centers largely on her life with her late husband, General George E. Pickett. Like many earlier writers and as she had done in her previous writings, Sallie Pickett used her memoirs as a vehicle to shore up her husband's reputation among Confederate celebrants. "Only a few days before he had ridden from Gettysburg to Richmond," she wrote, "cheer after cheer following him along the way. Men, women, and children were at the road side to welcome him and hang garlands on his horse. He had been the central figure in a scene so supreme that it needed not victory to crown it with glory," she concluded. To ensure that her history was entwined with the general's, Sallie claimed that the single most important moment in her life had been when, as a young girl, she first saw George Pickett: "Everyone has a point of beginning—a period back of which life, to present consciousness, was not. For me, this point stands out vividly in memory." Her description of that first encounter with Pickett strongly resembles Mary Anna Jackson's and Helen Dortch Longstreet's accounts of their first meetings with their future husbands. "He did not look as tall as the men in my family," Pickett noted, "but he carried himself so erectly and walked with such soldierly dignity that I was sure that any 'Good Prince' might have envied his appearance."[21] For all three women, life began with their first encounters with their military men.

La Salle Pickett later recalled meeting Colonel Robert E. Lee, just back from putting down John Brown's raid at Harpers Ferry. Lee's account of the event captivated the young girl: "To a child whose infancy had shuddered at the story of the Nat Turner insurrection," she noted, "the John Brown raid in 1859 was a subject of horrible fascination, and I listened intently as Col. Lee talked of this strange old fanatic and his followers." Neither Sallie nor Lee apparently understood at the time the importance of the raid. "The story of John Brown was graphically told and heard with absorbed attention but it is not likely that the Virginia planter, with all his knowledge and history and character, nor the great soldier with his military training, recognized the signs of the impending storm any more than did the wide-eyed child lost in breathless wonderment over the thrilling episode."[22] Although Pickett did not cast the story with a sense of foreboding that she did not experience in 1859, she did frame her memoirs with the incident, thus ensuring that *What Happened to Me* would be a story of the war.

According to Pickett, southerners quickly learned that the war of expectation and imagination did not match the war experienced by soldiers. After the Battle of Manassas, for example, Pickett noted, "We saw then only the bonfires of joy and heard only the paeans of victory." News of a friend's battle wound forced Pickett to reevaluate warfare, however: "When my friend, Maj. John W. Daniel, was brought to his home in Lynchburg with a wound received in that battle which we had celebrated with such triumphant delight, I began to feel that war meant something more than the thrill of martial music and the shouts of victory." She emphasized that sense of disconnect between reality and imagination when she later recalled that she and her fellow students at the Lynchburg Seminary "fancied that we knew something of war. We had cheered our flag, trembled for our soldiers at the front even while we prophetically gloried in their future triumph, and celebrated with great enthusiasm the battle of Manassas." They celebrated until a beau of one of the students was killed on the battlefield. "Now I was to learn something of what war meant," she lamented. Sallie Pickett certainly was not the first to recognize that reality failed to live up to an imagined war. Neither Pickett nor other southerners needed news from the battlefields of France to convince them that "courage's war" quickly lost to the war of combat.[23] They had already seen that transformation in the Civil War. But the Great War may well have influenced the ways in which Pickett told her story of the war. Rather than framing her narrative with the trope of the Lost Cause, Pickett instead told a story of a terrible war. The Confederate cause was glorious in Pickett's eyes, but battle was something else altogether.

Pickett's description of Richmond in the days following the Battle of Seven Pines, for example, both reflected the romantic language of earlier writers and signaled a way of telling about war that had been influenced by World War I. "Richmond was shaking with the thunders of battle," she remembered, "and the death-sounds thrilled through our agonized souls. The blood of the field was running in rivers of red through the hearts of her people. For days the dead-wagons and ambulances wended their tragic way from the battlefield to the Capital City, and every turn of their crunching wheels rolled over our crushed and bleeding hearts." Her attention to the blood-soaked battlefield and the mangled bodies of the dead and wounded may have suggested an interest in World War I as much as a desire to tell of the Civil War: "The wretched loads of wounded were emptied before the doors of the impoverished hospitals until they over-flowed with maimed humanity. . . . Wagons filled with dead rolled by, the stiff-ened bodies piled upon another in ghastly heaps, the rigid feet projecting from the ends of the vehicles. It was the most appalling sight that ever greeted human eyes." Indeed, battle seemed so terrible that she was willing to follow her hus-band's advice that they should "lay aside our war thoughts. After a while," he concluded, "we will take up the pen again and write down our memories."[24] Sallie Pickett waited until the turn of the twentieth century to lift her pen.

Rebecca Latimer Felton believed that "while we have Southern histories con-cerning the Civil War, compiled from data furnished by political and military leaders, the outside world really knows very little of how the people of Geor-gia lived in the long ago." And so, at the age of eighty-two, Felton published *Country Life in Georgia in the Days of My Youth* in 1919. In her memoirs, she maintained the position she had so often articulated in the decades following Reconstruction. According to Felton, ordinary southerners "were forced into a four-year bloody war to defend the institution of domestic slavery, and they lost their slaves, their real estate and personal property, lost their surplus money and lost their lives in many cases. Excepting those who retained their lands by self denial and self-sacrifice, this section was swept bare by war destruction." Felton snidely noted, "There was never a more loyal woman in the South after we were forced by our political leaders to go to battle to defend our rights in ownership of African slaves, but they called it 'State's Rights.' And all I owned was invested in slaves and my people were loyal and I stood by them to the end." Years of reflection on the issue, however, had forced Felton to conclude that "to fight for the perpetuation of domestic slavery was a mistake." Her position had little to do with "racial enlightenment," however. Rather, her conclusions sprung from a fear of a "race war," which she believed was inevitable. "Any reader of history will agree," she believed, "that the negro question is not half settled. Our fifty years of hard experience since the Civil War demonstrates one fact only," she believed. "The negro is in the United Sates to stay and according as he is dealt with, depends our own peace or disaster in his association with the whites."[25]

Felton proved her loyalty to the Confederate cause to her readers by chroni-cling the work she had performed during the war, a list that would have seemed familiar to those who had performed Red Cross work during World War I: "There was scarcely a week of war time that we did not feed soldiers going or coming. I knitted socks, gloves and sleeping caps continuously. We had wounded soldiers to stay with us, we carried food to trains, when wounded soldiers were being transported to points lower down. . . . We made a daily business of cooking and carrying baskets of good food to help them along. Some of the most tragic episodes of my life," she admitted, "happened in trying to relieve the distress of the time. It would take a larger book than this to set them down in detail." Felton's memoirs also included a chapter titled "Southern Women in the Civil War" that contained a synopsis of a 1900 address in which Felton listed valuable wartime services performed by Confederate women. Mindful of her audience, an Augusta, Georgia, UDC chapter, Felton had asserted that "upon nobody did the storm fall more dreadful and unexpectedly than upon the women of the South. . . . The women proceeded to send their blankets to the army and cut up their woolen carpets to help out the blanket proposition. We scraped lint from all the linen of worn towels and table cloths and stripped the sheets into bandages for the wounded in hospitals. We knitted socks and sleeping caps and mittens incessantly. We sent all the good things like jellies and preserves to the army."[26] Her account, refashioned and reprinted nearly twenty years after she had originally delivered it, would have resonated strongly with a generation of Americans that had sacrificed greatly during World War I.

Felton apparently did not use the recent U.S. experience in World War I to shape her memories of the Civil War; rather, she claimed that her memories of the earlier conflict had influenced the ways in which she thought about the Great War. The Confederate government's policy on conscription and exemptions, for example, compelled her to oppose the U.S. government's World War I conscription policy. "From what I then saw," Felton claimed, "I was strenuously opposed to conscription for Georgia boys in 1917. I had no objection to allowing volunteers to go to France or to serve in airplanes if they volunteered for such service," she clarified, "but I did my little best to convince Georgia readers that it would not do to force our soldiers into airships or to send them across the Atlantic ocean to dictate to foreign governments or fight for kings or queens or command the sorts of rulers they should have in the future." The Great War, then, might not have influenced how Felton told her story of the Civil War but might have influenced the timing her memoirs' publication. She prefaced her account by stating that she had originally intended to "allow my accumulated manuscripts to remain after my decease, when those who survive me might give them to [a] publisher if so desired."[27] But the spate of racial violence that occurred in 1917–19 convinced Felton that her version of the Civil War and its legacy was especially timely.

Susan Bradford Eppes, who published *Through Some Eventful Years* in 1926, when she was eighty, remained a bitter, unreconstructed southerner. Because Confederate defeat and Reconstruction were anathema to her, Eppes, more than Pickett and Felton, harked "back to the 1850s, which for her were an idyllic time." Eppes interspersed her memoirs of the antebellum South, the war, and Reconstruction with entries from a diary she allegedly had kept during the 1860s. Joseph D. Cushman, the editor of the most recent edition of her memoirs, points out, however, that the "diary that the author uses as a basis for her memoirs is in all probability a literary invention. There is no trace of the diary now."[28] Eppes's story of the war, then, was born out of twentieth-century realities.

Eppes saw *Through Some Eventful Years* as a companion to her 1925 publication, *The Negro of the Old South: A Bit of Period History*. "To those who have read 'the Negro of the Old South,' this book needs no introduction and no apology," she wrote in the introduction to her memoirs. In *The Negro of the Old South*, she offered a familiar defense of slavery as a benevolent institution maintained by kindly masters who rarely abused their power and oversaw contented slaves who were grateful for their removal from barbarism to civilization. "In spite of the John Brown episode, we felt every confidence in our dear black folks," Eppes argued predictably, "every faith in their affection for us, and never a doubt of their loyalty." She chose not to chronicle the history of the war in *The Negro of the Old South*, claiming that "everybody knows it," and moved on to a discussion of Reconstruction. White southerners had wanted peace, Eppes maintained, but carpetbaggers had had an alternative plan: "They appealed to race prejudice — they preached not only political, but social equality — they preached miscegenation — they preached and drew pictures of a day when no line would be drawn between the white and the black — and just here and on these unprincipled adventures — rests the blame for the crime of LYNCHING — the horrible — awful — unspeakable — outrage! punished swiftly and surely — in almost every instance, by the rope — was never known in the South until these apostles of negro equality put it in the minds of the newly made citizens."[29] A year later, when Eppes wrote *Through Some Eventful Years*, she no longer thought that the story of the war need not be told.

Eppes's "diary entries" advanced arguments familiar to most white southerners. The North, she asserted in an entry dated 11 June 1861, brought war to the peace-loving South. "We wanted peace but war was forced upon us and now that it has begun we will do our best to win," she wrote. Sensing that a profound shift in the direction of the war was about to occur, Eppes confided to her diary on 17 June 1863, "We seem to be upon the brink of a change some way. The army of Northern Virginia is on the move and we can only pray and work, for it grows more difficult with every passing day to provide the barest necessities for our brave boys at the front. Never did men fight under greater disadvantages." Eleven days later, Eppes recorded that as Lee's army pushed northward, "a curious species of fault finders has developed. While the men, the true men, are at the front, struggling with might . . . to save the South from destruction, there are others, poor weak-kneed cowards, who stand on street corners and criticize . . . the generals in command of our armies. These cowardly back-biters have never smelled gun powder," she contemptuously noted, "they are Carpet Generals and yet, to listen to them talk, you would think the only thing needed to insure victory would be to put them in command." Eppes's understanding of the Confederacy's loss at Gettysburg meshed with prevalent interpretations and confirmed Helen Dortch Longstreet's suspicions that southerners were taught spurious history. "The Battle of Gettysburg, which should have been a complete victory for the Confederates," Eppes asserted, "was lost by *a mistake*. We do not criticize, we have no unkind words to say," she feigned, "nevertheless, from that day the Confederacy, slowly but surely, lost ground. Such a magnificent display of courage and endurance was never before witnessed — such slaughter was sinful."[30] Eppes's recollections of the war's origins, the Confederacy's political positions, and the war's pivotal battles suggest, then, that her "diary" told a familiar story in a familiar way.

Eppes's telling of Confederacy's downfall resonated with the southern white postwar reading audience. She continued the practice of glorifying Confederate women's devotion to the cause. "The hours passed slowly in this Garden of Gethsemane," she wrote of the final days of the Confederacy, "and in those hours the Southern woman, throughout the poor conquered South, realized her *duty*; sacrificing *self* upon the altar of *love* and, putting shoulder to the wheel, she made ready to help her men." Although the men were "crushed and conquered" and could look forward only to "want and poverty," white southern women, Eppes insisted, ensured that their men had not lost their honor. Similarly, Eppes's description of the "dark days" of Reconstruction conformed to prevailing opinions of the period. Echoing what she had written in *The Negro of the Old South*, Eppes maintained in her second publication that "Negro rights" had brought a great abomination to the South. "Crimes, too vile for words[,] became of frequent occurrence," she asserted. Whites had to protect themselves against those "unspeakable crimes." "Guns and pistols were kept loaded and ready; yes, women and children, the larger ones, were taught to use these weapons for their personal protection." Eppes believed that other "horrors" besieged the South. The Reconstruction amendments were passed, and carpetbaggers infiltrated the former Confederacy, "sowing the seeds of hate and discord between white and black." The "nefarious" alliance between free blacks and carpetbaggers, according to Eppes, gave rise to the Ku Klux Klan, the redeemer of the South.[31] Redemption, however, had not restored the South to its former glory. The graciousness and refined culture of the 1850s were gone forever.

Pickett, Felton, and Eppes believed that, despite the recent glut in the market for Civil War stories, their tales needed to be heard. Some, like Pickett, still sought to set the record straight. Others, like Eppes, merely sought to use their narratives to confirm popular accounts of the war. All of these women recognized that the Confederate widow was a dying breed. There soon would be no more white southern women who could provide firsthand accounts of the war. These writers wanted to be sure that their accounts reached postwar reading audiences. And although only Felton alluded to the Great War and its aftermath, it surely influenced both Pickett and Eppes as well. Eppes's comments on racial violence and the birth of the Klan, for example, said as much about the South of the 1920s as about the South of the 1860s.[32] But these women did not follow the country's isolationist temper of the 1920s, instead concerning themselves with war and the telling of its story.

War Is the Only Hero of the Book

The nation's experiences with World War I, coupled with the South's confrontation with modernism, compelled many white southern novelists to look at the Civil War in new ways. Tennessee author Evelyn Scott, who had established her literary reputation in the early 1920s, offered her version of the Civil War in 1929 with the publication of The Wave. As Peggy Bach notes, Scott disagreed with southerners' "romantic view of the South, a view over-influenced by either a 'before the war' or 'after the war' time sense." Moreover, she believed that most white southern authors reviewing the past not only mourned a South destroyed by the war but also imagined a South that had never existed. Unlike the other authors examined in this book, Scott did not confine her treatment of the war to an exegesis on the South. Rather, she treated the political, economic, religious, and social problems wrought by the war "as universal dilemmas and used them as foundations for her novels."[33]

Scott took her title concept from a passage from *Physical Geography* by Philip Lake. "The water of the ocean is never still," she quoted in the preface to the novel. "It is blown into waves by the wind, it rises and falls with the tides. . . . The waves travel in some definite direction, but a cork thrown into the water does not travel with the waves. It moves up and down, to and fro, but unless it is blown by the wind or carried by a current it returns to the same position with each wave and does not permanently leave its place." Explaining the title of her novel, Scott argued, "War itself is the only hero of the book. Whatever the philosophy of an actor in a war, he must constantly be convinced of his feebleness when attempting to move in an emotional direction contrary to that of the mass. This propulsion of the individual by a power that is not accountable to reason is very obviously like the action of the wave." As Scott's biographer, Mary Wheeling White, explains, Scott did not demonstrate her argument by focusing on the experience of an individual: "Rather, it is the seemingly endless variety of war experiences seen through hundreds of pairs of eyes that bears out her thesis." Northerners, southerners, Christians, Jews, generals, foot soldiers, combatants, noncombatants, the elderly, children, slaves, and free blacks all tell the story of the war. Moreover, as White explains, everyone suffers in *The Wave*: "Scott did not need to demonstrate that one side or one race suffered more or that any one group perpetuated the most fiendish acts. As participants in the experience of war, all her characters together fill out the complex transracial, transnational story of the human struggle for survival."[34]

Scott described her writing method to Harry Salpeter for a 1931 *Bookman* piece. "I see the end of the novel," she explained, "not the stages. I write a rough draft in which I instruct myself in the stages necessary to achieve the end I see. The rough draft is a full book," she continued. "When I finish it, I throw it away." She never consulted the draft, which was frequently as long as the revised novel. She thus set aside a two-hundred-thousand-word draft for *The Wave*. "The continuing discipline of writing full-length rough drafts is necessary, partly as a counter-balance to my tendency to bite off larger chunks of the universe than I can chew," she claimed. "If I were to abandon the preliminary versions, I would be in danger of making all my books on the same pattern, of merely rewriting the same book, and each book is, and presents, a new problem." With each book, Scott attempted to "make my own universe recognizable to others; I want to communicate my sense of what life is to me. I don't expect anyone to know what my universe is until I'm dead and it has been completed," she continued. "One book can be only a partial attempt to create, or express, the universe." Each novel contributed to the general design, she believed. "And the design toward which she is striving," concluded Salpeter, "is that of a *comédie humaine* of America."[35]

The Wave generally received favorable reviews. Carl Van Doren declared it the "greatest novel on the American Civil War." Percy Hutchinson, reviewing the novel for the *New York Times*, was less impressed, however. *The Wave*, he noted, broke all the rules of the historical novel. It had no central protagonist, for example, no progression, and no plot. Indeed, Hutchinson had a hard time applying the word "narrative" to describe Scott's work. "For, except, in so far as everything set down in type with words following one after another is narrative," he wrote, "'The Wave' is an adaptation in an ancient field of all the newest methods of writing." Most readers unfamiliar with the basic story of the Civil War would abandon the novel, Hutchinson surmised. But "those who do not continue will miss the one striking feature of the book," Scott's "astonishing ability to project herself into widely different phases" of the war. Ultimately, however, the novel failed. Hutchinson predicted that the novel would be "acclaimed a work of more than usual significance and moment by those who are incurably addicted to the method pursued by Evelyn Scott." However, "the book is impressive but does not yield an impression. This is not the highest art," he concluded. "It is only a step on the way to art."[36]

Clifton Fadiman, whose review appeared in the *Nation*, was much more fulsome in his praise of Scott's novel than was Hutchinson. Rather than slighting Scott for failing to respect the rules of the traditional historical novel, Fadiman championed Scott's ability to transcend the genre. Fadiman opened his review by noting, "Historians and historical novelists of the conventional school have conspired to make us forget that wars happen to people as well as governments. It has long been supposed that the best way to encompass artistically a great national event was to take a bird's-eye view of it; and, of course, from an altitude a war would resolve itself into the movements of masses more or less controlled by the decisions of a few outstanding individuals and primarily actuated by some common ideal." Scott, however, eschewed tradition, instead offering "one of the few really formidable expressions of the anti-heroic viewpoint — or, if one may be permitted so lax a term, the modern viewpoint." Much to its credit, the novel recounts "no one man's war; it recounts the Civil War, whole and entire." Fadiman had no patience for those critics who cited the novel's "formlessness," pointing out that this shapelessness was deliberate: "It is in itself a way, a valid and exciting way, of viewing the national cataclysm which was the Civil War." In fact, Fadiman argued, the nebulousness was "the only way in which a thoroughly modern temperament *could* survey the war completely because only thus can the utter madness and senseless horror of strife be completely communicated." *The Wave*, according to Fadiman, achieved what other antiwar novels had failed to accomplish. Other novels rendered the tragedy of war in individual terms. What makes war tragic, however, is that it brings "wretchedness to millions of people—and in different ways." It took a gifted author, Fadiman argued, to suggest to readers "that the meanest Negro and General Robert E. Lee are both made sick to their very souls by the same event." This "multifariousness" of the novel rendered the "brutal variety and meaninglessness" of the war in a way unlike that of any other novel. In short, Fadiman proclaimed, the Civil War had received "its most adequate treatment in fiction" in *The Wave*.[37]

The New Republic's reviewer, Robert Morss Lovett, similarly praised Scott's revolutionary technique. Her method "allows her to combine the methods of all modern treatments of war—she sees it in the physical sufferings of fighting men, in the doubtful mental operations of their leaders, in the hope and fear, the love and grief of the helpless multitude of men and women behind lines." Lovett conceded that the novel demanded readers' patience and careful attention but believed that the reward justified the work. Lovett also wrote a piece for *Bookman* in which he traced Scott's career and praised her latest literary effort. Furthermore, he expounded on the importance of Scott's rendering of the Civil War, explaining that the war novel had "undergone a significant transformation during the last century. It remained for a long time in the mood of primitive literature in which the deeds of the warrior were the chief theme of the bard." Scott avoided celebrating "individual heroism and national glory," Lovett reiterated, focusing instead on "mass movement." According to Scott, "the individual is important only as an element of the mass, the organism in which he has a part through his unconscious self." The Civil War, Lovett concluded, had "taken Mrs. Scott out of the narrow round of specialization and case study and set her feet in the large ways of human life."[38]

The Literary Guild's decision to name *The Wave* its July 1929 selection bolstered the novel's critical reputation. The *New York Times* advertisement announcing the book club's choice boasted that Scott "makes the upheaval assume a reality which it can never have in the pages of history." According to White, *The Wave's* popularity persisted for another two decades. Fiction anthologies asked to reprint sections of the novel, and magazines published chapters as short stories. "Her 1929 effort was so massive and so inclusive," declared her biographer, "that very few American authors have since attained the heights and breadths she did in *The Wave*, her prose monument to the Civil War." Critical and popular acclaim for the novel, however, did not continue, and it has received scant attention from the critics who began an evaluation of Civil War literature at the war's centennial, for example. Literary scholar Bach suggests that "assumptions about such a complex and broad subject as the Civil War sometimes limit critics to only those novels created in the usual manner."[39] The novel faded from the popular imagination, in part, because of the tremendous success of Margaret Mitchell's 1936 literary coup, *Gone with the Wind*. Despite Scott's attempt to tell a truly national story of the Civil War in the broadest terms possible, her efforts were eclipsed by Mitchell's simple narrative, which captured the national reading audience's imagination like no other Civil War novel.

A Triumph over Pessimism, Obscurity, and Fatal Complexity

"The stirring drama of the Civil War and Reconstruction is brought vividly to life in this really magnificent novel," boasted Macmillan's spring 1936 catalog. Scarlett O'Hara, "the belle of the country," blossoms into young womanhood "just in time to see the Civil War sweep away the life for which her upbringing had prepared her." Shrewdness and a certain hardness, however, allow Scarlett to survive both the death of the Old South and the "turmoil of Reconstruction." *Gone with the Wind* "epitomizes the whole drama of the South under the impact of the War and its aftermath," the blurb concluded. "The ruggedness and strength of north Georgia's red hills are in the characters—bluff, blustering Gerald O'Hara; Ellen, his wife; Mammy, who both loved and chastened Ellen's daughters; the rollicking Tarleton twins; the quick-tempered and murderous Fontaines; stately John [sic] Wilkes, and a host of others, white and black, forming a rich picture of Southern life." Mitchell's "stirring drama" captivated the national reading audience like no other work of fiction. *Gone with the Wind* sold more than one million copies within six months of its publication. Printers could scarcely produce enough copies to stock bookstores; lending libraries could not keep copies on their shelves.[40] Mitchell had generated a literary phenomenon. The novel's success stemmed in part from Mitchell's ability to transform a southern story of the Civil War into a national story. In this respect, Mitchell succeeded where generations of southern white women authors had failed.

Mitchell unquestionably told a southern story of the war. For example, in her book, plantation life had failed to render southerners dissolute, contrary to northerners' claims: "Although born to the ease of plantation life, waited on hand and foot since infancy, the faces" of Scarlett O'Hara and the Tarleton twins "were neither slack nor soft," Mitchell observed. "They had the vigor and alertness of country people who have spent all their lives in the open." The people of North Georgia had a certain "vigor and energy." "They were a kindly people, courteous, generous, filled with abounding good nature, but sturdy, virile, easy to anger." The South was not strong enough to withstand the ravages of Civil War, however. Like many earlier white southern authors, Mitchell infused her tale of the war with a reading of the Lost Cause. Ashley Wilkes, the principled defender of the Old South, explains to his wife, Melanie, that he and his fellow Confederates "are fighting for a Cause that was lost the minute the first shot was fired, for our Cause is really our own way of living and that is gone already." Despite the inevitability of Confederate defeat, however, Ashley fights for his dying civilization. "I think of States' Rights and cotton and the darkies and the Yankees whom we have been bred up to hate," he muses, "and I know that none of these is the reason why I am fighting. Instead, I see Twelve Oaks and remember how the moonlight slants across the white columns, and the unearthly way the magnolias look, opening under the moon, and how the climbing roses make the side porch shady even at hottest noon." Wilkes also recalls his beloved mother, the cotton fields, "and the mist rising from the bottom lands in the twilight. And that's is why I am here who have no love of death or misery or glory and no hatred for anyone," he explains. Like many characters in southern novels of the war penned during the first half-century after its end, Confederates do not fight to defend slavery or states' rights: "Perhaps that is what is called patriotism, love of home and country."[41]

Mitchell populated her novel with white southern women who, save for Scarlett, offered unswerving support for the Confederacy. "They were all beautiful with the blinding beauty that transfigures even the plainest woman when she is utterly protected and utterly loved and is giving back that love a thousandfold," Mitchell wrote. "How could disaster ever come to women such as they when their stalwart gray line stood between them and the Yankees?" Mitchell asked disingenuously. These women, Mitchell noted, would willingly sacrifice their men "and bear their loss as proudly as the men bore their battle flags." Years of warfare, however, aged these women: "Throughout the South for fifty years there would be bitter-eyed women who looked backward, to dead times, to dead men," Mitchell surmised, "evoking memories that hurt and were futile, bearing poverty with bitter pride because they had those memories."[42] Ellen Glasgow's

Mrs. Blake and Augusta Wilson's Mrs. Maurice would have fit well in Mitchell's novel.

Despite these familiar elements common to many southern stories of the war, *Gone with the Wind* had unprecedented national appeal. Mitchell's decision to make the Gerald O'Hara a recent immigrant to the country, not a scion of antebellum southern society, contributed to the novel's success with the national reading audience. In this respect, the South did not differ greatly from the rest of the nation, which experienced an enormous influx of immigrants during the early twentieth century. In fact, Mitchell offered the southern story "as an only slightly special case of an inclusive national destiny." Gerald O'Hara "had come to America from Ireland when he was twenty-one," Mitchell explained early in the novel. "He had come hastily, as many a better and worse Irishman before and since, with the clothes he had on his back, two shillings above his passage money and a price on his head that he felt was larger than his misdeed warranted." Gerald's experience paralleled that of many recent immigrants to the United States: "He left home with his mother's hasty kiss on his cheek and her fervent Catholic blessing in his ears, and his father's parting admonition, 'Remember who ye are and don't be taking nothing off of no man.'" Moreover, Gerald O'Hara remained somewhat removed from his adopted culture. "He liked the South," Mitchell insisted, "and he soon became, in his own opinion, a Southerner. There was much about the South — and Southerners — that he would never comprehend," however. Gerald nevertheless, "with the whole-heartedness that was his nature, . . . adopted its ideas and customs, as he understood them, for his own — poker, and horse racing, red-hot politics and the code duello, States' Rights and damnation to all Yankees, slavery and King Cotton, contempt for white trash and exaggerated courtesy to women. He even learned to chew tobacco," Mitchell added. But "Gerald remained Gerald." He took what he found most useful about the South, "and the rest he dismissed."[43] Although Gerald eventually sees himself as a southerner, he nevertheless refuses to accept all of the region's customs. In many ways, he remains an interloper.

The appeal of *Gone with the Wind* also transcended regional borders because of Mitchell's ability to strip the Old South of its "peculiar institution," substituting racism for slavery and thereby rendering a story that the nation could embrace. As Elizabeth Fox-Genovese explains, Mitchell's early descriptions of Tara evoke a particular time and place, but "none of those descriptions bears any relation to the slave system." In the world that Mitchell made, house slaves regarded field hands with contempt: "In slave days, these lowly blacks had been despised by the house negroes and yard negroes as creatures of small worth." Plantation mistresses selected those slaves who performed well for positions of greater responsibility, and "those consigned to the fields were the ones least willing or able to learn, the least energetic, the least honest and trustworthy, the most vicious and brutish." According to Mitchell, then, the principles that governed the institution of slavery bore striking resemblance to "the prevailing capitalist ideology of work, schooling, and the promotion of merit, tempered by a harsh attitude toward crime." In other words, Mitchell's depiction of slavery more accurately reflected the governing ideology of the early-twentieth-century middle-class bourgeoisie than it did the "peculiar institution" of the Old South. Mitchell thus "brings her readers to accept a particular world without including any of the social features that structure it."[44]

Moreover, Mitchell's rendition of the horrors of Reconstruction would have resonated with a reading audience familiar with the Republican Party's abandonment of African-Americans during the late nineteenth century and with many of the overtly racist policies of the Progressives. Indeed, at the time of the novel's publication, scarcely twenty years had passed since Woodrow Wilson brought with him to Washington segregation, the "southern remedy" to the "Negro problem." The Reconstruction governments were, according to Mitchell, in desperate need of purging. Former slaves who had received positions of importance were "like monkeys or small children turned loose among treasured objects whose value is beyond their comprehension." They "ran wild—either from perverse pleasure in destruction or simply because of their ignorance." Their white allies fared no better in Mitchell's imagination. White Georgians wailed at the corruption in the state government. "But far and above their anger at the waste and mismanagement and graft was the resentment of the people at the bad light in which the governor represented them in the North," Mitchell noted. In response to white complaints, Georgia's Reconstruction governor "appeared before Congress and told of white outrages against negroes, of Georgia's preparation for another rebellion and the need for a stern military rule in the state." Because of his efforts, "the North saw only a rebellious state that needed a heavy hand, and a heavy hand was laid upon it." Thus, the Ku Klux Klan, which had witnessed a national resurgence during the Progressive era, figured in Mitchell's book as a corrective to Republican rule. Although Mitchell did not devote much space in *Gone with the Wind* to Klan activities, she did note that Frank Kennedy, Ashley Wilkes, "and all the men" in Scarlett's cohort had joined the Klan because they were "white men and Southerners" who needed to protect white women from rapacious black beasts and scurrilous Republican politicians.[45] The images of African-American men and corrupt politicians had changed little in the national imagination. Mitchell could be assured that her rendition of Reconstruction would strike a familiar chord.

Finally, Mitchell exposed the agrarian way of life as moribund. Initially, the major characters in *Gone with the Wind* had their destinies somehow tied to Tara, the O'Haras' thriving plantation. "There was an air of solidness, of stability and permanence about Tara," Mitchell claimed early in the novel, "and whenever Gerald galloped around the bend in the road and saw his own roof rising through green branches, his heart swelled with pride as though each sight of it were the first sight." Gerald constantly informs Scarlett that land is the only reliable source of wealth, encouraging her love of the place. "Land is the only thing in the world that amounts to anything," he proclaims, "for 'tis the only thing in the world that lasts, and don't you be forgetting it! 'Tis the only thing worth working for, fighting for—worth dying for." But Tara could not sustain its inhabitants through the war. Unlike so many novels examined in this book, with the notable exception of Mary Noailles Murfree's *Where the Battle Was Fought*, Mitchell's southern plantation is not reinvigorated after the war by the marriage of the returning, healthy Confederate veteran and the southern belle. The war has killed off the entire O'Hara clan, save Scarlett, and her future does not rest with Tara. Although she harbors a deep affection for Tara, it has become for her a place of retreat, not a source of livelihood. While in Atlanta, Scarlett yearns for Tara. She loves the city, "but—oh, for the sweet peace and country quiet of Tara, the red fields and the dark pines about it! Oh, to be back at Tara." Scarlett misses the "fresh smell of country air, the plowed earth and the sweetness of summer nights." On her return, she meets with "the soft gray mist in the swampy bottoms, the red earth and growing cotton, the sloping field with curving green rows and the black pines rising behind everything like sable walls."[46] Yet Scarlett knows she cannot remain at Tara.

Indeed, Scarlett recognizes that her future rests with the burgeoning industry of the New South. Scarlett turns to the Atlanta sawmills, not to the land, to raise money to pay the taxes on Tara: "In the ruin and chaos of that spring of 1866, she single mindedly turned her energies to making the mill pay," Mitchell wrote. "There was money in Atlanta. The wave of rebuilding was giving her the opportunity she wanted and she knew she could make money." Facing the birth of her daughter, Ella Lorena, Scarlett professes her disgust at the time she will miss from the mill. "What a mess it was to try to run a business and have a baby too!" Mitchell observed. "I'll never have another one," Scarlett declares. "I'm not going to be like other women and have a baby every year. Good Lord, that would mean six months out of the year when I'd have to be away from the mills. And I see now that I can't afford to be away from them even one day." Scarlett has adapted to changing times, becoming part of the enterprising southern bourgeoisie.[47]

Gone with the Wind thus resonated with a national reading audience because the novel offered a nostalgic depiction of the Old South but did not advocate its return. Indeed, Atlanta, the quintessential New South city, emerged triumphant as the Old South died away. The war forced Atlanta to become a manufacturing center for the Confederacy. "The little town was gone and the face of the rapidly growing city was animated with never-ceasing energy and bustle." Moreover, "In spite of war, fire and Reconstruction, Atlanta had again become a boom town," Mitchell informed her readers. "Underneath the surface were misery and fear, but all the outward appearances were those of a thriving town that was rapidly rebuilding from its ruins, a bustling hurrying town. Savannah, Charleston, Augusta, Richmond, New Orleans would never hurry," Mitchell declared. "It was ill-bred and Yankeefied to hurry. But in this period, Atlanta was more ill bred and Yankeefied that it had ever been before or would ever be again. With 'new people' thronging in from all directions, the streets were choked and noisy from morning till night. . . . The war," Mitchell concluded, "had definitely established the importance of Atlanta in the affairs of the South and the hitherto obscure town was now known far and wide." Mitchell professed astonishment that most people, even southerners, found it "difficult to understand how the Atlanta neighborhood differed from the rest of the South." She contended that although the story of the Old South "had been done many times and done beautifully, . . . this 'new South' was almost untouched." This unexplored territory, Mitchell once claimed, "made me want to write my book." As Fox-Genovese points out, in Mitchell's hands, the Civil War becomes "a national turning point in the transition from rural to urban civilization." Atlanta bore no relation to the moonlight and magnolias of the Old South but rather resembled the increasingly urbanized areas of the Northeast and Midwest. This interpretation allowed Mitchell to include the South in a "shared national drama."[48]

The novel's enormous popularity encouraged readers to question its author about her decision to write it. Mitchell told well-rehearsed but vague stories about her novel's origins. She began the book sometime in the 1920s, although, she claimed, "I can't quite place the date." To Julian Harris she said that she had started the project while recovering from an injury to her ankle. "I couldn't walk for a couple of years," she explained, "so I put in my time writing this book." But she also later contended that she could not remember why she had started on her novel. She told some people that it took her ten years to write *Gone with the Wind* but told others that she had spent only three years on the work. Few people knew of her project. Only her husband, John, had read the draft before publication, and Mitchell claimed in response to a rumor that John had coauthored the book that even he had read only portions of it before she handed the manuscript over to Macmillan. "If the story of *Gone with the Wind* is now part of the common heritage of English speakers everywhere on the planet," writes Mitchell's biographer, Darden Asbury Pyron, "its contemporary popularity is matched only the by obscurity in which the author herself conceived and executed the novel and the mystery with which she later surrounded its origins."[49]

Mitchell was clear, however, about her source material. Like many white southern women of her generation, Mitchell had been raised on stories of the war. As Fox-Genovese observes, Mitchell was of the last generation to come of age with little exposure to "the new culture of radio and film. Her experience of vicariously living the histories of grandparents, parents, and communities through the telling and retelling of tales" was common. These stories of the Civil War and Reconstruction "ensured," according to Fox-Genovese, "a widespread and living engagement with" the events of the past. Mitchell claimed that she had heard "so much when I was little about the fighting and the hard times after the war that I firmly believed Mother and Father had been through it all instead of being born long afterward. In fact I was about ten years old before I learned the war hadn't ended shortly before I was born," she confessed. As a child, she had listened to stories of the war as she sat on the "bony knees of veterans and the fat slippery laps of great aunts." Those stories "gradually became part of my life." She later noted that those skinny veterans and fat aunts were "a pretty outspoken, forthright, tough bunch of old timers and the things they said stuck in my mind much longer than the things the people of my parents' generation told me." Inspired, Mitchell voraciously read works on the Civil War era and hunted down private letters and diaries that helped her expand her knowledge. "Somehow, the period of the Sixties always seemed much more real to me than my own era, which Scott Fitzgerald called 'The Jazz Age.'"[50]

Mitchell often boasted of the novel's historical accuracy. Lauding Stephen Vincent Benet, who had reviewed *Gone with the Wind* in the *Saturday Review of Books*, for noticing the influence of Civil War diaries on her work, Mitchell wrote, "You're the only reviewer who has picked up the diaries and memoirs out of my background. . . . Of course I used everybody from Myrta Lockett Avary to Eliza Andrews and Mary Gay and Mrs. Clement Clay and Miss Fearn and Eliza Ripley and the Lord knows how many unpublished letters and diaries." She professed "horror" when Macmillan bought the manuscript, "for I realized that I had not checked a single fact" in it. As soon as she handed over the manuscript to the publisher, she read "the memoirs of Sherman, Johnston and Hood. I studied Cox's Atlanta campaign harder than I ever did Caesar's Gallic Wars," she continued. "And, if there was even a sergeant who wrote a book about that retreat, I read it." Elsewhere, she claimed that a bibliography for *Gone with the Wind* would run well over one thousand volumes. Indeed, while the novel was in production, Mitchell busied herself "rechecking her historical facts. However lousy the book may be as far as style, subject, plot, characters," she wrote to a friend, "it's as accurate historically as I can get it." Mitchell confessed that she did not "want to get caught out on anything that any Confederate Vet could nail me on, or any historian either."[51]

On more than one occasion, Mitchell singled out Mary Johnston's two volumes on the Civil War, *The Long Roll* and *Cease-Firing!* as being particularly helpful to her as she prepared her manuscript. One reviewer compared *Gone with the Wind* to Johnston's work, thereby enormously pleasing Mitchell. "Mary Johnston was a schoolmate of my mother's and before I could read, I had her books read to me," Mitchell told Paul Jordan-Smith of the *Los Angeles Times*. "Mother was strong minded but she never failed to weep over 'The Long Roll' and 'Cease Firing,' and I always bellowed too, but insisted on her not skipping sad parts." In trying to determine the weather during the Battle of Kennesaw Mountain, Mitchell turned to Johnston's work: "Unfortunately, I became so engrossed in the story that I read on through till the tragic end. And when I had finished," she continued, "I found that I couldn't possibly write anything on my own. I felt so childish and presumptuous for even trying to write about that period when she had done it so beautifully, so powerfully—better than anyone can ever do it, not matter how hard they try." Elsewhere, Mitchell confessed to suffering an attack of "the humbles" after rereading *Cease-Firing!*[52] She apparently recovered.

Writing about the Civil War was labor-intensive but provided Mitchell with no particular problems. Writing about Reconstruction, however, was another matter. "War can be made interesting, and peace," she confided to Herschel Brickell, "a muddled peace is hard to handle. I suppose it's because war has some design to it and reconstruction hasn't," she concluded. Moreover, she found little inspiration in nonfiction books on the subject; most "are dull beyond the belief," she declared. Fictional works might have proved more satisfying. Pyron writes that D. W. Griffith's film *Birth of a Nation* influenced Mitchell's vision of Reconstruction. In Griffith's view, "Appomattox came; the North and South prepared to work out their differences; Lincoln died; evil politicians took his place; they created a wicked coalition that immediately captured the governments of the Confederate states; their alliance consisted of spiteful, narrowminded politicians in Washington, former slaves, self-serving white collaborationists, and the nefarious Yankee mercenaries, the Carpetbaggers; while their wicked rule lasted for over a decade, finally, the local forces of righteousness, pressed beyond endurance, expelled the aliens; only then did peace as Lincoln had desired it, return to Dixie and to the nation." Mitchell's depiction of Reconstruction owes as much to Thomas Dixon as it does to D. W. Griffith, however. "I was practically raised on your books," she confessed to the author of *The Clansman* and other works on the Reconstruction South, "and love them very much."[53]

As Pyron explains, Mitchell published *Gone with the Wind* just as "historiography was on the brink of a monumental shift in its approach to Reconstruction, black history, slavery, and the South." W. E. B. Du Bois's important *Black Reconstruction* came out in 1935, just as Mitchell worked on the revisions to her manuscript, although Du Bois's work had little influence on Americans' historical imaginations, least of all Mitchell's. "Circumstances caught Mitchell's novel in a historiographical vise," Pyron notes. "The radical revision of scholarship of the forties, fifties, and much more afterward, made Mitchell's work appear especially reactionary." But, as Pyron notes, Mitchell imagined *Gone with the Wind* as a revisionist work of the planter class. "If she confirmed most of the racial stereotypes of Reconstruction," Pyron explains, "her emphasis on economic motives, in particular, challenged the old pieties and put her work in the vanguard of new interpretation of the Southern experience." After the book appeared, however, Mitchell denied that she had written a "triumph of materialism."[54]

Mitchell's manuscript was precisely the literary venture publisher Harold Latham of the Macmillan Company had sought when he began a much-vaunted trip throughout the South in the mid-1930s. Lois Cole, a friend of Mitchell's who had been working in Macmillan's New York offices since 1932, tipped off Latham about Mitchell's manuscript. Mitchell initially played coy, refusing to acknowledge that a manuscript existed. "I have nothing," Mitchell responded when Latham asked her directly about the novel's existence. She eventually recanted, however. The manuscript captured Latham's imagination from the moment he began reading it. "I see in it the making of a really important and significant book," he wrote to Mitchell in April 1935. "We are going to keep at this project until a novel is issued that is going to be regarded as a very significant publication." Latham closed his letter by asking Mitchell's permission to forward the manuscript to Macmillan's board of advisers. Mitchell reluctantly consented. Latham urged his superiors to consider seriously the manuscript. "We shall make a serious mistake if we do not immediately take it," he advised. As Pyron explains, Latham's enthusiasm aside, Macmillan required an outside reader to evaluate the manuscript. The company chose Charles W. Everett, a professor of English at Columbia University and a respected critic. Everett's report confirmed Latham's initial assessment: "I'm sure it is not only a good book but a best seller." Macmillan acted immediately, informing Mitchell that a contract would soon arrive.[55]

Mitchell spent mid-1935 revising her manuscript. She turned immediately to the first chapter, which she claimed that she had written the same day she handed over the manuscript to Latham. "I decided also that none of the many first chapters I had written were worth showing," she later explained to a friend, "yet I wanted Mr. Latham to have some notion of what the first chapter was about so I hastily knocked out a synopsis of the first chapter. . . . As it stands in the book is pretty much as I wrote it that afternoon." She later turned to the concerns Everett had raised in his evaluation. Everett particularly objected to Mitchell's rendition of Reconstruction, complaining that the author had allowed her opinion to cloud her narrative. Mitchell insisted that she had no idea that her "venom, bias, and bitterness" were so apparent. "All the V, B & B were to come through the eyes and head and tongues of the characters, as reactions from what they heard and felt," she assured Macmillan. Everett also took issue with the Mitchell's interpretation of the Ku Klux Klan. Mitchell suggested that Everett reread the manuscript, with the Klan material, once her revisions were completed. "If you do not like it and your advisers do not like it," she told the press, "I will be most happy to change it."[56]

While revising her novel, Mitchell also contended with concerns raised by her publishers. Echoing Ferris Greenslet, who had worried endlessly over the length of Mary Johnston's Civil War novel, Lois Cole advised Mitchell, "When the contract was drawn we visualized something between 250,000 and 300,000 words which could be made to sell for $2.50 . . . but the book has more than 400,000 words!" Cole calculated that the book would lose four cents per copy and requested that Mitchell consider accepting a cut in her royalties to offset the profit loss. Cole also informed Mitchell that changes in the galley proofs could prove expensive and reminded the author of her contractual commitment to pay for the alterations. These disputes greatly agitated Mitchell, raising her suspicions that Macmillan was not dealing with her fairly. She grudgingly agreed to the changes and mailed off the manuscript in March 1936.[57]

Macmillan aggressively marketed the novel. The firm solicited Ellen Glasgow, for example, to praise the book in an advertisement that appeared in the *New York Times*. "This book is absorbing," Glasgow claimed. "It is a fearless portrayal, romantic yet not sentimental, of a lost tradition and a way of life." Macmillan also created a pamphlet, *Margaret Mitchell and Her Novel* Gone with the Wind, that reprinted favorable reviews. The Book-of-the-Month Club's choice of *Gone with the Wind* as its main selection for July 1936 fueled speculation, according to Mitchell's biographer, "that Harold Latham had (as he knew all along) hit on something very hot indeed." Anticipating wide readership, Macmillan began circulating galley-proof editions as soon as they were available. "Yes, word was out," Pyron notes, "hot property."[58]

Macmillan's marketing strategies apparently pleased Mitchell. In June 1936 she confessed to Latham that she had finally accepted that Macmillan was committed to her book and to dealing with her fairly. "I thought, 'They are putting a lot of money behind my book for advertising purposes,'" she wrote to Latham, "'a lot more money than they usually put up for a new and unknown author.'" One month later, she exclaimed happily, "Good Heavens! The advertising you've put behind me! With all those ads and the grand publicity the newspapers have given me, Macmillan could have sold Karl Marx up here in these [North Georgia] hills!" Mitchell seemed especially grateful to Latham for excusing her from national autograph tours. "Such exploitation cheapens a person," she believed. When Macmillan requested that Mitchell come to New York on the publication date, she refused. Latham came south to persuade Mitchell to reconsider but eventually capitulated: "I was so happy to hear him say that he did not really think such 'literary circuses' sold books," she wrote to Julia Collier Harris. "I'm sure he wouldn't want to be quoted on that," Mitchell continued, "but he did say it. And he seemed to understand when I said I'd rather never sell a book than autograph in department stores." She nevertheless seemed thrilled when reports of the book's sales came in.[59]

As Pyron notes, the initial reviews from some of the New York papers were less than laudatory. Both Ralph Thompson's review in the *New York Times* and Isabel

Paterson's nationally syndicated column that appeared in the *New York Herald Tribune* offered "mixed assessments" of *Gone with the Wind*. The Mississippi-born Brickell, however, penned a much more enthusiastic review for the *New York Post*. Brickell had read "thousands" of books, none of which "left me feeling I'd much rather just go on thinking about them, savoring their truth and treasuring the emotional experience that reading them was, than to try to set down my impressions of them." *Gone with the Wind* was different. It was nothing short of the finest novel of the Civil War ever written. Edwin Granberry, writing for the *New York Sun*, was even more fulsome in his praise, comparing Mitchell favorably to the great novelists of the nineteenth century and claiming that she had "challenged the modernists who had abandoned plot for mood, ambiance, and angst." Her novel triumphed over the "pessimism, obscurity, and fatal complexity of most contemporary novelists."[60]

Mitchell thrilled at the positive reviews. She wrote to both Granberry and Brickell of her appreciation for their comments. "I am Margaret Mitchell of Atlanta, author of 'Gone with the Wind,'" she introduced herself to Granberry. "Your review of my book was the first review I read, and it made me so happy that I tried to write you immediately." She seemed especially pleased with the space Granberry devoted to his review: "I can never thank you enough for that! And when I read along to the breath-taking remark about being bracketed with Tolstoy, Hardy, Dickens, and Undset," she continued, "well, I gave out." After she finished reading that section of the review, she professed, "I lay down and called for an ice pack and my husband read the rest to me." She closed her letter rather disingenuously by stating, "I wish I could see you because I talk better than I write and perhaps I could make you understand what your review meant to me." She was similarly effusive in her letter to Brickell: "If you only knew how strange it felt to read your words about that book," she wrote less than a week after the book's official publication date. "And to finish up with your reference to Freeman's 'R. E. Lee' which is, to me, the most wonderful thing of its kind ever turned out—well, perhaps you contributed to a practical nervous collapse."[61]

Mitchell seemed especially pleased when historians praised her book. She confessed that she "positively cringed" when she heard that historian Henry Steele Commager would review *Gone With the Wind* for the *New York Herald Tribune Books*. "I cringed even though I knew the history in my tale was as water proof and air tight as ten years of study and a lifetime of listening to participants would make it," she told Commager. "Historians, like those who deal in the exact sciences, are prone to be tough!" she concluded. Mitchell was quite relieved, then, that her novel did not ruffle Commager's "historical feathers." Similarly, Douglas Southall Freeman's fan letter electrified Mitchell. "But any Southerner would be thrilled," she explained to Freeman, "and any Southerner, who had done a little research into the period with which you dealt, would naturally have palpitations." Freeman's letter afforded Mitchell the opportunity to tell him how much she had enjoyed his biography of Lee, which "is something that will make anyone who writes about the South of that period feel very humble. And also very proud that such a truly great book came out of our section." She believed that Freeman's work would continue to bring her pleasure in the years to come.[62]

Not surprisingly, Mitchell received batches of fan mail. "Readers dried their glasses one moment," explains Pyron, "and typed letters to the author the next." Fans professed their admiration for the author and her novel. If Mitchell reveled in the praise her novel received from adoring fans, she did not particularly enjoy being in the public eye. She complained bitterly and often about the loss of privacy she had suffered since the publication of Gone with the Wind. Mitchell felt besieged even before the novel's official publication date of 30 June 1936. "I did not realize that being an author meant this sort of thing," she confessed to Julia Collier Harris on 29 June, "autographing in book stores, being invited here and there about the country to speak, to attend summer schools, to address this and that group at luncheon. It all came as a shock to me," she maintained, "and not a pleasant shock." Indeed, the frenzy that followed the publication of Gone with the Wind forced Mitchell to flee Atlanta for the North Georgia mountains. "I am on the run," she confided to Brickell on 7 July. "I'm sure Scarlett O'Hara never struggled harder to get out of Atlanta or suffered more during her siege of Atlanta than I have suffered during the siege that has been on since publication day," she continued. Moreover, Mitchell resented the demands that fame placed on her. Exasperated, she wrote that she continued "to marvel as the mail mounts up with requests. . . . People seem to think that because an author can get a book published she can hop up on a minute's notice and make a forty-five minute address, but alas," Mitchell confessed, "this is not true in my case." Although she took pride in her novel's success, she was "neither proud nor grateful for the public interest in my private life or my personality. I resent it with a bitterness which I am unable to convey on paper," she told Brickell. On more than one occasion, she pleaded that she wished that her reputation could rest on the novel and not on her personal life.[63]

Some readers did not praise the book, of course. John Peale Bishop wrote a mixed review for the *New Republic*, ultimately claiming that the novel was "neither very good nor very sound." He praised Mitchell's deft handling of the historical material, noting that the author offered "an extraordinary sense of detail." But he faulted Mitchell for failing to address adequately the moral problem the novel raises. To Bishop, the novel seemed to ask, "In a society falling apart, upon what terms can the individual accord to survive?" The novel did not provide a suitable answer. "Scarlett wants only to last and takes any terms life offers," Bishop told his readers. "Miss Mitchell seems to approve of [Scarlett's] persistence. But [the author] also implies that civilization consists precisely in an unwillingness to survive on any terms save those of one's own determining." Bishop believed that Mitchell used Scarlett and Rhett indirectly to assert the virtues of the society whose destruction they witness. "By this device," he concluded, "she has clearly hoped to avoid sentimentality in treating a subject she fears as sentimental."[64]

Malcolm Cowley's review, which also appeared in the *New Republic*, damned *Gone with the Wind* with faint praise. Cowley located the novel firmly in the plantation school of southern fiction, which made it decidedly out of step with the literature of the southern renaissance. The novel, Cowley declared, "is an encyclopedia of the plantation legend. Other novelists by the hundreds have helped to shape this legend," he admitted, "but each of them has presented only a part of it. Miss Mitchell repeats it as a whole, with all its episodes and all its characters and all its stage settings — the big white-columned house sleeping under its trees among the cotton fields; the band of faithful retainers, including two who faintly resemble Aunt Jemima and Old Black Joe; the white-haired massa bathing in mint juleps." *Gone with the Wind* contained all of the potent stereotypes of the antebellum South, according to Cowley, including "every last bale of cotton and bushel of moonlight, every last full measure of Southern devotion working its lilywhite fingers uncomplainingly to the lilywhite bones." Cowley acknowledged that despite its triteness, *Gone with the Wind* resonated deeply with the reading public, and he ascribed this popularity to the novel's appeal to the readers' emotions. "But even if the legend is false in part and silly in part and vicious in its general effect on Southern life today," he wrote, "still it retains its appeal to the fundamental emotions. . . . I would never, never say that she has written a great novel," Cowley concluded, "but in the midst of triteness and sentimentality her book has a simple-minded courage that suggests great novelists of the past." No wonder, he mused, the book was "going like the wind."[65]

Evelyn Scott wrote the review for the *Nation*. Unlike many reviewers, Scott did not find Mitchell's story particularly compelling. "Neither the human incidents depicted nor the author's broad account of public events gripped this reader," Scott confessed, "until the widowed heroine, visiting Atlanta, found herself immured in a beleaguered city and responsible for her rival, the fragile Melanie." Not surprisingly, Scott chastised Mitchell for presenting only the white South's version of the war. "Margaret Mitchell gives us our Civil War through Southern eyes exclusively," she notes, "and no tolerant philosophy illumines the crimes of the invaders." Even worse, according to Scott, Mitchell had neither the talent nor the intellectual sophistication to render the true meanings of the war and Confederate defeat. Mitchell's "temperamental limitations as a critic both of mass movements and personal behavior are such that she often gives a shallow effect," Scott wrote. "She is vigorous enough to imbue her work with dramatic buoyancy," Scott conceded, "but unequal to the subtler demand she makes on herself with the tragedy fitly conceived as the climax of her story." Mitchell was insufficiently versed in modernist literature, Scott believed, to pull off her project. "The author seems handicapped by the undigested influence of that literature of pessimism," Scott mused, "which, though it is responsible for everlasting masterpieces and is a tonic antidote for easy romanticism, is too often misinterpreted among Anglo-Saxons as negativism." Only if Mitchell developed her talents would her version of the Civil War be worth reading. "If Miss Mitchell is able, later, to master the wide significances implicit in her own material and to convey her idealism as something more than a soporific," Scott concluded, "she may yet demonstrate the mature humanity absent in the works of so many among us who are 'disillusioned' in that adolescent fashion which follows a first boast of understanding and belief."[66]

Mitchell dismissed criticism with aplomb, at least publicly. She claimed that Bishop's review in the New Republic was "a very good one. Of course," she continued, "he thought it was necessary, before he finished, to chide me for not concerning myself with social significances, mass movements and economic problems, but I suppose that was to be expected in The New Republic, which apparently believes that 'if it isn't propaganda, it isn't art.' " Given the differences between her political views and those of the New Republic, Mitchell thought that "the magazine had done rather well by me." Cowley's more damning review "brought cries of joy" from Mitchell. "I suppose I must lack the exquisite sensitivity an author should have," she confessed rather disingenuously to Stark Young, "but the truth of the matter is that I would be upset and mortified if the Left Wingers liked the book. I'd have to do so much explaining to family and friends if the aesthetes and radicals of literature liked it." "Why should they like it or like the type of mind behind the writing of it?" she asked. "Everything about the book and the mind are abhorrent to all they believe in. One and all they have savaged me and given me great pleasure. However, I wish some of them would actually read the book and review the book I wrote, not the book they imagine I've written or the book they think I should have written." Elsewhere, she chastised critics who read reviews written by well-known commentators rather than her novel itself, "swallow[ing] [such reviews] whole" and rewriting them.[67]

Despite reviewers' claims to the contrary, Mitchell maintained that *Gone with the Wind* was not a "sweet sentimental novel of the Thomas Nelson Page type. My central woman character does practically everything that a lady of the old school should not do." Nor were her other characters "lavender-and-lace-moonlight-on-the-magnolias people." Mitchell based her characters on the "old ladies who had lived through [the Civil War] era who could scare the liver and lights out of you with one word and blast your vitals with a look." These tough women could not have been, according to Mitchell, "completely Thomas Nelson Page in their youths." But if Mitchell resisted writing a novel of the sentimental plantation school, she did not write a modern novel that characterized the post–World War I literary scene. Mitchell saw herself as a product of the Jazz Age, describing herself as a "short-haired, short-skirted, hard-boiled young woman who preachers said would go to hell or be hanged before [she was] thirty." Nonetheless, she believed that her novel belonged to a different tradition. In fact, Mitchell dismissed much of the writing of her contemporaries. "I've seen so much confused thinking," she confessed, "been so impatient with minds that couldn't start at the beginning of things and work them through logically to the end, etc., that when I sit down to read I don't want to have to read about muddled minds even if the muddled minds *are* muddling along in lovely prose." Mitchell singled out Erskine Caldwell's 1932 novel *Tobacco Road* and Ernest Hemingway's 1937 novel *To Have and Have Not* for special condemnation, believing the former to be silly and wrongheaded and the latter to be sadistic.[68]

Because *Gone with the Wind* did not fit the dominant literary tradition of the 1930s, Mitchell feared that her book would not be received favorably. "There was precious little obscenity in it, no adultery and not a single degenerate and I couldn't imagine a publisher being silly enough to buy it," she wrote. When sales and favorable reviews proved her fears unfounded, Mitchell seemed gratified. She did, however, chafe at readers and reviewers who were determined to ferret out a moral: "I had no aim or purpose in writing the book," she insisted, "didn't want to prove a point, prove a moral, give a lesson to the world." The novel was not, as many readers had argued, a "parallel to the Modern War and depression," she explained elsewhere. Exasperated, she exclaimed,

> Reviews and articles come out commending me on having written such a "powerful document against war . . . for pacifism." Lord! I think. I never intended that! Reviews speak of the symbolism of the characters, placing Melanie as the Old South and Scarlett the New. Lord! I never intended that either. Psychiatrists speak of the "carefully done emotional patterns" and disregard all the history part. "Emotional patterns?" Good Heavens! Can this be I? People talk and write of the "high moral lesson." *I* don't see anything very moral in it. I murmur feebly that "it's just a story" and my words are swallowed up while the storm goes over my head about "intangible values," "right and wrong" etc. Well, I still say feebly that it's just a story of some people who went up and some who went down, those who could take it and those who couldn't.[69]

Her simple story shook the literary world.

Gone with the Wind represented the culmination of a literary tradition. As Cowley pointed out in his review for the *New Republic*, although other novelists had contributed to the plantation legend, Mitchell articulated it fully. With *Gone with the Wind*, the legend became realized. In that respect, the novel also represented the death of a literary tradition. Although it remained a particular region in Mitchell's hands, the South lost much of its distinctiveness, instead becoming a regional variant of the national story. Moreover, the triumph of industrial capitalism, urbanization, and bourgeois individualism suggested the death of a worldview championed by many of the authors examined in this book. Unlike most of the authors under consideration, Mitchell did not turn to an antebellum or Confederate past as a source of comfort for present ills. Although defeat in the Civil War rendered a deathblow to southern civilization, Mitchell suggested, the loss gave birth to a society that proved compelling. Indeed, Scarlett looks not to Tara for the future but to Atlanta, the symbol of the New South. In the postwar world, Tara inspires nostalgia, but nothing more. Others, notably the Agrarians and their cohorts, would reject Mitchell's reading of history, but no one could eclipse the popularity and cultural prominence of *Gone with the Wind*.

Epilogue

Everything
That Rises
Must
Converge

There was the forlorn little man in search of his lost comrade, and the victory no longer seemed glorious. The warm, excited, curious feeling about the battle that he had had a few minutes before was gone. He thought dully that there had been a battle and that our arms, we were told, had been victorious. But he wanted only to stretch out, to sink into oblivion.

—CAROLINE GORDON, None Shall Look Back

In early September 1936 Caroline Gordon contemplated death, diarrhea, and her Civil War novel and became mightily irked. Her publisher had recently commented that the novel, *None Shall Look Back* (then titled *Cup of Fury*), was "all right so far as it went" but complained that the author "killed too many young men." An exasperated Gordon wrote to a friend that she returned home, "settled down and . . . killed one more young man, besides giving one chronic diarrhea and the other [a] gangrenous foot. I don't care whether he likes it or not."[1] Gordon's vision of her Civil War novel clearly differed from that of her publisher, whose expectations had undoubtedly been influenced by Margaret Mitchell's recently released *Gone with the Wind*.

Gordon found her inspiration elsewhere. The work of the Southern Agrarians, with whom Gordon was intimately connected, acutely influenced Gordon's understanding of the South and its part in the Civil War. Allen Tate, Gordon's husband, had written biographies of Stonewall Jackson (1928) and Jefferson

Davis (1929) as well as an "Ode to the Confederate Dead," and Andrew Lytle had published a biography of Nathan Bedford Forrest (1931), a chief figure in Gordon's novel of the war. By the time Gordon began work on *None Shall Look Back*, both Tate and Lytle had nearly completed their Civil War novels, *The Fathers* (1938) and *The Long Night* (1936). Moreover, she also worked in an era when the number of works published on the Civil War eclipsed the previous mark set in the post-Reconstruction years, aided by the release of novels by William Faulkner, Stark Young, Evelyn Scott, and of course Margaret Mitchell. Gordon was arguably the strongest woman author of this new generation, self-consciously pursuing the formal and stylistic innovations of modernism. In so doing, she not merely succeeded where others had failed but provided a model for later southern writers.

Like many other white southern women of her era, Gordon grew up steeped in the stories of the Civil War. "When my brothers and I were children," she wrote, "one of our favorite pastimes was to get into a hammock, three deep, and swing and sing." Their songs were not the popular ragtime songs of the day but those that celebrated famous Confederate heroes, notably Nathan Bedford Forrest. Their grandmother punctuated their singing with stories of bloodied battlefields and home-front heroics. Around 1940, Gordon recalled, "I do not think that my childhood experiences were very different from those of any other Southerner who is over thirty years old." But unlike Mary Johnston, Gordon intentionally set out to write a Civil War novel that defied the conventions of the genre. According to Eileen Gregory, one of Gordon's colleagues at the University of Dallas, Gordon noted in 1933 that she wanted to write an epic of the Civil War but "didn't think it could be done, at least not by a woman." Such comments suggested, at least to Gregory, that Gordon "had a particular kind of narrative in mind . . . and one that she saw as particularly 'masculine' in its demands on the writer." Gordon, reflecting on her life as a writer, wrote, "The work I do is not suitable for a woman. It is unsexing. I speak with real conviction here. I don't write 'the womanly novel.' I write the same kind of novel a man would write, only it is ten times harder for me to write it than it would be for a man who had the same degree of talent." Difficulties notwithstanding, Gordon remained faithful to her quest, and it is surely significant that her closest approximation of an autobiographical narrative may be found in her fictionalized first-person account of her father's life, *Aleck Maury, Sportsman*. Gordon's determination to write in the "male" mode embodied her visceral reaction against the sentimentalized, romanticized, and idealized Civil War romance usually associated with female authors. Unfortunately for Gordon, her novel was eclipsed by the publication of the greatest exemplar of that tradition, *Gone with the Wind*. Gordon immediately recognized that Mitchell's novel would outsell *None Shall Look Back* and wrote to a friend, Sally Wood, "Margaret Mitchell has got all the trade, damn her. They say it took her ten years to write that novel. Why couldn't it have taken twelve?"[2]

None Shall Look Back, which appeared in 1937, begins predictably enough, with a barbecue at the Allard plantation, but Gordon had no intention of focusing on the home front. Rather, she intended to "take a soldier through the four years of the war." Gordon considered her hero worthy of study and praise by writers who recited "his glorious deeds, pausing between recitals, to meditate on the mystery that sets him apart from his fellows." "From the beginning," writes Gregory, Gordon "seems to have envisioned a narrative difficult to achieve, one that should be epic in spirit—a tale memorializing the deeds of a hero, set in the context of the concrete, valuable, though flawed world for which he is willing to die." Most southern women authors had rejected the teleological structure of male war discourse—a soldier's story from righteous beginning to tragic or victorious end—because such narrative structures marginalized noncombatants. Gordon, in contrast, embraced the task of penetrating "masculine mysteries which she herself could never experience." She consistently emphasized the ways in which the difficulties of writing a Civil War epic, as opposed to a romance, peculiarly affected the woman writer. Some southern literary critics, however, have viewed the difficulties as more general and have argued that they prevented any southern novelist from producing a definitive story of the war. According to Louis D. Rubin, the greatest shortcoming of southern novels of the war results from their failure to predicate the picture of the war "on individual terms." In *None Shall Look Back*, however, Gordon sought precisely that individual perspective. Although she feared that she might have partially failed in her attempt to write the Civil War as an epic, she attributed the failure to her having written "the damn thing at top speed," even then qualifying, "I think it has some merit."[3]

Gordon's musings on her novel's merits did not hamper her expectations for the novel's sales. Anticipating poor sales in the wake of Mitchell's novel, Gordon confessed, "I think I might have made some money but for her." Although Gordon later noted that *None Shall Look Back* sold reasonably well, she nonetheless believed that external forces had limited the book's appeal. In addition to blaming *Gone with the Wind*'s overwhelming popularity for unfairly constricting the market, for example, she accused Scribner's of failing to market her novel aggressively. Her editor, Max Perkins, had worried about the "salability" of Gordon's proposed Civil War novel from the moment she sent him an outline. "The book will be written *directly*, I take it," he hopefully asked Gordon. He later accused "the rather oblique method of *Penhally*," Gordon's 1931 novel, of having "limited its audience to one on the higher levels, the more discriminating." Gordon charged that Scribner's never reassessed its initial evaluation of her as a highbrow author. Sometime after Scribner's published *None Shall Look Back*, Gordon fired off a letter to the firm, claiming,

> One of your writers told me years ago that the great difficulty at Scribner's is that "Once they have taken a certain tone towards your books they never change." I am convinced that you take the wrong tone towards my books. You have tried this non-committal advertising [*sic*]-on-the lowest-plane of action of four books. They have not sold. But my work has changed, steadily growing more human, easier to read. You are not going to get anywhere by saying "here is another good historical novel, remarkable for authentic detail." The idea is: At Last: A novel that combines historical reality with passion. . . . What's wrong with "passion?"

Gordon noted that Elizabeth Roberts's publishers did not market her works by claiming "Here is something nice about life in Kentucky" but instead wrote a brochure "telling the bookstore women what to think about her work." Moreover, Tate's Civil War novel, which "was higher-browed" than *None Shall Look Back* in Gordon's estimation, sold as well as her novel because "Putnam's had the book store women writing essays about it, competing for a prize." Gordon remained convinced that the "book store people" would be surprised to discover that Scribner's believed it had "something pretty good in me."[4]

Gordon's preparation for writing the novel might have induced Scribner's to maintain its policy toward the author. Like Mary Johnston, Gordon studied Civil War histories, papers of Confederate leaders, and the "Battles and Leaders" series published in *Century* magazine. She also studied classical accounts of war by Homer, Plutarch, and Thucydides, and she believed that this preparation paid off. Perkins initially expressed reservations about Gordon's ability to write battle scenes effectively. "War is so dramatic and colorful an element," he explained, "that when it fades out of a novel, it is very hard not to let the novel down." Presaging Rubin's, Edmund Wilson's, and others' criticisms of the American Civil

War novel, Perkins compared Gordon's plan, rather unfavorably, to *War and Peace*. That novel "almost ends with the end of the war," he recalled. "But in the book, there were intervals of peace between the wars, so that Tolstoi could do all that he wanted and yet not lose the climax of the war." Perkins then reminded Gordon that Tolstoy treated in an epilogue "all that part about Pierre and Natasha and Nicolai." Gordon proceeded undeterred and in the end believed that she had fared quite well. "One thing I really succeeded with," she explained, "each battle had to be treated in a different way or you'd get monotony. . . . I treated Ft. Donelson in Plutarchian style, reserving my personal impressions for Chickamauga. I worried about that but now after some months I believe it works out all right."[5]

Despite Gordon's confidence in her ability to write battle scenes, reviewers failed to reach a consensus on her success. Some found the scenes unconvincing: "Her pictures of cavalry and infantry maneuvers are somewhat bewildering to the uninitiated," wrote Jane Irdell Jones for the *Columbus (Georgia) Inquirer-Sun*, "and her battle scenes, all blood and horror[,] are . . . too long drawn out." The reviewer for the *New York World-Telegram* noted that although Gordon effectively portrayed the men and women of the plantation, "the captains and generals seem less convincing, and the military passages and dialogue are not lifelike." Elsie Ruth Chant of the *El Paso (Texas) Herald Post* found the battle scenes to be "manipulated," scarcely rising "above the history book descriptions." And Philip Russell of the *Savannah (Georgia) Press* believed Gordon incapable of writing believable battle scenes. "The author has undertaken a hard task," he admitted, "to see battles as men see them. But the authentic touch is not there. The descriptions are stirring and sound convincing, but the taste of blood and dirt does not come forth." Thus, according to Russell, Gordon's gender, not her artistic ability, prevented her from writing a true account of the Civil War.[6]

Other reviewers, however, found Gordon's ability to describe battle a singular feat. Gordon's mentor, Ford Madox Ford, confessed, "I do not know of any other book that so vitally renders the useless madness that is called war." Carl Van Doren proclaimed that the battle scenes were "the triumphs of her novel." The reviewer for the *Nation* agreed, noting that "the battle scenes . . . have a power and passion lacking and perhaps necessary in other sections of the book." Gordon's fellow writer and good friend, Katherine Anne Porter, pronounced the battle scenes "unbelievably fine and clear," adding that "there is an almost intolerable vividness in the landscape and the figures of men going into and coming away from battle. . . . I like the way you move around, a disembodied spectator in all places." Gordon could take small comfort from the fact that noted authors, critics, and personal friends penned the positive reviews, which appeared in national publications. But because Gordon cared less about specific battles than about the epic nature of war, the squabbling of reviewers probably mattered little to her. She likely took pleasure in the review published in the *Rocky Mount (North Carolina) Telegram*, which declared Gordon's style "vastly superior to Margaret Mitchell's."[7]

In addition to plumbing historical and classical influences, Gordon found models of literary technique and style in the works of Tolstoy and Dostoyevsky. The former suggested to Perkins a way to maintain readers' interest in the plot; the latter suggested to Gordon a way to assign moral responsibility for the sins of the South's past. Recognizing the formidable difficulties accompanying these tasks, however, she took solace from the consideration that her probable failure was not unprecedented. "The Brothers Karamazov, which hinges on the fact that each of the brothers is morally guilty of his father's death, does not," she noted, "really come off, as I found re-reading it last year. Comforting to think about that."[8]

The Brothers Karamazov probably did not figure prominently among other southern women writers' models for their narratives of the war. Even the more sophisticated authors, Mary Johnston and Ellen Glasgow, looked closer to home for their inspiration. Gordon, however, was writing during the high tide of literary modernism, and, perhaps more important, she lived in intimate association with the Southern Agrarians, who influenced both her developing conception of literary craft and her understanding of the South. Many of those who would become known as the Agrarians had first joined forces as the Fugitives, a group of poets dedicated to a modernist renewal and purification of their craft. In 1930, with a marked shift in focus, they published a collection of essays, *I'll Take My Stand*, with authorship credited to "Twelve Southerners," in which they advanced "traditional" southern values as an antidote to the destructive onslaught of capitalism and materialism.

The South of the Agrarian imagination bore little relation to the land of moonlight and magnolias except inasmuch as it was presented as the embodiment of an alternate and superior way of life. The Agrarian vision gave short shrift to slaves and slaveholders, virtually ignoring the purported chivalric tradition of the Old South. Rather, the Agrarians focused on the prevalence of independent yeoman households that cradled time-honored, classical virtues of liberty, moderation, and well-tempered individualism. Johnston's focus on aristocratic women was a legacy of the immediate postwar fiction that she had trouble releasing; she still thought in terms of a slaveholder's story. Gordon, however, drew heavily on the Agrarian vision, which powerfully shaped her sense of the most valuable aspects of southern society and traditions. Similarly, the Agrarians' distinct literary canons influenced hers, and, like them, she drew heavily on classical poetics, notably in relation to the epic and to tragedy. For Gordon as for the Agrarians, classical conceptions of the epic and tragedy focused on the abiding features of the human condition—those aspects of human character that recur in each generation. In such a view, historical specifics might change, but such manifestations of human character as greed, ambition, pride, heroism, and loyalty abided, and they, rather than the conditions in which they manifested themselves, merited the writer's attention. More tension than Gordon and the Agrarians admitted might have existed between this transhistorical vision of human character and the defense of the South as the last best hope of civilization, but Gordon's interest in writing an epic undoubtedly deterred her from presenting specific historical events as an end in themselves.

Gordon shared with her cohort a disdain for the crass materialism associated with the postwar South and perhaps even more explicitly with the post–World War I South. Late in *None Shall Look Back*, the Allards, forced to abandon their plantation, which has burned and been overrun by insolent slaves, have resorted to renting a modest cottage from the much socially inferior yet immensely practical Bradleys. To help pay the rent, Jim Allard works in the Bradley store and falls increasingly under the sway of the Bradley worldview. While gathering a few items for his father, who suffers from "shell shock" as a result of the loss of his plantation, "a lean country man whose boots were caked to the knees with red clay" walks in and asks, "Got any coffee?" Without checking the shelves, Jim immediately responds, "How are you going to pay for it?" When the stranger whips out a fat roll of Confederate bills, Jim shakes his head, apologizing: "Sorry, brother, but we aren't taking them." Desperate for coffee, the man fishes in his pocket for a "two-bit shin plaster." The exchange then proceeds smoothly, and the man leaves. The entire transaction, however, disgusts Jim's sister, Cally:

"Jim," she said coldly, "I should think you'd be ashamed to take that poor man's money." Jim tried to be airy. "Why? He wanted coffee and I wanted money. Fair exchange is no robbery." She hardly listened to what he said. She leaned over and brushed the shin-plaster off the counter. She set her heel on the paper and ground it into the floor. "You take the enemy's money.

. . . You're no better than a spy or a deserter." Jim's lip trembled and beads of sweat sprang out on his forehead but he kept his voice calm. "Now look here, Cally. I couldn't go to war as you very well know. But I've got to do something. You can't run a store without taking in money and there's no use taking in money that ain't worth the paper it's printed on."[9]

Gordon might have harbored a certain sympathy for Jim's position, but it is likely that she also found compelling Cally's loyalty to an increasingly untenable way of life.

Gordon originally intended Jim to be much more complicit in his conversion to the Yankee worldview. A late, corrected typescript of the novel contains a scene in which Jim invents a mechanical corn shucker. "There's money in this contraption," Mr. Bradley informs a bright-eyed Jim. Although the two men find the prototype promising, they realize that a problem lies in getting the machine to market. "How's a man going to run his business with the country all cut up the way it is?" asks Mr. Bradley. "Well, they're going to have to stop fighting pretty soon. Stop fighting and raise corn. Yes, they'll be raising corn long after they've stopped fighting and that's where you'll come in, my boy, with this little contraption." Bradley's musings force Jim to recall his failures while developing his machine, but "it was finished now, worked out to the last detail, a machine which would take the place of five, ten, Lord knows how many men. And Mr. Bradley would put it on the market for him."[10] Gordon's motivation for deleting Jim's participation in the South's nascent foray into industrialism remains unclear, but she may well have found his willingness to adopt the northern worldview too complete, his abandonment of southern traditions too easy.

Perhaps Gordon's inability to offer a specific program or remedy for the ills of industrialism convinced her to alter the scene. Gordon's inability or unwillingness to solve the ills of the modern age is not surprising, for *I'll Take My Stand* remained conspicuously silent on that score. Her description of the effects of industrialism reads much like the manifesto of the Southern Agrarians. John Crowe Ransom, who essentially wrote the book's Statement of Principles, explained,

The regular act of applied science is to introduce into labor a labor-saving machine. Whether this is a benefit depends on how far it is advisable to save the labor. The philosophy of applied science is generally quite sure that the saving of labor is a pure gain, and that the more of it the better. This is to assume that labor is an evil, that only the end of labor or the material product is good. On this assumption labor becomes mercenary and servile, and it is no wonder if many forms of modern labor are accepted without resentment though they are evidently brutalizing. The act of labor as one of the happy functions of human life has been in effect abandoned, and it is practiced solely for its rewards.

As Paul Conkin notes, however, neither Ransom nor the other Agrarians offered a specific remedy for industrialism, leaving "a set of glittering principles that are almost as obvious as respect for motherhood." Gordon may well have been similarly unprepared to provide the antidote to industrialism. She intended *None Shall Look Back* as a literary response to romanticism and sentimentalism, but as Conkin argues regarding the Agrarians' conception as presented in *I'll Take My Stand*, Gordon wanted "at the same time use the South as a concrete example of human fulfillment and as a way of pointing to the limitations of the generally unanchored platform of the New Humanists."[11] Perhaps, then, Gordon's decision to excise the discussion of industrialism and its attendant evils stemmed from her desire to avoid prescribing a particular solution, rooted in southern and American culture, to a modernist worldview.

Jim knows that Cally considers his "fall" unforgivable. Most egregious, perhaps, is Jim's abandonment of the Confederate war effort. Indeed, "in the last months he had almost forgotten that the war was going on." Cally, however, can never forget. In both the typescript and published versions, however, Cally receives reinforcement with the return of their brother, Ned, recently released from Johnson's Island through a prisoner-exchange program. A mere skeleton, with flesh around his eye sockets so shrunken and withered that "it was if the man had stopped seeing," Ned can think of nothing to do with his newfound freedom other than to reenlist in the Confederate army. Jim, reminded of his own inability to serve the South, becomes incensed. What possible use, he impatiently demands, could Ned be to the army when he was so weak that he was not even "worth feeding"? But although Jim convinces Ned that he would be more of a burden than an asset to the army, Jim cannot, in the published version, persuade Ned to stay on and help with the Bradleys' store. "Well," Ned complacently responds to Jim's tirade, "I reckon tomorrow or the next day I'll go on out to Brackets." Jim explodes at Ned's decision to return to the ruined family plantation, but this anger does not deter Ned, who understands that even if "there ain't anything there but a lot of niggers eating their heads off," the land remains.

"The Yankees couldn't burn that and they ain't strong enough to cart it off," he states simply. Ned's decision overjoys the rest of the Allard family, especially Cally, who regards her near-dead brother as her deliverer from the Bradleys and all that they represent. Cally readily grasps the implications of her decision to turn her back on the Bradleys and their way of life. "Old Man Bradley don't care about anything but making money," she explains. "And he's got all his money in United States bonds in a Cincinnati bank. The talk is he's traded in contraband cotton and I don't doubt it. . . . They say we're losing the war. I reckon if we do people like him'll rule this country."[12] And with that, Cally walks away to return to the land and way of life that was hers by birthright and inheritance.

Gordon's rejection of the trajectory of the New South does not, however, mean that she found the Old South untarnished. At one point in the novel, an opponent of secession dismisses the aristocratic Lower South, complaining, "It's too rich. . . . Those fellows down there got rich too quick and it's gone to their heads. If somebody don't hold them down they'll ruin the country." Yet Gordon populated *None Shall Look Back* with characters who were willing to die for this flawed South. In her view, their willingness to die did not diminish or trivialize the pathos of the Lost Cause but rather ennobled it. In a pivotal battle scene late in the novel, a desperate Nathan Bedford Forrest, "mounted on top of his saddle and standing there, seemingly unconscious of the target he presented, deliberately studied the field." His action is not without controversy. Riding past the general, Major Strange whispers with contempt, "Be killed. That's what he wants. Be killed." Rives Allard, Forrest's scout and the novel's hero, swears, "God damn . . . Lying . . . dirty . . . *coward!*" Allard is, of course, cursing Major Strange. Allard stands in his stirrups, waves his arms crazily, and shouts, "He's got the right. . . . Everyman. Got the right. To get killed."[13] Forrest escapes the battle unscathed, but Allard does not, proving perhaps that every man does indeed have the right to be killed.

Allard's fall forces upon Forrest the sudden realization that death "had been with him all the time and he had not known. . . . But they had all known. Hood, Bragg, Buckner, Floyd, His Excellency. . . . Those men, who weighed and considered, looked to this side, to that. They had whispered their constrained 'No's' not to him but to that dog, Death." Even Rives Allard, who had begun the war thinking that "the other men were in possession of some knowledge, of which he had only a part," finally understands what has heretofore eluded Forrest. Forrest has always taken personally disagreements with his supervisors about proper military procedure: dismissed because he did not attend West Point, envied because of his ingenuity, or resented by cowardly and recalcitrant ranking generals and statesmen, Forrest had believed that he had ample justification for his attitude. None of Forrest's superiors had escaped his contempt, but he seemed especially scornful of General Bragg, "the man with the iron hand, the iron heart, and the wooden head." As one of Forrest's scouts, Allard had been privy to many of these confrontations between Forrest and his superiors, and Allard initially "had been excited to think that he, a private, was receiving information about important maneuvers. That emotion seemed trivial now." Allard had spent the morning searching the body-strewn battlefield of Chickamauga looking for the remains of his cousin, George Rowan, an exercise that now "seemed trivial, too, and vain. He thought of George Rowan dead and buried on the field. He had felt pity for the dead man as he laid him in his grave but now he knew envy. If the Confederate cause failed—and for the first time he felt fear for its outcome—there could be no happiness for him except in the grave."[14] Allard's death, unremarkable in every other sense, triggers Forrest's sudden understanding of the nature of warfare and of his contributions to the fate of the Confederacy.

Gordon intended to end *None Shall Look Back* with Allard's death and Forrest's sudden realization that Death had always been his enemy. The published version, however, contains an additional chapter, which Gordon wrote after reviewing the final galley proofs. Gordon might have remembered Perkins's comments about *War and Peace*. More likely, she considered her original ending too grounded in a particular historical moment—the bloodied fields of Murfreesboro. The published epilogue removes the action from the battlefield to the home front, where Lucy Allard learns of her husband's death. Already destroyed by the war, Lucy wonders how "this death he had died was different from the other, imagined deaths." Gordon thus effectively put the action in the universal. At least one reader reassured Gordon on her "brilliant use of Death," believing that "it is in Lucy's defeat," not in the historical Nathan Bedford Forrest's, that the theme finds its ultimate significance."[15]

No more than other white southern women novelists did Gordon attribute the South's defeat to its past sins. No more than Johnston did Gordon believe that an inherently evil and destructive force had overcome the South. In other words, Gordon did not view the war through the prism of a morality play that pitted a good and a bad protagonist against one another. Unlike others, notably Johnston, however, Gordon did not regard war itself as the villain. Rather, following the canons of the epic, she suggested that the Confederacy had fallen because of the tragic flaws of individuals—of men like Forrest who manipulated the fates of those around them. Gordon's vision allowed for the possibility that the fall of the Confederacy had been predetermined, but not because of some nostalgic myth of moonlight and magnolias and not because all war is an inherently destructive and leveling force. She never denied that some wars had to be fought to defend the higher good of civilization, she never claimed that no cause could justify the loss of a single human life in war, and she never suggested that all wars were inherently meaningless. To the contrary, she seems to have believed that war might uniquely test a person's mettle and character and thus reveal something important about human nature. In the end, Forrest comes to understand that he has failed precisely the test he had thought he was acing, and his hard-won self-knowledge offers an object lesson in the Aristotelian theory of tragedy. Some readers may feel that Gordon did not fully execute her vision — that *None Shall Look Back* retains a heavier dose of social and historical commentary and offers less reflection on human character than Gordon might have hoped — but the possibility of a less-than-perfect execution does not gainsay the aspiration.

This perspective helps to identify Gordon as the last adherent of a tradition that her work effectively laid to rest. Many writers would continue to try their hands at the conventional myth-of-moonlight-and-magnolias romance and would enjoy impressive sales. But the living force of the tradition had drained away under the combined pressures of newly deadly wars, modernism, and the emergence of the New South. The realities of that world exposed nostalgia as precisely nostalgia — the antithesis of literary vitality and innovation. But it remains striking that, in Gordon's case, the attempt to break free of the nostalgia led not away from war but to a new way of telling its story.

Speaking in 1974 before the Flannery O'Connor Foundation, Caroline Gordon proudly proclaimed, "I am a totally unreconstructed Confederate." She seemed to revel in her position as an oddity, a "rarity." "You won't find many of us around these days," she noted. Her political position stemmed in part from her association with the "parlor pinks" of the 1930s. "I came to believe," she confessed, "that the fact that we lost the Civil War was not only a disaster for the South but for the whole nation." The cultural silencing of works sympathetic to the Confederacy contributed to Gordon's unpopular political stance. Citing historian E. D. Dodd, Gordon noted that "the trouble with us was not that we were defeated but that we were licked. The side that wins the war writes the histories, of course," she mused. "The true history of our great conflict yet remains to be told." The literary scene had changed considerably, however, since Dodd's proclamation. Indeed, Gordon found solace in the "contemporary literary scene." In her view, the best fiction writers were southerners. Although many commentators had recognized that southerners dominated the literary market, few had "discerned any connection between the prevalence of good writers in the South and history." For Gordon, that connection was "vital." Alluding to the title of one of Flannery O'Connor's most famous short stories, Gordon ended her lecture by stating, "Everything that rises must converge but everything that converges must have risen. Hold your Confederate money, boys!" she advised. "The South has risen again."[16]

This book belies the claims of those who feared that the winners would write history. The results of the Civil War proved notoriously difficult for white southerners to understand and to negotiate. They turned to their pens at the outset of the hostilities to explain themselves to their society and increasingly the nation. Women contributed to this project with vigor and a keen appreciation of the significance of their endeavors. Their narratives did not necessarily supplant those of southern men but rather intertwined with them to help fashion both a cultural memory of the war and a postbellum identity for the region.

Notes

Abbreviations

CV *Confederate Veteran*

ESC Special Collections Department, Robert W. Woodruff Library, Emory
   University, Atlanta

GHS Georgia Historical Society, Savannah

PL   Special Collections Department, William R. Perkins Library, Duke University,
   Durham, North Carolina

SC   South Caroliniana Library, University of South Carolina, Columbia

SHC Southern Historical Collection, Louis R. Wilson Library, University of North
   Carolina, Chapel Hill

SHSP *Southern Historical Society Papers*

UDC United Daughters of the Confederacy

UGA Hargrett Rare Books and Manuscripts Library, University of Georgia, Athens

UVA Special Collections Department, University of Virginia Library, Charlottesville

Introduction

1. Faulkner, *Flags*, 13–14; Faulkner, *Absalom, Absalom!* 7–8. Earlier in this novel, Quentin Compson, ruminating on Rosa Coldfield's intent desire to tell him about Thomas Sutpen, concludes, "*It's because she wants it told* he thought *so that people whom she will never see and whose names she will never hear and who have never heard her name nor seen her face will read it and know at last why God let us lose the war: that only through the blood of our men and the tears of our women could He stay this demon and efface his name and lineage from the earth*" (6).

2. Henry Fleming, John Carrington, and Basil Ransom are, respectively, the protagonists of Stephen Crane's 1895 novel, *The Red Badge of Courage*; Henry Adams's 1880 novel, *Democracy*; and Henry James's 1884 novel, *The Bostonians*.

3. Lady of Virginia, *Diary*, 219–20; McDonald, *Woman's Civil War*, 231.

4. See, for example, Aaron, *Unwritten War*; Simpson, *Mind*; R. P. Warren, *Legacy*; E. Wil-

son, *Patriotic Gore*. For an account of southern women's writings during the war years, see Fahs, *Imagined Civil War*, esp. chap. 4. Sizer's *Political Work* examines the lives and works of nine northern women who write during the Civil War period. See also E. Young, *Disarming*, for an account of women's writings during the war. For a reading that considers specifically "Victorian" Americans' efforts to tailor "the facts of the war to their own cultural ends" by carefully crafting their reminiscences and memoirs, see Rose, *Victorian America*, 235–55. On Mary Chesnut, see, for example, Hayhoe, "Mary Boykin Chesnut"; Muhlenfeld, *Mary Boykin Chesnut*; Woodward, "Mary Chesnut." On Margaret Mitchell, see, for example, Cullen, *Civil War*; Fox-Genovese, "Scarlett O'Hara"; Hale, *Making Whiteness*; Pyron, *Southern Daughter*; "Coming to Terms with Scarlett."

5. Katherine Anne Porter to Caroline Gordon, New York, 11 February 1937, Caroline Gordon Papers, Princeton University Library, Rare Books and Special Collections Department, Princeton, New Jersey. Porter later savaged *So Red the Rose* in a *New Republic* review of Gordon's 1937 novel, *None Shall Look Back*. I do not mean to suggest that Porter did not embellish, alter, or fabricate her family history. Rather, I wish to highlight Porter's disgust with Young's version of the Civil War story and his misrepresentation of what she believed to be the significance of her family's memories. On Porter, see Brinkmeyer, *Katherine Anne Porter's Artistic Development*; Busby and Heaberlin, *From Texas*; Stout, *Katherine Anne Porter*.

There is a large body of feminist theory literature on the relations among women, war, and war narrative. See, for example, M. Cooke and Woollacott, *Gendering War Talk*; M. Cooke, *Women*; Elshtain, "On Beautiful Souls"; Elshtain, *Women and War*; Huston, "Tales"; Huston, "Matrix." These theorists challenge the assumption that war is solely a male phenomenon, arguing that because women are generally noncombatants, their roles in war are as disseminators of information, tellers of tales, and creators of history. Once the stories of the battlefield filter back to the home front, they become part of the public domain and fodder for women's narratives.

Miriam Cooke points out that "most wars were recounted within a narrative frame that the British military historian John Keegan argues has remained unchanged since Thucydides." Cooke refers to this narrative frame as the War Story and argues that it forces a grid on chaos. Although wars are usually experienced as confusion, their narratives are neat. The War Story arranges "experience and actors into neat pairs: beginning and ending; foe and friend; aggression and defense; war and peace; front and home; combatant and civilian." She later explains that "the dichotomies of the War Story organize the confusion so that aggression should not be confused with defense, victory with defeat, civilian with combatant, home with front, women's work with men's work" (*Women*, 15–16). Many southern women did not draw the dichotomies so neatly—the divide between civilian and combatant, home and front, women's work and men's work, for example, often did not exist. These women's war narratives thus can offer an alternative to the conventional War Story.

6. In an effort to counter the already prevailing opinion that the South had lost because of inadequate war matériel and an inferior army, Pollard insisted instead that "the Confederates, with an abler Government and more resolute spirit, might have accomplished their independence." Moreover, despite this defeat, "the Confederates have gone out of this war

with the proud, secret, deathless, *dangerous* consciousness that they are THE BETTER MEN, and there was nothing wanting but a change in a set of circumstances and a firmer resolve to make them the victors." The memory of defeat, coupled with this knowledge that theirs was a nobler cause, reasoned Pollard, had left southerners with a "deathless heritage of glory." "Under these traditions," Pollard proclaimed, "sons will grow to manhood and lessons sink deep that are learned from the lips of widowed mothers" (*Lost Cause*, 729, 752). Pollard's version of the Confederacy's downfall became the foundation for a myth of the Lost Cause, which, as some historians argue, dominated the postwar white southern consciousness. For a fine historiographical essay on the myth of the Lost Cause, see Nolan, "Anatomy."

7. In the political area, Coulter's 1947 work, *The South during Reconstruction*, for example, confirms Pollard's assertion that the Lost Cause could be regained in the field of politics. For Coulter, the creation of the myth coincided with the South's triumph over Reconstruction. Southerners created the Lost Cause myth not only to celebrate the Confederacy but also to promote a political agenda for the postwar South based on white supremacy. Defeated white southerners had viewed their new battle with the federal government in terms of racial survival. The end of Reconstruction and the ascendancy of the Democratic Party in the South signaled the triumph of the white race. With this victory, "the Confederate tradition . . . cast its resplendent light throughout the South — the Lost Cause had been regained" (Coulter, *South*, 180). Coulter was not without his critics. Four years after the publication of his book, Woodward published *The Origins of the New South*, in which he disparages Coulter's celebration of the resurgence of white supremacy in the South and argues that this goal was at the center of the Lost Cause myth. In the chapter "The Divided Mind of the New South," Woodward suggests that along with the industrialization and urbanization of the postbellum South came a "cult of archaism, a nostalgic vision of the past" (154–55). This reading of southern history not only validated the past but allowed the South to forge a new identity necessary to assume the position of an industrialized region. Twenty years later, Paul Gaston offered a reading of the Lost Cause myth that was very much in line with Woodward's. Gaston connects the creation of the Lost Cause myth with the development of the New South creed, a philosophy that advocates regional distinction, racial harmony, and the creation of a new economic and social order based both on industry and a diversified agriculture, "all of which would lead, eventually, to the South's dominance in the reunited union" (*New South Creed*, 6–7; see also Holden, "'Is Our Love?'").

Scholars examining the religious aspects of the myth maintain that the South understand its history in Christian terms, complete with iconography, with Robert E. Lee as the Christ figure and James Longstreet as the Antichrist. Southerners created the myth, which became a civil religion, to advance the position that they lost the Civil War because they had grown complacent in their belief that they were God's chosen people. Defeat, however, did not signal the South's fall from grace but rather God's providence at work. Just as colonial New England had deciphered its jeremiad, the South interpreted its downfall as a sign that God had selected its people to endure this travail. Defeat confirmed southerners' chosen status and did not indicate that the South was wrong in its intentions. Once southerners recognized that they were the servants of God, they would eventually triumph over evil. The South had lost a holy war, but because God was on the side of the Confederacy, the mythmakers could expect, according to historian Charles Reagan Wilson, a "joyful resurrection" of the southern cause (*Baptized in Blood*, 13; see also Connelly and Bellows, *God and General Longstreet*; L. A. Hunter, "Immortal Confederacy").

Both Cash and Foster argue that the myth had such a profound cultural resonance on the South that it generated a set of memories common to all white southerners. Although southerners were not the first to sentimentalize defeat, Cash doubts that the process had ever been carried to the length it had in the South. Southerners responded to their "absorbing need" to glorify not only the Confederacy but also the entire antebellum way of life. This glorification led, in turn, to an unshakable belief in the legitimacy of the Old South's social hierarchy and an unflinching acceptance of the former master class's right to guide and command the New South. Cash thus contends not only that the progress of the New South stems from the past but also that its language and figures are those from the Civil War (*Mind*, 145). In *Ghosts of the Confederacy*, Foster agrees with Cash that a creation of a southern collective memory lies at the core of the Lost Cause myth, though Foster disputes Cash's pronouncement that the myth's greatest proponents came from the old planter aristocracy. Foster argues instead that the myth's creators, most notably the United Confederate Veterans and the United Daughters of the Confederacy, came from the newly emerging urban and professional classes. Indeed, when Confederate celebrations became elite social events rather than grassroots activities, the myth began to lose its cultural currency(see also Bohannon, "'These Few Gray-Haired, Battle-Scarred Veterans"; Carmichael, "New South Visionaries").

Scholars who address the literary manifestations of the myth have erroneously posited that southerners created the myth not to assert their superiority or even separateness from the North but to reconcile themselves with their erstwhile foes. According to Buck, an early historian of the postwar southern consciousness, the Lost Cause myth was a defense of the South couched in literary conventions, giving southerners a "heritage of courage, energy, and strength" without offending the North (*Road*, 205). According to Osterweis, who agreed with Buck's interpretation of southern history, the myth found its first expression in the literature of a defeated people anxious over a lost identity. Southerners quickly fixated on a cast of familiar characters drawn from the prewar plantation tradition in order to legitimate their past, to ease the sense of defeat and displacement, and, most importantly, to reintegrate themselves into the Union. The bitterness of wartime rhetoric gave way to the expressed desire for national unity (Osterweis, *Myth*). Gallagher cast doubt on Buck's and Osterweis's arguments, however, in "Jubal A. Early, the Lost Cause, and Civil War History," an essay on Early's literary efforts to defend the Confederate cause.

8. Smiley, "Quest."

9. Works by southern male writers include, among others, J. Davis, *Rise and Fall*; Eggleston, *History*; Gildersleeve, *Creed*; C. W. Harris, *Sectional Struggle*; J. Longstreet, *From Manassas to Appomattox*; Page, *Old South*; Page, *Meh Lady*; Page, *Red Rock*; Stephens, *Constitutional View*. For histories of the war sympathetic to the northern position, see, for example, Burgess, *Civil War*; S. Cox, *Union-Disunion-Reunion*; Draper, *History*; Duyckinck, *National History*; Formby, *American Civil War*; Greeley, *American Conflict*; Headley, *Great Rebellion*; George, *Popular History*; Rhodes, *History of the United States*; Rhodes, *Lectures*.

A list of pro-North fiction includes but is not limited to Adams, *Democracy*; Avery, *Rebel General's Loyal Bride*; Bierce, *Civil War Short Stories*; Craig, *Was She?* Crane, *Red Badge*; Dickinson, *What Answer?* De Forest, *Kate Beaumont*; De Forest, *Miss Ravenel's Conversion*; De Forest, *Bloody Chasm*; Norris, *Grapes*; James, *Bostonians*; Pearson, *The Poor White*; Tourgée, *Bricks*.

10. Gallagher, introduction, 9. My interpretation of the significance of the Civil War directly contradicts that of Michael Kammen in *A Season of Youth*, which argues that the Revolutionary War has been the single most important event in the formation of an American imagination. As historian John G. Barrett notes, in 1866 John Russell Bartlett published *Literature of the Rebellion*, in which he cited more than six thousand books, articles, and pamphlets on the Civil War and slavery ("Confederate States," 277). By the late twentieth century, a similar appraisal would include well over ten thousand titles.

11. Faust's controversial argument, presented in full in *Mothers of Invention*, that the withdrawal of southern women's support for the war led, in large measure, to the Confederacy's ultimate defeat, did not translate into southern women's narratives of the war. For an argument similar to Faust's, see Edwards, *Scarlett*. For the most part, southern women cast themselves as unwavering supporters of the Confederacy. A fascinating and notable exception to this rule was Rebecca Latimer Felton, who changed dramatically her interpretation of the meanings and legacies of the war for her widely differing audiences. See also Evelyn Scott's *The Wave* for an exception to this generalization.

12. Here, my work has been influenced by recent studies that explicate the inextricable link between history and memory. See, for example, Butler, *Memory*; Finley, "Myth, Memory, and History"; Halbwachs, *On Collective Memory*; Hobsbawm and Ranger, *Invention*; Lowenthal, *Past*; Wachtel, "Memory and History"; Nora, "Between Memory and History"; Cohen, *Production*; McNeill, "Mythistory." For specific discussions on collective memory and the American context, I cite here only Blight, *Race and Reunion*; Thelen, *Memory and American History*; and Kammen's monumental work, *Mystic Chords of Memory*. For specific discussions of memory in the southern context, see two recent articles by Hall, "Open Secrets" and "'You Must Remember This.'" In both articles, Hall considers Katherine Du Pre Lumpkin's efforts to fashion a New South history that escaped the myth of the Lost Cause. For more scientific discussions of memory, see, for example, Bolles, *Remembering*; Middleton and Edwards, *Collective Remembering*; Neisser, *Memory Observed*; G. L. Wells and Loftus, *Eyewitness Testimony*.

13. As another example of the shifting boundaries of the Lost Cause myth, I offer a reading of two scenes, one from Augusta Jane Evans's 1864 war story, *Macaria*, and one from Mary Johnston's 1912 novel, *Cease Firing!* In the first scene, Evans wrote of a heavy, square morocco ambrotype of a Confederate soldier's sweetheart that miraculously spares the life of the hero, Russell Aubrey, by preventing a deadly bullet from penetrating his chest. The locket's glass cracks, but the image escapes damage. When Russell looks at the face of his beloved Irene, "nobler associations, [and] purer aims" possess him and he beams "with 'triumphant joy for the [southern] Nation's first great victory'" (320). Nearly fifty years later, Mary Johnston wrote of a bullet striking the image of a soldier's sweetheart. In this instance, the scene is not Manassas, where the Confederates had prevailed, but the bloodied fields of Gettysburg, and the daguerreotype fails to stop the bullet. The bullet not only

shatters the image but kills the unnamed soldier. Johnston, who knew *Macaria*, was explicitly referring to it when she turned on its head the story of the bullet, the image of the southern belle, and the soldier. Although only brief incidents in much larger works, these scenes signal the transformations of war narratives that transpired during the postwar period.

14. See Augusta Jane Evans to Mrs. J. K. Chrisman, Mobile, Alabama, 3 February 1866, Augusta Jane Evans Wilson Papers, Alabama Department of Archives and History, Montgomery; Augusta Jane Evans to Alexander H. Stephens, Mobile, Alabama, 29 November 1865, Alexander H. Stephens Papers, ESC; Faust, introduction to A. J. Evans, *Macaria*, xvi. Evans returned to southern history as the catalyst for the action of her novel *A Speckled Bird*.

15. Cornelia Branch Stone, report of the president-general of the UDC, in UDC, *Minutes of the Fourteenth Annual Convention of the United Daughters of the Confederacy, Held in Norfolk, Virginia, 13–16 November 1907* (Opelika, Ala.: Post, 1908), 71.

16. These works, when studied at all, have not fared much better with southern literary critics. Indeed, critics have dismissed as wretched stuff most of the postbellum fiction on the war — and not just the stories written by southern women. These observers have nevertheless reserved their harshest criticism for southern authors, who, because they were writing for the vanquished, should have written the definitive novel of the war modeled on Tolstoy's *War and Peace*. The greatest failing of these novels, charged Louis D. Rubin, is that "the picture of the war is not predicated on individual terms." The characters merely "serve as spokesmen for the region's attitudes, as the authors conceive them" ("Image," 51, 56–57). Other critics who share this view include Aaron, *Unwritten War*; Sullivan, "Fading Memory"; and E. Wilson, *Patriotic Gore*. In other words, southern authors "fail" to portray the southern crisis writ small, the established criterion for the definitive Civil War novel. If women writers have rejected the teleological structure of male war discourse — a soldier's story from a righteous beginning to a tragic or victorious end — it does not follow that they do not make significant contributions to war narratives. Feminist critics argue that women are marginalized by such a narrative structure because they are, for the most part, noncombatants. Rather than a world of armed conflict, theirs is a world of rumors, tales, and stories of the war. They are from the outset participants in a newly generated discourse (see, for example, Elshtain, *Women and War*; Faust, "Altars"). Search as they might, Rubin and others will never find the "definitive" war narrative in the accounts of these women. Rather than exploring the ways in which the sectional crisis manifested itself in the individual, southern women concerned themselves with the connections between the individual and the larger southern community. Most of all, these women writers wished to explore the connections between the community and its past in order to comprehend its future. Through evocations of time and memory, such authors connect the reader or the participant to the historic and imagined past. Although not writing specifically of the imaginative works on the Civil War written by women, C. Vann Woodward stresses southern fiction's importance for the historian precisely because of the genre's concern not with an individual at sea fighting with a whale but with community. The southern author deals with humans "as an inextricable part of a community, attached and determined in a thousand ways to other wills and destinies of a people he [*sic*] has only heard about" (Woodward, *Burden*, 37).

Chapter One

1. Emma Edwards Holmes diary, 13, 27 February, June 1861, TS, Emma Edwards Holmes Papers, South Caroliniana Library, University of South Carolina, Columbia. Holmes's position was a popular one among South Carolinian women. Grace Elmore claimed, for example, "How proud have I been of Carolina[,] of her untarnished career from the time of the Revolution when she was amongst the first to free herself from a tyrant's sway to the time that she was the first to break the links that bound the States together" (Elmore diary, 7 December 1861, Grace B. Elmore Papers, SHC; see also 27 February 1861 entry).

2. Fox-Genovese, *Within the Plantation Household*, 247–52; S. Stowe, "City, Country, and the Feminine Voice," 316. In this chapter, I am concerned primarily with those diaries kept during the Civil War that exist only in manuscript form or that were published during the war. I did not, for the most part, examine for this chapter those wartime diaries/journals that were published in the postbellum period. I have made this decision because, as I argue throughout this work, any given Civil War narrative was as much a product of its historical context as it was of the events of the war. In no way should the list of works cited in this chapter be considered exhaustive. I have chosen diaries that best illustrate the issues confronted by Confederate women who kept wartime chronicles of events. Much fine work has been published on Confederate women's wartime diaries. For more detailed discussion, see, for example, Faust, *Mothers*; Rable, *Civil Wars*.

3. Louisiana Burge diary, 4 May 1860, Burge Family Papers, ESC; Temple and Bunkers, "Mothers, Daughters, Diaries."

4. Moss, *Domestic Novelists*, 4. For an account of the wartime literary market, see Fahs, *Imagined Civil War*, chap. 1. For an introduction to domestic fiction, see D. Anderson, *House Undivided*; Baym, *Woman's Fiction*; Kelley, *Private Woman*; Tompkins, *Sensational Designs*; Voloshin, "Limits." For works specifically on domesticity in southern fiction, see Moss, *Domestic Novelists*. For an account of women's literary professionalism, the literary marketplace, and the cultural context of nineteenth-century women writers, see Coultrap-McQuin, *Doing Literary Business*. The *Southern Literary Messenger* detailed the duties of antebellum southern authors: "Let Southern authors, men [*sic*] who see and know slavery as it is, make it their duty to deluge all the realms of literature with a flood of light upon this subject. Let them dispel with the sun of genius the mists and clouds which ignorance and fanaticism have thrown around slavery, purposely involving it in an obscurity and darkness, through which men will not grope to find the truths upon which it reposes. This, then, is the 'Duty of Southern Authors'" (W.R.A., "Duty," 242). Despite the gendered nature of the journal's call, southern white women also met the challenge.

5. Augusta Jane Evans to P. G. T. Beauregard, [Mobile, Alabama?], 4 August 1862, in McMillan, *Alabama Confederate Reader*, 354. For a discussion of the "feminized war," see Fahs, *Imagined Civil War*, chap. 4.

6. McDonald, *Woman's Civil War*, 21. In reviewing southern white women's diaries of the Civil War, Faust observes that the "very process of authorship itself nurtured new female self-consciousness" (*Mothers*, 161–68) Although I do not disagree with Faust's interpretation, I do place stronger emphasis than she does on the act of writing about war rather than on merely writing.

7. Kate Rowland diaries (microfilm), 29 October 1863, ESC; Margaret Junkin Preston diary, 3 April 1862, in Allan, *Life and Letters*, 134–35. Preston noted on 14 April 1862 that

she did not intend to indulge in "moaning in these bald pages; nor to write down any opinions; merely to essay a very brief record of such *facts* as I am personally concerned with, for future reference" (Allan, *Life and Letters*, 137). Grace B. Elmore (1839–1912), daughter of South Carolina Senator and John C. Calhoun supporter Franklin Harper Elmore, began her war diary on 8 November 1861. She later revised and edited her diary, probably sometime in the 1880s or 1890s and probably with the intention of publication. Significantly, she began her revised account with an 18 October 1860 "entry" that offered her musings on Lincoln and foreshadowing the war. The diary is contained in the Elmore Papers.

8. Loula Kendall Rogers diary, 31 December 1861, Loula Kendall Rogers Papers, ESC. Eugenia Phillips ended her short diary of her imprisonment with a similar sentiment but added an unusual twist: "The incidents of a life, however humble the individual, are full of instruction," she noted. "The narrative of such events which I have made may afford amusement if not instruction to such of my family of intimates as may hereafter peruse it. It was written however without any such motive," she added, "my sole inducement being to kill time which finally kills us all" (Eugenia Phillips diary, 26 September 1861, P. Phillips Family Papers, Manuscript Reading Room, Library of Congress, Washington, D.C.).

9. Rable, *Civil Wars*, 156; Rogers diary, 27 December 1864; Loughborough, *My Cave Life*, 35; Sarah Lois Wadley diary, 21, 26 April 1861, Sarah Lois Wadley Papers, ESC Edmondson, *Lost Heroine*, 126, 129; Elmore diary, 8 February 1865. See also, for example, Wadley's 28 July 1861 story of the Confederate Army's capture of Scott's sword and epaulettes at the Battle of Manassas. Rowland made a pronouncement similar to Edmondson's: "Reports are rife as to raid having been made upon Milledgeville and all the public buildings burnt but I do not credit anything of the kind, there are many false reports that I have determined to believe nothing I hear except what is official" (Rowland diaries, 1 August 1864).

10. Rogers diary, 14 June 1862; Rowland diaries, 5 July 1864; Wadley diary, 25 March 1864, ESC. As Rable notes, "At best, civilians received widely conflicting accounts of battles and casualties. With haphazard mail service and the telegraph lines between the eastern and western parts of the Confederacy regularly cut by Yankee cavalry, the only news was often no news" (*Civil Wars*, 65).

11. Rogers diary, 21 February 1862; Elmore diary, 20, 26 November 1864.

12. Wadley diary, 28 December 1862, 12 July 1863, ESC.

13. Rable, *Civil Wars*, 155; Wadley diary, 18 April 1861, ESC; Rogers diary, 17 November 1864. Rable also notes that such enmity belied "popular images of morally superior women." He quotes Kate Sperry as admitting that she took her hatred "out in 'cussing'" and had "become reckless—stonehearted and everything, hard and pitiless—never knew I was so vengeful" (155).

14. Faust, *Mothers*, esp. chap. 9; Whites, *Civil War*; McDonald, *Woman's Civil War*, 30; Rowland diaries, 26 November 1864; Elmore diary, 6 March 1865. For a study of southern women's diary entries regarding Sherman's March to the Sea, see Schultz, "Mute Fury."

15. Wadley diary, 11 February 1864, ESC; Elmore diary, 17 September 1864; see also Faust, *Mothers*, 163–64.

16. Elsie Bragg to Braxton Bragg, "Bivouac," [Louisiana], 9 May 1862, TS, Writings: Books, Bell Irvin Wiley Papers, ESC (original in correspondence files, Braxton Bragg Papers, University of Texas, Austin).

17. Elsie Bragg to Braxton Bragg, "Bivouac," [Louisiana], 20 April 1862, TS, Writings: Books, Wiley Papers (original in correspondence files, Braxton Bragg Papers, University of Texas, Austin); Mary Ann Cobb to Howell Cobb, Athens, Georgia, 13 July 1862, correspondence files, Howell Cobb Papers, UGA.

18. Augusta Jane Evans to J. L. M. Curry, Mobile, Alabama, 20 December 1862, correspondence files, J. L. M. Curry Papers, Manuscript Reading Room, Library of Congress, Washington, D.C.; Evans, *Macaria*, 304.

19. Varina Davis to Mary Boykin Chesnut, Richmond, 27 April 1862, TS, Writings: Books, Wiley Papers (original TS in Mary Boykin Miller Chesnut Papers, "Letters in Chesnut Letterbook," SC).

20. Faust, *Mothers*, 162; Mary Ann Cobb to Howell Cobb, Athens, Georgia, 5 August 1861, correspondence files, Cobb Papers.

21. Loughborough, *My Cave Life* (1881), 8; Loughborough, *My Cave Life* (1864), 43–44, 95.

22. Greenhow, *My Imprisonment*, 1, 59, 324.

23. Excerpts from review quoted in Tardy, *Living Female Writers*, 273. Evans, author of the tremendously successful 1859 novel *Beulah*, already carried significant moral authority with the southern reading public. See, for example, a review of *Macaria* in *Southern Literary Messenger* 38 (Fall 1864): 317; Faust, *Mothers*, 175–78; on Evans, see esp. Bakker, "Overlooked Progenitors"; Faust, "Altars"; Faust, *Mothers*, 168–78; Fidler, "Augusta Evans Wilson"; Fidler, *Augusta Evans Wilson*. On Ford, see Tardy, *Living Female Writers*, 57–62. On the readership of these novels, see Fidler, "Augusta Jane Evans," 39 n.24; Tardy, *Living Female Writers*, 58. Davidson noted that Ford's novel "appeared in 1864, while the fame of the great guerilla was fresh, and about the time of—but I believe just before—his death. It was May or June, I think, that General Rosecrans, of the Department of the West, issued orders forbidding the circulation and sale of this book in the Northern Army, then occupying Tennessee" (*Living Writers*, 204).

24. Evans, *Macaria*, 218, 365; Ford, *Raids and Romance*, 4.

25. Ford, *Raids and Romance*, 26; Evans, *Macaria*, 308.

26. Evans, *Macaria*, 366. For the challenges and "problems" of Confederate nationalism, see Faust, *Creation*; Rable, *Confederate Republic*; E. M. Thomas, *Confederate Nation*. For a discussion of the historiography of Confederate nationalism, see Gallagher, *Confederate War*, 63–72. Gallagher notes that "the aroma of moral disapprobation envelops most arguments denying the existence of Confederate nationalism," forcing many historians to argue that the absence of nationalism was both the cause and the symptom of Confederate defeat. Gallagher suggests that historians' unwillingness to ascribe "nationality" to a people they find morally repugnant blinds them to two important developments: "First, Confederates by the thousands from all classes exhibited a strong identification with their country and ended the war still firmly committed to the idea of an independent southern nation. Second, although these people finally accepted defeat because Union armies had overrun much of their territory and compelled major southern military forces to surrender, that acceptance should not be confused with an absence of a Confederate identity" (70–71). Southern white women were not exempt from or immune to this process.

27. Augusta Jane Evans to P. G. T. Beauregard, Mobile, [Alabama,] 17 March 1863, correspondence files, Pierre Gustave Toutant Beauregard Papers, PL. For Beauregard's response,

see *War of the Rebellion*, vol. 51, pt. 2, 688–89. For an account of Beauregard's leadership in the Battle of Manassas, see McPherson, *Battle Cry*, 339–46; T. H. Williams, *P. G. T. Beauregard*, 66–95. Johnston was in charge of Confederate troops in the Shenandoah Valley in the weeks that preceded the Battle of Manassas. Successfully outmaneuvering Union General Robert Patterson's troops, Johnston and his men left the Valley and joined with Beauregard's troops at Manassas, ensuring that the Confederate forces were equal in size to the Union force under the command of Irwin McDowell. Greenhow, a Washington socialite and Confederate spy, had tipped off Beauregard to McDowell's impending advance. Allen Pinkerton, head of General George McClellan's secret service, later arrested and imprisoned Greenhow for her involvement with Confederate espionage. Centreville, located three miles from the Confederate defenses at Bull Run, was under Federal control (McPherson, *Battle Cry*, 339–46; Greenhow, *My Imprisonment*). Evans's fear may have been a bit disingenuous, since she and Beauregard had corresponded often during the course of the war. Beauregard's biographer, T. H. Williams, wrote that Beauregard "found much pleasure in the company of Augusta Evans" and once professed that " 'it would not do for me to see [her] too often . . . for I might forget 'home and country' in their hour of need and distress.' " An enthusiastic admirer of Evans's work, Beauregard had said that " 'many and many pages were read through a flow of tears' " (*P. G. T. Beauregard*, 160).

28. Evans, *Macaria*, 332–33.

29. Ibid., 334–35.

30. Ford, *Raids and Romance*, 34, 43–44.

31. Ibid., 210. For an account of Morgan's invasion of Kentucky, see Nevins, *War*, 3:279–90.

32. Evans, *Macaria*, 414; Ella Gertrude Clanton Thomas diaries, 28 June 1864, TS, PL. Of course, not all of Evans's readers expressed such unqualified enthusiasm. Emma Edwards Holmes noted during the course of reading *Macaria* that although she liked the book "very much," she believed that Evans had "certainly tried to display all her learning in a small space & has only shown herself thoroughly pedantic." Holmes accused Evans of trying "to show how the minds of such peculiarly gifted persons, as her heroines, were led from the sublime faith of their childhood to the utter indifference of the Transcendentalists, by the study of such works, & then purified through suffering. I should not be at all surprised," Holmes continued, "it if was only her own experience written out" (Holmes diary, 15 August 1864).

33. For discussions of the crises in southern households, see Faust, *Mothers*, chap. 2; Rable, *Civil Wars*, chap. 3; Whites, *Civil War*, chap. 2. For discussions of the disruption of the literary market, see Muhlenfeld, "Civil War and Authorship."

34. O'Connor, *Heroine*, 357, 79–80.

35. McIntosh, *Two Pictures*, 434, 472–73. On the importance of *Uncle Tom's Cabin* in American culture, see, for example, Moss, *Domestic Novelists*, esp. 101–36; Gossett, *Uncle Tom's Cabin*; Potter, *Impending Crisis*; Tandy, "Pro-Slavery Propaganda"; E. Wilson, *Patriotic Gore*, 3–58. For a discussion of southern clerics' insistence that slavery was divinely sanctioned but that masters must bring slavery up to biblical standards or face God's wrath, see Genovese's provocative study, *A Consuming Fire*.

36. McIntosh, *Two Pictures*, 475. See Moss, *Domestic Novelists*, 101–3, for a similar reading of *Two Pictures*.

37. O'Connor, *Heroine*, 353, 354.

38. Ibid., 153, 187.

39. McIntosh, *Two Pictures*, 277; O'Connor, *Heroine*, 94.

40. O'Connor, *Heroine*, 118–19.

41. Ibid., 329, 334. See Boyd, *Belle Boyd*, for her accounts of her activities as a spy for Jackson.

42. O'Connor, *Heroine*, 337–38.

43. Ibid., 21.

44. Ford, *Raids and Romance*, 318.

45. Elmore diary, 22 March 1867. See also Fox-Genovese, *Within the Plantation Household*, 370–71, for a discussion of women's reluctance to write in their diaries immediately following Confederate defeat.

Chapter Two

1. Sarah Lois Wadley diary, 20 April, 13 May 1865, Sarah Lois Wadley Papers, SHC.

2. Historiographical essays on Reconstruction include E. Anderson and Moss, *Facts*; Foner, "Reconstruction Revisited"; Kolchin, "Myth"; L. Cox, "From Emancipation to Segregation"; A. Robinson, "Beyond the Realm"; J. D. Smith, "'Work'"; Woodman, "Economic Reconstruction." See also Foner, *Reconstruction*. Important works on Reconstruction include Carter, *When the War Was Over*; Du Bois, *Black Reconstruction*; Franklin, *Reconstruction*; Perman, *Road*. Information for the following discussion has been culled from these works.

3. Wadley diary, 26 April, 13 May 1865, SHC; E. G. C. Thomas diaries, 8 May 1865.

4. Wadley diary, 13 May 1865, SHC; Rogers diary, 15 July 1865. As Roark notes, despite the mad rush of oath swearing, male southerners too remained privately unrepentant: "The South adopted a public stance of acquiescence that was superficial and misleading, occasioned by military necessity" (*Masters*, 185). Rable notes that because of contradictory policies of the various military departments, some women had to take oaths: "In areas under Federal occupation, both sexes had to swear allegiance to the United States to receive mail, collect rent, run a business, qualify for Army relief rations, or even get married" (*Civil Wars*, 232).

5. Holmes diary, 17, 22 April 1865; Rogers diary, 11 May 1865.

6. Augusta Jane Evans to Mrs. J. K. Chrisman, Mobile, Alabama, 3 February 1866, Augusta Jane Evans Wilson File, ADAH.

7. Augusta Jane Evans to Alexander H. Stephens, Mobile, Alabama, 29 November 1865, Stephens Papers; Augusta Jane Evans to Mrs. J. K. Chrisman, Mobile, Alabama, 3 February 1866, Augusta Jane Evans Wilson File; Faust, introduction to A. J. Evans, *Macaria*, xvi. For the desire to reestablish the prewar patriarchal order, see Edwards, *Gendered Strife*; Faust, *Mothers*; Whites, *Civil War*.

8. Augusta Jane Evans to P. G. T. Beauregard, Mobile, [Alabama], 30 March 1867, Beauregard Papers, PL.

9. Augusta Jane Evans Wilson to W. A. Seaver, Mobile, [Alabama], 7 September 1876, Augusta Jane Evans Wilson Collection, UVA. For other examples of Wilson's antipathy toward *Harper's*, see Evans to Seaver, Mobile, [Alabama], 8 November 1875, Augusta Jane Evans Wilson Collection, UVA.

10. See Augusta Jane Evans to P. G. T. Beauregard, Mobile, [Alabama], 30 March 1867, Beauregard Papers, PL.

11. Dorsey, *Recollections*, 9. For the Percy clan, see Wyatt-Brown, *House*.

12. Headley, *Great Rebellion*, 1:10; Greeley, *American Conflict*, 1:352; Lunt, *Origin*, xi. For additional northern accounts of the war published during Reconstruction, see Draper, *History*; Duyckinck, *National History*.

13. Dorsey, *Recollections*, 13.

14. Ibid., 219. Critics had spared Johnston from such ignominious slurs regarding Vicksburg because had not handed over his army (McPherson, *Battle Cry*, 626–38).

15. J. E. Cooke, *Stonewall Jackson*, 450–51; J. E. Cooke, *Life*, 3, 2.

16. Boyd, *Belle Boyd*, 73, 267, 20. For biographical information on Boyd and for other strategies she employed to elicit readers' sympathy, see Kennedy-Nolle's introduction to Boyd, *Belle Boyd*, 1–53.

17. Lady of Virginia, *Diary*, 5, 6–7, 250, 8.

18. Cornelia Phillips Spencer to John W. Graham, Chapel Hill, [North Carolina], 22 February 1866, Cornelia Phillips Spencer Papers, SHC; C. P. Spencer, *Last Ninety Days*, 13, 14.

19. E. J. Hale to Cornelia Phillips Spencer, Fayetteville, North Carolina, 11 January 1866, Thomas Atkinson to Cornelia Phillips Spencer, Wilmington, [North Carolina], 30 January 1866, and Verina M. Chapman to Cornelia Phillips Spencer, Hendersonville, North Carolina, 8 May 1866, Spencer Papers. Portions of Atkinson's letter appeared in C. P. Spencer, *Last Ninety Days*, 61–64. Spencer claimed that Chapman's account was "the most characteristic production I think I ever saw. She is certainly a smart woman, and very womanish" (Cornelia Phillips Spencer to Zebulon B. Vance, Chapel Hill, North Carolina, 24 August 1866, Spencer Papers).

20. Zebulon B. Vance to Cornelia Phillips Spencer, Charlotte, North Carolina, 14 October 1865, Spencer Papers; C. P. Spencer, *Last Ninety Days*, 61, 70. For Spencer's views on the proper conduct of war, see *Last Ninety Days*, 54–61.

21. C. P. Spencer, *Last Ninety Days*, esp. 71–72; Cornelia Phillips Spencer to Zebulon B. Vance, Chapel Hill, North Carolina, 11 November 1865, Spencer Papers. Given such views, it is no small wonder that Vance pleaded with Spencer to portray him as a "brave and true man" rather than as a "wise one" (Vance to Spencer, Charlotte, North Carolina, 27 April 1866, Spencer Papers).

22. Zebulon B. Vance to Cornelia Phillips Spencer, Charlotte, North Carolina, 31 August 1866, R. L. Beall to Cornelia Phillips Spencer, Lenoir, North Carolina, 16 January 1867, and clippings and typed transcripts of reviews, Spencer Papers. Vance was not an unbiased critic: he later wrote that Spencer was the smartest woman in North Carolina—"and the smartest *man* too" (Vance, *My Beloved Zebulon*, xxiii).

23. Putnam, *Richmond*, 15.

24. Ibid., 26.

25. Ibid., 385.

26. Ibid., 389.

27. Sallie A. Brock Putnam to Loula Kendall Rogers, New York, 16 May 1868, Rogers Papers. For Putnam's fiction, see her *Kenneth*.

28. Ives, *Princess*, 16–17, 68.

29. Ibid., 69–70, 70–71.

30. Ibid., 70. Ives never made explicit the South's putative sins; see Faust, *Creation*, 41–57; Hobson, *Tell*, 86, for accounts of what southerners believed their sins to be. The best secondary source on the religion of the Lost Cause remains C. R. Wilson, *Baptized*.

31. Chapin, *Fitz-Hugh St. Clair*, 39, 40, vii; "Book Notice," *SHSP* 5 (June 1878): 304.

32. Chapin, *Fitz-Hugh St. Clair*, 73–74.

33. Ibid., 209.

34. See Buck, *Road*; Appleby, "Reconciliation"; Silber, *Romance*. In a study of short fiction appearing in national and regional magazines from 1861 to 1876, Diffley noted that the metaphor of national reunification did not always guide these stories. "Elastic as Romances proved to be while the terms of 'restoration' were contested, more than two stories out of every three attended to local affairs rather than to national reunion," Diffley explains, suggesting that the case for the "romance of reunion" may have been overstated (*Where My Heart Is Turning Ever*, 58). See Higonnet, "Civil Wars and Sexual Territories," for a discussion of the relationships between sexual politics and national political upheavals. See also Silber, *Romance*, 110–11, for a discussion of the gendered implications of *Miss Ravenel's Conversion.*, 164. For other northern reconciliation romances of the Reconstruction period, see, for example, M. J. Holmes, *Rose Mather*; B. Spencer, *Tried and True*. De Forest, a former Union officer, wrote many of these reconciliation romances, including *Bloody Chasm* and *Kate Beaumont* as well as *Miss Ravenel's Conversion*. On the politics of "redemption," see Pollard, *Lost Cause Regained*. See also Ayers, *Promise*; Woodward, *Origins*; Woodward, *Reunion and Reaction*.

35. *SHSP* 1 (January 1876): 41–43. For a history of the Southern Historical Society, see Starnes, "Forever Faithful."

36. M. F. Maury, "A Vindication of Virginia and the South," *SHSP* 1 (February 1876): 49–60; C. W. Read, "Reminiscences of the Confederate States Navy," *SHSP* 1 (May 1876): 331–62; J. E. B. Stuart, "General J. E. B. Stuart's Report of Operations after Gettysburg," *SHSP* 3 (February 1877): 72–77; "Causes of the Defeat of General Lee's Army at the Battle of Gettysburg—Opinions of Leading Confederate Soldiers," *SHSP* 5 (January–February 1877): 38–93; for the reaction to Boynton's work, see *SHSP* 1 (February 1876): 76.

37. Helena J. Harris, "Cecil Gray; or, the Soldier's Revenge," in *Southern Sketches*, 1–20. A notable exception to the general southern formulation was Virginia's Mary Virginia Terhune, who wrote under the name of Marion Harland. Harland had already garnered a favorable literary reputation when she and her husband, Reverend Edward Payson Terhune, relocated from the South to Newark, New Jersey, where her husband became pastor of the First Reformed Dutch Church in 1858. The outbreak of the Civil War tested Harland's loyalties, and in the end she sided with the Union. In 1866 she penned *Sunnybank*, a quasi-sequel to her first novel, *Alone*, published in 1854. Unlike the other novels studied in this chapter, *Sunnybank* extolled the virtues of unionism and warned of the perils of secession. The heroine, Elinor, remains steadfastly loyal to the Union, as do the other members of her family, except for one old eccentric maiden aunt, who seems long ago to have lost all ability to reason, and her brothers, who swear their allegiance to the Union by the novel's end. Elinor has two suitors—Harry Wilton, a Union man, whom she eventually marries, and Rolf Kingston, a lascivious, scheming Confederate, who meets an appropriate end. In a scene that foreshadows the plot of Avery's *The Rebel General's Loyal Bride*, Rolf extorts Elinor's promise of marriage in exchange for the release of her father,

whom the Confederates hold. Fortunately for the family at Sunnybank, Yankee raiders kill Rolf, freeing Elinor to marry Harry. At the end of the war, with Richmond safely in Federal hands and law and order returned to the South, Harry exclaims, "Let our dead past bury its dead" (404). Proving Harry's sentiments, Elinor notes, "We talk little of the events of the four years war" (414). The past was anything but dead to southerners, and as the following chapters will demonstrate, southerners talked incessantly about the war. Not surprisingly, southern journalists denounced Harland's politics, while northern reviewers praised *Sunnybank*. For excerpts from selected contemporary reviews, see Tardy, *Living Female Writers*, 433–36. For Virginia Terhune's account of the Civil War and her wartime politics, see *Marion Harland's Autobiography*, esp. 360–407.

38. Whittlesey, *Bertha*, 148.

39. Ibid., 358–59, 374.

40. Dorsey, *Lucia Dare*, 9, 28, 30. Anna Dickinson was an active participant in the abolition movement and author of the 1868 Civil War novel *What Answer?*

41. Ibid., 97, 106.

42. Magill, *Women*, 177.

43. Ibid., vi, x.

44. Ibid., 162–63.

45. Higonnet, "Civil Wars and Sexual Territories," 80. For southern women acting as nurses, see Culpepper, *Trials and Triumphs*, 315–58; Faust, *Mothers*, 92–112; Massey, *Bonnet Brigades*, 43; Rable, *Civil Wars*, 121–28; Simkins and Patton, *Women*, 82–99.

46. Whitson, *Gilbert St. Maurice*, viii, 10.

47. Ibid., 223, vii.

48. Cruse, *Cameron Hall*, 5. *Cameron Hall* fared well with both readers and reviewers, although at least one contemporary critic noted that it "would be improved by judicious pruning." This reviewer continued, "To read it after reading a sensational novel is like getting up early in the morning; it was very hard to start, and awful dull and sleepy to dress in the shuttered, dark room; but once up and out, how fresh and pure and sweet!" (Tardy, *Living Female Writers*, 257). *Surry of Eagle's Nest* reportedly "found a place in practically every Southern library, as an example of all that this conquered and occupied people held most dear in what remained of their devastated civilization" (J. E. Cooke, *Surry*, 6). Cooke had served as a captain under his cousin-in-law, J. E. B. Stuart, and later under Robert E. Lee after Stuart's death. Cooke's war novel offered readers a mix of character sketches, historical anecdotes, and the imaginings of one of the antebellum South's greatest defenders. See also J. E. Cooke, *Mohun* (the sequel to *Surry*); Aaron, *Unwritten War*, chap. 16; E. Wilson, *Patriotic Gore*, 192–96.

49. Cruse, *Cameron Hall*, 513–14, 78, 81.

50. Ibid., 78, 308.

51. Ibid., 489, 529–30.

52. Ibid., 5, 81, 172–73, 517–18.

53. Ibid., 518, 520.

54. Ibid., 537; J. E. Cooke, *Mohun*, 370. Cruse's position echoed, in part, that of Spencer, although Cruse seemed much more sympathetic toward Confederate men.

55. For an example of an anthology, see Putnam, *Southern Amaranth*. Putnam had no

shortage of material: "Like Ruth after the gleaners of Boaz," she explained in the anthology's preface, "I entered the field in expectation of finding only an occasional *idyl* for my culling; but the growth of Southern sentiment seems destined to be perennial and inexhaustible, and I deeply regret that a vast number of beautiful and worthy productions are compelled for want of space to be crowded out of this volume" (v).

General Daniel Harvey Hill founded *The Land We Love: A Monthly Magazine Devoted to Literature, Military History, and Agriculture* in May 1866. Although Hill preferred manuscripts by men who fought in the war, amateur poets inundated his office with their unsolicited works. Hill rejected many of these compositions, but a significant number still found their way in print, a situation that undoubtedly pleased the authors, for Hill paid his contributors, a practice that was rare immediately following the war. Never profitable, the magazine folded in December 1869. Circulation probably never exceeded twelve thousand (Riley, *Magazines*, 97–100; Atchison, "*The Land We Love*").

Stephen D. Pool, a North Carolina artillery colonel, founded *Our Living and Our Dead* in 1873. In addition to camp and battlefield reminiscences, the magazine ran excerpts from women's journals and poetry. Unlike *The Land We Love*, Pool's magazine welcomed poetry, claiming that "the poetry that would be run in *Our Living and Our Dead* will be commemorative of the events which occurred during the war, or of the sentiments and feelings of those who participated in it, and memorial sketches in verse of gallant officers and men who fell in battle, or significantly distinguished themselves" (Riley, *Magazines*, 164). Like *The Land We Love*, *Our Living and Our Dead* was never profitable, and it folded in 1876. Circulation has been estimated at around two thousand (Riley, *Magazines*, 163–66; Atchison, "*Our Living and Our Dead*").

56. Margaret Junkin Preston, "Acceptance," *The Land We Love* 1 (August 1866): 240.

57. Fanny Downing, "They Are Not Dead," *Our Living and Our Dead* 1 (February 1875): 566; Lou Belle Custiss, "Hallow'd Ground," *Atlanta Constitution*, 3 August 1869, p. 1; Catherine M. Warfield, "Manassas," in *Southern Amaranth*, ed. Putnam, 246; L. Virginia French, "Shermanized," in *Southern Amaranth*, ed. Putnam, 342. For the work of Ladies Confederate Memorial Associations, see, for example, report of the Confederate Memorial Association of Lynchburg, Virginia, *Atlanta Constitution*, 9 April 1869, p. 3; report of the Georgia Memorial Association, *Atlanta Constitution*, 12 December 1869, p. 1; Ladies Association to Commemorate the Confederate Dead Records, South Caroliniana Library, University of South Carolina, Columbia; Ladies Memorial Association Records, SHC; Greenville Ladies Association in Aid of the Volunteers of the Confederate Army Records, South Caroliniana Library, University of South Carolina, Columbia; Ladies Confederate Memorial Association Records, UVA; Ladies Memorial Association Records, Atlanta History Center, Atlanta. See also Foster, *Ghosts*, 38–45; Rable, *Civil Wars*, 237–39.

58. Loula Kendall Rogers copying book, 1854–78, Rogers Papers; Elmore diary, vol. 2, 1864–72. Because diarists rarely cited the authors of particular poems, it is frequently difficult to identify whether the poem was original or had been copied from another source.

59. Foster, *Ghosts*, 63, 70.

60. Sallie A. Brock, "The Fall of Richmond," in *Southern Amaranth*, ed. Putnam, 45.

Chapter Three

1. Political theorist Nancy Huston makes the point that in writing war narratives, each side must see itself as heroic. As she put it, "there is no such thing as enemic verse" ("Tales," 273).

2. Cumming, *Gleanings*, 10, 11. The standard work on New South boosterism remains Gaston's *New South Creed*, in which he argues that the men of the postwar south consciously set out to promote southern industry and culture by manipulating images of the Old South. As Cumming's *Gleanings* demonstrates, this activity was by no means restricted to men.

3. Rebecca Latimer Felton, untitled MS, 2, n.d., Rebecca Latimer Felton Papers, UGA. This bitterness and contemptuousness pervades much of Felton's writings. Although she always maintained that she, along with all white southern women, firmly supported the Confederacy during the war, she also asserted that had white southern women been consulted, the Civil War never would have been fought, for they realized that the cause was lost and the sacrifices were too great. See Felton, *Country Life*.

4. T. E. Watson, "Negro Question," 548. For the promise and failures of Populism and the significance of the Wilmington race riot, see Gilmore, *Gender and Jim Crow*.

5. Ayers, *Promise*, 63.

6. General works on the post-Reconstruction South include Ayers, *Promise*; Daniel, *Breaking the Land*; Litwack, *Trouble*; Woodward, *Origins*; G. Wright, *Old South, New South*.

7. Buck, *Road*, viii; Appleby, "Reconciliation"; Silber, *Romance*, 65; E. Wilson, *Patriotic Gore*, 540.

8. Cauthen and Jones, "Coming," 226; Page, *Old South*, 253–54; George, *Popular History*, 21–22; J. A. Logan, *Great Conspiracy*, 671, 674. The devil theory posited that "southern slaveowners were evil men lacking even the rudiments of Christian morality, while northern abolitionists and the Republican party were as pure as the driven snow" (Cauthen and Jones, "Coming," 227).

9. Silber, *Romance*, 4; Cumming, *Gleanings*, 13. For information on Federal and Confederate reunions, see, for example, Foster, *Ghosts*, esp. chap. 5; Linderman, *Embattled Courage*, esp. the epilogue; Silber, *Romance*, esp. chap. 4. On the theme of forgetfulness, see Silber, *Romance*, 3–4. If, in fact, "forgetfulness, not memory, appears to be the dominant theme in the reunion culture," as Silber argues, it is curious that veterans, both northern and southern, felt a collective need for meetings. Forgetting would seem to be much easier without the trappings of ritualized cultural remembrance.

10. Ayers, *Promise*, 340; John, *Best Years*, esp. 125–80.

11. Richard Watson Gilder to the editor of a southern periodical, n.p., 16 October 1886, in Gilder, *Letters*, 392.

12. S. Davis, "'A Matter.'" See also preface to Johnson and Buel, *Battles and Leaders*, 1:ix–xi; Johnson, *Remembered Yesterdays*, 189–237.

13. Editorial, *Century* 28 (October 1884): 943–44. See also John, *Best Years*, 127, for additional information on the timing of the series.

14. Johnson, *Remembered Yesterdays*, 189–90, 208; S. Davis, "'A Matter,'" 339–40; John, *Best Years*, 129.

15. Mrs. E. J. Beale to the Century Company, Suffolk, Virginia, 18 May [?]; Susie Bishop to the editor of *Century* magazine, 26 March 1891, Century Company Records, Brooke

Russell Astor Reading Room for Rare Books and Manuscripts, New York Public Library, New York. The files of the Century Company records are brimming with letters such as these, but I mention only those written by Mary M. Guy (Charleston, South Carolina, 29 February 1892), Mrs. S. A. Elliott (Oxford, North Carolina, 11 November 1885), Mrs. E. W. Kyle (San Marcos, Texas, 16 April 1889), and Mrs. William Mueller (St. Louis, Missouri, 27 August 1885). For information on the remuneration received by the former generals, see S. Davis, "'A Matter,'" 340–41 n.8. For figures on the payments received by southern women who sent their manuscripts to the Century, see, for example, Mary Bedinger Mitchell to editor, 21 May 1885; Orra Langhorne to the Century Company, Lynchburg, Virginia, 11 May 1885; Margaret Junkin Preston to Clarence Buel, Lexington, Virginia, 17 May 1886, Century Company Records.

16. Mrs. Herbert Ellerbe to the editor of Century magazine, Atlanta, 16 September 1885; Lucy R. Mayo to the editor of Century magazine, Hague, Virginia, n.d.; Mary Bedinger Mitchell to the editor of Century magazine, Long Island, New York, 18 September 1884; Mary Bedinger Mitchell to the editor of Century magazine, 21 March 1885; Mrs. Jonathan Coleman to "Sirs," Halifax County, Virginia, n.d., Century Company Records.

17. Varina Davis to John D. Howe and Charles E. Duffie, New York, 9 June 1902, and Fannie Conigland Farinholt to the editor of Century magazine, Asheville, North Carolina, 1 April 1891, Century Company Records.

18. Margaret Junkin Preston to Clarence Buel, Lexington, Virginia, 7 October [1886], Century Company Records.

19. Johnson, Remembered Yesterdays, 191; Constance Cary Harrison, "Virginia Scenes in '61," in Battles and Leaders, ed. Johnson and Buel, 1:161, 162; Thomas Nelson Page to Constance Cary Harrison, Richmond, 1 August 1885, in the Burton Norvell Harrison Family Papers, Manuscript Reading Room, Library of Congress, Washington, D.C. During the 1880s and early 1890s, Page had begun to shore up his reputation as a conciliatory writer of plantation fiction. See esp. his In Ole Virginia, first collected in 1887, and Old South. See L. H. MacKethan, Dream, for a fine study of plantation fiction. For praise similar to Page's on Constance Cary Harrison's piece, see also, for example, Sara A. Pryor to Constance Cary Harrison, n.p., n.d., and Frank R. Stockton to Constance Cary Harrison, Charlottesville, Virginia, 30 August 1885, Harrison Family Papers.

20. Robert U. Johnson to Constance Cary Harrison, New York, 15 November 1888, Harrison Family Papers; Constance Cary Harrison, "Richmond Scenes in '62," in Battles and Leaders, ed. Johnson and Buel, 2:448; Constance Cary Harrison to Robert U. Johnson, New York, n.d., Century Company Records.

21. Annie Laurie Harris Broidrick, "A Recollection of Thirty Years Ago," [1, 23–24], SHC.

22. Hague, Blockaded Family, 176.

23. R. Taylor, Destruction and Reconstruction, 269; Dabney H. Maury, "Grant as Soldier and Civilian," SHSP 5 (May 1878): 227; Rev. R. L. Dabney, "George W. Cable in the Century Magazine, a Review," SHSP 13 (March 1885): 148–49; J. A. P. Campbell, "The Lost Cause: A Masterly Vindication of It," SHSP 16 (July 1888): 319.

24. Thomas Nelson Page to Grace King, quoted in E. Wilson, Patriotic Gore, 606. Page was not the only southern male author to succumb to the romance of reunion. William C. Falkner, great-grandfather of William Faulkner, published The White Rose of Memphis in

1881. In a recent biography of Faulkner, Singal notes that Falkner was "resolved in this novel to avoid any mention of the recent war in which he had so actively participated, save for a few short speeches in the standard New South mode concerning the need to forget politics and get on with the business of reunion. There was also a minor subplot, so typical of the literature of this period, in which the daughter of a northern carpetbagger is won over by a gallant southern Ivanhoe. . . . But other than these stock devices of the reconciliation novel, Falkner stayed notably clear of the intersectional conflict." Singal suggests that this concession to a popular literary trend stemmed largely from Falkner's desire to see his novel in print. Falkner's next novel, *The Little Brick Church*, published in 1882, made no such concession. "Perhaps because his reputation had become reasonably well established," argues Singal, "Falkner now felt free to vent . . . some of his real attitudes toward the North" (*William Faulkner*, 36–37).

25. Bonner, *Like unto Like*, 214, 213.

26. Bryan, *1860–1865*, 172; Constance Cary Harrison, "Crow's Nest," in *Belhaven Tales*, 150.

27. McClelland, *Broadoaks*, 10–11, 45.

28. Ibid., 45, 261.

29. Meriwether, *Recollections*, 227; Meriwether, *Master*, 3:9–10.

30. Silber, *Romance*, esp. 2–9, 122. See also Appleby, "Reconciliation."

31. Bonner, *Like unto Like*, 11.

32. Jeannette L. Gilder to Constance Cary Harrison, New York, 15 April 1890, Harrison Family Papers.

33. "New Books," *Boston Transcript*, 13 December 1890, Jonathan Hubert Claiborne to Constance Cary Harrison, [New York], 28 February 1891, and Constance Cary Harrison diary, 24 February 1890, Harrison Papers. For additional correspondence of this ilk, see Mrs. Burton Harrison correspondence files, Harrison Family Papers. Harrison was in the habit of recording favorable notices and comments on her work in her diary. After some encouraging words from her editor, for example, Harrison confessed that she was "so grateful for words like this—not in the least vain, I think, rather humbly glad that my hopes and longings [for success] may be coming true" (C. C. Harrison diary, 13 March 1890, Harrison Family Papers).

34. C. C. Harrison, *Flower de Hundred*, 13, 44, 43.

35. Ibid., 185.

36. F. M. Williams, *Who's the Patriot?* 35. This tactic of using a nonslaveholder to defend the position of the Confederacy was popular. See also, for example, Meriwether, *Master*, 3:60.

37. Cable, *Dr. Sevier*, 367, 371; Aaron, *Unwritten War*, 274.

38. Grace B. Elmore, "Light and Shadows," pt. 2, pp. 7–8, n.d., MS, Elmore Papers; Bryan, *1860–1865*, 50; F. M. Williams, *Who's the Patriot?* 37.

39. Loula Kendall Rogers, "Capture of President Jefferson Davis," 26 April 1886, unidentified clipping in Rogers Papers.

40. Margaret Junkin Preston, "Personal Reminiscences of Stonewall Jackson," *Century* 32 (October 1886): 927, 936. For a discussion of the relationship between Stonewall Jackson and his sister-in-law, see Gardner, "'Sweet Solace.'"

41. Jackson, *Life and Letters*, esp. 56–88; Margaret J. Preston to the editor of *Century*

magazine, Lexington, Virginia, 23 February 1892, Century Company Records. The second printing of the biography bears an apology from the publishers: "On pages 56 to 88 there appear frequent and extended extracts from an interesting article by Mrs. Margaret J. Preston. . . . The appropriate credit for the use of these extracts was inadvertently omitted from the first edition of this work, and the Publishers are glad of the opportunity to make this acknowledgement to the author of the article referred to." Harper and Brothers also apologized personally to Preston, claiming that the failure to cite the original author was purely inadvertent (Harper and Brothers to Margaret Junkin Preston, New York, 11 March 1892, correspondence files, Margaret Junkin Preston Papers, SHC).

42. Jackson, *Life and Letters*, 67; Margaret Junkin Preston to the editor of *Century* magazine, Lexington, Virginia, 23 February 1892, Century Company Records. In one instance, Anna Jackson wrote, "It is the Rev. Dr. Dabney who thus sketches the figure of the chief," pulling two paragraphs from Dabney's *Life and Campaigns of the Lieut.-General Thomas J. Jackson*, published in 1866 (Jackson, *Life and Letters*, 65–66). It is not surprising that Anna Jackson named Dabney as her source but failed to name Preston. In claiming his authority for writing his work, Dabney explained that "the widow and family of General Jackson" entrusted him with the task. Moreover, he noted his position as Jackson's chief of staff during the Valley and Chickahominy campaigns, claiming possession of "personal knowledge of the events on which the structure of his military fame was first reared" (*Life and Campaigns*, v–vi). That Anna Jackson was so careful to respect Dabney's personal knowledge of her late husband but not Preston's is telling, indeed. Perhaps even Jackson recognized the near impossibility of inserting herself into the military narrative while realizing the possibilities of claiming the "personal" narrative of her late husband.

Mary Anna Jackson was a bit more forthright in a biographical sketch she wrote of her late husband for *Hearst Magazine*. Describing her return to Lexington as a new bride, she wrote that "the General's sister-in-law . . . greeted me in the sweetest manner. 'You are taking the place that my sister had,' she said, 'and so you shall be a sister to me. This was Margaret Junkin Preston, whose influence left such a strong impress upon the General" ("With 'Stonewall' Jackson," 386). It is important to note that this sketch appeared more than twenty years after the book-length biography was published.

Henry M. Field, who wrote the introduction to Anna Jackson's *Life and Letters*, perpetuated this fiction that the general's widow held a proprietary claim to the his life story: "Knowing, as she only can know, all his worth . . . she is right to let him speak for himself [in letters] in these gentle words that are whispered from the dust. And sure we are that those who have read all the great histories of war will turn with fresh interest to this simple story, written out of a woman's heart" (Jackson, *Life and Letters*, xvi).

43. Jackson, *Life and Letters*, v–vi, 89.

44. Ibid., 284. For a good discussion of the importance of Christianity in the formation of the myth of the Lost Cause, see C. R. Wilson, *Baptized*.

45. Jackson, *Life and Letters*, 240, 223–24; Robertson, *Stonewall Brigade*, 57–67. See also Gardner, "Sweet Solace," 59–60. For an account of the Bath-Romney campaign suggesting that Jackson's men questioned their leader, see Imboden, "Stonewall Jackson." The reminiscences appear in Jackson, *Memoirs*, 466–647.

46. J. Davis, *Rise and Fall*, 2:763; Wyatt-Brown, *House*, 160. See also Bleser, "Marriage," 23–27.

47. Wyatt-Brown, *House*, 163–64.

48. V. Davis, *Jefferson Davis*, 2:1–2, 71, 346. One of Jefferson Davis's harshest critics was General William T. Sherman, who, at a 1884 meeting of the Grand Army of the Republic, for example, charged Davis with designing to turn the masses in the North into slaves of southerners. For a reprint of this allegation, see V. Davis, *Jefferson Davis*, 2:833–47.

49. V. Davis, *Jefferson Davis*, 2:1; Jackson, *Life and Letters*, v.

50. V. Davis, *Jefferson Davis*, 2:94, 137.

51. Elshtain, "Reflections on War and Political Discourse," 42; Higonnet, "Civil Wars and Sexual Territories," 94. See also M. Cooke, "Wo-Man"; Higonnet, "Not So Quiet."

52. V. Davis, *Jefferson Davis*, 2:203–4; *New York Times*, 30 November 1891, sec. 1, p. 4.

53. Pember, *Southern Woman's Story*, 13–14.

54. Clara D. Maclean, "The Last Raid," *SHSP* 13 (December 1885): 473; Grace Pierson James Beard, "A Series of True Incidents Connected with Sherman's March to the Sea— The Experiences of a Lady Who Lived in the Line of His March," 6, n.d., TS, SHC.

55. See Pember, *Southern Woman's Story*, 173–75.

56. Meriwether, *Master*, 2:226–27;

57. Murfree, *Where the Battle Was Fought*, 96–97, 174. For a discussion of the uneven development of southern industry and the ways in which industry influenced the lives of southerners, see Ayers, *Promise*, esp. chap. 5.

58. Murfree, *Where the Battle Was Fought*, 107–8.

59. Ibid., 89, 96.

60. Ibid., 123–34, 6, 113. For a discussion of women local colorists in the second half of the nineteenth century, see A. D. Wood, "Literature," esp. 16–22. Murfree's family plantation, Grantland, was overrun and destroyed during the war, and this experience provided Murfree with much of the plot for *Where the Battle Was Fought*. For basic biographical information on Murfree, see, for example, Bain, Flora, and Rubin, *Southern Writers*, 325.

61. James R. Osgood to Mary Noailles Murfree, n.p., 9 July 1884, Mary Noailles Murfree Papers, ESC. Sales and earnings figures for the novel while it was published by Osgood's firm are unavailable. Houghton Mifflin, however, picked up the reprint rights by 1889, and although their records indicate that *Where the Battle Was Fought* certainly was not a runaway best-seller, it sold steadily from 1889 through at least 1915. During that period, it sold almost 2,500 copies and earned Murfree more than one thousand dollars. See the firm's book sales and book earnings records in the Houghton Mifflin Company Correspondence and Records, Houghton Library, Harvard University, Cambridge, Massachusetts. For a decade-by-decade breakdown of the publication of Civil War literature, see Lively, *Fiction Fights*, 22.

62. Rebecca Latimer Felton, "The Industrial School for Girls," 73, 18 February 1891, galley proof, Felton Papers.

63. Rebecca Latimer Felton, "Race Antipathy in the United States," n.d., MS, 6, 4, Felton Papers; Gilmore, *Gender and Jim Crow*. On Felton and the racial tensions of the late 1890s, see Whites, "Love."

64. George Washington Cable, "The Freedman's Case in Equity," in Cable, *Negro Question*, 51–52, 73–74. Williamson explained that Cable's orthodox position on race was shattered "when a mob of white men invaded the Girls' High School [in New Orleans] and

forcibly expelled every girl suspected of African descent, some of whom were visibly indistinguishable from other students who were undeniably white." Cable "was outraged. He simply could not accept a racial system in which people who were perfectly white in appearance were designated black" (*Rage*, 77).

65. Grady quoted in Cable, *Negro Question*, 76. See Henry Grady, "In Plain Black and White," *Century* 29 (April 1885): 909–17.

66. Cable, *Silent South*, 116, 118; Aaron, *Unwritten War*, 274–77; Grace King quoted in Rubin et al., *History*, 203.

67. Bonner, *Like unto Like*, 198–99, 217–18.

68. Meriwether, *Master*, 2:14, 3:91.

69. Ibid., 3:90–91, 88–89, 190.

70. J. M. Cronly, "After the War," 6, n.d. [1883?], MS, Jane Cronly Papers, PL; Flora K. Overman, "Bushwacker's Retreat: An Incident of 1865," 3, Maverick and Van Wyck Family Papers, South Caroliniana Library, University of South Carolina, Columbia.

71. Lively, *Fiction Fights*, 22, 28.

72. Beard, "Series of True Incidents," 15.

Chapter Four

1. Glasgow, *Deliverance*, 4, 71;Glasgow, *Certain Measure*, 27; see also 35–36.

2. Evans, *Speckled Bird*, 12–14.

3. Mrs. James Mercer Garnett, report of the Historical Committee, in UDC, *Minutes of the Twelfth Annual Convention of the United Daughters of the Confederacy, Held in San Francisco, California, November 19–21, 1905* (Opelika, Ala.: Post, 1906), 217; Green, *Southern Strategies*, 71. As Green notes, the UDC was one of the few organizations that "purposely limited its membership to women from the middle and upper middle classes" (*Southern Strategies*, 71). Ever preoccupied with "firsts," a nasty battle raged within the UDC over its origins. In fact, the 1900 convention formed a special committee to investigate the rivaling claims of Caroline D. M. Goodlett of Nashville, Tennessee, and Mrs. L. H. Raines of Savannah, Georgia, to having founded the UDC. The committee eventually sided with Raines ("Claim as Presented by Mrs. L. H. Raines, Savannah, Ga., United Daughters of the Confederacy," Mildred Lewis Rutherford Papers, UGA). For published histories of the UDC, see L. B. MacKethan, *Chapter Histories*; Poppenheim et al., *History*. See also published UDC state division and national minutes UDCfor this time period. Many private collections contain rich and valuable material on the formation of local chapters of the UDC. The following collections are particularly helpful: John Grammar Brodnax Papers, PL; Sarah Rebecca Cameron Papers, SHC; James Mercer Garnett Papers, UVA; Adeline Burr Davis Green Papers, PL; Mrs. Thomas Baxter Gresham Papers, PL; Elizabeth Seawell Hairston Papers, SHC; Elvira Evelyna Moffitt Papers, SHC; Eliza Hall Parsley Papers, SHC; Rutherford Papers, UGA. A number of secondary works have been published on women's organizations in the late nineteenth and early twentieth centuries. Most deal with clubs in the northeast, but these works are, nevertheless, useful. See, for example, Blair, *Clubwoman*; Martin, *Sound*; A. F. Scott, *Natural Allies*; Solomon, *In the Company*. For examples of women addressing the United Confederate Veterans, see "Women as Patriots," *CV* 11 (November 1903): 496–501; "Miss Lumpkin to Georgia Veterans," *CV* 12 (February 1904): 69–70.

4. Numbers on members and chapters were compiled from figures in membership reports printed in the minutes of the UDC annual conventions, 1896–1905.

5. Garnett, report of the Historical Committee, 199.

6. Stone, report of the president-general, 71; Mrs. D. Giraud Wright, "Maryland and the South," *SHSP* 31 (May 1903): 214.

7. "A Nashville Daughter," *CV* 3 (October 1895): 302.

8. "South Carolina Daughters," *CV* 5 (January 1897): 14. As Green explains, "The Daughters did not politicize domesticity as much as they reinforced it. While the work of the UDC had a decidedly political agenda (the defense of the Confederate rebellion), it carefully maintained its nonpolitical façade. The organization insisted that the nonpolitical role was the only proper public role available to women" (*Southern Strategies*, 71). See "The Veteran in 1895," *CV* 3 (February 1895): 31, for an eight-point plan for the magazine.

9. Rebecca Cameron to Elvira Evelyna Moffitt, Hillsboro, North Carolina, 8 September, 12 December 1903, Moffitt Papers.

10. See, for example, Ross, "Historical Consciousness."

11. Pressly, *Americans*, 136, 151, 154, 156. See Dodd, "Some Difficulties," 121. See also, for example, W. Wilson, *History*; Trent, *Southern Statesmen*; Bassett, *Short History*; Brown, *Lower South*; Dodd, *Expansion*. On providential versus secular conceptions of history and their historical development in the United States, see Ross, "Historical Consciousness." Ross further developed these ideas in *Origins*, 22–97. On southerners' conviction that they were God's chosen people and that God would vindicate their defeat, see Faust, *Creation*, esp. chaps. 2–3; C. R. Wilson, *Baptized*. The standard work on objectivity and history and the development of American graduate schools is Novick, *That Noble Dream*. See also Kraus, *History*, esp. chap. 9; Loewenberg, *American History*, esp. chaps. 19–23; Wish, *American Historian*, esp. chap. 9. Had members of the UDC been familiar with Henry Adams's 1909 essay, "The Rule of Phase Applied to History," in which he proclaimed confidently that "the future of Thought, and therefore of History, lies in the hands of the physicists, and that the future historian must seek his education in the world of mathematical physics" (283), they would have vehemently disagreed.

12. Adelia Dunovant, historical paper, address to the UDC, in UDC, *Minutes of the Fifth Annual Meeting of the United Daughters of the Confederacy, Hot Springs, Arkansas, November 9–12, 1898* (Nashville: Foster and Webb, 1899), 75.

13. E. F. Andrews, address of welcome, in UDC, Georgia Division, *Minutes of the Second Annual Convention of the Georgia Division of the United Daughters of the Confederacy, held in Macon, Georgia, October 21–22, 1896* (Augusta, Ga.: Chronicle Job Printing, 1897), 20–21. Irwin Huntington, in his preface to Mary Frances Seibert's 1897 novel, "*Zulma*," similarly indicted realism: "In introducing 'Zulma' to the reading public," he wrote, "I believe that in this day of progress and despite the influence of the so-called realistic literature, there are still some who care to pause now and then and cast a backward glance at those institutions laid low by Time, the arch iconoclast" (vii).

14. Shi, *Facing Facts*, 47; Aaron, *Unwritten War*, 218; Glasgow, quoted in Shi, *Facing Facts*, 65.

15. Dunovant, historical paper, 78.

16. B. B. Munford, "The Vindication of the South," *SHSP* 27 (February 1899): 82–83; Allan, *Life and Letters*, 44; Merrick, *Old Times*, 5.

17. "To the Historians of the Several State and Territorial Divisions," circular, n.d., C. C. Clay Papers, PL. Dating of the document was verified by the report of the Historical Committee, in UDC, *Minutes of the Eighth Annual Convention of the United Daughters of the Confederacy, Held in Wilmington, North Carolina, November 1901* (Opelika, Ala.: Post, 1902), 126–28. The 1901 Historical Committee comprised some of the UDC's most influential members and was chaired by Adelia Dunovant. Other members included Mildred Lewis Rutherford, Mary B. Poppenheim, Virginia Clay-Clopton, and S. T. McCullough.

18. Record Book, 1906–27, Secessionville Chapter of the UDC, James Island, South Carolina, 16 December 1909, 17 February, 17 March, 21 April, 19 May 1910, June 1911, UDC, South Carolina Division, Secessionville Chapter Records, South Caroliniana Library, University of South Carolina, Columbia; Mary B. Poppenheim, Mrs. August Kohn, and Lulah Ayer Vandiver, open letter "To the Chapters of the South Carolina Division of the United Daughters of the Confederacy," n.d., Cameron Papers; "Historical Study for West Virginia Division, 1912–13," MS, Mary Calvert Stribling Papers, PL.

19. Rutherford, *Open Letter*, 2.

20. Mildred Lewis Rutherford, "State History," in UDC, Georgia Division, *Minutes of the Fifth Annual Convention of the Georgia Division of the United Daughters of the Confederacy, Held in Athens, Georgia, October 11–13, 1899* (Rome, Ga.: Fletcher Smith, 1900), 27.

21. Harriet Cobb Lane, "Some War Reminiscences," 4, Lillie Vause Archbell Papers, SHC; Mrs. George Reid, untitled TS, [1911?], 3, Agatha Abney Woodson Papers, PL. In the margin of Lane's paper, Lillie Vause Archbell claims to have recorded the story as dictated by Lane, yet internal evidence suggests heavy editing by Archbell. For examples of Rutherford's writings, see her *Address . . . University Chapel*; *Jefferson Davis*; *South Must Have Her Rightful Place*; *South in History*; *Address: Thirteen Periods*; *Historical Sins*; *Truths*.

22. Harriott Horry Ravenel, "Burning of Columbia, February 17th 1865," 12 March 1898, 2, Harriott Horry Ravenel Papers, South Caroliniana Library, University of South Carolina, Columbia.

23. "Report of the Historical Committee," *CV* 3 (June 1895): 163, 167, 169; Mrs. James Garnett, historical report, in UDC, *Minutes of the Eleventh Annual Convention of the United Daughters of the Confederacy, Held in St. Louis, Missouri, October 4–8, 1904* (Opelika, Ala.: Post, 1905), 197–201; "Review of Histories Used in Southern Schools and Southern Homes," reprint of address by Anna Caroline Benning before the eighth annual convention of the Georgia Division, United Daughters of the Confederacy, La Grange, Georgia, 28–30 October 1902, in *CV* 10 (December 1902): 550. See also "Patriotic School Histories," *CV* 5 (September 1897): 450–52; Dr. S. H. Stout, "Confederate History," *CV* 11 (October 1903): 462–63; "Official Report of the History Committee of the Grand Camp, C.V., Department of Virginia," *CV* 12 (March 1904): 161–69. For secondary literature on the United Confederate Veterans and its efforts to fight the battles of the histories, see Bailey, "Textbooks"; Hattaway, "Clio's Southern Soldiers."

24. Pryor, *Reminiscences*, 7.

25. Avary, *Virginia Girl*, vi–vii; "Myrta Lockett Avary," *CV* 11 (April 1903): 174.

26. Avary, *Virginia Girl*, 8–9; Mrs. D. G. Wright, *Southern Girl*, 77.

27. Clay-Clopton, *Belle*, 142–43; Pryor, *Reminiscences*, 320–21.

28. Ada Sterling to Virginia Clay-Clopton, [New York], 14 July 1903, 17 January, 21 April 1904, and Ada Sterling to Mrs. Humes and Virginia Clay-Clopton, New York, 14 Novem-

ber 1905, Virginia Clay-Clopton correspondence files, Clay Papers. The UDC's alleged refusal to endorse *A Belle of the Fifties* seems odd, since Virginia Clay Clopton was a revered member of the Alabama Division. The UDC later endorsed the book.

29. Henry Watterson to Virginia Clay-Clopton, Louisville, [Kentucky], 6 November 1905, and Letitia Dowdell Ross to Virginia Clay-Clopton, Auburn, [Alabama], 20 February 1905, Virginia Clay-Clopton correspondence files, Clay Papers; Emily Ritchie McLean to Myrta Lockett Avary, New York, 8 May 1903, Myrta Lockett Avary Papers, Atlanta History Center, Atlanta.

30. My ideas on Longstreet were developed and first presented in a somewhat different form in Gardner, "Making."

31. H. D. Longstreet, *Lee and Longstreet*, 8–9, 32–33; J. Longstreet, *From Manassas to Appomattox*, xvi, 405. Wert, one of Longstreet's biographers, notes that the general's memoirs "engendered both praise and censure. His detractors especially condemned him for his criticisms of Lee. He was also accused of shoddy research and of lacking a 'facile' pen. On balance, the work enjoyed a good reception," however (*General James Longstreet*, 423). For an account of the shifting memories of Pickett's charge, see Reardon, *Pickett's Charge*.

32. Connelly argues that the greatest postbellum "sin" committed against the South's cause was an attack on Lee. Because Gettysburg was the greatest tarnish on Lee's military record, his followers sought to cast the blame elsewhere, resuscitating the image of Lee as an invincible warrior. Longstreet provided a convenient target (*Marble Man*, esp. 83–90).

33. Wert, "James Longstreet," 128. Pendleton was an Episcopal minister who spoke throughout the South in the 1870s. The sermon to which Helen Dortch Longstreet directly referred was delivered by Pendleton on 17 January 1873 for the dedication of the Lee Chapel at Washington and Lee University in Lexington, Virginia. See H. D. Longstreet, *Lee and Longstreet*, 33–34, 31, 56–57; see also Connelly, *Marble Man*, 84–85. For a transcript of the sermon, see Helen Dortch Longstreet, "Lee and Longstreet at Gettysburg," n.d., TS, Helen Dortch Longstreet Papers, Atlanta History Center, Atlanta. For additional information on the controversy, see, for example, J. William Jones, "The Longstreet-Gettysburg Controversy: Who Commenced It?" *SHSP* 23 (January–December 1895): 342–48; Walter H. Taylor, "Lee and Longstreet," *SHSP* 24 (January–December 1896): 73–79; Henry Alexander White, "Gettysburg Battle," *SHSP* 27 (January–December 1899): 52–60. For an account of the Battle of Gettysburg, see, for example, McPherson, *Battle Cry*, chap. 21.

34. J. B. Gordon, *Reminiscences*, 161, xxvii; "Report of the Historical Committees, UDC," *CV* 12 (February 1904): 65.

35. "Gen. James Longstreet," *CV* 12 (February 1904): 86–87. For Gordon's obituaries, see, for example, "Texas Daughters Honor General Gordon," *CV* 12 (March 1904): 159; "UDC's President's Report at St. Louis," *CV* 12 (December 1904): 570.

36. H. D. Longstreet, *Lee and Longstreet*, 7.

37. L. J. Gordon, *General George E. Pickett*, 172; Pickett, *Pickett*, vii, 7. For an insightful biography of the Picketts and a description of La Salle's efforts to bolster her husband's tarnished reputation, see L. J. Gordon, *General George E. Pickett*.

38. Pickett, *Pickett*, 267, 270, 312; La Salle Corbell Pickett, "General George E. Pickett: His Appointment to West Point — A Letter from His Widow," *SHSP* 24 (January–December 1896): 153. Interestingly, in this letter, La Salle Pickett was much more contemptuous of

other Confederate officers who allowed the debacle to take place and who, in the post-war era, envied Pickett's renowned fame: "The glory of Pickett's charge at Gettysburg . . . will shine, in spite of [General John B.] Gordon's jealousy, with ever increasing lustre as time rolls on, and the purity of patriotism is more and more refined and the truth more and more clearly revealed." Historian Carol Reardon explores the postwar dissections of Pickett's charge in *Pickett's Charge*. She notes the struggles between Virginians, who claimed unparalleled glory, and veterans from other states, who insisted that Virginians inaccurately portrayed their role in the battle to exclude the participation of non-Virginians. Pickett's widow played a decisive role in this debate: "Sallie's active partisanship helped to breathe new life into the image of Pickett and his men," Reardon wrote. "New cockiness emerged in Virginians' narratives of the events of July 3. They showed no fear of the criticism heaped on them by North Carolina and her allies. Nor did they respond to the barbs of fellow Virginians. They simply dismissed all challenges. Richmond's wartime version of the charge had proved sufficiently durable to suggest its entire truthfulness" (*Pickett's Charge*, 164).

39. Pickett, *Pickett*, 153, 419.

40. H. D. Longstreet, *Lee and Longstreet*, 94.

41. Helen Dortch Longstreet to Sears W. Cabell, May 1938, Helen Dortch Longstreet Collection, GHS; Mrs. L. H. Watson, "Address of Mrs. L. H. Watson," in UDC, *Minutes of the Sixteenth Annual Convention of the United Daughters of the Confederacy, Held in Houston, Texas, October 19–22, 1909* (Opelika, Ala.: Post, 1909), 367.

42. UDC tributes printed in the appendix of H. D. Longstreet's *Lee and Longstreet*, 277–78, 309, 310; Wert, "James Longstreet," 142.

43. Evans, *Speckled Bird*, 14, 228. Mrs. Maurice's low opinion of Kent is further justified when it is revealed that he had been involved in embezzlement and bribery schemes during his tenure as a U.S. senator.

44. Ibid., 75–76, 119–20.

45. See, for example, reviews of *A Speckled Bird* in *Bookman* 16 (October 1902): 178–89, and *Dial* 33 (October 1902): 333. For Wilson's response to her critics, see A. J. E. Wilson, "Author and Critic," *Bookman* 16 (November 1902): 230–32.

46. Glasgow, *Certain Measure*, 28. Standard critical biographies on Glasgow include Raper, *Without Shelter*; Rubin, *No Place*. See also A. G. Jones, *Tomorrow*, chap. 4; Singal, *War Within*, chap 4. Glasgow published an autobiography, *The Woman Within*. A partial list of critical essays on Glasgow's fiction pertinent to this discussion includes Atteberry, "Ellen Glasgow"; B. Harrison, "Ellen Glasgow's Revision"; Holman, "Ellen Glasgow."

47. Ellen Glasgow to Paul Reynolds, Richmond, 10 December 1899, Ellen Glasgow Papers, UVA; Ellen Glasgow to Walter Hines Page, 2 December 1899, in Glasgow, *Letters*, 28–29.

48. Glasgow, *Certain Measure*, 61; Glasgow, *Voice*, 10, 94–95, 216. Standard works on Populism include Ayers, *Promise*; Goodwyn, *Democratic Promise*; Hahn, *Roots*; McMath, *Populist Vanguard*; Palmer, "*Man over Money*"; Woodward, *Origins*. Glasgow chose Virginia as the setting for these social histories because of its symbolic importance in the course of southern history. Contrary to the picture painted by Glasgow, however, Virginia was not a hotbed for Populist activity. As Dailey points out, though, Virginia did give rise

to an interracial alliance, the Readjuster movement, in the immediate postemancipation period. Dailey reads *The Voice of the People* as a commentary on the Readjusters' failure: "Ellen Glasgow saw the Readjusters' defeat," Dailey writes, "as representative of the processes that transformed the idea of black-white coalition in the South from hopeful possibility to failure." For Dailey, however, "the most important thing about the Readjusters was not their failure but their existence and their legacy" (*Before Jim Crow*, 168).

49. Glasgow, *Voice,*, 10, 346.

50. Ibid., 442.

51. Glasgow, *Certain Measure*, 49, 59, 15. For the relation of Glasgow's works to Victorianism and modernism, see, for example, Singal, *War Within*, chap. 4.

52. Glasgow, *Certain Measure*, 55, 12.

53. Glasgow, *Voice*, 27, 44–45, 409, 52, 111, 114. In this sense, Uncle Ish resembles Thomas Nelson Page's Sam, the nostalgic slave from Page's most popular story, "Marse Chan." In one of the most oft-quoted passages from "Marse Chan," Sam wistfully reminisces about his days in bondage. "Dem wuz good ole times, marster—de bes' Sam ever see! Niggers didn't hed nothin' 't all to do," Sam explained, "jus' hed to 'ten' to de feedin' an cleanin' de hosses, en' doin' what de marster tell 'em to do" (*In Ole Virginia*, 10).

54. Review of *The Voice of the People*, *Louisville Courier-Journal*, 21 April 1900, clippings files, Glasgow Papers; review of *The Voice of the People*, *Dial* 29 (July 1900): 24; Ellen Glasgow to Walter Hines Page, 12 May 1900, in Glasgow, *Letters*, 32. For a comparison similar to that in the *Dial*, see *Bookman* 11 (June 1900): 398.

55. Ellen Glasgow to Walter Hines Page, 18 April 1900, in Glasgow, *Letters*, 30; Glasgow, *Certain Measure*, 20, 12. For a minor work published a few years before *The Battle Ground* that offers the standard Lost Cause plot, see Cairns, *"Bobbie."*

56. Glasgow, *Battle-Ground*, 323.

57. Ibid., 443.

58. Ibid., 278, 411.

59. Ibid., 299–300, 307; for the battle, see 299–313.

60. Ibid., 48. For the lady in southern fiction, see, for example, A. G. Jones, *Tomorrow*, chap. 1; Wolfe, "Southern Lady"; on plantation mistresses, see Fox-Genovese, *Within the Plantation Household*. For an opposing view, see Clinton, *Plantation Mistress*.

61. Glasgow, *Battle-Ground*, 510. The most important work on paternalism and southern slaveholding remains Genovese, *Roll, Jordan, Roll*.

62. Glasgow, *Certain Measure*, 5; Glasgow, *Battle-Ground*, 332, 512.

63. Review of *The Battle-Ground*, *Critic*, n.s., 41 (1902): 279; Benjamin W. Wells, "Southern Literature of the Year," *Forum* 29 (December 1900): 508; review of *The Battle-Ground*, *Louisville Courier-Journal*, 29 March 1902, clippings files, Glasgow Papers; B. W. Wells, "Southern Literature," 508; Glasgow, *Certain Measure*, 24–25. See also Carl Hovey, "Seven Novels of Some Importance," *Bookman* 15 (May 1902): 258. For a comment similar to that of the *Courier-Journal* reviewer, see *Dial* 32 (June 1902): 385.

64. Page, *Red Rock*, 17–19.

65. Ibid., viii; Hobson, *Tell*, 149; Cecelski and Tyson, introduction to *Democracy Betrayed*, 5; Thomas H. Carter to Thomas Nelson Page, December 1, 1898, quoted in Hobson, *Tell*, 150.

66. Glasgow, *Certain Measure*, 13; Gray, *Southern Aberrations*, 71; Glasgow, *Deliverance*, 15, 16, 28, 31, 29, 50. Louisiana author Ruth McEnery Stuart also offered an "inversion plot" in her 1902 tale of Reconstruction, *Napoleon Jackson*. Unlike Glasgow, who inverted the social classes of southern whites, however, Stuart inverted the position of the races in southern society. Napoleon Jackson, the "gentleman," was as black "as a crow" and of the purest African blood. Moreover, Stuart wrote her tale so readers could see the "romance," "tragedy, and fortunately for all concerned," the "comedy" of the lives of African-Americans in the Reconstruction South (*Napoleon Jackson*, 4). Glasgow hardly offered her novel in the spirit of comedy.

67. Glasgow, *Deliverance*, 27, 70.

68. Glasgow, *Certain Measure*, 34, 33; Glasgow, *Deliverance*, 199, 92. Glasgow challenged Page's contention that the plantations served as a "breeding ground" for chivalric heroes. The dissolute Christopher Blake offers a great contrast to Gordon Keith, "the son of a gentleman" and the eponymous hero of Page's novel of Reconstruction. Gordon is the son of General McDowall Keith, who survived the downfall of the slaveholding South "unchanged, unmoved, unmarred, an antique memorial of the life of which he was a relic." Page noted that Keith's lineage "was his only patrimony" but that this legacy has served him well, helping "him over many rough places. He carried it with him as a devoted Romanist wears a sacred scapulary next to the heart." The plantation is Gordon's world; "the woods that rimmed it were his horizon, as they had been that of the Keiths for generations." The collapse of his world, however, fails to divest Gordon of his patrimony. Gordon, too, is a southern gentleman (Page, *Gordon Keith*, 2, 4). See also L. H. MacKethan, "Thomas Nelson Page," 322.

69. Dixon, *Clansman*, 2; Williamson, *Rage*, 113.

70. Ellen Glasgow to Walter Hines Page, 26 December 1902, in Glasgow, *Letters*, 40–41. Glasgow never commented on her inversion of the standard plot of the sexually charged construction of African-American men's lust and white women's virtue. But the image of the vigorous white male protecting the southern belle from the rapacious black beast seems to be maintained largely by white men. Perhaps southern men were covering their own inadequacies, their own loss in the war. By recasting themselves as dashing cavaliers, protectors, southern men could atone from the sin of defeat. Although southern women vigorously participated in this reconfiguration of history and the legacies of the war, they were seemingly uninterested in constructing the white male protector, thereby signaling their unwillingness to participate in—or at least their unease with—the articulation of a powerful racial stereotype.

71. William Morton Payne, review of *The Deliverance*, *Dial* 36 (February 1904): 118, 119; review of *The Deliverance*, *Louisville Courier-Journal*, 16 January 1904, clippings files, Glasgow Papers; Archibald Henderson, review of *The Deliverance*, *Sewanee Review* 12 (October 1904): 462; review of *The Deliverance*, *Nation* 78 (March 1904): 235.

Chapter Five

1. Florence Faison Butler to Mary Anna Jackson, Washington, D.C., 20 March 1912, Florence Faison Butler correspondence files, Florence Faison Butler Papers, SHC. See also Mrs. Alexander B. White to Florence F. Butler, North Adams, Massachusetts, 11 January

1912, and Hilary A. Herbert, open letter to UDC members, Washington, D.C., April 1912, Florence Faison Butler correspondence files, Butler Papers, for the significance convention organizers placed on the meeting's location.

2. Mary Anna Jackson to Florence F. Butler, Charlotte, North Carolina, 2 April 1912, Florence Faison Butler to Mary Anna Jackson, Washington, D.C., 20 March 1912, Mildred Lewis Rutherford to Florence F. Butler, Athens, Georgia, 24 September, 3 October 1912, and Florence Faison Butler to Mrs. Alexander B. White, Washington, D.C., 30 September 1912, Florence Faison Butler correspondence files, Butler Papers.

3. Mrs. L. Eustace Williams, Leonora Rogers Schuyler, and Mrs. (A. A.) Susie S. Campbell, "Report of Committee on War between States," in UDC, *Minutes of the Nineteenth Annual Convention of the United Daughters of the Confederacy, Held in Washington, D.C., November 13–16, 1912* (Jackson, Miss.: McCowat Mercer, 1913), 315–16.

4. "Address of President Taft to the United Daughters of the Confederacy, November 1912," Florence Faison Butler correspondence files, Butler Papers.

5. "Address of the President," in UDC, *Minutes*, 1912, 8–9. It is noteworthy that Wilson segregated Washington, D.C., thus lending increased credence to the southern solution to the "Negro problem."

6. Isabell Worbell Ball, "The U.D.C.," *Washington (D.C.) National Tribune*, 21 November 1912, Florence Faison Butler clippings files, Butler Papers. Ball incurred the wrath of the UDC leadership for this article: Butler contacted a lawyer regarding the matter (see Florence F. Butler to James Tanner, Washington, D.C., 25 December 1912, and James Tanner to Florence F. Butler, Washington, D.C., 27 November 1912, Florence Faison Butler correspondence files, Butler Papers).

7. Rhodes's major works on the Civil War include *History of the United States* (7 vols.), *Lectures*, and *History of the Civil War*. For information on Rhodes, see, for example, Pressly, *Americans*, 142; see also 135–49.

8. Dunning, *Reconstruction*, xv, 204, 213–14.

9. Rutherford, *Wrongs*, 3; Rutherford, *Address . . . New Willard Hotel*, 4, 6; Mildred Lewis Rutherford, "Report of the Historian-General," in UDC, *Minutes of the Twenty-first Annual Convention of the United Daughters of the Confederacy, Held in Savannah, Georgia, November 11–14, 1914* (Raleigh, N.C.: Edwards and Broughton, 1915), 162. See also "Loyalty to the South and the South's Ideals," n.d., MS, Rutherford Papers, UGA.

10. Mrs. J. Enders Robinson, "Report of the Historian-General," in UDC, *Minutes of the Eighteenth Annual Convention of the United Daughters of the Confederacy, Held in Richmond, Virginia, November 1–11, 1911* (Paducah, Ky.: Paducah Printing, 1911), 109; Mrs. L. H. Watson, "Address," 366–67.

11. Annah Robinson Watson, "Report of Committee on Endorsement of Books," in UDC, *Minutes*, 1914, 291, 292; Rosa H. Mullins to Mary Calvert Stribling, Clay, West Virginia, 28 February 1911, Stribling Papers.

12. Mrs. A. R. Howard, resolution, in UDC, *Minutes*, 1911, 29, 31; A. S. Salley Jr. to Louisa B. Poppenheim, Columbia, South Carolina, 28 February 1909, Louisa B. and Mary B. Poppenheim Correspondence, PL.

13. Rutherford, *South in the Building*, 5–6.

14. "Sketch of David C. Milling," by his daughter, and Lucy Davis King, "Sketch of

John K. McIver," in UDC, South Carolina Division, John K. McIver Chapter, *Treasured Reminiscences*, 34, 13–14.

15. Kate Mason Rowland, "English Friends of the South," in UDC, *Three Papers*, 10; Mrs. Samuel Posey, "The Fight between the First Ironclads," n.d., TS, and Mrs. George B. Russell, "The Women of the Sixties," n.d., TS, *Confederate Veteran* Papers, PL. See also, for example, Posey's "Lee at Lexington," n.d., *Confederate Veteran* Papers.

16. *Carolina and the Southern Cross* 1 (November 1912): 1; 1 (March 1913): 1; Mrs. Lloyd K. Wooten, "Lee Did Not Apologize," *Carolina and the Southern Cross* 1 (December 1913): 20. Archbell faced difficulties in her publication schedule. After the inaugural issue of her magazine, she suspended publication for four months. When she resumed, she restarted the numbering with volume 1, number 1.

17. Editorial, *Carolina and the Southern Cross* 2 (July 1914): 10.

18. C. Harris, *Recording Angel*, 82–83. See Carrey S. Johnston to Corra Harris, Cambridge, Massachusetts, 15 March 1912, Corra Harris Papers, UGA.

19. In 1896, the first year for which membership figures are available for the national organization, more than 85 percent of the UDC's chapters were located in the states of the former Confederacy. Twenty years later, the number had decreased to 73 percent. While only a handful of chapters existed in states outside of the South during the UDC's early years, nearly every state soon boasted a chapter, with New York home to the largest number of chapters.

20. Muhlenfeld, *Mary Boykin Chesnut*, 191; Woodward, introduction to Chesnut, *Mary Chesnut's Civil War*, xxv.

21. Muhlenfeld, *Mary Boykin Chesnut*, 3–11; Chesnut, *Mary Chesnut's Civil War*, xv–liii.

22. Isabella D. Martin and Myrta Lockett Avary to Francis W. Halsey, Columbia, South Carolina, 9 January 1904, Avary Papers.

23. Francis W. Halsey to Myrta Lockett Avary, [New York], 3, 30 September 1904, and Myrta Lockett Avary to Francis W. Halsey, Mecklenburg, Virginia, 19 October 1904, Avary Papers.

24. Myrta Lockett Avary to Francis W. Halsey, Columbia, South Carolina, 2 December 1904, W. W. Appleton to Isabella D. Martin, [New York], 5 December 1904, and Francis W. Halsey to Isabella D. Martin, [New York], 13 December 1904, Avary Papers.

25. Myrta Lockett Avary to Francis W. Halsey, Columbia, South Carolina, 26 January 1905, Avary Papers. See also Myrta Lockett Avary to Roger Bowen, Columbia, South Carolina, 31 January 1905, Avary Papers, for a fuller discussion of Avary and Martin's objections to the term "Civil War," including Avary's fears that she would forever be condemned by her friends and family if she were associated with the phrase.

26. M. M. Kirkman to Isabella D. Martin, 28 March 1905, quoted in Muhlenfeld, *Mary Boykin Chesnut*, 8; Selene Ayer Armstrong, review of *A Diary from Dixie*, by Mary Boykin Chesnut, n.d., 39, clipping in Avary Papers.

27. Woodward, introduction to Chesnut, *Mary Chesnut's Civil War*, xxvii.

28. Andrews, *War-Time Journal*, 1, 5–6.

29. Ibid., 4, 9.

30. Ibid., 127, 11, 13.

31. Ibid., 14.

32. De Saussure, *Old Plantation Days*, 9–10, 17, 18.

33. Ibid., 19–20, 102. Dixon, the author of thirty novels, wrote *The Leopard's Spots* in 1902. This work and Dixon's follow-up novel, *The Clansman* (1905), tell the "history" of the white southern race after the war. The two volumes formed the basis for the 1914 epic film *Birth of a Nation*.

34. Battle, *Forget-Me-Nots*, 11, 25–26, 33, 37.

35. Ibid, 11–12, 137.

36. Ibid., 33, 37.

37. Ibid., 167–68. For an exploration of the ways in which newly emancipated African American women exercised their rights, see T. W. Hunter, *To 'Joy My Freedom*.

38. Battle, *Forget-Me-Nots*, 171–74.

39. S. M. Dawson, *Confederate Girl's Diary*, x. Charles East, editor of the 1991 edition of the diary, noted that Morgan made some alterations to the diary as she transcribed it, including "marginal comments, excisions, and occasional corrections of spellings." East also reported that Morgan wrote entirely in ink, enabling him in some cases "to determine whether her notations between the lines in the margins of the page were contemporaneous by comparing the ink with the original entry." East asserted in a footnote that "the manuscript diary vindicates Sarah" (East, introduction to S. M. Dawson, *Civil War Diary*, xxx, xxxiii n.30).

40. S. M. Dawson, *Confederate Girl's Diary*, xiii.

41. Ibid., 31–32.

42. R. E. Blackwell to Warrington Dawson, Ashland, Virginia, 6 October 1913, Francis Warrington Dawson Papers, PL; Elise Ripley Noyes to Warrington Dawson, Stamford, Connecticut, 13 February 1914, Dawson Papers.

43. Reviews of *A Confederate Girl's Diary*, by S. M. Dawson, in *Philadelphia Enquirer*, 27 September 1913, *Springfield (Illinois) Republican*, 1 October 1913, *Charleston (South Carolina) Sunday News*, 2 November 1913, and *Milwaukee Free Press*, 20 October 1913, Francis Warrington Dawson Scrapbook, 1884–1915, Dawson Papers.

44. Thruston, *Called*, vii–viii; R. H. Warren, *Southern Home*, 65–66; Seabrook, *Daughter*, 7.

45. Thruston, *Called*, 64–65; R. H. Warren, *Southern Home*, 14.

46. Selph, *Texas*, 46; Kennedy, *Cicely*, 26, 201; Annah Robinson Watson, "Report of Committee," in UDC, *Minutes*, 1914, 292; Thruston, *Called*, 120.

47. Pickett, *Bugles*, 5, 14–15.

48. Ibid., 100–101, 162 66–67.

49. Ibid., 116, 14, 124.

50. Reardon, *Pickett's Charge*, 186, 198; Gallagher, *Lee and His Generals*, 228, 229, 233–41; J. Longstreet, "Lee" (also published in *SHSP* 5 [January–February 1877]: 54–86; J. Longstreet, "Mistakes" (also published in *SHSP* 5 [June 1878]: 257–70); Edward Porter Alexander, "Letter from General E. P. Alexander, Late Chief of Artillery, First Corps, A.N.V.," *SHSP* 4 (September 1877): 97–111.

51. Selph, *Texas*, 7–8.

52. Kennedy, *Cicely*, 51, 305.

53. Seabrook, *Daughter*, 47, 275–77.

54. A. G. Jones, *Tomorrow*, 253, 238; Glasgow, *Virginia*, 5, 12, 21–22.

55. Ibid., 102, 105, 297, 476; A. G. Jones, *Tomorrow*, 240.

56. Glasgow, *Virginia*, 13, 45, 47.

57. Ibid., 369–70.

58. See the following reviews of *Virginia*, by Ellen Glasgow: *Sewanee Review* 21 (October–December 1913): 500; *Nation* 96 (22 May 1913): 524; *North American Review* 197 (June 1913): 856.

59. A. G. Jones, *Tomorrow*, 240, 253.

60. Mary Johnston, "Autobiography," n.d. [1900–10?], edited and typed by Elizabeth Johnston, 1953, Mary Johnston Papers, UVA; Mary Johnston to Thomas Nelson Page, Birmingham, Alabama, 28 April 1899, Thomas Nelson Page Papers, PL; Mary Johnston diary, 10 August 1908, Johnston Papers. See also Ferris Greenslet to Mary Johnston, Boston, 9 June 1909, Johnston Papers. For biographical information on Mary Johnston, see Cella, *Mary Johnston*; for an assessment of her historical fiction, see L. G. Nelson, "Mary Johnston"; Wagenknecht, "World."

61. Singal, *War Within*, 35–36; Glasgow, *Certain Measure*, 12.

62. Sales and earnings figures compiled from the Houghton Mifflin Account files, Johnston Papers; see also Houghton Mifflin Company, sales and earnings books, 1898–1914, Houghton Mifflin Company Correspondence and Records; royalty figures for the play production of *Audrey*, 1902–10, and statements from the Famous Player Film Company, 1916–21, Johnston Papers. *The Goddess of Reason* had sold only 908 copies by 1916 (sales figures compiled from the Houghton Mifflin Account files, Johnston Papers; see also sales and earnings books, Houghton Mifflin Company Correspondence and Records).

63. Robert A. Lively notes that after a drop in the number of Civil War novels published during Reconstruction, the numbers begin to steadily rise, peaking in the first decade of the twentieth century. Between 1862 and 1869, 69 war novels were published; in 1870–79, 17; in 1880–89, 49; in 1890–99, 76; in 1900–1909, 110; and in 1910–19, 59 (*Fiction Fights*, 22).

64. Johnston diary, 24 August, 7 September 1908. Johnston's background reading list included Henderson, *Stonewall Jackson*; Maury, *Recollections*; Alexander, *War*; J. E. Johnston, *Narrative*; Wyeth, *Life*; Chesnut, *Diary from Dixie* (which Johnston found "heart breaking"); R. Taylor, *Destruction and Reconstruction*; J. B. Gordon, *Reminiscences*; and Long, *Memoirs*, as well as thirty volumes of the *Southern Historical Society Papers* and "the hundred + odd" volumes in the *War of the Rebellion* series. "Weary work," she noted on 24 September 1908 (Johnston diary, August–September 1908).

65. Johnston diary, 25 May 1909; Ferris Greenslet to Mary Johnston, Boston, 9 June 1909, Johnston Papers.

66. Ferris Greenslet to Mary Johnston, Boston, 24, 30 December 1910, Mary Otto Kyllman to Mary Johnston, London, [England], 24 January 1911, Johnston Papers.

67. Ferris Greenslet to Mary Johnston, Boston, 16 October 1909, 24 May 1910, Johnston Papers. Greenslet did not find fault with all of Johnston's descriptions of battles (see Ferris Greenslet to Mary Johnston, Boston, 15 November, 16 December 1910, Johnston Papers).

68. M. Johnston, *Long Roll*, 201, 203.

69. Ferris Greenslet to Mary Johnston, Boston, 8 March 1911, Johnston Papers.

70. Mary Johnston to Ferris Greenslet, [Warm Springs, Virginia], n.d. [8–11 March 1911], Ferris Greenslet to Mary Johnston, Boston, 11 March 1911, Johnston Papers. Johnston later gave a great deal of thought to her financial future. Acknowledging that her writing had

changed dramatically since her early efforts, she affirmed her later works but admitted, "I am very truly and really concerned as to my future earning capacity" (Mary Johnston to Ferris Greenslet, Warm Springs, [Virginia], 29 October 1914, Houghton Mifflin Company Correspondence and Records).

71. Houghton Mifflin Earnings Book, 1911, Houghton Mifflin Company Correspondence and Records; M. Johnston, *Long Roll*, 38.

72. M. Johnston, *Long Roll*, 8, 16.

73. Johnston diary, 7 September 1908; M. Johnston, *Long Roll*, 22–23, 157.

74. Mary Johnston to Mrs. Henry Tracey, Warm Springs, Virginia, 20 June 1912, Johnston Papers.

75. "Prose Epic of the Civil War," *Baltimore Sun*, 4 June 1911, clipping in Johnston Papers.

76. "The Long Roll: Miss Johnston's Story of Stonewall Jackson and His Battles," *Charleston (South Carolina) News*, 28 May 1911, "Mary Johnston Has Splendid New Book," *Dallas News*, 26 July 1911, and *New York Evening Globe*, 13 May 1911, clippings in Johnston Papers.

77. M. Johnston, *Long Roll*, 141, 142, 152.

78. Ibid., 163–64.

79. Mary Anna Jackson, "Mrs. 'Stonewall' Jackson Denounces 'The Long Roll,'" *New York Times Sunday Magazine*, 29 October 1911, pp. 6–7; see also "Mrs. Jackson Writes of 'The Long Roll,'" *CV* 19 (December 1911): 591.

80. Captain J. P. Smith, "Stonewall Jackson: His Character," *CV* 19 (October 1911): 496.

81. Ibid., 497–98.

82. Mary Johnston, "Mary Johnston Defends 'The Long Roll,'" *CV* 19 (November 1911): 548.

83. Minutes Book, 1906–27, Secessionville Chapter of the UDC, James Island, South Carolina, 19 October, 16 November 1911, UDC, South Carolina Division, Secessionville Chapter Records; Joseph Ames to Mary Johnston, Baltimore, 29 October 1911, Johnston Papers; William Clayton Torrence, "General Stonewall Jackson and 'The Long Roll': A Reply to Miss Johnston's Critics," *Richmond Times-Dispatch*, 19 November 1911, p. 9, clipping in Johnston Papers; Ferris Greenslet to Mary Johnston, Boston, 31 October 1911, Johnston Papers.

84. Ferris Greenslet to Mary Johnston, Boston, 8 February 4 August 1912, Johnston Papers.

85. Ferris Greenslet to Mary Johnston, Boston, 28 September 1912, Johnston Papers.

86. M. Johnston, *Cease Firing!* 417, 426; Ferris Greenslet to Mary Johnston, Boston, 18 September 1912, Johnston Papers.

87. Ferris Greenslet to Mary Johnston, 18 September 1912, Johnston Papers; M. Johnston, *Cease Firing!* 439.

88. M. Johnston, *Cease Firing!* 73, 327.

89. Joseph Ames to Mary Johnston, Baltimore, 28 November 1912, Johnston Papers; *Wilmington (Delaware) Every Evening*, 16 November 1912, and *Minneapolis Journal*, 5 January 1913, clippings in Johnston Papers.

90. Murfree, *Storm Centre*, 214–19, 246–47, 253.

91. Murfree, *Raid*, 7, 28, 50–51.

92. Murfree, "The Lost Guidon," in *Raid*, 143, 147, 163.

Chapter Six

1. Helen Dortch Longstreet to manager, Scribner's Publishers, Washington, D.C., 9 August 1934, Helen Dortch Longstreet Collection, GHS.

2. Charles Scribner's Sons to Helen Dortch Longstreet, New York, 23 August 1934, Helen Dortch Longstreet Collection, GHS.

3. Helen Dortch Longstreet, "The Gallant Southron," n.d., TS, Helen Dortch Longstreet Collection, GHS.

4. Freeman, *R. E. Lee*, 1:vii, xiv.

5. Mrs. Dunbar Rowland, "Report of the Peace Committee," in UDC, *Minutes of the Twenty-third Annual Convention of the United Daughters of the Confederacy, Held in Dallas, Texas, November 8–11, 1916* (Raleigh, N.C.: Edwards and Broughton, 1917), 315; Birdie A. Owen, "Report of the President, Tennessee Division, U.D.C.," in UDC, *Minutes of the Twenty-fifth Annual Convention of the United Daughters of the Confederacy, Held in Louisville, Kentucky, April 1–5, 1919* (Kansas City: Kellog Baxter, 1919), 492.

6. Cordelia Powell Odenheimer, "Report of the President General," in UDC, *Minutes of the Twenty-fourth Annual Convention of the United Daughters of the Confederacy, Held in Chattanooga, Tennessee, November 14–17, 1917* (Richmond: Richmond Press, 1918), 113; "Resolution Offered by the J. Z. George Chapter and Adopted by the Mississippi Division in Convention at Greenwood, Miss., May 3, 1917," *CV* 25 (July 1917): 329.

7. "From the President General," *CV* 25 (May 1917): 230; "From the President General," *CV* 25 (June 1917): 280; "From the President General," *CV* 25 (August 1917): 376.

8. "From the President General," *CV* 26 (January 1918): 36; H. C. L. to Mary Calvert Stribling, Washington, D.C., 10 January 1918, Stribling Papers; "Georgia Division United Daughters of the Confederacy War Relief," *Report of the Twenty-fourth Year's Work, Georgia Division United Daughters of the Confederacy; Convention to Have Been Held in Atlanta, Georgia, October 22–25, 1918* (n.p., n.d.), 37–41; Mrs. Cabell Smith, "Report of the Virginia Division," *CV* 26 (February 1918): 87; Agnes Halliburton, "Report of the Arkansas Division," *CV* 26 (February 1918): 88.

9. Louise Ayer Vandiver, "Report of the South Carolina Division," *CV* 26 (March 1918): 127; Anne Bachman Hyde, "Report of the Historian-General," in UDC, *Minutes*, 1919, 183; "UDC Program for March 1918," *CV* 26 (March 1918): 130; "UDC Program for June 1918," *CV* 26 (May 1918): 226; "UDC Program for August 1918," *CV* 26 (July 1918): 320.

10. Anne Bachman Hyde to state historians, Chattanooga, Tennessee, February 1919, Stribling Papers. See also "Prizes for 1922," "World War Record Committee," and "Hero Scholarships," in *Minutes of the Twenty-eighth Annual Convention of the United Daughters of the Confederacy, Held in St. Louis, Missouri, November 8–12, 1921* (Jackson, Tenn.: McCowat-Mercer, 1922), 23, 190, 125; Mrs. John W. Goodwin, "Confederate Descendants in the World War," in UDC, *Minutes of the Twenty-ninth Annual Convention of the United Daughters of the Confederacy, Held in Birmingham, Alabama, November, 14–18, 1922* (Jackson, Tenn.: McCowat-Mercer, 1923), 328.

11. Miss E. H. Hanna, "Report on the Committee of Southern Literature and Endorsement of Books," in *Minutes*, 1919, 398; Mrs. Alexander B. White, "Report of the Editor of the UDC's Department of the *Confederate Veteran*," in UDC, *Minutes of the Twenty-sixth Annual Convention of the United Daughters of the Confederacy, Held in Tampa, Florida, November 11–15, 1919* (Jackson, Tenn.: McCowat-Mercer, 1920), 262.

12. Mrs. J. A. Rountree, "Report of the Insignia Committee," in UDC, *Minutes of the Thirtieth Annual Convention of the United Daughters of the Confederacy, Held in Washington, D.C., November 20–24, 1923* (Jackson, Tenn.: McCowat-Mercer, 1924), 203, 205; minutes, Executive Board, Georgia Division, United Daughters of the Confederacy, 29 January 1924, Carswell Collection, GHS; Mrs. J. A. Rountree, "Report of the Insignia Committee," in UDC, *Minutes of the Thirty-third Annual Convention of the United Daughters of the Confederacy, Held in Richmond, Virginia, November 16–20, 1926* (Jackson, Tenn.: McCowat-Mercer, 1927), 192.

13. "State Historical Program," 1920, and "Women of the South in War Times," [1930s?], Carswell Collection.

14. Selph, *The South*, 5, 39, 164. For an account of historians' use of nationalism, see Potter, *The South*, 34–83.

15. Cauthen and Jones, "Coming," 233, 234; Potter, review, 400. See also Malvasi, *Unregenerate South*; Pressly, *Americans*, 239–53; Twelve Southerners, *I'll Take My Stand*, 61–91.

16. Helen Dortch Longstreet to the editor of the *Washington (D.C.) Star*, Washington, D.C., 9 May 1934, Helen Dortch Longstreet to Eleanor Patterson, Washington, D.C., 9 May 1934, Helen Dortch Longstreet to "Dearly beloved Margaret," Washington, D.C., 9 May 1934, Helen Dortch Longstreet to Mr. McFadden, Washington, D.C., 16 June 1934, and Helen Dortch Longstreet to Mr. Meyer, Washington, D.C., 12 October 1934, Helen Dortch Longstreet Collection, GHS.

17. Helen Dortch Longstreet to the editor of the *Burlington (Vermont) Free Press*, Lorton, Virginia, 1937. See also, for example, Helen Dortch Longstreet to Mr. Lay, Lorton, Virginia, 17 August 1937, and Bruce Rae to Helen Dortch Longstreet, New York, 19 August 1937, Helen Dortch Longstreet Collection, GHS.

18. See "Introduction to Glory's Bivouac," [1936–37?], TS, Helen Dortch Longstreet Collection, GHS.

19. "Glory's Bivouac — Contents," "The Bugles are Calling," and cover page of "Glory's Bivouac," n.d. [1937?], TS, Helen Dortch Longstreet Collection, GHS.

20. Pressly, *Americans*, 240.

21. Pickett, *What Happened*, 126, 30, 34.

22. Ibid., 85, 86.

23. Ibid., 89, 91–92. See Linderman, *Embattled Courage*, for a discussion of the ways in which the experience of combat changed perceptions of war.

24. Pickett, *What Happened*, 105, 107, 200–201.

25. Felton, *Country Life*, 5, 83, 86–87. 84. See Hale, *Making Whiteness*, for a discussion of Felton's role in "domestic reconstruction."

26. Felton, *Country Life*, 88–89, 101.

27. Ibid., 91, 5.

28. Cushman, introduction to Eppes, *Through Some Eventful Years*, xxi.

29. Eppes, *Through Some Eventful Years*, 9; Eppes, *Negro*, 106–7, 115, 148–49.

30. Eppes, *Through Some Eventful Years*, 154, 202, 213. If the diary were authentic, Eppes's prescience on the significance of the Battle of Gettysburg would be remarkable, considering that according to Reardon, most contemporaries did not distinguish Gettysburg as the war's turning point (see Reardon, *Pickett's Charge*).

31. Eppes, *Through Some Eventful Years*, 267, 355, 358.

32. See, for example, Brundage, *Lynching*; MacLean, *Behind the Mask*.

33. Bach, "The Wave," 21. See also Bach, "Evelyn Scott," 715. For a discussion of the southern literary renaissance, see for example, Gray, *Writing*; R. King, *Southern Renaissance*; Kreyling, *Inventing*.

34. E. Scott, *Wave*, preface; Scott quoted in Bach, "The Wave," 21, and in White, *Fighting*, 119; White, *Fighting*, 119, 121.

35. Harry Salpeter, "Portrait of a Disciplined Artist," *Bookman* 74 (November 1931): 285–86.

36. Carl Van Doren, review of *The Wave*, by Evelyn Scott, *Saturday Review of Literature*, 6 July 1929, 16; Percy Hutchinson, "A Panoramic Civil War Novel," *New York Times Book Review*, 30 June 1929, pp. 1, 19.

37. Clifton P. Fadiman, "A Great National Drama," *Nation*, 31 July 1929, 119.

38. Robert Morss Lovett, review of *The Wave*, by Evelyn Scott, *New Republic*, 7 August 1929, 319; Robert Morss Lovett, "The Evolution of Evelyn Scott," *Bookman* 70 (October 1929): 155, 156.

39. Literary Guild advertisement, *New York Times Book Review*, 30 June 1929, 11; White, *Fighting*, 123; Bach, "The Wave," 25.

40. Macmillan 1936 spring catalog, reprinted in Mitchell, *Letters*, photo insert; Pyron, *Southern Daughter*, 337.

41. Mitchell, *Gone with the Wind*, 4, 55, 212, 211.

42. Ibid., 171, 428.

43. Fox-Genovese, "Scarlett O'Hara," 397; Mitchell, *Gone with the Wind*, 42–43, 44–45.

44. Mitchell, *Gone with the Wind*, 654; Fox-Genovese, "Scarlett O'Hara," 408.

45. Mitchell, *Gone with the Wind*, 654, 905, 798. In answering a series of questions from a fan, Mitchell explained that the Klan's first purpose was "to protect women and children. Later it was used to keep the Negroes from voting eight or ten times at every election. But it was used equally against the Carpetbaggers who had the same bad habit where voting was concerned. Members of the Klan knew that if unscrupulous or ignorant people were permitted to hold office in the South the lives and property of Southerners would not be safe" (Margaret Mitchell to Ruth Tallman, Atlanta, 30 July 1937, in Mitchell, *Letters*, 162).

46. Mitchell, *Gone with the Wind*, 48, 36, 686, 691.

47. Ibid., 660, 744; Fox-Genovese, "Scarlett O'Hara," 398.

48. Mitchell, *Gone with the Wind*, 147, 657; Margaret Mitchell to Gilbert E. Govan, Atlanta, 15 October 1937, in Mitchell, *Letters*, 172–73; Fox-Genovese, "Scarlett O'Hara," 398.

49. Margaret Mitchell to Julian Harris, Atlanta, 21 April 1936, and Margaret Mitchell to Harry Slattery, Atlanta, 3 October 1936, in Mitchell, *Letters*, 1, 70. A. G. Jones, *Tomorrow*, 333; Pyron, *Southern Daughter*, 223–29. See also Margaret Mitchell to Julia Collier Harris, Atlanta, 28 April 1936, in Mitchell, *Letters*, 5.

50. Fox-Genovese, "Scarlett O'Hara," 395; Margaret Mitchell to Julia Collier Harris, Atlanta, 28 April 1936, Margaret Mitchell to Joseph Henry Jackson, Atlanta, 1 June 1936, and Margaret Mitchell to Harriet Ross Colquitt, Atlanta, 7 August 1936, in Mitchell, *Letters*, 3–4, 13, 50.

51. Margaret Mitchell to Stephen Vincent Benet, Gainesville, Georgia, 9 July 1936, Margaret Mitchell to Achmed Abdullah, Atlanta, 14 April 1937, Margaret Mitchell to Robert C. Taylor, Atlanta, 15 August 1936, and Margaret Mitchell to Julian Harris, Atlanta, 21 April 1936, in Mitchell, *Letters*, 36, 140, 53, 2.

52. Margaret Mitchell to Paul Jordan-Smith, Atlanta, 27 May 1936, and Margaret Mitchell to Stephen Vincent Benet, Gainesville, Georgia, 9 July 1936, in ibid., 7–8, 35.

53. Margaret Mitchell to Herschel Brickell, Atlanta, 13 November 1936, and Margaret Mitchell to Thomas Dixon Jr., Atlanta, 15 August 1936, in ibid., 87, 52; Pyron, *Southern Daughter*, 310.

54. Pyron, *Southern Daughter*, 311; Margaret Mitchell to Henry Steele Commager, Atlanta, 10 July 1936, in Mitchell, *Letters*, 37.

55. Pyron, *Southern Daughter*, 306, 307. For a detailed account of the fate of Mitchell's manuscript, see 294–99.

56. Ibid., 308, 312. Pyron's chapter "Bloody Work Done" offers a detailed account of Mitchell's revisions to her manuscript.

57. Ibid., 318–19.

58. Glasgow quoted in Mitchell, *Letters*, 57 n.1; Margaret Mitchell to Herschel Brickell, Atlanta, 22 October 1936, in Mitchell, *Letters*, 81; Pyron, *Southern Daughter*, 324.

59. Margaret Mitchell to Harold Latham, Atlanta, 1 June, 13 August 1936, Margaret Mitchell to George Brett, Gainesville, Georgia, 8 July 1936, Margaret Mitchell to Julia Collier Harris, Atlanta, 29 June 1936, and Margaret Mitchell to Herschel Brickell, Atlanta, 22 February 1937, in Mitchell, *Letters*, 9, 50–51, 22, 17, 122. Mitchell made an exception and held autograph sessions in Atlanta. In a few instances, Mitchell professed dismay at the novel's popularity, which guaranteed her prolonged exposure to the public gaze; see, for example, Margaret Mitchell to Herschel Brickell, Atlanta, 9 October 1936, 17 January 1937, in Mitchell, *Letters*, 74, 109–10.

60. Pyron, *Southern Daughter*, 331.

61. Margaret Mitchell to Edwin Granberry, Gainesville, Georgia, 8 July 1936, and Margaret Mitchell to Herschel Brickell, Gainesville, Georgia, 7 July 1936, in Mitchell, *Letters*, 27–30, 21.

62. Margaret Mitchell to Henry Steele Commager, Atlanta, 10 July 1936, and Margaret Mitchell to Douglas S. Freeman, Atlanta, 13 October 1936, in ibid., 39, 77.

63. Pyron, *Southern Daughter*, 338–39; Margaret Mitchell to Julia Collier Harris, Atlanta, 29 June 1936, Margaret Mitchell to Herschel Brickell, Gainesville, Georgia, 7 July, 18 September 1936, Margaret Mitchell to Julia Peterkin, Atlanta, 14 August 1936, Margaret Mitchell to Herschel Brickell, Atlanta, 18 September 1936, 17 January 1937, and Margaret Mitchell to William Lyon Phelps, Atlanta, 21 January 1938, in Mitchell, *Letters*, 17, 19, 52, 62, 109, 181–82.

64. John Peale Bishop, "All War and No Peace," *New Republic*, 15 July 1936, 301.

65. Malcolm Cowley, review of *Gone with the Wind*, by Margaret Mitchell, *New Republic*, 16 September 1936, 161–62.

66. Evelyn Scott, "War between the States," *Nation*, 4 July 1936, 19–20.

67. Margaret Mitchell to Stark Young, Atlanta, 1, 29 September 1936, and Margaret Mitchell to Jackson P. Dick Jr., Atlanta, 16 February 1937, in Mitchell, *Letters*, 59, 66, 120.

68. Margaret Mitchell to Julia Collier Harris, Atlanta, 28 April 1936, Margaret Mitchell to Paul Jordan Smith, Atlanta, 27 May 1936, Margaret Mitchell to Gilbert Govan, Gainesville, Georgia, 8 July 1936, Margaret Mitchell to Mark Allan Patton, Atlanta, 11 July 1936, Margaret Mitchell to Mark Millikin, Atlanta, 3 September 1936, and Margaret Mitchell to Herschel Brickell, Atlanta, 20, 30 October 1937, in ibid., 5, 8, 24, 42, 60, 173, 174–75.

69. Margaret Mitchell to Julia Collier Harris, Atlanta, 21 April 1936, Margaret Mitchell to Kate Duncan Smith, Atlanta, 24 July 1936, Margaret Mitchell to Mordecai M. Thurman, Atlanta, 6 February 1937, 115, and Margaret Mitchell to Herschel Brickell, Atlanta, 9 October 1936, in ibid., 1–2, 46, 115, 75.

Epilogue

1. Caroline Gordon to Sally Wood, Monteagle, Tennessee, 10 September 1936, in S. Wood, *Southern Mandarins*, 201–2.

2. Untitled TS beginning "When my brothers and I were children," n.d. [1939–45], Gordon Papers; Gregory, preface to Gordon, *None Shall Look Back*, viii; Makowsky, "Caroline Gordon on Women Writing," 43; Caroline Gordon to Sally Wood, Monteagle, Tennessee, 10 September 1936, in S. Wood, *Southern Mandarins*, 201–2. For biographical information on Caroline Gordon, see, for example, Fraistat, *Caroline Gordon*; Jonza, *Underground Stream*; Waldron, *Close Connections*; Makowsky, *Caroline Gordon*. After the phenomenal success of *Gone with the Wind*, few reviewers questioned the appearance of a Civil War novel written by a woman. Still, some felt compelled to comment on Gordon's gender: "The battle scenes are excellent," wrote Robert E. Betts for the *Raleigh (North Carolina) Times*. "One is surprised to find that a woman could write so well about such a subject" (27 February 1937, clipping in Gordon Papers). The reviewer for the *Memphis Appeal* apparently could not resist a touch of sarcasm: "Oh what discipline it must have taken to do such a masculine lot of writing on those battle scenes! Once, tis said, after finishing a particularly fierce battle violently as to rush out and down town, to buy a whole store of feminine frills" (28 February 1937, clipping in Gordon Papers). Not surprisingly, Ford Madox Ford, Gordon's mentor, made the most sympathetic comment on the connection between Gordon's gender and writing ability: "She writes with the intelligence of a man about the intimate details of men's occupations. You cannot say that she writes like a man—or for the matter of that, like a woman" (Ford, review of *None Shall Look Back*, unidentified clipping in Gordon Papers).

3. Gregory, preface to Gordon, *None Shall Look Back*, viii–ix; Makowsky, "Caroline Gordon on Women Writing," 44, 45; Rubin, "Image," 51; Caroline Gordon to Sally Wood, Clarksville, Tennessee, May 1937, in S. Wood, *Southern Mandarins*, 208–9. Some reviewers noted the familiarity of the opening scene and of other formulaic episodes in Gordon's plot: see, for example, Elsie Ruth Chant, "Stirring Deeds," *El Paso (Texas) Herald-Post*, 3 June 1937, *Milwaukee Sentinel*, 28 February 1937, Carl Van Doren, "Another Civil War Novel," *Boston Herald*, 27 February 1937, clippings in Gordon Papers. For more on the shortcomings of southern novels of the war, see Aaron, *Unwritten War*; Simpson, *Mind*; Sullivan, "Fading Memory"; R. P. Warren, *Legacy*; E. Wilson, *Patriotic Gore*. Gordon apparently fretted a good deal over her work. Katherine Anne Porter offered some advice to Gordon after the publication of *None Shall Look Back*: "I hope you feel better about it

now it is finished and published. Take time all you need on your next one, and try not to suffer always that sense of haste and the feeling that you have not done all you might have done on any given piece of work. . . . You felt that way about the other two, also; it is possible you may never be satisfied with anything you do—I know I have never been—but still, it is something to be able to say that, at any given time, you have done exactly all you could do, and if it is not enough, why then, begin again on something else" (Porter to Gordon, New York, 22 February 1937, Gordon Papers).

4. Caroline Gordon to Sally Wood Kohn, Clarksville, Tennessee, postmarked 8 January 1937, Max Perkins to Caroline Gordon, New York, 8 July 1935, and Caroline Gordon to Mr. Weber, n.p., n.d., Gordon Papers.

5. Max Perkins to Caroline Gordon, New York, 7 August 1935, Caroline Gordon to Sally Wood Kohn, Clarksville, Tennessee, 19 May 1937, Gordon Papers.

6. Jane Irdell Jones, "Caroline Gordon Writes Telling Story of Plantation Life in Novel, 'None Shall Look Back,'" *Columbus (Georgia) Inquirer-Sun*, 8 March 1937, "Civil War—With a Difference," *New York World-Telegram*, 4 March 1937, Chant, "Stirring Deeds," Philip Russell, review of *None Shall Look Back*, *Savannah (Georgia) Press*, 10 April 1937, clippings in Gordon Papers.

7. Van Doren, "Another Civil War Novel"; F. M. Ford, review; review of *None Shall Look Back*, by Caroline Gordon, *Nation*, 20 March 1937, clipping in Gordon Papers; Katherine Anne Porter to Caroline Gordon, New York, 22 February 1937, Gordon Papers; review of *None Shall Look Back*, *Rocky Mount (North Carolina) Telegram*, 6 March 1937, clipping in Gordon Papers. Not surprisingly, many reviewers compared *None Shall Look Back* with *Gone with the Wind*. The reviewer for *Time* magazine noted the unfortunate timing of the publication of Gordon's novel: "When Allen Tate, critic and poet, had written most of a long-planned life of Robert E. Lee, Douglass Southall Freeman's four-volume, definitive *Robert E. Lee* . . . appeared, blew his house down before the roof was on. Last week," the reviewer continued, "the same meteorological hard luck seemed to be pursuing Caroline Gordon (Mrs. Allen Tate). For her Civil War novel came out in the wake of that typhoon of best-sellers, *Gone with the Wind*" ("After the Big Wind," *Time*, 1 March 1937). For other reviews comparing *None Shall Look Back* to *Gone with the Wind*, see, for example, *St. Paul (Minnesota) Dispatch*, 27 February 1937, *Macon (Georgia) Telegraph*, 9 March 1937, *Nation*, 20 March 1937, Elrich B. Davis, "Caroline Gordon's New Novel of the South, 'None Shall Look Back,' Is a Noble Book," *Cleveland Press*, clippings in Gordon Papers. Long after the publication of *None Shall Look Back*, Gordon remembered Tate "saying when 'Gone With the Wind' appeared that the enormous popularity which it achieved would set the art of the novel back at least two hundred years. It almost looks as if he was right!" (Gordon to Frederick McDowell, Princeton, New Jersey, 22 January 1965, Gordon Papers).

8. Caroline Gordon to Sally Wood, Clarksville, Tennessee, May 1937, in S. Wood, *Southern Mandarins*, 209.

9. C. Gordon, *None Shall Look Back*, 330–31.

10. Caroline Gordon, "None Shall Look Back," 354–56, n.d., TS, Gordon Papers.

11. Twelve Southerners, *I'll Take My Stand*, xl–xli; Conkin, *Southern Agrarians*, 74. See also Malvasi, *Unregenerate South*.

12. C. Gordon, *None Shall Look Back*, 357, 336–37, 340–41.

13. Ibid., 8, 316, 319.

14. Ibid, 375, 107, 298, 285–86.

15. Ibid., 378; Lon Cheney to Caroline Gordon, Smyrna, Tennessee, 3 December [1951?], Gordon Papers.

16. Caroline Gordon, "Rebels and Revolutionaries," lecture delivered to the Flannery O'Connor Foundation, April 1974, TS, Gordon Papers.

Bibliography

Manuscript Sources
Athens, Georgia
University of Georgia, Hargrett Library Special Collections
  Howell Cobb Papers
  Rebecca Latimer Felton Papers
  Corra Harris Papers
  Ladies Volunteer Aid Association Records
  Eunice Williams Reed Papers
  Mildred Lewis Rutherford Papers
  United Daughters of the Confederacy, Laura Rutherford Chapter Records

Atlanta, Georgia
Atlanta History Center
  1900 Study Club Records
  1908 History Class Records, Mary Connally Spalding Papers
  Atlanta Ladies Memorial Association Records
  Myrta Lockett Avary Papers
  Nellie Peters Black Papers
  Mrs. D. Mitchell Cox Papers
  Sarah Clayton Crane Papers
  Every Saturday Club Records
  History Class of 1884 Collection
  Helen Dortch Longstreet Papers
  Emma Slade Prescott Reminiscences
  Mary Rawson Diary
  Mildred Rutherford Papers
  United Daughters of the Confederacy Collection
Emory University, Robert W. Woodruff Library, Special Collections
  G. T. Beauregard Papers

Burge Family Papers
Every Saturday Club Programs
James Longstreet Papers
Mary Noailles Murfree Papers
Sue Richardson Diary
Loula Kendall Rogers Papers
Kate Whitehead Rowland Diaries
Alexander H. Stephens Papers
Sarah Lois Wadley Papers
Bell Irvin Wiley Papers
Georgia Department of Archives and History
Zilla Lee Bostick Redd Agerton Papers
Nellie Peters Black Papers
Louisa Warren Patch Fletcher Papers
Julia B. Reed Papers
Birdie Varner Sanders Papers
United Daughters of the Confederacy, Atlanta Chapter Records
United Daughters of the Confederacy, La Grange Chapter Records
United Daughters of the Confederacy, Frankie Lyle Chapter Records
United Daughters of the Confederacy, Lizzie Rutherford Chapter Records

Cambridge, Massachusetts
Harvard University, Houghton Library
Houghton Mifflin Company Correspondence and Records
Mary Noailles Murfree Papers

Chapel Hill, North Carolina
University of North Carolina, Wilson Library, Southern Historical Collection
Lillie Vause Archbell Papers
Lucy Hull Baldwin Papers
Grace Pierson James Beard Manuscript
Annie Laurie Harris Broidrick Manuscript
Florence Faison Butler Papers
Sarah Rebecca Cameron Papers
Annie Jeter Carmouche Papers
Grace B. Elmore Papers
Mrs. Nicholas Ware Eppes Papers
Gale and Polk Family Papers
Josephine Clay Habersham Habersham Diary
Elizabeth Seawell Hairston Papers
Maria L. Haynsworth Letter
Rachel Lyons Heustis Papers
Annie Hyde Papers
Belle Kearney Manuscript
Ladies Memorial Association Records

Judith White Brockenbrough McGuire Diary Excerpts
Elvira Evelyna Moffitt Papers
Harriet Ellen Moore Diary
Matilda Lamb Morton Manuscript
Eliza Hall Parsley Papers
Phoebe Yates Levy Pember Papers
Sarah Ellen Phillips Manuscript
Margaret Junkin Preston Papers
Catherine McAlprin Wray Pritchard Papers
J. G. M. Ramsey Papers
Emma Lydia Rankin Papers
Louisa Campbell Sheppard Recollections
Cornelia Phillips Spencer Papers
Sarah Lois Wadley Papers

Charlottesville, Virginia
University of Virginia Library, Special Collections Department
James Mercer Garnett Papers
Ellen Glasgow Papers
Mary Johnston Papers
Ladies Confederate Memorial Association Records
United Daughters of the Confederacy, Virginia Division, Albemarle Chapter Papers
Augusta Jane Evans Wilson Collection

Columbia, South Carolina
University of South Carolina, South Caroliniana Library
Current Literature Club (Columbia) Records
Emily Caroline Searson Ellis Manuscript
Girls of the Sixties Records
Emily Geiger Goodlett Papers
Greenville Ladies Association in Aid of the Volunteers of the Confederate Army Records
Mary Y. Harth Papers
Emma Edwards Holmes Papers
Ladies Aid Society Records
Ladies Association to Commemorate the Confederate Dead Records
Maverick and Van Wyck Family Papers
Harriott Horry Ravenel Papers
United Daughters of the Confederacy, South Carolina Division, Black Oak Chapter
    Records
United Daughters of the Confederacy, South Carolina Division, Marion Chapter
    Records
United Daughters of the Confederacy, South Carolina Division, Secessionville Chapter
    Records
Mrs. Clark Waring Papers

Durham, North Carolina
Duke University, Perkins Library Special Collections
  Pierre Gustave Toutant Beauregard Papers
  John Grammar Brodnax Papers
  I. H. Carrington Papers
  C. C. Clay Papers
  Confederate Veteran Papers
  Cronly Family Papers
  J. L. M. Curry Papers
  Francis Warrington Dawson Papers
  Kate D. Foster Diary
  Adeline Burr Davis Green Papers
  Greenville Ladies' Association in Aid of the Volunteers of the Confederate Army
    Minutes
  Mrs. Thomas Baxter Gresham Papers
  Hemphill Family Papers
  Hinsdale Family Papers
  T. H. Holmes Papers
  Gertrude Jenkins Papers
  Montrose Jonas Papers
  Clara Victoria Dargan Maclean Papers
  McMullen Family Papers
  John Singleton Mosby Papers
  Munford-Ellis Families Papers
  Thomas Nelson Page Papers
  Pope-Carter Family Papers
  Louisa B. and Mary B. Poppenheim Correspondence
  Mary Calvert Stribling Papers
  Ella Gertrude Clanton Thomas Diaries
  United Daughters of the Confederacy, Miscellaneous Records
  United Daughters of the Confederacy, South Carolina Division, Black Oak Chapter
    Records
  United Daughters of the Confederacy, South Carolina Division, Edgefield Chapter
    Records
  Agatha Abney Woodson Papers
  Elvira L. Woodson Papers

Montgomery, Alabama
Alabama Department of Archives and History
  Sarah Rodgers Espy Diaries
  Sarah Lowe Journals
  Mary D. Waring Diary
  Mary L. Williamson Diary
  Augusta Jane Evans Wilson File
  Haynie Brandon Zillah Diaries

New York, New York
New York Public Library
  Century Company Records

Princeton, New Jersey
Princeton University Library, Rare Books and Special Collections Department
  Caroline Gordon Papers
  Allen Tate Papers

Savannah, Georgia
Georgia Historical Society
  Carswell Collection
  Helen Dortch Longstreet Collection

Washington, D.C.
Library of Congress
  J. L. M. Curry Papers
  Burton Norvell Harrison Family Papers
  P. Phillips Family Papers

Printed Sources

Aaron, Daniel. *The Unwritten War: American Writers and the Civil War*. New York: Knopf, 1973.

Adams, Henry. *Democracy: An American Novel*. Foreword by Henry D. Aiken. New York: New American Library, 1961.

———. "The Rule of Phase Applied to History." In Adams, *The Degradation of the Democratic Dogma*, 267–311. New York: Macmillan, 1919.

Alexander, Edward Porter. "Letter from General E. P. Alexander, Late Chief of Artillery First Corps, A. N. V.," *SHSP* 4 (September 1877): 97–111.

Allan, Elizabeth Preston. *The Life and Letters of Margaret Junkin Preston*. Boston: Houghton, Mifflin, 1903.

Anderson, Douglas: *A House Undivided: Domesticity and Community in American Literature*. New York: Cambridge University Press, 1990.

Anderson, Eric, and Alfred A. Moss Jr., eds. *The Facts of Reconstruction: Essays in Honor of John Hope Franklin*. Baton Rouge: Louisiana State University, 1991.

Andrews, Eliza Frances. *The War-Time Journal of a Georgia Girl, 1864–1865*. Ed. Spencer Bidwell King Jr. Macon, Ga.: Ardivan Press, 1960.

Appleby, Joyce. "Reconciliation and the Northern Novelist, 1865–1880." *Civil War History* 10 (June 1964): 117–29.

Arnold, Thomas Jackson. *Early Life and Letters of General Thomas J. Jackson, "Stonewall" Jackson*. New York: Fleming H. Revell, 1916.

Atchison, Ray M. "*The Land We Love*: A Southern Post-Bellum Magazine of Agricultural, Literary, and Military History." *North Carolina Historical Review* 37 (October 1960): 506–15.

————. "*Our Living and Our Dead*: A Post-Bellum North Carolina Magazine of Literature and History." *North Carolina Historical Review* 40 (Autumn 1963): 423–33.

Atteberry, Phillip D. "Ellen Glasgow and the Sentimental Novel of Virginia." *Southern Quarterly* 23 (Summer 1985): 5–14.

Avary, Myrta Lockett. *Dixie after the War: An Exposition of Social Conditions Existing in the South during the Twelve Years Succeeding the Fall of Richmond.* New York: Doubleday, Page, 1906.

————, ed. *A Virginia Girl in the Civil War, 1861–1865: Being a Record of the Actual Experiences of the Wife of a Confederate Officer.* New York: Appleton, 1903.

Avery, M. A. *The Rebel General's Loyal Bride: A True Picture of Scenes in the Late Civil War.* Springfield, Mass.: W. J. Holland, 1873.

Ayers, Edward L. *The Promise of the New South: Life after Reconstruction.* New York: Oxford University Press, 1992.

Bach, Peggy. "Evelyn Scott: The Woman in the Foreground." *Southern Review* 18 (October 1982): 703–17.

————. "*The Wave*: Evelyn Scott's Civil War." *Southern Literary Journal* 17 (Spring 1985): 18–32.

Bacon, Eugenia Jones. *Lyddy: A Tale of the Old South.* New York: Continental, 1898.

Bailey, Fred Arthur. "The Textbooks of the 'Lost Cause': Censorship and the Creation of Southern State Histories." *Georgia Historical Quarterly* 75 (Fall 1991): 507–33.

Bain, Robert, Joseph M. Flora, and Louis D. Rubin Jr. *Southern Writers: A Biographical Dictionary.* Baton Rouge: Louisiana State University Press, 1979.

Bakker, Jan. "Overlooked Progenitors: Independent Women and Southern Renaissance in Augusta Jane Evans Wilson's *Macaria; or Altars of Sacrifice.*" *Southern Quarterly* 25 (Winter 1987): 131–42.

Ballard, Michael B. "Yankee Editors on Jefferson Davis." *Journal of Mississippi History* 43 (November 1981): 316–32.

Bargainnier, Earl. "The Myth of Moonlight and Magnolias." *Louisiana Studies* 15 (Spring 1976): 5–20.

Barrett, John G. "The Confederate States of America at War on Land and Sea." In *Writing Southern History: Essays in Historiography in Honor of Fletcher M. Green*, ed. Arthur S. Link and Rembert W. Patrick, 273–94. Baton Rouge: Louisiana State University Press, 1965.

Baskerville, W. M. "Southern Literature since the War." *Vanderbilt Observer*, 15 (May 1893): 207–11.

Bassett, John Spencer. *A Short History of the United States.* New York: Macmillan, 1913.

Battle, Laura Elizabeth Lee. *Forget-Me-Nots of the Civil War: A Romance, Containing Reminiscences and Original Letters of Two Confederate Soldiers.* St. Louis, Mo.: A. R. Fleming, 1909.

Baym, Nina. *Woman's Fiction: A Guide to Novels by and about Women in America, 1820–1870.* Ithaca: Cornell University Press, 1978.

Beers, Fannie A. *Memories: A Record of Personal Experience and Adventure during Four Years of War.* Philadelphia: Lippincott, 1888.

Beringer, Richard E., Herman Hattaway, Archer Jones, and William N. Still. *Why the South Lost the Civil War.* Athens, Ga.: University of Georgia Press, 1986.

Bierce, Ambrose. *The Civil War Short Stories of Ambrose Bierce.* Comp. and foreword by Ernest Jerome Hopkins. Lincoln: University of Nebraska Press, 1988.

Bishir, Catherine W. "Landmarks of Power: Building a Southern Past, 1855–1915." *Southern Cultures* 1 (special issue 1993): 5–45.

Blair, Karen J. *The Clubwoman as Feminist: True Womanhood Redefined, 1868–1914.* Preface by Annette K. Baxter. New York: Holmes and Meier, 1980.

Bleser, Carol K. "The Marriage of Varina Howell and Jefferson Davis: A Portrait of the President and the First Lady of the Confederacy." In *Intimate Strategies of the Civil War: Military Commanders and Their Wives,* ed. Carol K. Bleser and Lesley J. Gordon, 3–31. New York: Oxford University Press, 2001.

Blight, David W. *Race and Reunion: The Civil War in American Memory.* Cambridge: Belknap Press of Harvard University Press, 2001.

Bohannon, Keith S. "'These Few Gray-Haired, Battle-Scarred Veterans': Confederate Army Reunions in Georgia, 1885–1895." In *The Myth of the Lost Cause and Civil War History,* ed. Gary W. Gallagher and Alan T. Nolan, 89–110. Bloomington: Indiana University Press, 2000.

Bolles, Edmund Blair. *Remembering and Forgetting: An Inquiry into the Nature of Memory.* New York: Walker, 1988.

Bonner, Sherwood. *Like unto Like: A Novel.* Intro. Jane Turner Censer. 1878; Columbia: University of South Carolina Press, 1997.

Boyd, Belle. *Belle Boyd in Camp and in Prison.* Foreword by Drew Gilpin Faust; intro. Sharon Kennedy-Nolle. 1865; Baton Rouge: Louisiana State University Press, 1998.

Boynton, H. V. *Sherman's Historical Raid: The Memoirs in Light of the Record: A Review Based upon Compilations from the Files of the War Office.* Cincinnati: Wilstach, Baldwin, 1875.

Brinkmeyer, Robert H. *Katherine Anne Porter's Artistic Development: Primitivism, Traditionalism, and Totalitarianism.* Baton Rouge: Louisiana State University Press, 1993.

Brock, Sallie A. *See* Putnam, Sallie A. Brock.

Brown, William Garrott. *The Lower South in American History.* New York: Macmillan, 1902.

Bryan, Emma Lyon. *1860–1865: A Romance of the Valley of Virginia.* Harrisonburg, Va.: J. Taliaffero, 1892.

Brundage, W. Fitzhugh. *Lynching in the New South: Georgia and Virginia, 1880–1930.* Urbana: University of Illinois Press, 1993.

Buck, Paul H. *The Road to Reunion, 1865–1900.* Boston: Little, Brown, 1937.

Burge, Dolly Sumner Lunt. *A Woman's Wartime Journal: An Account of the Passage over a Georgia Plantation of Sherman's Army on the March to the Sea, as Recorded in the Diary of Dolly Sumner Lunt (Mrs. Thomas Burge).* Intro. and notes by Julian Street. New York: Century, 1918.

Burgess, William. *The Civil War and the Constitution, 1859–1865.* New York: Scribner's, 1901.

Busby, Mark, and Dick Heaberlin, eds. *From Texas to the World and Back: Essays on the Journeys of Katherine Anne Porter.* Fort Worth: Texas Christian University Press, 2001.

Butler, Thomas, ed. *Memory: History, Culture, and the Mind.* Oxford: Basil Blackwell, 1989.

Cable, George Washington. *Dr. Sevier.* 1884; New York: Scribner's, 1902.

————. *The Negro Question: A Selection of Writings on Civil Rights in the South.* Ed. Arlin Turner. New York: Norton, 1968.

————. *The Silent South.* 1885; Montclair, N.J.: Patterson Smith, 1969.

Cairns, Kate. *"Bobbie."* Richmond: B. F. Johnson, 1899.

Caldwell, Erskine. *Tobacco Road.* New York: Scribner's, 1932.

Carmichael, Peter S. "New South Visionaries: Virginia's Last Generation of Slaveholders, the Gospel of Progress, and the Lost Cause." In *The Myth of the Lost Cause and Civil War History*, ed. Gary W. Gallagher and Alan T. Nolan, 111–26. Bloomington: Indiana University Press, 2000.

Carter, Dan T. *When the War Was Over: The Failure of Self-Reconstruction in the South, 1865–1867.* Baton Rouge: Louisiana State University Press, 1985.

Cash, W. J. *The Mind of the South.* New York: Knopf, 1941.

Castille, Philip, and William Osborne, eds. *Southern Literature in Transition: Heritage and Promise.* Memphis, Tenn.: Memphis State University Press, 1983.

Cauthen, C. E., and Lewis P. Jones. "The Coming of the Civil War." In *Writing Southern History: Essays in Historiography in Honor of Fletcher M. Green*, ed. Arthur S. Link and Rembert W. Patrick, 224–72. Baton Rouge: Louisiana State University Press, 1965.

Cecelski, David S., and Timothy B. Tyson, eds. *Democracy Betrayed: The Wilmington Race Riot of 1898 and Its Legacy.* Chapel Hill: University of North Carolina Press, 1998.

Cella, C. Ronald. *Mary Johnston.* Boston: Twayne, 1981.

Chapin, Sallie F. *Fitz-Hugh St. Clair: The South Carolina Rebel Boy; or, It's No Crime to Be Born a Gentleman.* Philadelphia: Claxton, Remsen, and Haffelfinger, 1872.

Chesnut, Mary Boykin. *A Diary from Dixie, as Written by Mary Boykin Chesnut.* Ed. Isabella D. Martin and Myrta Lockett Avary. New York: Appleton, 1905.

————. *Mary Chesnut's Civil War.* Ed. C. Vann Woodward. New Haven: Yale University Press, 1981.

————. *The Private Mary Chesnut: The Unpublished Civil War Diaries.* Ed. C. Vann Woodward and Elisabeth Muhlenfeld. New York: Oxford University Press, 1984.

Chigaski, Hisako. *Three Confederate Women: Mary Boykin Chesnut, Kate Stone, Kate Cumming.* N.p., 1972.

Clack, Louise. *Our Refugee Household.* New York: Blelock, 1866.

Clay-Clopton, Virginia. *A Belle of the Fifties: Memoirs of Mrs. Clay of Alabama, Covering Social and Political Life in Washington and the South, 1853–1866.* New York: Doubleday, Page, 1904.

Clayton, Bruce. *The Savage Ideal: Intolerance and Intellectual Leadership in the South, 1890–1914.* Baltimore: Johns Hopkins University Press, 1972.

Clinton, Catherine. *The Plantation Mistress: Woman's World in the Old South.* New York: Pantheon, 1982.

Cohen, David William. *The Combing of History.* Chicago: University of Chicago Press, 1994.

————. *The Production of History.* N.p., 1986.

"Coming to Terms with Scarlett." *Southern Cultures* 5 (Spring 1999): 6–48.

Conkin, Paul. *The Southern Agrarians.* Knoxville: University of Tennessee Press, 1988.

Connelly, Thomas L. *The Marble Man: Robert E. Lee and His Image in American Society.* New York: Knopf, 1977.

Connelly, Thomas L., and Barbara L. Bellows. *God and General Longstreet: The Lost Cause and the Southern Mind.* Baton Rouge: Louisiana State University Press, 1982.

Cook, Anna Marie Green. *The Journal of a Milledgeville Girl, 1861–1867.* Ed. James C. Bonner. Athens: University of Georgia Press, 1964.

Cooke, John Esten. *A Life of General Robert E. Lee.* New York: Appleton, 1871.

———. *Mohun; or, The Last Days of Lee and His Paladins.* 1869; Ridgewood, N.J.: Gregg Press, 1968.

———. *Stonewall Jackson: A Military Biography.* 1863; New York: Appleton, 1866.

———. *Surry of Eagle's Nest; or, The Memoirs of a Staff-Officer Serving in Virginia.* 1866; Ridgewood, N.J.: Gregg Press, 1968.

Cooke, Miriam. "Wo-Man, Retelling the War Myth." In *Gendering War Talk*, ed. Miriam Cooke and Angela Woollacott, 177–204. Princeton: Princeton University Press, 1993.

———. *Women and the War Story.* Berkeley: University of California Press, 1996.

Cooke, Miriam, and Angela Woollacott, eds. *Gendering War Talk.* Princeton: Princeton University Press, 1993.

Cooper, Helen M., Adrienne Auslander Munich, and Susan Merrill Squier, eds. *Arms and the Woman: War, Gender, and Literary Representation.* Chapel Hill: University of North Carolina Press, 1989.

Core, Deborah. "Caroline Gordon, Ford Madox Ford: A Shared Passion for the Novel." *Southern Quarterly* 28 (Spring 1990): 33–42.

Coulter, E. Merton. *The South during Reconstruction, 1865–1877.* Baton Rouge: Louisiana State University Press, 1947.

———. "What the South Has Done about Its History." *Journal of Southern History* 2 (February 1936): 3–28.

Coultrap-McQuin, Susan. *Doing Literary Business: American Women Writers in the Nineteenth Century.* Chapel Hill: University of North Carolina Press, 1990.

Cox, LaWanda. "From Emancipation to Segregation: National Policy and Southern Blacks." In *Interpreting Southern History: Historiographical Essays in Honor of Sanford W. Higginbotham*, ed. John B. Boles and Evelyn Thomas Nolen, 199–253. Baton Rouge: Louisiana State University Press, 1987.

Cox, Samuel. *Union—Disunion—Reunion: Three Decades of Federal Legislation, 1855–1885.* Washington, D.C.: J. M. Stoddart, 1885.

Coxe, Elizabeth Allen. *Memories of a South Carolina Plantation during the War.* N.p.: privately published, 1912.

Craig, Mrs. Benjamin H. *Was She? A Novel* New York: Neale, 1906.

Crane, Stephen. *The Red Badge of Courage: An Episode of the American Civil War.* New York: Appleton, 1895.

Croly, Jane Cunningham. *The History of the Woman's Club Movement in America.* New York: H. G. Allen, 1898.

Cruse, Mary Ann. *Cameron Hall: A Story of the Civil War.* Philadelphia: Lippincott, 1867.

Cullen, Jim. *The Civil War in Popular Culture: A Reusable Past.* Washington, D.C.: Smithsonian Institution Press, 1995.

Culpepper, Marilyn Mayer. *Trials and Triumphs: Women of the American Civil War.* East Lansing: Michigan State University Press, 1991.

Cumming, Kate. *Gleanings from Southland: Sketches of Life and Manners of the People of* the South before, during, and after the War of Secession, with Extracts from the Author's Journal and Epitome of the New South. Birmingham, Ala.: Roberts and Son, 1895.

————. A Journal of Hospital Life in the Confederate Army of Tennessee, from the Battle of Shiloh to the End of the War. Louisville, Ky.: John P. Morton, 1866.

Curry, J. L. M. Civil History of the Government of the Confederate States of America, with Some Personal Reminiscences. Richmond: B. F. Johnson, 1901.

Dabney, Robert Lewis. Life and Campaigns of the Lieut.-Gen. Thomas J. Jackson (Stonewall Jackson). New York: Blelock, 1866.

Dailey, Jane Elizabeth. Before Jim Crow: The Politics of Race in Postemancipation Virginia. Chapel Hill: University of North Carolina Press, 2000.

Dameron, J. Lasley, and James W. Mathews, eds. No Fairer Land: Studies in Southern Literature before 1900. Troy, N.Y.: Whitston, 1986.

Daniel, Pete. Breaking the Land: The Transformation of Cotton, Tobacco, and Rice Cultures since 1880. Urbana: University of Illinois Press, 1985.

Davidson, James Wood. The Living Writers of the South. New York: Carleton, 1869.

Davis, Jefferson. The Rise and Fall of the Confederate Government. New York: Appleton, 1881.

Davis, Mary Evelyn Moore. In War Times at La Rose Blanche. Boston: D. Lothrop, 1888.

Davis, Stephen. "'A Matter of Sensational Interest': The Century's 'Battles and Leaders' Series." Civil War History 27 (December 1981): 338–49.

Davis, Varina. Jefferson Davis, Ex-President of the Confederate States of America. New York: Belford, 1890.

Dawson, Francis Warrington. Our Women in the War: An Address. Charleston, S.C.: Walker, Evans, and Cogswell, 1887.

Dawson, Sarah Morgan. The Civil War Diary of Sarah Morgan. Ed. Charles East. Athens: University of Georgia Press, 1991.

————. A Confederate Girl's Diary. Intro. Warrington Dawson. Boston: Houghton, Mifflin, 1913.

Dean, Henry Clay. Crimes of the Civil War, and Curse of the Funding System. Baltimore: J. Wesley Smith and Brothers, 1869.

De Forest, John William. The Bloody Chasm: A Novel. New York: Appleton, 1881.

————. Kate Beaumont. Boston: J. R. Osgood, 1872.

————. Miss Ravenel's Conversion from Secession to Loyalty. 1867; New York: Harper and Brothers, 1939.

De Saussure, Nancy Bostwick. Old Plantation Days: Being Recollections of Southern Life before the Civil War. New York: Duffield, 1909.

Dickinson, Anna E. What Answer? Boston: Ticknor and Fields, 1868.

Diffley, Kathleen. Where My Heart Is Turning Ever: Civil War Stories and Constitutional Reform, 1861–1876. Athens: University of Georgia Press, 1992.

Dillon, Mary C. Johnson. In Old Bellaire. New York: Century, 1906.

Dixon, Thomas, Jr. The Clansman: An Historical Romance of the Ku Klux Klan. New York: Doubleday, Page, 1905.

————. The Leopard's Spots: A Romance of the White Man's Burden, 1865–1900. New York: Doubleday, Page, 1902.

Dodd, William E. Expansion and Conflict. Boston: Houghton Mifflin, 1915.

————. "Some Difficulties of the History Teacher in the South." *South Atlantic Quarterly* 3 (April 1904): 117–22.

Dorsey, Sarah A. *Lucia Dare: A Novel.* New York: M. Doolady, 1867.

————. *Recollections of Henry Watkins Allen, Brigadier-General, Confederate States Army, Ex-Governor of Louisiana.* New York: M. Doolady, 1866.

Douglas, Ann. *The Feminization of American Culture.* New York: Knopf, 1977.

Draper, John William. *History of the American Civil War.* 3 vols. New York: Harper, 1867–70.

Du Bois, W. E. B. *Black Reconstruction: An Essay toward a History of the Part Which Black Folk Played in the Attempt to Reconstruct Democracy in America, 1860–1880.* New York: Harcourt, Brace, 1935.

Dunning, William A. *Reconstruction, Political and Economic, 1865–1870.* New York: Harper and Brothers, 1907.

Duyckinck, Evert A. *National History of the War for the Union, Civil, Military, and Naval: Founded on Official and Other Authentic Documents.* 3 vols. New York: Johnson, Fry, 1861–65.

Edmondson, Belle. *A Lost Heroine of the Confederacy: The Diaries and Letters of Belle Edmondson.* Ed. Loretta Galbraith and William Galbraith. Jackson: University Press of Mississippi, 1990.

Edmondston, Catherine Devereux. *Journal of a Secesh Lady: The Diary of Catherine Anne Devereux Edmondston.* Ed. Beth G. Crabtree and James W. Patton. Raleigh, N.C.: Division of Archives and History, Department of Cultural Resources, 1979.

Edwards, Laura F. *Gendered Strife and Confusion: The Political Culture of Reconstruction.* Urbana: University of Illinois Press, 1997.

————. *Scarlett Doesn't Live Here Anymore: Southern Women in the Civil War Era.* Urbana: University of Illinois Press, 2000.

Eggleston, George Cary. *The History of the Confederate War: Its Causes and Its Conduct: A Narrative and Critical History.* New York: Sturgis and Walton, 1910.

Ellis, William A. *The Theory of the American Romance: An Ideology in American Intellectual History.* Ann Arbor, Mich.: UMI Research Press, 1989.

Elshtain, Jean Bethke. "On Beautiful Souls, Just Warriors, and Feminist Consciousness." *Women's Studies International Forum* 5 (1982): 341–48.

————. "Reflections on War and Political Discourse: Realism, Just War, and Feminism in a Nuclear Age." *Political Theory* 13 (February 1985): 39–57.

————. *Women and War.* New York: Basic Books, 1987.

Elson, Henry William. *A History of the United States of America.* New York: Macmillan, 1927.

Emerson, Bettie Alder Calhoun, comp. *Historic Southern Monuments: Representative Memorials of the Heroic Dead of the Southern Confederacy.* New York: Neale, 1911.

Eppes, Susan Bradford. *The Negro of the Old South: A Bit of Period History.* Chicago: Joseph C. Branch, 1925.

————. *Through Some Eventful Years.* Intro. Joseph D. Cushman Jr. 1926; reprint, Gainesville: University of Florida Press, 1968.

Evans, Augusta Jane. *Beulah.* Ed., intro., and notes by Elizabeth Fox-Genovese. 1859; Baton Rouge: Louisiana State University Press, 1992.

———. *Macaria; or, Altars of Sacrifice*. Ed., intro., and notes by Drew Gilpin Faust. 1864; Baton Rouge: Louisiana State University Press, 1992.

———. *A Speckled Bird*. New York: G. W. Dillingham, 1902.

Fahs, Alice. *The Imagined Civil War: Popular Literature of the North and South, 1861–1865*. Chapel Hill: University of North Carolina Press, 2001.

Falkner, William C. *The Little Brick Church: A Novel*. Philadelphia: Lippincott, 1882.

———. *The White Rose of Memphis: A Novel*. New York: Carleton, 1881.

Faulkner, William. *Absalom, Absalom! The Corrected Text* 1936; New York: Vintage, 1990.

———. *Flags in the Dust*. Ed. and intro. Douglas Day. New York: Vintage, 1974.

Faust, Drew Gilpin. "Altars of Sacrifice: Confederate Women and the Narratives of War." *Journal of American History* 76 (March 1990): 1200–1228.

———. *The Creation of Confederate Nationalism: Ideology and Identity in the Civil War South*. Baton Rouge: Louisiana State University Press, 1988.

———. "In Search of the Real Mary Chesnut." *Reviews in American History* 10 (March 1982): 54–59.

———. *Mothers of Invention: Women of the Slaveholding South in the American Civil War*. Chapel Hill: University of North Carolina Press, 1996.

Felton, Rebecca Latimer. *Country Life in Georgia in the Days of My Youth, Also Addresses before Georgia Legislature, Woman's Clubs, Woman's Organizations, and Other Noted Occasions*. Atlanta: Index Printing, 1919.

Ferrel, Charles Clifton. "The Daughter of the Confederacy: Her Life, Character, and Writings." *Publications of the Mississippi Historical Society* 2 (1899): 69–84.

Fidler, William Perry. *Augusta Evans Wilson, 1853–1909, a Biography*. University: University of Alabama Press, 1951.

———. "Augusta Evans Wilson as Confederate Propagandist." *Alabama Review* 2 (January 1949): 32–44.

Finley, M. I. "Myth, Memory, and History." *History and Theory* 4 (1965): 281–302.

———. *The Use and Abuse of History*. London: Chatto C. Winders, 1975.

Fleming, Walter L., J. A. C. Chandler, Franklin Lafayette Riley, James Curtis Ballagh, John Bell Henneman, Edwin Mims, Thomas E. Watson, Samuel Chiles Mitchell, H. Walker McSpadden. *The South in the Building of the Nation: A History of the Southern States Designed to Record the South's Part in the Making of the American Nation; to Portray the Character and Genius, to Chronicle the Achievements and Progress, and to Illustrate the Life and Traditions of the Southern People*. 13 vols. Richmond: Southern Historical Publication Society, 1909–13.

Foner, Eric. *Reconstruction: America's Unfinished Revolution, 1863–1877*. New York: Harper and Row, 1988.

———. "Reconstruction Revisited." *Reviews in American History* 10 (December 1982): 82–100.

Ford, Sallie Rochester. *Raids and Romance of Morgan and His Men*. New York: Charles B. Richardson, 1864.

Formby, John. *The American Civil War: A Concise History of Its Causes, Progress, and Results*. New York: Scribner's, 1910.

Foster, Gaines M. *Ghosts of the Confederacy: Defeat, the Lost Cause, and the Emergence of the New South, 1865 to 1913*. New York: Oxford University Press, 1987.

Fox-Genovese, Elizabeth. "The Anxiety of History: The Southern Confrontation with Modernity." *Southern Cultures* 1 (special issue 1993): 65–82.

———. "Scarlett O'Hara: The Southern Lady as New Woman." *American Quarterly* 33 (Autumn 1981): 391–411.

———. *Within the Plantation Household: Black and White Women of the Old South.* Chapel Hill: University of North Carolina Press, 1988.

Fraistat, Rose Ann C. *Caroline Gordon as Novelist and Woman of Letters.* Baton Rouge: Louisiana State University Press, 1984.

Franklin, John Hope. *Reconstruction after the Civil War.* Chicago: University of Chicago Press, 1961.

Fraser, Walter J., Jr., and Winfred B. Moore Jr., eds. *From the Old South to the New: Essays on the Transitional South.* Westport, Conn.: Greenwood Press, 1981.

Freeman, Douglas Southall. *R. E. Lee, a Biography.* 4 vols. New York: Scribner's, 1934–35.

Frisch, Michael. "American History and the Structures of Collective Memory: A Modest Exercise in Empirical Iconography." In *Memory and American History,* ed. David Thelen, 1–26. Bloomington: Indiana University Press, 1990.

Fussell, Paul. *The Great War and Modern Memory.* New York: Oxford University Press, 1975.

Gallagher, Gary W. *The Confederate War: How Popular Will, Nationalism, and Military Strategy Could Not Stave Off Defeat.* Cambridge: Harvard University Press, 1997.

———. Introduction to *The Myth of the Lost Cause and Civil War History,* ed. Gary W. Gallagher and Alan T. Nolan, 1–10. Bloomington: Indiana University Press, 2000.

———. "Jubal A. Early, the Lost Cause, and Civil War History: A Persistent Legacy." In *The Myth of the Lost Cause and Civil War History,* ed. Gary W. Gallagher and Alan T. Nolan, 35–59. Bloomington: Indiana University Press, 2000.

———. *Lee and His Generals in War and Memory.* Baton Rouge: Louisiana State University Press, 1998.

Gardner, Sarah E. "Every Man Has Got the Right to Get Killed? The Civil War Narratives of Mary Johnston and Caroline Gordon." *Southern Cultures* 5 (Winter 1999): 14–40.

———. "The Making of a Model Confederate Soldier: Helen Dortch Longstreet and the 'Reconstruction' of General James Longstreet." Paper presented at the Southern Association of Women Historians Conference, Houston, Texas, June 1994.

———. "'A Sweet Solace to My Lonely Heart': 'Stonewall' and Mary Anna Jackson and the Civil War." In *Intimate Strategies of the Civil War: Military Commanders and Their Wives,* ed. Carol K. Bleser and Lesley J. Gordon, 49–68. New York: Oxford University Press, 2001.

Gaston, Paul M. *The New South Creed: A Study in Southern Mythmaking.* New York: Knopf, 1970.

Gay, Mary Ann Harris. *Life in Dixie during the War, 1861–1862–1863–1864–1865.* Atlanta: Foote and Davies, 1894.

———. *Life in Dixie during the War, 1861–1862–1863–1864–1865.* 3d ed. Atlanta: C. P. Byrd, 1897.

———. *Life in Dixie during the War, 1863–1864–1865.* Atlanta: Constitution Job Office, 1892.

Genovese, Eugene D. *A Consuming Fire: The Fall of the Confederacy in the Mind of the White Christian South*. Athens: University of Georgia Press, 1998.

————. *Roll, Jordan, Roll: The World the Slaves Made*. New York: Vintage, 1976.

George, Herbert B. *The Popular History of the Civil War in America (1861–1865)*. New York: F. M. Lupton, 1884.

Gilbert, Sandra. "Soldier's Heart: Literary Men, Literary Women, and the Great War." *Signs* 8 (Spring 1983): 422–50.

Gilder, Rosamond, ed. *Letters of Richard Watson Gilder*. Boston: Houghton Mifflin, 1916.

Gildersleeve, Basil L. *The Creed of the Old South*. Baltimore: Johns Hopkins Press, 1915.

Gilmore, Glenda Elizabeth. *Gender and Jim Crow: Women and the Politics of White Supremacy in North Carolina, 1896–1920*. Chapel Hill: University of North Carolina Press, 1996.

Glasgow, Ellen. *Barren Ground*. Garden City, N.Y.: Doubleday, Page, 1925.

————. *The Battle-Ground*. New York: Doubleday, Page, 1902.

————. *A Certain Measure: An Interpretation of Prose Fiction*. New York: Harcourt, Brace, 1943.

————. *The Deliverance: A Romance of the Virginia Tobacco Fields*. New York: Doubleday, Page, 1904.

————. *Letters*. Comp. and ed. Blair Rouse. New York: Harcourt, Brace, 1958.

————. *The Sheltered Life*. Garden City, N.Y.: Doubleday, Doran, 1932.

————. *Vein of Iron*. New York: Harcourt, Brace, 1935.

————. *Virginia*. Garden City, N.Y.: Doubleday, Page, 1913.

————. *The Voice of the People*. New York: Doubleday, Page, 1900.

————. *The Woman Within: An Autobiography*. 1954; New York: Hill and Wang, 1980.

Glenwood, Ida [Mrs. C. M. R. Gorton]. *Lily Pearl and the Mistress of Rosedale*. Chicago: Dibble, 1892.

Godbold, E. Stanly, Jr. "A Battleground Revisited: Reconstruction in Southern Fiction, 1895–1905." *South Atlantic Quarterly* 73 (Winter 1974): 99–116.

Goodwyn, Lawrence. *Democratic Promise: The Populist Moment in America*. New York: Oxford University Press, 1976.

Gordon, Caroline. *Aleck Maury, Sportsman*. New York: Scribner's, 1934.

————. *None Shall Look Back*. Preface by Eileen Gregory. 1937; Nashville: J. S. Sanders, 1992.

————. *Penhally*. New York: Scribner's, 1931.

Gordon, John B. *Reminiscences of the Civil War*. Intro. Ralph Lowell Eckert. 1903; Baton Rouge: Louisiana State University Press, 1993.

Gordon, Lesley J. *General George E. Pickett in Life and Legend*. Chapel Hill: University of North Carolina Press, 1998.

Gossett, Thomas F. *Uncle Tom's Cabin and American Culture*. Dallas: Southern Methodist University Press, 1985.

Grady, Benjamin. *The Case of the South against the North; or, Historical Evidence Justifying the Southern States of the American Union in Their Long Controversy with the Northern States*. Raleigh, N.C.: Edwards and Broughton, 1899.

Granger, A. O. "The Effect of Club Women in the South." *Annals of the American Academy of Political and Social Science* 28 (March 1906): 51–58.

Gray, Richard J. *Southern Aberrations: Writers of the American South and the Problem of Regionalism.* Baton Rouge: Louisiana State University Press, 2000.

———. *Writing the South: Ideas of an American Region.* Cambridge: Cambridge University Press, 1986.

Greeley, Horace. *The American Conflict: A History of the Great Rebellion in the United States of America, 1860–'64.* Hartford, Conn.: O. D. Case, 1864–66.

Green, Elna C. *Southern Strategies: Southern Women and the Woman Suffrage Question.* Chapel Hill: University of North Carolina Press, 1997.

Greenhow, Rose O'Neal. *My Imprisonment and the First Year of Abolition Rule at Washington.* London: R. Bentley, 1863.

Hackett, Alice Payne. *Fifty Years of Best Sellers, 1895–1945.* New York: R. R. Bowker, 1945.

Hague, Parthenia Antoinette Vardaman. *A Blockaded Family: Life in Southern Alabama during the Civil War.* Boston: Houghton, Mifflin, 1888.

Hahn, Steven. *The Roots of Southern Populism: Yeoman Farmers and the Transformation of the Georgia Upcountry, 1850–1890.* New York: Oxford University Press, 1983.

Halbwachs, Maurice. *On Collective Memory.* Ed., trans., and intro. Lewis A. Coser. Chicago: University of Chicago Press, 1992.

Hale, Grace Elizabeth. *Making Whiteness: The Culture of Segregation in the South, 1890–1940.* New York: Pantheon, 1998.

Hall, Jacquelyn Dowd. "Open Secrets: Memory, Imagination, and the Refashioning of Southern Identity." *American Quarterly* 50 (March 1998): 109–24.

———. "'You Must Remember This': Autobiography as Social Critique." *Journal of American History* 85 (September 1998): 439–65.

Hamilton, J. G. de Roulhac. "History in the South — A Retrospect of Half a Century." *North Carolina Historical Review* 31 (April 1954): 173–81.

Hamilton, Sylla W. *Forsaking All Others: A Story of Sherman's March through Georgia.* New York: Neale, 1905.

Hardin, Elizabeth Pendleton. *The Private War of Lizzie Hardin: A Kentucky Confederate Girl's Diary of the Civil War in Kentucky, Virginia, Tennessee, Alabama, and Georgia.* Ed. G. Glenn Clift. Frankfort: Kentucky Historical Society, 1963.

Harland, Marion [Mary Virginia Terhune]. *Alone.* 1854; New York: Arno Press, 1981.

———. *Marion Harland's Autobiography: The Story of a Long Life.* New York: Harper and Brothers, 1910.

———. *Sunnybank.* New York: Sheldon, 1866.

Harris, Cicero W. *The Sectional Struggle: An Account of the Troubles between the North and the South, from the Earliest Times to the Close of the Civil War.* Philadelphia: Lippincott, 1902.

Harris, Corra May White. *The Recording Angel.* Garden City, N.Y.: Doubleday, Page, 1912.

Harris, Helena J. *Southern Sketches.* New Orleans: Crescent, 1866.

Harris, Mrs. L. H. "The Confederate Veteran." *Independent* 53 (October 1901): 257–58.

Harrison, Beth. "Ellen Glasgow's Revision of the Southern Pastoral." *South Atlantic Review* 55 (May 1990): 47–70.

Harrison, Constance Cary [Mrs. Burton Harrison]. *Belhaven Tales: Crow's Nest, Una and King David.* New York: Century, 1892.

———. *The Carlyles: A Story of the Fall of the Confederacy.* New York: Appleton, 1905.

————. *A Daughter of the South, and Shorter Stories*. New York: Cassell, 1892.

————. *Flower de Hundred: The Story of a Virginia Plantation*. New York: Century, 1899.

————. *Recollections Grave and Gay*. New York: Scribner's, 1912.

Harrison, Walter. *Pickett's Men: A Fragment of War History*. Intro. Gary W. Gallagher. 1870; Baton Rouge: Louisiana State University Press, 2000.

Hattaway, Herman. "Clio's Southern Soldiers: The United Confederate Veterans and History." *Louisiana History* 12 (Spring 1971): 213–42.

Hayhoe, George F. "Mary Boykin Chesnut: The Making of a Reputation." *Mississippi Quarterly* 35 (Winter 1981–82): 60–72.

Headley, J. T. *The Great Rebellion: A History of the Civil War in the United States*. 2 vols. Hartford, Conn.: American Publishing, 1865–66.

Hemingway, Ernest. *To Have and Have Not*. New York: Scribner's, 1937.

Henderson, G. F. R. *Stonewall Jackson and the American Civil War*. New York: Longmans, Green, 1900.

Hendrix, James P., Jr. "From Romance to Scholarship: Southern History at the Take-Off Point." *Mississippi Quarterly* 30 (Spring 1977): 193–212.

Henry, Josephine K. "The New Woman of the New South." *Arena* 11 (1895): 353–62.

Herbert, Hilary A. *The Abolition Crusade and Its Consequences*. New York: Scribner's, 1912.

Hesseltine, William Best. *Confederate Leaders in the New South*. Baton Rouge: Louisiana State University Press, 1950.

Heyward, Pauline DeCaradeuc. *A Confederate Lady Comes of Age: The Journal of Pauline DeCaradeuc Heyward, 1863–1888*. Ed. Mary D. Robertson. Columbia: University of South Carolina Press, 1992.

Higonnet, Margaret R. "Civil Wars and Sexual Territories." In *Arms and the Woman: War, Gender, and Literary Representation*, ed. Helen M. Cooper, Adrienne Auslander Munich, and Susan Merrill Squier, 80–96. Chapel Hill: University of North Carolina Press, 1989.

————. "Not So Quiet in No-Woman's-Land." In *Gendering War Talk*, ed. Miriam Cooke and Angela Woollacott, 205–26. Princeton: Princeton University Press, 1993.

Hilldrup, Robert LeRoy. "Cold War against the Yankees in the Ante-Bellum Literature of Southern Women." *North Carolina Historical Review* 31 (July 1954): 370–84.

Hobsbawm, Eric, and Terence Ranger, eds. *The Invention of Tradition*. New York: Cambridge University Press, 1983.

Hobson, Fred C. *Tell about the South: The Southern Rage to Explain*. Baton Rouge: Louisiana State University Press, 1983.

Holden, Charles J. "'Is Our Love for Wade Hampton Foolishness?' South Carolina and the Lost Cause." In *The Myth of the Lost Cause and Civil War History*, ed. Gary W. Gallagher and Alan T. Nolan, 60–88. Bloomington: Indiana University Press, 2000.

Holliday, Carl. *A History of Southern Literature*. New York: Neale, 1906.

Holman, C. Hugh. "Ellen Glasgow and Southern Literary Tradition." In *Southern Writers: Appraisals in Our Time*, ed. R. C. Simonini Jr., 103–23. Charlottesville: University Press of Virginia, 1964.

————. *The Immoderate Past: The Southern Writer and History*. Athens: University of Georgia Press, 1977.

Holmes, Mary Jane. *Rose Mather: A Tale*. New York: Carleton, 1868.

Holmes, Sarah Katherine Stone. *See* Stone, Kate.

Howe, Daniel Wait. *Civil War Times, 1861–1865*. Indianapolis, Ind.: Bowen-Merrill, 1902.

Hubbell, Jay B. *The South in American Literature, 1607–1900*. Durham, N.C.: Duke University Press, 1954.

Humphries, Jefferson, ed. *Southern Literature and Literary Theory*. Athens: University of Georgia Press, 1990.

Hunter, Lloyd A. "The Immortal Confederacy: Another Look at Lost Cause Religion." In *The Myth of the Lost Cause and Civil War History*, ed. Gary W. Gallagher and Alan T. Nolan, 185–218. Bloomington: Indiana University Press, 2000.

Hunter, Tera W. *To 'Joy My Freedom: Southern Black Women's Lives and Labors after the Civil War*. Cambridge: Harvard University Press, 1997.

Huston, Nancy. "The Matrix of War: Mothers and Heroes." *Poetics Today* 6 (1985): 153–70.

———. "Tales of War and Tears of Women." *Women's Studies International Forum* 5 (1982): 271–82.

Imboden, John D. "Stonewall Jackson in the Shenandoah." In *Battles and Leaders of the Civil War: Being for the Most Part Contributions by Union and Confederate Officers*, ed. Robert Underwood Johnson and Clarence Clough Buel, 2:282–98. New York: Thomas Yoseloff, 1956.

Ingraham, Ellen M. [Grace Lintner, pseud.]. *Bond and Free: A Tale of the South*. Indianapolis, Ind.: C. B. Ingraham, 1882.

"Insiders and Outsiders in American Historical Narrative and American History." *American Historical Review* 87 (April 1982): 390–423.

Ives, Cora Semmes. *The Princess of the Moon: A Confederate Fairy Story*. Baltimore: Sun Book and Job Office, 1869.

Jackson, Mary Anna. *Life and Letters of General Thomas J. Jackson*. Intro. Henry M. Field. New York: Harper and Brothers, 1892.

———. *Memoirs of Stonewall Jackson*. Intro. Lieut.-Gen. John B. Gordon and Rev. Henry M. Field. 2d ed. Louisville, Ky.: Prentice Press, 1895.

———. "With 'Stonewall' Jackson in Camp: More Confederate Memories." *Hearst Magazine* 24 (1913): 386–94.

Jacoway, Elizabeth, Dan T. Carter, Lester C. Lamon, and Robert C. McMath, eds. *The Adaptable South: Essays in Honor of George Brown Tindall*. Baton Rouge: Louisiana State University Press, 1991.

James, Henry. *The Bostonians*. Ed., intro., and notes by Charles R. Anderson. New York: Penguin, 1988.

John, Arthur. *The Best Years of the Century: Richard Watson Gilder, Scribner's Monthly and the Century Magazine, 1870–1909*. Urbana: University of Illinois Press, 1981.

Johnson, Robert Underwood. *Remembered Yesterdays*. Boston: Little, Brown, 1923.

Johnson, Robert Underwood, and Clarence Clough Buel, eds. *Battles and Leaders of the Civil War: Being for the Most Part Contributions by Union and Confederate Officers*. Intro. Ray F. Nichols. 4 vols. New York: Thomas Yoseloff, 1956.

Johnston, Joseph E. *Narrative of Military Operations, Directed, during the Late War between the States*. New York: Appleton, 1874.

Johnston, Mary. *Audrey*. Boston: Houghton Mifflin, 1902.

———. *Cease Firing!* Boston: Houghton, Mifflin, 1912.

————. *Dedication of the Virginia Tablet in the Vicksburg National Military Park.* Vicksburg: Mississippi Printing, 1907.

————. *The Goddess of Reason.* Boston: Houghton Mifflin, 1907.

————. *Lewis Rand.* Boston: Houghton Mifflin, 1908.

————. *The Long Roll.* Boston: Houghton, Mifflin, 1911.

————. *Prisoners of Hope: A Tale of Colonial Virginia.* Boston: Houghton Mifflin, 1899.

————. *To Have and to Hold.* Boston: Houghton Mifflin, 1900.

Jones, Anne Goodwyn. *Tomorrow Is Another Day: The Woman Writer in the South, 1859–1936.* Baton Rouge: Louisiana State University Press, 1981.

Jones, Katherine M. *When Sherman Came: Southern Women and the "Great March."* Indianapolis: Bobbs-Merrill, 1964.

Jonza, Nancylee Novell. *The Underground Stream: The Life and Art of Caroline Gordon.* Athens: University of Georgia Press, 1995.

Kammen, Michael G. *Mystic Chords of Memory: The Transformation of Tradition in American Culture.* New York: Knopf, 1991.

————. *A Season of Youth: The American Revolution and the Historical Imagination.* New York: Knopf, 1978.

Kaufman, Janet E. "'Under the Petticoat Flag': Women in the Confederate Army." *Southern Studies* 23 (Winter 1984): 363–75.

Kearney, Belle. *A Slaveholder's Daughter.* New York: Abbey Press, 1900.

Keely, Karen A. "Marriage Plots and National Reunion: The Trope of Romantic Reconciliation in Postbellum Literature." *Mississippi Quarterly* 51 (Fall 1998): 621–48.

Kelley, Mary. *Private Woman, Public Stage: Literary Domesticity in Nineteenth-Century America.* New York: Oxford University Press, 1984.

Kennedy, Sarah Beaumont. *Cicely: A Tale of the Georgia March.* Garden City, N.Y.: Doubleday, Page, 1911.

King, Grace. *Monsieur Motte.* New York: A. C. Armstrong and Son, 1888.

King, Richard H. *A Southern Renaissance: The Cultural Awakening of the American South, 1930–1955.* New York: Oxford University Press, 1980.

Kolchin, Peter. "The Myth of Radical Reconstruction." *Reviews in American History* 3 (June 1975): 228–36.

Kondert, Nancy T. "The Romance and Reality of Defeat: Southern Women in 1865." *Journal of Mississippi History* 35 (May 1973): 141–52.

Kraus, Michael. *A History of American History.* New York: Farrar and Rinehart, 1937.

Kreyling, Michael. *Figures of the Hero in Southern Narrative.* Baton Rouge: Louisiana State University Press, 1987.

————. *Inventing Southern Literature.* Jackson: University Press of Mississippi, 1998.

————. "Southern Literature: Consensus and Dissensus." *American Literature* 60 (March 1988): 83–95.

Kuklick, Bruce. "Myth and Symbol in American Studies." *American Quarterly* 24 (October 1972): 435–50.

Kunitz, Stanley J., and Howard Haycraft, eds. *American Authors, 1600–1900: A Biographical Dictionary of American Literature.* New York: H. W. Wilson, 1938.

A Lady of Virginia [Judith B. McGuire]. *Diary of a Southern Refugee during the War.* New York: E. J. Hale and Son, 1867.

Lake, Philip. *Physical Geography*. Cambridge: Cambridge University Press, 1915.

Lee, Susan P. *The New Primary History of the United States*. Richmond: B. F. Johnson, 1899.

Linderman, Gerald F. *Embattled Courage: The Experience of Combat in the American Civil War*. New York: Free Press, 1987.

Linenthal, Edward Tabor. *Changing Images of the Warrior Hero in America: A History of Popular Symbolism*. New York: E. Mellen, 1982.

Litwack, Leon F. *Been in the Storm So Long: The Aftermath of Slavery*. New York: Knopf, 1979.

————. *Trouble in Mind: Black Southerners in the Age of Jim Crow*. New York: Knopf, 1998.

Lively, Robert Alexander. *Fiction Fights the Civil War: An Unfinished Chapter in the Literary History of the American People*. Chapel Hill: University of North Carolina Press, 1957.

Loewenberg, Bert James. *American History in American Thought: Christopher Columbus to Henry Adams*. New York: Simon and Schuster, 1972.

Logan, Celia Connelly [L. Fairfax, pseud.]. *The Elopement: A Tale of the Confederate States of America*. London: W. Freeman, 1863.

Logan, John Alexander. *The Great Conspiracy: Its Origin and History*. New York: A. R. Hart, 1886.

Long, A. L. *Memoirs of Robert E. Lee*. New York: J. M. Stoddart, 1886.

Longstreet, Helen Dortch. *Lee and Longstreet at High Tide: Gettysburg in Light of Official Records*. Gainesville, Ga.: by the author, 1904.

Longstreet, James. *From Manassas to Appomattox: Memoirs of the Civil War in America*. Philadelphia: Lippincott, 1896.

————. "Lee in Pennsylvania" and "The Mistakes of Gettysburg." In *The Annals of War, Written by Leading Participants North and South, Originally Published by the* Philadelphia Weekly Times, ed. A. K. McClure, 414–46. Philadelphia: Times Publishing, 1879.

Lossing, Benson John. *A History of the Civil War, 1861–65, and the Causes That Led Up to the Great Conflict*. New York: War Memorial Association, 1912.

Loughborough, Mary Webster. *My Cave Life in Vicksburg: With Letters of Trial and Travel*. New York: Appleton, 1864.

————. *My Cave Life in Vicksburg: With Letters of Trial and Travel*. New York: Appleton, 1881.

Lowenthal, David. *The Past Is a Foreign Country*. New York: Cambridge University Press, 1985.

————. "The Timeless Past: Some Anglo-American Historical Preconceptions." In *Memory and American History*, ed. David Thelen, 134–52. Bloomington: Indiana University Press, 1990.

Lunt, George. *The Origin of the Late War: Traced from the Beginning of the Constitution to the Revolt of the Southern States*. New York: Appleton, 1866.

Lytle, Andrew Nelson. *Bedford Forrest and His Critter Company*. New York: G. P. Putnam's Sons, 1931.

————. *The Long Night*. Indianapolis: Bobbs-Merrill, 1936.

MacKethan, Lucinda Hardwick. *Daughters of Time: Creating Woman's Voice in Southern Story*. Athens: University of Georgia Press, 1990.

————. *The Dream of Arcady: Place and Time in Southern Literature.* Baton Rouge: Louisiana State University Press, 1980.

————. "Thomas Nelson Page: The Plantation as Arcady." *Virginia Quarterly Review* 54 (1978): 314–32.

MacKethan, Lulie Biggs, comp. *Chapter Histories, 1897–1947: North Carolina Division, United Daughters of the Confederacy.* Raleigh: North Carolina Division, United Daughters of the Confederacy, 1947.

MacLean, Nancy. *Behind the Mask of Chivalry: The Making of the Second Ku Klux Klan.* New York: Oxford University Press, 1994.

Magill, Mary Tucker. *Women; or, Chronicles of the Late War.* Baltimore: Turnbull Brothers, 1871.

Mainiero, Lina, ed. *American Women Writers: A Critical Reference Guide from Colonial Times to the Present.* 5 vols. New York: Ungar, 1979–84.

Makowsky, Veronica A. *Caroline Gordon: A Biography.* New York: Oxford University Press, 1989.

————. "Caroline Gordon: Amateur to Professional Writer." *Southern Review* 23 (Autumn 1987): 778–93.

————. "Caroline Gordon on Women Writing: A Contradiction in Terms?" *Southern Quarterly* 28 (Spring 1990): 43–52.

Malvasi, Mark G. *The Unregenerate South: The Agrarian Thought of John Crowe Ransom, Allen Tate, and Donald Davidson.* Baton Rouge: Louisiana State University Press, 1997.

Manning, Carol S., ed. *The Female Tradition in Southern Literature.* Urbana: University of Illinois Press, 1993.

Martin, Theodora Penny. *The Sound of Our Own Voices: Women's Study Clubs, 1860–1910.* Boston: Beacon, 1987.

Mason, Emily. *Popular Life of Gen. Robert Edward Lee.* Baltimore: J. Murphy, 1872.

Massey, Mary Elizabeth. *Bonnet Brigades.* New York: Knopf, 1966.

Maury, Dabney H. *Recollections of a Virginian in the Mexican, Indian, and Civil Wars.* New York: Scribner's, 1894.

May, Robert E. "Southern Elite Women, Sectional Extremism, and the Male Political Sphere: The Case of John A. Quitman's Wife and Female Descendants, 1847–1931." *Journal of Mississippi History* 50 (Winter 1988): 251–85.

McClelland, Mary G. *Broadoaks.* St. Paul, Minn.: Price-McGill, 1893.

McCracken, Elizabeth. "The Women of America — Third Paper — The Southern Woman and Reconstruction." *Outlook,* November 21, 1903, 697–703.

McDonald, Cornelia Peake. *A Diary with Reminiscences of the War and Refugee Life in the Shenandoah Valley, 1860–1865.* Nashville: Cullom and Ghertner, 1935.

————. *A Woman's Civil War: A Diary with Reminiscences of the War from March 1862.* Ed. and intro. Minrose C. Gwin. Madison: University of Wisconsin Press, 1992.

McIntosh, Maria. *Charms and Counter-Charms.* New York: Appleton, 1848.

————. *The Lofty and the Lowly; or, Good in All and None All-Good.* 1851.

————. *Two Pictures; or, What We Think of Ourselves, and What the World Thinks of Us.* New York: Appleton, 1863.

McMath, Robert C., Jr. *Populist Vanguard: A History of the Southern Farmers' Alliance.* Chapel Hill: University of North Carolina Press, 1975.

McMillan, Malcolm M., ed. *The Alabama Confederate Reader*. University: University of Alabama Press, 1963.

McNeill, William H. "Mythistory, or Truth, Myth, History, and Historians." *American Historical Review* 91 (February 1986): 1–10.

McPherson, James M. *Battle Cry of Freedom: The Civil War Era*. New York: Oxford University Press, 1988.

McPherson, James M., and William J. Cooper Jr., eds. *Writing the Civil War: The Quest to Understand*. Columbia: University of South Carolina Press, 1998.

McWhiney, Grady. "Jefferson Davis: The Unforgiven." *Journal of Mississippi History* 42 (Spring 1980): 113–27.

Mendenhall, Marjorie S. "Southern Women of a 'Lost Generation'" *South Atlantic Quarterly* 33 (October 1934): 334–53.

"Men's Views of Women's Clubs." *Annals of the American Academy of Political and Social Sciences* 28 (March 1906): 85–93.

Meriwether, Elizabeth Avery [George Edmonds, pseud.]. *Facts and Falsehoods Concerning the War on the South, 1861–1865*. Memphis, Tenn.: A. R. Taylor, 1904.

———. *The Master of Red Leaf: A Tale*. 3 vols. London: Samuel Tinsley, 1879.

———. *Recollections of Ninety-two Years, 1824–1916*. Nashville: Tennessee Historical Commission, 1958.

Merrick, Caroline E. *Old Times in Dixie Land: A Southern Matron's Memories*. New York: Grafton Press, 1901.

Meyerson, Joel, ed. *Antebellum Writers in New York and the South*. Vol. 3 of *Dictionary of Literary Biography*. Detroit: Gale Research, 1979.

Middleton, David, and Derek Edwards, eds. *Collective Remembering*. London: Sage, 1990.

Miller, Olive Thorne. *The Woman's Club: A Practical Guide and Hand-Book*. New York: American Publishers, 1891.

Minor, Kate Pleasants, ed. *From Dixie: Original Articles Contributed by Southern Writers for Publication as a Souvenir of the Memorial Bazaar for the Benefit of the Monument to the Private Soldiers and Sailors of the Confederacy and the Establishment of the Museum for Confederate Relics, with Heretofore Unpublished Poems by Some Who Have "Crossed over the River."* Richmond, Va.: West, Johnston, 1893.

Mitchell, Margaret. *Gone with the Wind*. 1936; New York: Scribner's, 1996.

———. *Margaret Mitchell's "Gone with the Wind" Letters, 1936–1949*. Ed. Richard Harwell. New York: Macmillan, 1976.

Mixon, Wayne. *Southern Writers and the New South Movement, 1865–1913*. Chapel Hill: University of North Carolina Press, 1980.

———. "Traditionalist and Iconoclast: Corra Harris and Southern Writing, 1900–1920." In *Developing Dixie: Modernization in a Traditional Society*, ed. Winfred B. Moore Jr., Joseph F. Tripp, and Lyon G. Tyler Jr., 235–44. New York: Greenwood Press, 1988.

Morgan, Sarah. See Dawson, Sarah Morgan.

Moss, Elizabeth. *Domestic Novelists in the Old South: Defenders of Southern Culture*. Baton Rouge: Louisiana State University Press, 1992.

Muhlenfeld, Elisabeth. "The Civil War and Authorship." In *The History of Southern Literature*, ed. Louis D. Rubin Jr., Blyden Jackson, Raybun S. Moore, Lewis P. Simpson, and Thomas Daniel Young, 178–187. Baton Rouge: Louisiana State University Press, 1985.

————. *Mary Boykin Chesnut: A Biography*. Baton Rouge: Louisiana State University Press, 1981.

Murfree, Mary Noailles [Charles Egbert Craddock, pseud.]. *The Raid of the Guerilla and Other Stories*. Philadelphia: Lippincott, 1912.

————. *The Storm Centre: A Novel*. New York: Macmillan, 1905.

————. *Where the Battle Was Fought: A Novel*. Boston: Houghton Mifflin, 1884.

Neisser, Ulric. *Memory Observed: Remembering in Natural Contexts*. San Francisco: W. H. Freeman, 1982.

Nelson, Lawrence G. "Mary Johnston and the Historic Imagination." In *Southern Writers: Appraisals in Our Time*, ed. R. C. Simonini Jr., 71–102. Charlottesville: University Press of Virginia, 1964.

Nelson, Richard Current. *Arguing with Historians: Essays on the Historical and the Unhistorical*. Middletown, Conn.: Wesleyan University Press, 1987.

Nevins, Allan. *The War for the Union*. 4 vols. New York: Scribner's, 1959–71.

Nolan, Alan T. "The Anatomy of the Myth." In *The Myth of the Lost Cause and Civil War History*, ed. Gary W. Gallagher and Alan T. Nolan, 11–34. Bloomington: Indiana University Press, 2000.

Nora, Pierre. "Between Memory and History: *Les Lieux de Mémoire*." *Representations* 26 (Spring 1989): 7–24.

Norris, Mary Harriott. *The Grapes of Wrath: A Tale of North and South*. Boston: Small, Maynard, 1901.

Novick, Peter. *That Noble Dream: The "Objectivity Question" and the American Historical Profession*. New York: Cambridge University Press, 1988.

O'Brien, Michael. *The Idea of the American South, 1920–1941*. Baltimore: Johns Hopkins University Press, 1979.

————. "Intellectual History and the Search for Southern Identity." In O'Brien, *Rethinking the South: Essays in Intellectual History*, 207–18. Baltimore: Johns Hopkins University Press, 1988.

O'Connor, Florence J. *The Heroine of the Confederacy; or, Truth and Justice*. London: Harrison, 1864.

Olson, Otto H., ed. *Reconstruction and Redemption in the South*. Baton Rouge: Louisiana State University Press, 1980.

Osterweis, Rollin G. *The Myth of the Lost Cause, 1865–1900*. Hamden, Conn.: Archon, 1973.

"Our Women in the War": The Lives They Lived; the Deaths They Died. Charleston, S.C.: News and Courier Book Presses, 1885.

Page, Thomas Nelson. *Gordon Keith*. New York: Scribner's, 1903.

————. *In Ole Virginia; or, Marse Chan and Other Stories*. 1887; New York: Scribner's, 1892.

————. *Meh Lady: A Story of the War*. New York: Scribner's, 1893.

————. *The Old South: Essays Social and Political*. New York: Scribner's, 1892.

————. *Red Rock: A Chronicle of Reconstruction*. New York: Scribner's, 1899.

Palmer, Bruce. *"Man over Money": The Southern Populist Critique of American Capitalism*. Chapel Hill: University of North Carolina Press, 1980.

Pearson, Emily C. *The Poor White; or, the Rebel Conscript*. Boston: Graves and Young, 1864.

Pember, Phoebe Yates. *A Southern Woman's Story*. New York: Carleton, 1879.

Perman, Michael. *The Road to Redemption: Southern Politics, 1869–1879*. Chapel Hill: University of North Carolina Press, 1984.

Peterson, Merrill D. *Lincoln in American Memory*. New York: Oxford University Press, 1994.

Pickett, La Salle Corbell. *The Bugles of Gettysburg*. Chicago: F. G. Browne, 1913.

———. *Literary Hearthstones of Dixie*. Philadelphia: Lippincott, 1912.

———. *Pickett and His Men*. 2d ed. Atlanta: Foote and Davies, 1900.

———. *What Happened to Me*. New York: Brentano's, 1917.

———, ed. *The Heart of a Soldier: As Revealed in the Intimate Letters of General George E. Pickett, C.S.A.* New York: Seth Moyle, 1913.

Pizer, Donald, and Earl N. Harbert, eds. *American Realists and Naturalists*. Vol. 12 of *Dictionary of Literary Biography*. Detroit: Gale Research, 1982.

Pollard, Edward A. *The Lost Cause: A New Southern History of the War of the Confederates*. New York: E. B. Treat, 1867.

———. *The Lost Cause Regained*. New York: Carleton, 1868.

Poppenheim, Mary, et al. *The History of the United Daughters of the Confederacy*. Raleigh, N.C.: Edwards and Broughton, 1956.

Porter, Katherine Anne. Review of *None Shall Look Back*, by Caroline Gordon. *New Republic*, April 1937, 244–45.

Potter, David M. *The Impending Crisis, 1848–1861*. New York: Harper and Row, 1976.

———. Review of *Americans Interpret Their Civil War*, by Thomas T. Pressly. *Journal of Southern History* 20 (August 1954): 400–406.

———. *The South and the Sectional Conflict*. Baton Rouge: Louisiana State University Press, 1968.

Pressly, Thomas J. *Americans Interpret Their Civil War*. Princeton: Princeton University Press, 1954.

Preston, Margaret Junkin. *Beechenbrook: A Rhyme of the War*. Richmond, Va.: J. W. Randolph, 1865.

Pryor, Sara [Mrs. Roger A. Pryor]. *My Day: Reminiscences of a Long Life*. New York: Macmillan, 1909.

———. *Reminiscences of Peace and War*. New York: Macmillan, 1904.

Putnam, Sallie A. Brock. *Kenneth, My King: A Novel*. New York: Carleton, 1873.

———. *Richmond during the War: Four Years of Personal Observation*. New York: Carleton, 1867.

———, ed. *The Southern Amaranth: A Carefully Selected Collection of Poems Growing out of and in Reference to the Late War*. New York: G. S. Wilcox, 1869.

Pyron, Darden Asbury. *Southern Daughter: The Life of Margaret Mitchell*. New York: Oxford University Press, 1991.

Rable, George C. *But There Was No Peace: The Role of Violence in the Politics of Reconstruction*. Athens: University of Georgia Press, 1979.

———. *Civil Wars: Women and the Crisis of Southern Nationalism*. Urbana: University of Illinois Press, 1989.

———. *The Confederate Republic: A Revolution against Politics*. Chapel Hill: University of North Carolina Press, 1994.

Raper, J. R. *Without Shelter: The Early Career of Ellen Glasgow.* Baton Rouge: Louisiana State University Press, 1971.

Reardon, Carol. *Pickett's Charge in History and Memory.* Chapel Hill: University of North Carolina Press, 1997.

Rhodes, James Ford. *History of the Civil War, 1861–1865.* New York: Macmillan, 1917.

———. *History of the United States from the Compromise of 1850 to the Final Restoration of Home Rule at the South in 1877.* 7 vols. New York: Harper and Brothers, 1893–1906.

———. *Lectures on the American Civil War.* New York: Macmillan, 1913.Riley, Franklin L., J. A. C. Chandler, and J. G. de Roulhac Hamilton. *Our Republic: A History of the United States for Grammar Grades.* Richmond: Riley and Chandler, 1910.

Riley, Sam G. *Magazines of the American South.* New York: Greenwood Press, 1986.

Ripley, Eliza Moore Chinn McHatton. *From Flag to Flag: A Woman's Adventures and Experiences in the South during the War, in Mexico, and in Cuba.* New York: Appleton, 1889.

Roark, James L. *Masters without Slaves: Southern Planters in the Civil War and Reconstruction.* New York: Norton, 1977.

Robertson, James I. *The Stonewall Brigade.* Baton Rouge: Louisiana State University Press, 1963.

Robinson, Armstead L. "Beyond the Realm of Social Consensus: New Meanings of Reconstruction and the Rise of the New South." *Journal of American History* 68 (September 1981): 276–97.

Rose, Anne C. *Victorian America and the Civil War.* New York: Cambridge University Press, 1992.

Ross, Dorothy. "Historical Consciousness in Nineteenth-Century America." *American Historical Review* 89 (October 1984): 909–28.

———. *Origins of American Social Science.* Cambridge: Cambridge University Press, 1991.

Rubin, Louis D., Jr. "The American South: The Continuity of Self-Definition." In *The American South: Portrait of a Culture,* ed. Louis D. Rubin Jr., 3–23. Baton Rouge: Louisiana State University Press, 1980.

———. "The Image of an Army: The Civil War in Southern Fiction." In *Southern Writers: Appraisals in Our Time,* ed. R. C. Simonini Jr., 50–70. Charlottesville: University Press of Virginia, 1964.

———. *No Place on Earth: Ellen Glasgow, James Branch Cabell, and Richmond-in-Virginia.* Austin, University of Texas Press, 1959.

———. *The Writer in the South: Studies in Literary Community.* Athens: University of Georgia Press, 1972.

Rubin, Louis D., Jr., Blyden Jackson, Raybun S. Moore, Lewis P. Simpson, and Thomas Daniel Young, eds. *The History of Southern Literature.* Baton Rouge: Louisiana State University Press, 1985.

Rutherford, Mildred Lewis. *Address.* Athens, Ga.: n.p., 1912.

———. *Address Delivered at the University Chapel, Georgia Day, February 12, 1914.* Athens, Ga.: n.p., 1914.

———. "Address, Delivered by Mildred Lewis Rutherford, New Willard Hotel, Washington, D.C., Thursday, November 19th, 1912." Athens, Ga.: MacGregor, 1912.

————. *Address Delivered by Miss Mildred Lewis Rutherford . . . Historian General*. Athens, Ga.: MacGregor, 1916.

————. *Address Delivered by Miss Mildred Lewis Rutherford, Historian General, United Daughters of the Confederacy: Thirteen Periods of United States History*. New Orleans, Louisiana, Thursday, November 21st, 1912. n.p.: J. Standish Clark, 1916.

————. *Facts and Figures vs. Myths and Misrepresentations, Henry Wirz and the Andersonville Prison*. Athens, Ga.: n.p., 1921.

————. *Four Addresses by Miss Mildred Lewis Rutherford*. Birmingham, Ala.: Mildred Rutherford Historical Circle, 1916.

————. *Historical Sins of Omission and Commission: Address Delivered by Miss Mildred Lewis Rutherford, Historian General*. Athens, Ga.: MacGregor, 1915.

————. *Jefferson Davis, the President of the Confederate States, and Abraham Lincoln, the President of the United States, 1861–1865*. Richmond: Virginia Stationery, 1916.

————. *A Measuring Rod to Test Text Books and Reference Books in Schools and Colleges and Libraries*. Athens, Ga.: n.p., 1920.

————. *An Open Letter to All State Historians, Chairmen of the Historical Committees and Chapter Historians of the United Daughters of the Confederacy*. Athens, Ga.: MacGregor, 1912.

————. *The South in History and Literature: A Hand-Book of Southern Authors, from the Settlement of Jamestown, 1607, to Living Writers*. Atlanta: Franklin-Turner, 1907.

————. *The South in the Building of the Nation [and] Thirteen Periods of United States History: Two Addresses Delivered at Washington, D.C., and New Orleans, La*. Athens, Ga.: n.p., 1913.

————. *The South Must Have Her Rightful Place in History*. Athens, Ga.: M. L. Rutherford, 1923.

————. *Truths of History . . . A Fair, Unbiased, Impartial, Unprejudiced, and Conscientious Study of History: Object: To Secure a Peaceful Settlement of the Many Perplexing Questions Now Causing Contention between the North and the South*. Athens, Ga.: n.p., 1920.

————. *What the South May Claim; or, Where the South Leads*. Athens, Ga.: MacGregor, 1916.

————. *Wrongs of History Righted: Address Delivered by Miss Mildred Lewis Rutherford, Historian General, United Daughters of the Confederacy, Savannah, Georgia, Friday, November 13, 1914*. Athens, Ga.: n.p., 1914.

Saunders, Catherine E. *Writing the Margins: Edith Wharton, Ellen Glasgow, and the Literary Tradition of the Ruined Woman*. Cambridge: Department of English and American Literature and Language, Harvard University, 1987.

Saxon, Elizabeth Lyle. *A Southern Woman's War Time Reminiscences*. Memphis, Tenn.: Pilcher Printing, 1905.

Schultz, Jane E. "Mute Fury: Southern Women's Diaries of Sherman's March to the Sea, 1864–65." In *Arms and the Woman: War, Gender, and Literary Representation*, ed. Helen M. Cooper, Adrienne Auslander Munich, and Susan Merrill Squier, 57–79. Chapel Hill: University of North Carolina Press, 1989.

Schuman, Howard, and Jacqueline Scott. "Generations and Collective Memories." *American Sociological Review* 54 (June 1989): 359–81.

Schwartz, Barry. "The Social Context of Commemoration: A Study in Collective Memory." *Journal of Social Forces* 61 (December 1982): 374–402.

Scott, Anne Firor. *Natural Allies: Women's Associations in American History.* Urbana: University of Illinois Press, 1991.

———. *The Southern Lady: From Pedestal to Politics, 1830–1930.* Chicago: University of Chicago Press, 1970.

Scott, Evelyn. *The Wave.* 1929; Baton Rouge: Louisiana State University Press, 1996.

Scura, Dorothy M. "A Knowledge in the Heart: Ellen Glasgow, the Women's Movement, and *Virginia*." *American Literary Realism, 1870–1910* 22 (Winter 1990): 30–43.

Sea, Sophie Fox. *A Brief Synoptical Review of Slavery in the United States.* Louisville, Ky.: Albert Sidney Johnson Chapter, U.D.C., 1916.

Seabrook, Phoebe Hamilton. *A Daughter of the Confederacy: A Story of the Old South and the New.* New York: Neale, 1906.

Seibert, Mary Frances. *"Zulma" a Story of the Old South.* Natchez, Miss.: Natchez Printing and Stationery, 1897.

Selph, Fannie Eoline. *The South in American Life and History.* Nashville: McQuiddy Printing, 1928.

———. *Texas; or, The Broken Link in the Chain of Family Honors: A Romance of the Civil War.* West Nashville, Tenn.: n.p., 1905.

Severance, Caroline M. "The Genesis of the Club Idea." *Women's Journal* 33, no. 22 (1902): 174.

Sewall, May Wright. "The General Federation of Woman's Clubs." *Arena* 6 (1892): 362–66.

Shaw, Christopher, and Malcolm Chase, eds. *The Imagined Past: History and Nostalgia.* Manchester, Eng.: Manchester University Press, 1989.

Shi, David E. *Facing Facts: Realism in American Thought and Culture, 1850–1920.* New York: Oxford University Press, 1995.

Shils, Edward. "Tradition." *Comparative Studies in Society and History* 13 (1971): 122–59.

———. "Tradition and the Generations: On the Difficulties of Transmission." *American Scholar* 53 (Winter 1983–84): 27–40.

Silber, Nina. *The Romance of Reunion: Northerners and the South, 1865–1900.* Chapel Hill: University of North Carolina Press, 1993.

Simkins, Francis Butler, and James Welch Patton. *The Women of the Confederacy.* Richmond: Garrett and Massie, 1936.

Simpson, Lewis P. *The Brazen Face of History: Studies in the Literary Consciousness in America.* Baton Rouge: Louisiana State University Press, 1980.

———. *The Dispossessed Garden: Pastoral and History in Southern Literature.* Baton Rouge: Louisiana State University Press, 1983.

———. *Mind and the American Civil War: A Meditation on Lost Causes.* Baton Rouge: Louisiana State University Press, 1989.

Singal, Daniel. *The War Within: From Victorian to Modernist Thought in the South, 1919–1945.* Chapel Hill: University of North Carolina Press, 1982.

———. *William Faulkner: The Making of a Modernist.* Chapel Hill: University of North Carolina Press, 1997.

Singmaster, Elsie. *Gettysburg: Stories of the Red Harvest and the Aftermath.* Boston: Houghton, Mifflin, 1913.

Sizer, Lyde Cullen. *The Political Work of Northern Women Writers and the Civil War, 1850–1872.* Chapel Hill: University of North Carolina Press, 2000.

Slotkin, Richard. "Part I: Myth is the Language of Historical Memory." In Slotkin, *The Fatal Environment: The Myth of the Frontier in the Age of Industrialization, 1800–1890,* 1–47. Middletown, Conn.: Wesleyan University Press, 1986.

Smedes, Susan Dabney. *Memorials of a Southern Planter.* Ed., intro., and notes by Fletcher M. Green. New York: Knopf, 1965.

Smiley, David L. "The Quest for the Central Theme in Southern History." *South Atlantic Quarterly* 71 (Summer 1972): 307–25.

Smith, C. A. "The Possibilities of the South in Literature." *Sewanee Review* 6 (1898): 298–305.

Smith, John David. "An Old Creed for the New South: Southern Historians and the Revival of the Proslavery Argument, 1890–1920." *Southern Studies* 18 (Spring 1979): 75–87.

———. "'The Work It Did Not Do Because It Could Not': Georgia and the 'New' Freedmen's Bureau Historiography." *Georgia Historical Quarterly* 82 (Summer 1998): 331–49.

Snyder, Ann E. *The Civil War from a Southern Standpoint: Revised and Arranged for Use in Schools and Colleges.* Nashville: Publishing House of the M. E. Church, 1890.

Snyder, Robert E. "Telling about the South." *American Quarterly* 41 (June 1989): 391–401.

Solomon, Barbara Miller. *In the Company of Educated Women: A History of Women and Higher Education in America.* New Haven: Yale University Press, 1985.

Spencer, Bella. *Tried and True; or, Love and Loyalty.* Springfield, Mass.: W. J. Holland, 1866.

Spencer, Cornelia Phillips. *The Last Ninety Days of the War in North Carolina.* New York: Watchman, 1866.

———. *Selected Papers.* Ed. and intro. Louis Round Wilson. Chapel Hill: University of North Carolina Press, 1953.

Starnes, Richard D. "Forever Faithful: The Southern Historical Society and Confederate Historical Memory." *Southern Cultures* 2 (Summer 1996): 177–94.

Stephens, Alexander H. *A Constitutional View of the Late War between the States; Its Causes, Character, Conduct, and Results, Presented in a Series of Colloquies at Liberty Hall.* 2 vols. Philadelphia: National Publishing, 1868–70.

Stone, Kate. *Brokenburn: The Journal of Kate Stone, 1861–1868.* Ed. John Q. Anderson. Baton Rouge: Louisiana State University Press, 1955.

Stonebraker, J. Clarence. *The Unwritten South: Cause, Progress, and Result of the Civil War. Relics of Hidden Truth after Forty Years.* 7th ed. N.p.: Privately published, 1908.

Stout, Janis P. *Katherine Anne Porter: A Sense of the Times.* Charlottesville: University Press of Virginia, 1995.

Stovall, Pleasant A. *Robert Toombs, Statesman, Speaker, Soldier, Sage: His Career in Congress and on the Hustings—His Work in the Courts—His Record with the Army—His Life at Home.* New York: Cassell, 1892.

Stowe, Harriet Beecher. *Uncle Tom's Cabin; or, Life among the Lowly.* Ed. Ann Douglas. New York: Penguin, 1986.

Stowe, Steven M. "City, Country, and the Feminine Voice." In *Intellectual Life in Antebellum Charleston,* ed. Michael O'Brien and David Moltke-Hansen, 295–324. Knoxville: University of Tennessee Press, 1986.

Stuart, Ruth McEnery. *Napoleon Jackson: The Gentleman of the Plush Rocker*. New York: Century, 1902.

Sullivan, Walter. "The Fading Memory of the Civil War." In *The American South: Portrait of a Culture*, ed. Louis D. Rubin Jr. 245–53. Baton Rouge: Louisiana State University Press, 1980.

Sutherland, Daniel E. "Southern Fraternal Organizations in the North." *Journal of Southern History* 53 (November 1987): 587–612.

Swierenga, Robert P., ed. *Beyond the Civil War Synthesis: Political Essays of the Civil War Era*. Westport, Conn.: Greenwood Press, 1975.

Tandy, Jeannette Red. "Pro-Slavery Propaganda in American Fiction in the Fifties." *South Atlantic Quarterly* 21 (January–March 1922): 41–50, 170–78.

Tardy, Mary T. *The Living Female Writers of the South*. Philadelphia: Claxton, Remsen, and Haffelfinger, 1872.

————. *Southland Writers: Biographical and Critical Sketches of the Living Female Writers of the South*. 2 vols. Philadelphia: Claxton, Remsen, and Haffelfinger, 1870.

Tate, Allen. *The Fathers*. New York: G. P. Putnam's Sons, 1938.

————. *Jefferson Davis: His Rise and Fall*. New York: Minton, Balch, 1929.

————. *"Ode to the Confederate Dead," Being the Revised and Final Version of a Poem Previously Published on Several Occasions; to Which Are Added "Message from Abroad" and "The Cross"*. New York: published for the author by Minton, Balch, 1930.

————. *Stonewall Jackson: The Good Soldier*. New York: Minton, Balch, 1928.

Taylor, Richard. *Destruction and Reconstruction: Personal Experiences of the Late War*. New York: Appleton, 1879.

Taylor, William R. *Cavalier and Yankee: The Old South and American National Character*. Cambridge: Harvard University Press, 1979.

Temple, Judy Nolte, and Suzanne L. Bunkers. "Mothers, Daughters, Diaries: Literacy, Relationship, and Cultural Context." In *Nineteenth-Century Women Learn to Write*, ed. and intro. Catherine Hobbs, 197–216. Charlottesville: University Press of Virginia, 1995.

Thelen, David, ed. *Memory and American History*. Bloomington: Indiana University Press, 1990.

Thomas, Ella Gertrude Clanton. *The Secret Eye: The Journal of Ella Gertrude Clanton Thomas, 1848–1889*. Ed. Virginia Ingraham Burr, intro. Nell Irvin Painter. Chapel Hill: University of North Carolina Press, 1990.

Thomas, Emory M. *The Confederate Nation, 1861–1865*. New York: Harper and Row, 1979.

Thomas, Mary Martha. "The 'New Woman' in Alabama, 1890–1920." *Alabama Review* 43 (July 1990): 163–80.

Thompson, Lawrence S. "The Civil War in Fiction." *Civil War History* 2 (March 1956): 83–95.

Thruston, Lucy Meacham. *Called to the Field: A Story of Virginia in the Civil War*. Boston: Little, Brown, 1906.

Tillett, Wilbur Fisk. "Southern Womanhood as Affected by the War." *Century* 43 (1891–92): 9–16.

Tindall, George B. "Mythology: A New Frontier in Southern History." In *The Idea of the South: Pursuit of a Central Theme*, ed. Frank E. Vandiver, 1–15. Chicago: University of Chicago Press, 1964.

Tompkins, Jane. *Sensational Designs: The Cultural Work of American Fiction, 1790–1860.* New York: Oxford University Press, 1985.

Tourgée, Albion W. *Bricks without Straw.* Ed. Otto H. Olsen. Baton Rouge: Louisiana State University Press, 1969.

———. *A Fool's Errand.* Ed. John Hope Franklin. 1879; Cambridge: Belknap Press of Harvard University Press, 1961.

———. "The South as a Field for Fiction." *Forum* 6 (1888–89): 404–11.

Trent, William P. *Southern Statesmen of the Old Régime: Washington, Jefferson, Randolph, Calhoun, Stephens, Toombs, and Jefferson Davis.* New York: T. Y. Crowell, 1897.

Twelve Southerners. *I'll Take My Stand: The South and the Agrarian Tradition.* 1930; Baton Rouge: Louisiana State University Press, 1977.

Underwood, John Levi. *The Women of the Confederacy, in Which Is Presented the Heroism of the Women of the Confederacy with Accounts of Their Trials during the War and the Period of the Reconstruction, with Their Ultimate Triumph over Adversity.* New York: Neale, 1906.

United Daughters of the Confederacy. *Three Papers Written for and Read on the Third Historical Evening, Richmond, Virginia, Thursday, November 9, 1911.* Richmond: n.p., [1911?].

United Daughters of the Confederacy, Georgia Division, Atlanta Chapter. *History of the Atlanta Chapter of the United Daughters of the Confederacy, 1897–1922.* Atlanta: United Daughters of the Confederacy, 1922.

United Daughters of the Confederacy, Georgia Division, Lizzie Rutherford Chapter. *A History of the Origin of Memorial Day as Adopted by the Ladies' Memorial Association of Columbus, Georgia, and Presented to the Lizzie Rutherford Chapter of the Daughters of the Confederacy.* Columbus, Ga.: T. Gilbert, 1898.

United Daughters of the Confederacy, South Carolina Division. *Recollections and Reminiscences, 1861–1865 through World War I.* 7 vols. [South Carolina]: South Carolina Division, United Daughters of the Confederacy, 1990–97.

———. *South Carolina Women in the Confederacy.* Columbia, S.C.: State Company, 1903–7.

United Daughters of the Confederacy, South Carolina Division, John K. McIver Chapter. *Treasured Reminiscences: Including Accounts of the 1st, 6th, 9th, and 21st Regiments, South Carolina Volunteer Infantry, the 6th South Carolina Cavalry Regiment, and the 1st, 15th, and Pee Dee Volunteer Artillery Battalions, Confederate States Army, 1861–1865.* 1911; University, Ala.: Confederate Publishing, 1982.

Van Auken, Sheldon. "The Southern Historical Novel in the Early Twentieth Century." *Journal of Southern History* 14 (May 1948): 157–91.

Vance, Zebulon Baird. *My Beloved Zebulon: The Correspondence of Zebulon Baird Vance and Harriett Newell Espy.* Ed. Elizabeth Roberts Cannon; intro. Frances Gray Patton. Chapel Hill: University of North Carolina Press, 1971.

Velazquez, Loreta Janeta. *The Story of the Civil War; or, The Exploits, Adventures, and Travels of Mrs. L. J. Velazquez (Lieutenant H. T. Buford, C.S.A.).* Ed. C. J. Worthington. New York: Worthington, 1890.

Voloshin, Beverly R. "The Limits of Domesticity: The Female Bildungsroman in America, 1820–1870." *Women's Studies* 10 (1984): 283–302.

W. R. A. "The Duty of Southern Authors." *Southern Literary Messenger* 23 (October 1856): 241–47.

Wachtel, Nathan. "Memory and History: An Introduction." *History and Anthropology* 2 (October 1986): 207–24.

Wagenknecht, Edward. "The World and Mary Johnston." *Sewanee Review* 44 (1936): 188–206.

Waldron, Ann. *Close Connections: Caroline Gordon and the Southern Renaissance.* Knoxville: University of Tennessee Press, 1989.

The War of the Rebellion: A Compilation of the Official Records of the Union and Confederate Armies. 128 vols. Washington, D.C.: Government Printing Office, 1880–1901.

Warren, Robert Penn. *The Legacy of the Civil War: Meditations on the Centennial.* New York: Random House, 1961.

Warren, Rose Harlow. *A Southern Home in War Times.* New York: Broadway, 1914.

Watson, Thomas E. "The Negro Question in the South." *Arena* 6 (1892): 540–50.

Waugh, John C. *Surviving the Confederacy: Rebellion, Ruin, and Recovery—Roger and Sara Pryor during the Civil War.* New York: Harcourt, 2002.

Weems, Mrs. Albert G. "Work of the United Daughters of the Confederacy." *Publications of the Mississippi Historical Society* 4 (1901): 73–78.

Wells, Gary L., and Elizabeth F. Loftus, eds. *Eyewitness Testimony: Psychological Perspectives.* New York: Cambridge University Press, 1984.

Wert, Jeffry D. *General James Longstreet: The Confederacy's Most Controversial Soldier: A Biography.* New York: Simon and Schuster, 1993.

———. "James Longstreet and the Lost Cause." In *The Myth of the Lost Cause and Civil War History*, ed. Gary W. Gallagher and Alan T. Nolan, 127–36. Bloomington: Indiana University Press, 2000.

White, Mary Wheeling. *Fighting the Current: The Life and Work of Evelyn Scott.* Baton Rouge: Louisiana State University Press, 1998.

Whites, LeeAnn. *The Civil War as a Crisis in Gender: Augusta, Georgia, 1860–1890.* Athens: University of Georgia Press, 1995.

———. "Love, Hate, Rape, Lynching: Rebecca Latimer Felton and the Gender Politics of Racial Violence." In *Democracy Betrayed: The Wilmington Race Riot of 1898 and Its Legacy*, ed. David S. Cecelski and Timothy B. Tyson, 143–62. Chapel Hill: University of North Carolina Press, 1998.

Whitson, Mrs. L. D. *Gilbert St. Maurice.* Louisville, Ky.: Bradley and Gilbert, 1875.

Whittlesey, Sarah J. C. *Bertha the Beauty: A Story of the Southern Revolution.* Philadelphia: Claxton, Remsen, and Haffelfinger, 1872.

Wiley, Bell I. *Confederate Women.* Westport, Conn.: Greenwood Press, 1975.

Williams, Flora McDonald. *Who's the Patriot? A Story of the Southern Confederacy.* Louisville, Ky.: Press of the Courier-Journal Job Printing Company, 1886.

Williams, T. Harry. *P. G. T. Beauregard: Napoleon in Gray.* Baton Rouge: Louisiana State University Press, 1955.

Williamson, Joel. *A Rage for Order: Black/White Relations in the American South since Emancipation.* New York: Oxford University Press, 1986.

———. *William Faulkner and Southern History.* New York: Oxford University Press, 1993.

Wilson, Augusta Jane Evans. *See* Evans, Augusta Jane.

Wilson, Charles Reagan. *Baptized in Blood: The Religion of the Lost Cause, 1865–1920.* Athens: University of Georgia Press, 1980.

Wilson, Edmund. *Patriotic Gore: Studies in the Literature of the American Civil War.* New York: Oxford University Press, 1962.

Wilson, Woodrow. *A History of the American People.* New York: Harper and Brothers, 1902.

Windberry, John. "'Lest We Forget': The Confederate Monument and the Southern Townscape." *Southeastern Geographer* 23 (November 1983): 107–21.

Wish, Harvey. *The American Historian: A Social-Intellectual History of the Writing of the American Past.* New York: Oxford University Press, 1960.

Wolfe, Margaret Ripley. "The Southern Lady: Long Suffering Counterpart of the Good Ole' Boy." *Journal of Popular Culture* 11 (Summer 1977): 18–27.

Wood, Ann Douglas. "The Literature of Impoverishment: The Women Local Colorists in America, 1865–1914." *Women's Studies* 1 (1972): 3–45.

Wood, Mary I. *The History of the General Federation of Women's Clubs for the First Twenty-two Years of Its Organization.* New York: History Department, General Federation of Women's Clubs, 1912.

Wood, Sally, ed. *The Southern Mandarins: Letters of Caroline Gordon to Sally Wood, 1924–1937.* Baton Rouge: Louisiana State University Press, 1984.

Woodman, Harold. "Economic Reconstruction and the Rise of the New South, 1865–1900." In *Interpreting Southern History: Historiographical Essays in Honor of Sanford W. Higginbotham,* ed. John B. Boles and Evelyn Thomas Nolen, 254–307. Baton Rouge: Louisiana State University Press, 1987.

Woodward, C. Vann. *The Burden of Southern History.* 3d ed. Baton Rouge: Louisiana State University Press, 1993.

———. "Mary Chesnut in Search of Her Genre." *Yale Review* 73 (January 1984): 199–209.

———. *The Origins of the New South, 1877–1913.* Rev. ed. with a critical essay by Charles B. Dew. Baton Rouge: Louisiana State University Press, 1971.

———. *Reunion and Reaction: The Compromise of 1877 and the End of Reconstruction.* 2d ed. Garden City, N.Y.: Doubleday, 1956.

Wright, Mrs. D. Giraud [Louise Wigfall Wright]. *Address of Mrs. D. Giraud Wright, President of the Maryland Division, United Daughters of the Confederacy, to the State Convention, Baltimore, 7 December 1903.* N.p., [1904?].

———. *A Southern Girl in '61: The War-Time Memories of a Confederate Senator's Daughter.* New York: Doubleday, Page, 1905.

Wright, Gavin. *Old South, New South: Revolutions in the Southern Economy since the Civil War.* New York: Basic Books, 1986.

Wyatt-Brown, Bertram. *The House of Percy: Honor, Melancholy, and Imagination in a Southern Family.* New York: Oxford University Press, 1994.

Wyeth, John A. *Life of General Nathan Bedford Forrest.* New York: Harper and Brothers, 1899.

Young, Elizabeth. *Disarming the Nation: Women's Writing and the American Civil War.* Chicago: University of Chicago Press, 1999.

Young, Stark. *So Red the Rose.* New York: Scribner's, 1934.

Magazines, Newspapers, and Periodicals

Atlanta Constitution

Atlanta Journal

Bookman

Carolina and the Southern Cross

Century Magazine

Confederate Veteran

Critic

The Dial

Keystone

The Land We Love

The Lost Cause

The Nation

The New Republic

Our Living and Our Dead

Southern Bivouac

Southern Historical Society Papers

Index

federate women; Gettysburg, battle of; Manassas, battle of; Union soldiers

Clay-Clopton, Virginia, 128, 130–31

Cobb, Mary Ann, 22–23

Cole, Lois, 242, 243–44

Commager, Henry Steele, 245–46

Confederate defeat, 39, 42–43, 45, 71; in fiction, 54–69; in poetry, 69–71

Confederate nationalism, 273 (n. 26)

Confederate soldiers, 22–23, 62, 96–99, 131–34, 166, 194, 197, 198–99; in fiction, 55, 58, 61, 67, 91, 93, 94–95, 105–6, 117, 147, 148–50, 183–84, 207, 251, 252, 253, 257, 260–61

Confederate Veteran, 119, 167, 201–2, 215, 216, 218

Confederate women, 2–3, 13–14, 15, 16–25, 36–37, 39, 42–45, 48–54, 82, 83–85, 97, 128–31, 169–71, 173–79, 223–30; in fiction, 1–2, 30, 34–36, 61–66, 67, 69, 88, 90–91, 110–12, 115–17, 141–47, 150–52, 181, 182–83, 186, 235–36, 238–39, 261

Cooke, John Esten, 48, 69; *Surry of Eagle's Nest*, 66, 278 (n. 48)

Cowley, Malcolm, 247, 248, 249, 250

Craddock, Charles Egbert. *See* Murfree, Mary Noailles

Crane, Stephen: *The Red Badge of Courage*, 11, 122, 149

Critic, 152

Cronly, Jane, 112

Cruse, Mary Ann: *Cameron Hall*, 7, 66–69, 278 (n. 48)

Cumming, Kate: *Gleanings from the Southland*, 76, 78, 80–81

Davis, Jefferson, 23–24, 79–84, 96, 99–100; *Rise and Fall of the Confederate Government*, 99

Davis, Varina, 23–24; on Jefferson Davis, 99–102

Dawson, Sarah Morgan. *See* Morgan, Sarah

De Forest, John W., 277 (n. 34); *Miss Ravenel's Conversion from Secession to Loyalty*, 57–58

De Saussure, Nancy Bostick: *Old Plantation Days*, 175–76

Dial, 142, 147, 157

Dixon, Thomas: *The Clansman*, 156, 242; *The Leopard's Spots*, 156, 175

Dodd, William E., 121

Domestic fiction, 14–15, 25–36

Dorsey, Sarah A.: and collaboration with Jefferson Davis, 99–100; *Lucia Dare*, 62–64; *Recollections of Henry Watkins Allen*, 46–48

Dunning, William A., 163

Dunovant, Adelia, 121, 123

Edmondson, Belle, 17

Elmore, Grace: Civil War diary of, 17, 19, 21, 37, 71; unpublished novel of, 95

Eppes, Susan Bradford: *The Negro of the Old South*, 228, 229; *Through Some Eventful Years*, 227–30

Evans, Augusta Jane, 15–16, 23; and abandoned history of Confederacy, 45–46; on Reconstruction, 45–46; *Macaria; or, Altars of Sacrifice*, 7, 13, 15–16, 23, 25–30, 274 (n. 32); *A Speckled Bird*, 117, 140–42

Fadiman, Clifton, 232

Falkner, William: *White Rose of Memphis*, 281 (n. 24)

Faulkner, William C., 10, 252; *Absalom, Absalom!*, 2, 265 (n. 1); *Flags in the Dust*, 1–2

Felton, Rebecca Latimer, 76, 107–8; *Country Life in Georgia*, 226–27

Feminist theory: on war and warfare, 101, 266 (n. 5), 277 (n. 34), 280 (n. 1)

Ford, Ford Madox, 255

Ford, Sallie Rochester: *Raids and Romance of Morgan and His Men*, 26–27, 29–30

Forrest, Nathan Bedford, 260–62

Fort Donelson, 19, 29

Forum, 152

Freeman, Douglas Southall, 246: *R. E. Lee: A Biography*, 10, 209–12

Garnett, Kate Noland, 117–18

George, Herbert, 80

Gettysburg, battle of, 134–35, 136–37, 139, 229

Gilder, Richard Watson, 81

Glasgow, Ellen, 4, 9, 142, 256; on *Gone with the Wind*, 244; on southern literature, 122–23, 142–44, 146, 147, 148, 156; *Battle-Ground*, 9, 145–52; *The Deliverance: A Romance of the Virginia Tobacco Fields*, 9,

Murfree, Mary Noailles: *The Raid of the Guerilla and Other Stories*, 206–7; *The Storm Centre*, 206–7; *Where the Battle Was Fought*, 8, 75, 78, 104–7

The Nation, 189, 232–33, 247–48, 255
The New Republic, 233, 247, 248
New South, 8, 75–78, 86, 112–13; in fiction, 168–69, 187–90, 257–60
New York Times, 199, 232, 233, 244

Oaths of allegiance, 42, 51–52, 67, 275 (n. 4)
O'Connor, Florence J.: *Heroine of the Confederacy*, 31–36
Odenheimer, Cordelia Powell, 214–15
Our Living and Our Dead, 69–70, 278–9 (n. 55)
Owen, Birdie A., 213–14
Overman, Flora K., 112

Page, Thomas Nelson, 79, 85, 87, 190, 249; *Gordon Keith*, 154, 291 (n. 68); "Marse Chan," 290 (n. 53); *Red Rock; A Chronicle of Reconstruction*, 152–54
Page, Walter Hines, 147
Pember, Phoebe Yates, 103
Pemberton, John C., 47–48
Perkins, Maxwell, 254, 255
Phillips, Eugenia, 272 (n. 8)
Pickett, La Salle Corbell: and *Carolina and the Southern Cross*, 168; on George Pickett, 288 (n. 38); *Bugles of Gettysburg*, 183–84; *The Heart of a Soldier*, 184–85; *Pickett and His Men*, 131, 136–38; *What Happened to Me*, 212, 223–26
Plantation romances, 247, 249, 262, 291 (n. 68)
Pollard, Edward, 5, 55, 266 (n. 6)
Poppenheim, Louisa, 165, 168
Poppenheim, Mary, 124, 168
Populism, 9, 77; in fiction, 144–47
Porter, Katherine Anne, 4, 255–56, 301 (n. 3)
Posey, Mary Johnson, 167
Powell, Mrs. J. Norment, 215
Preston, Margaret Junkin, 16, 70, 123; and contributions to "Battles and Leaders of the Civil War" series, 84, 96–97
Pryor, Sara, 128–31
Putnam, Sallie Brock: *Richmond During the War*, 52–54

Ransom, John Crowe, 258–59
Ravenel, Harriott Horry, 126–27
Readjuster movement, 289 (n. 48)
Reconciliation romances, 57–60, 79–80, 277 (nn. 34, 37), 280 (n. 9), 281 (n. 24); southerners' refutation of, 57, 60–66, 80–81, 86–91, 148, 151–52, 186, 281 (nn. 19, 24); southerners' contributions to, 81–86, 132, 185–86
Reconstruction, 40–42, 163, 166, 175–76, 177–78; in fiction, 54–57, 59–60, 79, 87–90, 110–12, 152–57, 237–38, 241–42
Reid, Mrs. George, 126
Rhodes, James Ford, 162–63
Robinson, Mrs. J. Enders, 164
Rogers, Loula Kendall, 16–17, 19–20, 42–43, 71, 96
Roosevelt, Franklin D., 221–22
Rountree, Mrs. J. A., 217
Rowland, Kate, 16, 21, 167
Russell, Mrs. George B., 167
Rutherford, Mildred Lewis, 125–26, 159, 162–64, 166

Scott, Evelyn, 10, 252; and review of *Gone with the Wind*, 247–48; *The Wave*, 212–13, 230–34
Seabrook, Phoebe Hamilton: *A Daughter of the Confederacy*, 181, 186
Secession, 27, 31, 95, 181, 185, 196
Seibert, Mary Frances, 286 (n. 13)
Selph, Fannie, 182, 219
Sewanee Review, 157, 189
Sherman, William T., 19, 50, 102, 182
Slavery: and Civil War, 46–47, 67, 93, 108, 118, 126, 127, 148, 161, 162, 175, 176, 228; in fiction, 32–33, 92–93, 150, 236–37
Southern Historical Society, 60–61, 87, 123, 137, 184
Spanish-American War, 209
Spencer, Cornelia Phillips: *The Last Ninety Days of the War in North Carolina*, 49–52
States' rights, 25, 26, 80, 93, 102, 127, 137, 162, 163, 196, 214
Stephens, Alexander H., 43
Sterling, Ada, 130–31
Stone, Cornelia Branch, 118
Stowe, Harriet Beecher: *Uncle Tom's Cabin*, 32, 33, 175